DISSERTATIONS

ON THE

APOSTLES' CREED.

Reprinted 1993
The den Dulk Christian Foundation
Escondido, California

Distributed by
Presbyterian and Reformed Publishing Company
Phillipsburg, New Jersey

ISBN: 0-87552-871-6

PUBLISHER'S PREFACE

BY

SINCLAIR B. FERGUSON

───────

THE NAME of Herman Witsius is today little known among Christians generally, nor as well known in the English-speaking Reformed churches as it was a century and a half ago. Then William Pringle could write that it was "familiarly known to the English Reader"; but, alas no more. It is therefore welcome news to those who love the best Christian literature of the past that Witsius's exposition of the Apostles' Creed is again made available after a long absence even from second-hand bookshops. It now joins his better-known *The Economy of the Covenants Between God and Man,* re-published in 1990.

The present work, written in Latin, was first published in Franeker in 1681. This English translation, by Donald Fraser, from the third edition (Amsterdam 1697) was published in Glasgow, Scotland, in 1823. Fraser lived in an era of pastoral ministry a little different from that to which most of us are accustomed today. Not only did he engage in the translation of Witsius in what he modestly calls "part of his leisure," but to it he added well over two hundred pages of his own endnotes and commentary.

Little could Donald Fraser have realized, as his lamp burned in the manse study at Kennoway while he patiently compared texts and worked over his translation, that late twentieth-century Christians would feel themselves enormously in his debt. But in our non-Latinate age, deeply indebted many who open this book will be; for Witsius's *On the Apostles' Creed* is a great treasure. I, for one, am excited that it should be in the hands of Christian people today.

A brief account of Witsius's life is prefaced to this edition. It was largely uneventful as lives are ordinarily measured. But there is special significance in the fact that, even after he left parish ministry to serve as a professor of theology, he served simultaneously both as a theological teacher and as a preacher. This marriage of lectern and pulpit was important to him, as is evident throughout his study of the Creed.

The work itself began life in lectures he gave to his students on what he called "the principal articles of our religion," first when he was professor at the University of Franeker and later at the University of Utrecht. Their tone is captured in Witsius's own principle, urged frequently on his students: "He alone is a true Theologian, who adds the practical to the theoretical part of Religion." This beautiful biblical balance is what we find throughout his exposition of the Creed. He seeks to expound the truth of Scripture and apply it to life in a way that simultaneously expresses the spirit of Scripture.

The exposition begins with a series of introductory studies. These discuss such questions as the title of the Creed (Witsius recognizes that "Apostles'" should be taken to refer to the apostolicity of the doctrine, not of the authors), the role of fundamental articles and the nature of saving faith. Thereafter follows his phrase-by-phrase exposition of the substance of the Creed.

Some readers will have an instinctive desire to turn immediately to check "Witsius's position" on a variety of topics. There is much here of interest. Those who wonder whether he was a presuppositionalist or an ev-identialist in his apologetical method will be intrigued by his comments on the existence of God and his Calvi-nesque allusion to the "innate knowledge of God." In fact, lovers of Calvin's theology will find more than one echo in both content and style in these pages. His abil-ity to pull the reader into an understanding of the gospel which marries the intellect with the heart is one of them. Many will turn immediately to see what Wit-sius had to say on the variously interpreted clause "he descended into hell," and few will fail to be intrigued by his discussion of such questions as: Are there other inhabited worlds? Will our sins be publicly made known on the day of judgment?

A word of counsel may be in order, therefore, to those who are inveterate "dippers" rather than patient readers. Witsius yields his best fruit to those who will work over the whole soil with him. The most enduring benefits of his work come to those who sit at his feet and absorb exposition and application, substance and style, not those who come merely to pick his brain. The latter will miss what to Witsius was central: medita-tion on the truth of the gospel, and especially on the God who has made himself known as Father, Son, and Holy Spirit.

"Dip in" then, if you must. But once you have picked over your special interest, return to the beginning, and savor Witsius's wisdom and his wide learning; appreciate his judicious mind and be challenged, humbled, encouraged, and uplifted by his teaching.

Witsius himself—student, pastor, scholar, professor, preacher—well states his own burden and points us in the direction of discovering the chief blessing to be found in the pages that follow:

> Religion is not seated in the tongue, but in the mind; . . . it consists not in words, but in deeds; not in the subtlety of speculation, but in purity of heart; not in the affection of new discoveries, but in the prosecution of a new life.

No doubt if the Reverend Donald Fraser had been a twentieth-century American, rather than a nineteenth-century Scotsman, his Translator's Introduction could appropriately have ended with a one-word sentence. Enjoy!

SINCLAIR B. FERGUSON
Westminster Theological Seminary
Philadelphia, Pennsylvania

Eng^dby R.Scott Edin^r.

HERMAN WITSIUS, D.D.

Professor of Divinity in the Universities of Franeker, Utrecht, and Leyden.

Pub^d by A.Fullarton & Co.Edinburgh, and by Khull, Blackie, & Co Glasgow.

SACRED DISSERTATIONS,

ON WHAT IS COMMONLY CALLED THE

APOSTLES' CREED.

BY

HERMAN WITSIUS, D.D.

PROFESSOR OF DIVINITY IN THE UNIVERSITIES OF
FRANEKER, UTRECHT, AND LEYDEN.

———

TRANSLATED FROM THE LATIN,

AND FOLLOWED WITH

NOTES, CRITICAL AND EXPLANATORY,

BY

DONALD FRASER,

MINISTER OF THE GOSPEL, KENNOWAY.

———

IN TWO VOLUMES.

———

VOL. I.

———

EDINBURGH:

PRINTED FOR A. FULLARTON & Co. EDINBURGH;
AND KHULL, BLACKIE & Co. GLASGOW:
AND SOLD BY J. OFFOR, LONDON.

———

1823·

CONTENTS

OF

THE FIRST VOLUME.

DISSERTATIONS.*

DISSERTATION I.

On the Authors, and the Authority of the Apostles' Creed.

Pages 1—15.

* The *Contents* of the *Dissertations* in both Volumes are faithfully translated from the Latin. T.

VOL. I. *a*

CONTENTS.

DISSERTATION II.

On Fundamental Articles.

Pages 16—33.

DISSERTATION III.

On Saving Faith.

Pages 34—68.

SECT.

DISSERTATION IV.

On the Faith of the Existence of God.

Pages 69—98.

DISSERTATION V.

On Faith IN GOD.

Pages 99—120.

DISSERTATION VI.

On Faith in a THREE-ONE GOD.

Pages 121—145.

DISSERTATION VII.

On Faith in GOD THE FATHER.

Pages 146—177.

DISSERTATION VIII.

On the Creation.

Pages 178—230.

DISSERTATION IX.

On the Name Jesus.

Pages 231—254.

DISSERTATION X.

On the Name CHRIST.

Pages 255—290.

DISSERTATION XI.

On the name CHRISTIANS.

Pages 291—322.

DISSERTATION XII.

On Jesus Christ, the ONLY-BEGOTTEN SON OF GOD.

Pages 323—348.

DISSERTATION XIII.

On Jesus Christ, our Lord.

Pages 349—370.

THE

TRANSLATOR'S PREFACE.

———

AMONGST the numerous treatises, which have been published at different periods and in various languages, on what is usually styled the APOSTLES' CREED, there is a great diversity of merit. By all who have the least acquaintance with the subject, it will be readily admitted, that whilst some of them are extremely superficial and inaccurate, if not essentially defective or grossly erroneous, others are distinguished as well for soundness of doctrine and richness of sentiment, as for correctness of arrangement and elegance of language.

Of those to which the latter description applies, the EXERCITATIONS (or DISSERTATIONS, as with equal propriety they may be called,) of the celebrated WITSIUS on this ancient summary of the Christian faith, unquestionably hold an eminent place. They form a work, which, with regard to its illustrations and defences of the grand articles which this summary embraces, is probably, at least, equal to the best and most popular publications on the Creed that have appeared in the English tongue; and, with regard to the piety of its spirit, its skilful application of doctrine to practice, and its powerful appeals to the conscience and the

heart, is decidedly superior.   Fervent piety, indeed,
was so prominent a feature in the character of WIT-
SIUS, that it tinged every discussion which occupied his
pen, and gave an indescribable charm to all his works.
It is not without reason that the devout and evangelical HERVEY commends him as " a most excellent
" author, all of whose works have such a delicacy of
" composition, and such a sweet savour of holiness,
" that I know not," he adds, " any comparison more
" proper to represent their true character than *the*
" *golden pot which had manna,* and was outwardly
" bright with burnished gold, inwardly rich with hea-
" venly food." *   A similar encomium is pronounced
by the learned Dr JOHN GILL, who describes him as
" a writer not only eminent for his great talents and
" particularly solid judgment, rich imagination, and
" elegance of composition, but for a deep, powerful,
" and evangelical spirituality, and savour of godli-
" ness." †

How far the DISSERTATIONS on the CREED may
be expected to correspond with the general character
which these distinguished Divines have given to the
works of WITSIUS, the reader may be able, in some
degree, to judge, from the author's own Dedication and
Preface, in both of which he expressly states, that his
original and principal design, in preparing these Discourses, was to furnish his pupils with a specimen of
the practical tendencies of all the doctrines of the
Christian religion.

Some years ago, it occurred to the Translator that

---

* Theron and Aspasio, vol. ii. p. 73. Edin. Edit. 1812.

† See a Recommendation prefixed to the Translation of the Economy of the Covenants, subscribed by Dr Gill and some other Ministers.

part of his leisure could not be employed with greater pleasure to himself, or, perhaps, greater advantage to the Church, than in writing a Translation of this excellent treatise. After having made a little progress in the work, he mentioned his intention to a few friends, who approved of his design, and encouraged him to proceed. To his Reverend Fathers and Brethren, who have attentively perused some parts of his manuscript, and concurred in recommending the Translation, and most of whom also favoured him with critical remarks on the version, or with general suggestions for its improvement, his unfeigned gratitude and cordial acknowledgments are due. It seems proper, at the same time, to state, that, as these respectable Clergymen have all of them read only specimens of this Translation, and no one has perused the whole, the Translator alone is responsible for its faults and defects. This remark applies, in particular, to the Notes subjoined; none of which, owing to circumstances which it is unnecessary to mention, have had the advantage of being submitted to the review of his Brethren.

The Translation is executed from the third edition, printed at Amsterdam in the year 1697, and probably the last that was corrected under the author's eye, collated with the first edition, which was printed at Franeker in the year 1681. A few unimportant sentences, which occur in the first edition, but are dropt by the author in the third, are also omitted in the version; whilst all the enlargements added to the third, which are considerably numerous and valuable, are faithfully retained. On the same principle, it seemed proper to retain the whole Preface to the third edition, which differs from the original Preface in the two following points.

In the first place, it concludes with some strictures which the venerable Author, in deference to the judgment of his friends, deemed proper to add, respecting the uncandid treatment which he had experienced from a Divine of some note, who differed from him on certain theological questions at that time warmly contested. Although that portion of the Preface may now appear to many somewhat uninteresting, it supplies a striking evidence that no attainments in learning or piety are sufficient to prevent the outrageous assaults of misguided zeal; and affords, at the same time, a happy instance of that amiable meekness and candour with which WITSIUS was disposed to treat the most virulent adversary.

The only other particular in which the third Preface deviates from the first, is that it omits a short apology, which had originally been made to the reader, for certain coincidences between this work and the treatise on the Covenants. Those coincidences, however, are few, and scarcely any of them required an apology, with the exception of the Dissertation on Saving Faith, a great part of which is nearly the same as the chapter on that subject in the other work. The fact is, that these two elaborate publications are, on the whole, quite distinct, and that both are necessary to form a complete system of theology. Not to mention various other important discussions peculiar to this Treatise, it contains ample and interesting illustrations of some of the most significant and delightful characters of our blessed Redeemer, and of the several steps of his abasement and exaltation, which the plan of his admirable work on the Covenants did not include. The characteristical excellence, in short, of the treatise on the Creed, and the circumstance which suggested the idea of making it accessible to the English reader, is its singular tendency to enrich the understanding with the knowledge, and to warm the heart with the love of that Saviour, who is " altogether lovely," and whose divinity and atonement constitute the grand basis of the Christian hope.

Regarding fidelity as the most essential quality of any version, the Translator has attempted to produce an exact transcript in English of the original Latin. If he has ever, in any degree, misrepresented the sense of the Author, he can affirm, with confidence, that this is owing to misconception or inadvertency, not to design. He never lost sight of the principle, that, in translating, his business was not to express his own sentiments, but to state, without the slightest modification, the sentiments of another—of one, however, with whom he had the happiness, in almost every case, to agree. Yet, as tame servility is not essential but rather hostile to fidelity, he has freely made use of those necessary and reasonable liberties to which all Translators are entitled. He has endeavoured to supply the reader with an English book, perspicuously written, and composed in accordance with the genius and principles of the English tongue. In spite of his vigilance, however, a critical eye, he doubts not, will be able to detect a variety of instances in which the Latin idiom is inadvertently retained, as well as other deviations from purity of stile.

There was, originally, no intention of subjoining Notes to this Translation. But the work was not far advanced when it appeared that a few Explanatory remarks would be necessary, in order to elucidate some arguments and expressions which to many readers might seem difficult and obscure. It was natural, in

consequence, to proceed a step further, and to hazard
some Critical observations on various passages which
either obviously required, or easily admitted of them.
In many instances the writer has cheerfully availed
himself of the lights furnished by esteemed Authors,
his obligations to whom are uniformly acknowledged;
and, to prevent the Notes from extending to an undesirable length, he has frequently referred, on subjects
of moment, to Critics and Divines who treat them
fully.   Such references, he presumes, may perhaps be
acceptable to pious and intelligent youths, who delight
in biblical and theological researches.

It has been his earnest wish, not only to direct the
attention of such Students and Ministers of the Gospel
as may have hitherto neglected them, to these instructive Dissertations of WITSIUS, but also to render them
intelligible and useful to those classes of Christians,
who have no pretensions to literature.   For their sake
he has inserted a number of Notes, which would otherwise have been unnecessary; and principally for their
accommodation, too, an Index is appended of nearly
all the Authors, ancient and modern, quoted in the
course of the work, containing short notices of the character and history of most of them.   The useful Indexes
subjoined to the original are also preserved.

A few immaterial alterations, it may be right to
mention, have been made in the form of the work.
The numerous references to the Book, Chapter and
Verse, in which the quotations from Scripture are to be
found, are removed from the text to the bottom of the
page.   A few sentences, also, in different parts of the
book, consisting chiefly of verbal criticisms, which the
English reader might not well understand, are transferred to the bottom.   When short Notes are added in

the course of the work, instead of being subjoined at the end of the Volumes, they are carefully distinguished from those transposed sentences which occur in the original.*

A Memoir of Witsius is prefixed, the materials of which are collected principally from the Oration delivered on occasion of his funeral by the celebrated Dr John Marck. It necessarily coincides, in a great measure, with " the Life of Witsius" prefixed to the Translation of the Economy of the Covenants, and with the account of him which appears in the fourth Volume of Middleton's "Evangelical Biography :"— the substance of both of which is avowedly extracted from the same original and authentic source.

That this attempt to render more extensively useful a highly valuable Work, may, by the blessing of God, be rendered, in some degree, conducive to the glory of the Saviour, and to the best interests of men, is the prayer of

THE TRANSLATOR.

* The distinctive mark of the Translator's observations in the places referred to, is the subscription of the letter T.

RECOMMENDATIONS.

―――――――

" WE have perused part of Mr FRASER's Translation of WITSIUS's excellent and instructive Work on the CREED, and compared it in various places with the Original; and we do not hesitate to pronounce it a good Translation. It is faithful, not more free than the genius of the two languages requires, and conveys in good English not only the sense of the Author, but a considerable portion of his spirit and manner.

WITSIUS is known to the mere English reader, only by a very indifferent translation of his Economy of the Covenants, and by his Irenical Animadversions translated a few years ago by the late Mr Bell of Glasgow. His Treatise on the Apostles' Creed is not inferior to either of these; and we feel much satisfaction in the prospect that a work which has so long benefited the student and divine, and which is so well calculated to give instruction and delight to every class of Christians, is now about to be given to our countrymen in their own tongue.

JAMES PEDDIE, D.D.
JOHN COLQUHOUN, D.D.
THOMAS M'CRIE, D.D.
DAVID DICKSON."

EDINBURGH, *January* 1st, 1822.

" WE have perused, with much pleasure, a part of Mr Fraser's Translation of WITSIUS on the CREED, and consider it as a faithful expression of the sense of the original. We recommend the work to the public as a scriptural, luminous, and pious exposition of that short summary of the Christian faith.

JOHN DICK, D.D.
JOHN MITCHELL, D.D."

GLASGOW, *November 15th*, 1821.

" TO all who are in some measure familiar with the writings of the orthodox continental Divines, it must often have been the subject of regret, that, from their being composed in a dead language, the stores of theological learning and evangelical truth with which they are so liberally replenished, are in a great measure inaccessible to Christians in this country. Among these theologians, few occupy a higher place than WITSIUS —who, to profound learning and fervent piety, added a taste for classical elegance, in his days rather uncommon among his countrymen. Of his voluminous and valuable works, none, so far as we know, have ever been translated into English, except his *Œconomia Fœderum* and his *Animadversiones Irenicæ*, both of which have been favourably received by the religious public. His work on the Apostles' CREED appears to us to have at least equal claims on a kind reception. It is learned, perspicuous, pious and practical, and free of that tediousness which often characterises the Dutch divines. In Mr Fraser, (part of whose Manuscript we have had

the satisfaction of perusing,) Witsius has met with a
Translator, capable, in no ordinary degree, of transfu-
sing not merely the meaning, but the spirit of his original
into his version.   Though not a slavish, he is a faithful interpreter; and while the reader is furnished with
the sentiments of Witsius, he is not frequently reminded by the foreign turn of expression, that he is not
reading an original work.

We have no hesitation in saying, that the original
work of Witsius is equally worthy of the public pa-
tronage as any of that Author's treatises which have
yet been translated, and that the Version is superior
in merit to that of either of his works which have appeared in an English dress.

> JOHN BROWN, *Whitburn.*
> JOHN BROWN, Jun. *Biggar.*"

WHITBURN, *November* 12*th*, 1821.

MEMOIR

OF

HERMAN WITSIUS, D.D.

THIS eminent Divine was born on the 12th of February, 1636, at *Enchuysen* in the province of WEST
FRIESLAND,—a town distinguished not only by the
magnanimous efforts made by its inhabitants in the
cause of liberty, when the United Provinces threw off
the yoke of Spain, but also by their zealous attachment
to learning and religion. Several individuals who attained celebrity in the religious and literary world,
were natives of Enchuysen.

The parentage of Witsius was highly respectable.
His father NICHOLAS WITS, or WITSIUS, was universally beloved by his fellow-citizens as a man of unfeigned piety and primitive simplicity; and sustained,
with much reputation, the character of a deacon and an
elder in the Church, as well as some honourable offices
in the state with which he was successively invested.
To the laudable attention of this good man, the Church
of Holland was indebted for an excellent collection of
Sacred Songs. JOHANNA, his wife, a godly and prudent woman, was the daughter of HERMAN GERARD,
who, after experiencing numerous vicissitudes, and esca-
ping the most imminent dangers, obtained a peace-

able settlement as a Minister of the Gospel at
Enchuysen, and exercised his office in that place for
more than thirty years, with great fidelity and zeal.
The subject of this Memoir was not the only child of
his parents. They had at least one son more, viz.
JAMES, who died at Enchuysen in the prime of life,
leaving a family of amiable daughters, who proved a
comfort to their uncle.

Witsius, it is said, was, even previously to his birth,
devoted by his parents to the service of God and the
Church; and they gave him the name of his mother's
Father, earnestly praying that their young Herman
might equal or even surpass his Grandfather in gifts
and graces, inherit his excellencies, and imitate his
example. His birth, it appears, was premature, and
had almost cost both mother and son their lives. On
his first appearance, he was so uncommonly small and
feeble, that it was concluded he could not live above a
few hours. It pleased God, however, to disappoint
the fears of his relatives, and not merely to preserve
alive this puny infant, but to make him at length a
truly great man, distinguished for mental vigour,
though not for corporeal size and strength, and renown-
ed throughout the whole Christian world for his valuable labours and useful writings.

His parents, whilst they found it necessary to take
particular care of his health, did not neglect his education. In conformity with their vows and prayers,
they were at pains, above all, to instruct him early in
the first principles of the Christian religion. In his
sixth year they sent him to the public school of his native town, to learn the rudiments of Latin. After he
had been kept there three years, and promoted to the
highest class, PETER GERARD, his mother's brother,

a learned and devout man, took him to his own
house, and favoured him with his immediate tuition.
Under the care of this venerable uncle, who treated
him as his own son, Witsius made so rapid a progress,
that before he was fifteen years old, he could not only
speak and write the Latin language correctly, but was
minutely acquainted with Greek and Hebrew. With
the utmost facility, he could read and interpret the
Scriptures in the original tongues, as also the Orations
of Isocrates, and the Hebrew Commentaries of Samuel.
He had now acquired, also, a tolerable knowledge of
Logic, Metaphysics, Ethics, and Natural Philosophy,
and had accurately studied *Windelin's* Compendium
of Theology. The pious conversation of the good
uncle, his ready command of the Scriptures in the
Greek and Hebrew, and his happy talent in accommo-
dating pertinent passages to the ordinary occurrences
of life, had a salutary effect upon the dispositions and
habits of the nephew, and laid the foundation of that
intimate acquaintance with the sacred volume for
which he was distinguished in the subsequent periods
of life. " O rare felicity of Witsius," exclaims Dr
Marck, " and nobly improved! Were similar prepara-
" tions to be made in the present age, many would
" enter the University far better instructed than they
" now are, when they leave it to engage in the various
" pursuits of life."

In the year 1651, and the fifteenth of his age, he
was sent to the University of Utrecht; where he studied Philosophy under *Paul Voetius;* the oriental languages, Hebrew, Syriac and Arabic, under the celebrated *Leusden;* and Theology under *Gisbert Voetius,
John Hoornbeeck, Walter Bruinius,* and *Andrew
Essenius. Maatsius,* another excellent Professor of

divinity, died just before his arrival; and he had only
the melancholy satisfaction of hearing Hoornbeeck pronounce the funeral oration over his lamented colleague.
Here Witsius applied himself with unwearied assi-
duity to oriental learning; and he gave a specimen of
his proficiency, by composing an elegant oration in the
Hebrew language *On the Messiah of the Jews and
the Christians,* which, at the request of Leusden his
master, he pronounced with great applause before the
University, in the eighteenth year of his age.

In the year 1654, attracted by the fame of *Samuel
Maresius,* he repaired to the University of Groningen,
where he devoted himself wholly to divinity. Under
the guidance of that eminent Professor, he engaged in
the usual exercises preparatory for preaching, and performed them in the French tongue, to the entire satisfaction of his teacher. Having continued a whole year
at Groningen, he returned to Utrecht. While now,
as formerly, he heard with attention the different Professors of divinity both in public and private, he cultivated a peculiar familiarity with *Justus van der
Bogaerdt,* a man of uncommon judgment, gravity, and
piety. The admirable gifts of Bogaerdt, and the savour of evangelical and vital religion, which pervaded
alike his public discourses, his prayers, and his private
conversation, greatly endeared him to Witsius. According to his own acknowledgment, it was chiefly by
the divine blessing on the instructions of this excellent
divine, that he was preserved from the pride of science,
taught to receive the kingdom of heaven as a little
child, led beyond the outer court in which he had previously been inclined to linger, and conducted to the
sacred recesses of vital Christianity. His increased attention to spiritual religion, however, was far from

abating his ardour or retarding his progress in literary pursuits. About this time he wrote, and publicly debated in the University, under the presidency of Leusden, his *Theses* on the Trinity; in which, with great learning and ability, he proved that important doctrine from the writings of the ancient Jews, and showed how far their descendants have degenerated in that article from the sentiments of their ancestors.

The time was now come, when it was proper for Witsius to enter on the public service of the Church. Accordingly, having received ample testimonials from the Professors at Groningen and Utrecht, he presented himself for what is called the preparatory examination at Enchuysen in the month of May 1656. He gave full satisfaction to the Ministers, and was licensed to preach the Gospel. His endowments as a Preacher were soon perceived, and procured for him the cordial approbation of the churches. At the instigation of that excellent man, *John Boisus,* Minister of the French Protestant church at Utrecht, Witsius, too, though naturally bashful and diffident, was prevailed with to apply to the French divines assembled at Dort for license to preach publicly, and in the French language, in their churches. This he easily obtained, partly from the influence of the celebrated *Anthony Hulsius,* to whom, at the request of Boisus, he had written an excellent epistle in Hebrew. Availing himself of the privilege thus acquired, he often preached in French at Utrecht, Amsterdam, and other places. He entertained a design, also, of taking an excursion to France, that he might visit the eminent Divines of that country, and make further improvements in the language. Providence, however, prevented the execution of that design.

Having received a regular call from the church of *West-wouden*, he was ordained on the 8th of July 1657, in the 21st year of his age. For the space of four years and a-half, he laboured here with much alacrity, zeal, and success. The young people of his charge obtained his particular attention. In catechising and exhorting them, he accommodated himself, with great suavity and condescension, to their tender capacities; and such was their progress in knowledge, and such the accuracy with which they confirmed the doctrines of Christianity by appropriate passages of Scripture, and repeated the substance of the discourses they heard, that their parents and other elderly people around them at once blushed and rejoiced.

The growing reputation of Witsius attracted the notice of other churches. The church of *Wormeren* in the same tract of North Holland, a very numerous society but at that time distracted by intestine jars and animosities, thought they could not choose a pastor better qualified than Witsius to restore unanimity, and edify their souls. Judging it his duty to acquiesce in the call of that church, he was translated in October 1661. In this new sphere of usefulness, he exerted himself with exemplary discretion and fidelity, and not without remarkable success. He was universally esteemed and beloved; and although the people of *Sluice* in Flanders earnestly solicited him to come to them and preach the Gospel both in Dutch and French, he could not think of removing. He considered it right, however, to accept of a call which he afterwards received from the congregation of *Goes* in Zealand, and accordingly he was translated to that town in the year 1666.

At *Goes* his labours were signally acceptable and

useful. Enjoying favourable opportunities for retirement and study, and blessed with three excellent Colleagues, of whom he venerated two as his fathers, and loved the third as a brother, he often wished to live to old age in that tranquil retreat. But in November 1667, a most earnest and affectionate invitation was given to him by the church of *Leewarden*, the capital of West Friesland; and, after mature deliberation, he accepted their call, and commenced his ministry amongst them in the month of April 1668. The fidelity, prudence, and vigilance, which he discovered in this important station, and the courage and firmness he displayed in a season of extraordinary difficulty, when the United Provinces were harassed and alarmed by the tumults of war and the incursions of the enemy, commanded universal admiration. Dr Marck, who was then a student, and residing in that district, affirms that he knew no other man of God, whose labours were more abundantly blessed. To the church, the nobility, and the court, his services were equally grateful. Nor should it be omitted, that he was for some time tutor to HENRY CASIMIR, the most serene Prince of NASSAU, who was cut off by an early death;—that, with happy effect, he instructed AMELIA, the sister of HENRY, a Princess of eminent piety, who afterwards gave her hand to the Duke of SAXE-EISENACH;— and that he had the honour to preside when, in the presence of their illustrious mother ALBERTINA, both of them, much to the edification of the church, made a public profession of faith.

In the year 1675, in order to repair the heavy losses sustained by the death of the venerable CHRISTIANUS SCHOTANUS, and that of JOHN MELCHIOR STEINBERG, Witsius was elected Professor of divinity in the

University of FRANEKER, and also invited to take
the pastoral charge of the church in that city.   He removed, in consequence, to Franeker, where, after being
honoured with the degree of Doctor in Divinity, he was
installed Professor, April 15th ; on which occasion he
delivered before a numerous audience an excellent oration upon the character of a True Divine.   In this new
situation, he filled both the pulpit and the academical
chair with great dignity and extensive success ; and the
most perfect cordiality subsisted between him and NI-
CHOLAS ARNOLD, his aged and venerable colleague.

But the superior endowments, and increasing celebrity of Witsius, procured for him further honours. In
the year 1679, he was invited by the patrons of the
University of GRONINGEN to succeed the excellent
JAMES ALTINGIUS, as well in the theological and philological chairs, as in the university-church.   This
proposal, however, he was prevailed with to decline.
But at the beginning of the year immediately following, after the death of the celebrated BURMAN, the
citizens of UTRECHT despatched an honourable depu-
tation to Franeker, to importune him to adorn their
university and church with his residence ; and notwithstanding the opposition made to his removal by his
friends in Friesland, he considered himself bound in
duty and gratitude to embrace the opportunity thus
presented, of advancing the interests of literature and
religion in a city to which he had been indebted for
inestimable advantages in the days of youth.   Accordingly, having come to that city, he was invested with
the ministry of the church on the 25th of April, and,
four days after, commenced Professor of Divinity.   He
introduced himself to his academical labours with an
elegant oration on the excellence of Evangelical Truth,

which fully equalled the high expectations previously formed. At Utrecht he spent more than eighteen* years of his valuable life, discharging his various functions with indefatigable industry, and enjoying great happiness in the society of JOHN LEUSDEN his former tutor, PETER MAESTRICHT that illustrious divine, and his other learned and pious colleagues in the university, and in the church. His public sermons produced strong impressions on his audiences; his academical lectures were numerously attended, and exceedingly valued; his talents, integrity, and prudence, secured universal esteem. He was twice honoured with the supreme government and headship of the university; first in the year 1686, and afterwards in 1697. It deserves also to be recorded, that in the year 1685, when the States of Holland sent a splendid embassy to James II. King of Great Britain, who at that time was pursuing measures which led to his ruin, the three Ambassadors, at the suggestion of Lord DYKEVELT, himself one of the three, agreed in making choice of Witsius to accompany them to England, in the capacity of chaplain. In this appointment he cheerfully acquiesced; and after a stay of four months in England, he expressed, on his return, a sincere regard for the English divines, both conformists and dissenters, and acknowledged that he had found their company at once agreeable and highly instructive. The English, too, thought themselves happy in that opportunity of

---

* In Middleton's Evang. Biography, vol. iv. p. 163. it is said, that Witsius continued Professor at Utrecht "more than 22 years." But this is obviously a mistake of the respectable Author or his printer. The expression of Dr Marck is *ultra duodeviginta annos.* See his *Funebris Oratio* subjoined to his *Scripturariæ Exercitationes,* p. 723.

becoming more intimately acquainted with Witsius, and did not conceal the great respect and esteem in which they subsequently held him.   One striking expression of the veneration which the Divines of England bore for him, was, that towards the conclusion of the seventeenth century, when controversies respecting several articles of faith were keenly agitated amongst them, under the discordant names of Antinomians and Neonomians, they agreed to refer their differences to him as an able and impartial umpire.   Nor did Witsius perform a slight office of kindness to them, when, after carefully perusing the books they sent to him on each side of the question, which, from his imperfect acquaintance with the English language, cost him considerable labour, and after thoroughly unraveling the subtleties and intricacies in which the question was involved, he wrote his " Conciliatory Animadversions," which were first printed at Utrecht in the year 1696 ; and which, from the judgment, candour, impartiality, and perspicuity with which they are composed, were excellently calculated to unite the sentiments and allay the animosities of the contending theologians.

In the year 1698, when the death of SPANHEIM seemed to be approaching, the governors of the university of LEYDEN resolved to give Witsius an invitation to succeed that great man, in the professorship of divinity.   And, notwithstanding his obligations to the citizens of Utrecht, and their unwillingness to part with him, he complied with the invitation to Leyden ; partly because he was informed by HEINSIUS, the administrator of Holland, that it had the marked approbation of WILLIAM III., Stadtholder of the United States and King of Great Britain, a Prince for whom

he entertained a profound respect,* and who afterwards
assured him, in a personal conference with which he
was honoured, that he was highly pleased with his acquiescence in that call, and that himself had been the
first mover of it; and partly because he deemed it
equally conducive to the interest of the Church and his
own comfort, that he should now desist from the labours of the pulpit, and devote exclusively his few remaining years to academical employments. He commenced the duties of his office at Leyden on the 16th
of October 1698, by delivering an oration on the character of a candid and modest Divine; and for the
space of ten years he continued to perform them, with
unwearied diligence, and universal applause. Here he
was attended, as he had formerly been at Franeker
and Utrecht, by a numerous circle of promising youths
from every part of the Protestant world, who listened
with delight to his pious, learned, and eloquent instructions. Many candidates for the ministry from
Holland, Germany, France, Poland, Prussia, Switzer-
land, and Great Britain, and even individuals from
America, amongst whom, too, were some native Indians,
resorted to the seats of learning where he successively
taught; and after finishing their studies, returned to
their several native countries, equally built up in piety,
and improved in learning. Even Doctors in divinity
and Professors of the sciences, in great numbers, did
him the honour to hear him daily. His acquaintance,
too, was prized and solicited by the learned SELDEN,

* Witsius had an equally sincere regard for MARY, the Queen;
as appears, according to Dr Marck, from a discourse which he
preached and published on occasion of her death, and in which he
celebrated her virtues with peculiar dignity and elegance.

and by many eminent scholars and divines throughout
Europe.

Scarcely had he passed one year at Leyden, when,
in compliance with the importunate request of the
States of Holland and West Friesland, he reluctantly
accepted the office of Regent of the theological college
in the room of MARK ESSIUS, then just deceased.
In this arduous and honourable office, he discovered
strict fidelity, tempered with uncommon mildness and
affection towards his pupils.   He retained it till the
8th of February 1707, when, upon account of his advanced years and increasing infirmities, he resigned the
situation with all its emoluments.   At his own earnest
request, he was, at the same time, exempted from the
public duties of his professorship in the university, for
discharging which with his former accuracy and spirit,
he found himself, notwithstanding the unimpaired vigour of his mind, in a great degree disabled by bodily
indisposition.   On that occasion, he often declared to
an intimate friend, that he thought it much better to
desist altogether from his work, than not to perform it
in a becoming manner.

Amidst the arduous and incessant labours of his
useful life, Witsius was blessed with all that is soothing in domestic felicity.   In the year 1660, he married
ALETTA VAN BORCHORN, daughter to WESSAL VAN
BORCHORN, a citizen and merchant of good character
at Utrecht, and an esteemed elder in the church.
With this excellent woman, who was equally eminent
for the sweetness of her natural temper, and the amiable graces which adorn the Christian, he lived in unin-
terrupted harmony till the year 1684, when, after a
painful and lingering illness, she died in a manner or-
namental to the gospel.   He was no less happy in his

children.   Not to mention two sons who died young,
he had three pious and accomplished daughters, who
showed their venerable father every possible mark of
filial affection and respect.   Two of them, to wit,
MARTINA and JOHANNA, were respectably married
some time before his death.   PETRONELLA, however,
determined to remain with him to the last, and continued, with the most affectionate solicitude, to attend
and comfort him, amidst the growing infirmities of age.

Witsius never had the advantage of a vigorous constitution, or of a long course of confirmed health.   He
was often afflicted with certain painful and alarming
distempers, which threatened an early dismission from
the service of the Church on earth.   In advanced life,
he had several violent attacks of the gout and the
stone : and six years previous to his death, whilst sitting in the Professor's chair and delivering an academical lecture, he was seized, for the first time, with a
temporary dizziness, accompanied with a suspension of
memory and absence of thought.   These disorders,
though mitigated by medicine, were never thoroughly
cured.   It is perhaps worthy of notice that, notwithstanding his other ailments, arising, no doubt, in a
great degree, from his long continued habits of intense
application to reading and writing, he retained his eye-
sight in such perfection, that, within a few months of
his death, he was able, by moon-light, and without the
assistance of spectacles, to read the Greek New Testament in the smallest type.   His last illness was
ushered in by an universal languor, and, according
to the accounts of the celebrated BOERHAAVE, it
commenced in a fever, with which he was suddenly
seized on the 18th of October 1708, about one
o'clock in the morning ; and which, although it soon

subsided, was followed by an extreme debility of body and torpor of mind. The good man, perceiving these symptoms, with great serenity and composure told the physician and others around him, that he knew he had but few days to live. Nor was he mistaken. His senses were gradually weakened by repeated slumbers, whilst his soul was fixed on invisible objects, and sustained by the hope of a blessed immortality. In his very last hour, when Dr Marck stood by administering consolation to his much-revered friend, he signified his perseverance in the same faith and hope which he had often expressed before; and then, about noon, on the 22d of October 1708, he sweetly departed this life, and entered into the joy of his Lord, in the 73d year of his age, and 52d of his ministry.

His death was deeply regretted by the friends of religion in Holland and other countries. And on the 29th of October, after his mortal remains had been committed to the dust amidst the tears of a vast concourse of mourners, Dr Marck, the same worthy Divine who attended him in his last moments, by appointment of the Professors of the university of Leyden, pronounced a Funeral oration, which contains interesting details of his history. In the course of that oration, he takes occasion to specify, with much feeling, the friendly services which Witsius had done to himself, and the great advantages which he had derived, in youth, from the public discourses, academical lectures, personal intercourse, salutary counsels, and engaging example of this eminent man of God.

It only remains to present the reader with a rapid sketch of his Character, and a short notice of his Works.

His talents were of the first order. The force of his genius, the accuracy of his judgment, the strength of his memory, and the charms of his eloquence, were extensively known and admired. His learning was various and profound. Deeply skilled in languages, philosophy, and history, he improved them to the noblest purposes. He discovered an uncommon dexterity in availing himself of the aids of human literature for the elucidation of divine truth, and in bringing forth from his copious treasures whatever seemed most conducive to the illustration of the subject before him. With Theology in all its departments, he possessed an intimate acquaintance. He devoted himself, in particular, to the study of the BIBLE. Few have ever acquired either so complete a command of the expressions of Scripture in the original tongues, or so great a facility in expounding its most difficult passages. Instead of relying upon human authority, or suffering himself to be led by the greatest names, whether ancient or modern, he constantly appealed to the sacred volume as the only infallible standard, and implicitly acquiesced in the dictates of the Holy Spirit. His zeal for " the faith once delivered to the saints" conspicuously appeared in his discourses and writings. When dangerous opinions in philosophy and divinity prevailed, and when reason was extolled to the prejudice of faith and to the overthrow of the essential doctrines of the Christian religion, he vindicated the cause of truth with pious ardour and unshaken fidelity, most happily blended with meekness and prudence. With regard to the less important differences of sentiment which took place among sound and faithful theologians, no one could exercise greater mildness and forbearance. He was an admirer of that excellent saying; " Una-

" nimity in what is necessary, liberty in what is not ne-
" cessary, in all things prudence and charity." To
heal the breaches of Zion and promote peace and concord amongst brethren, was to him a delightful office.
In suavity of disposition and benignity of manners, few
have equalled, and perhaps none surpassed him. CAN-
DIDE was the motto inscribed upon his seal, and CAN-
DOUR shone forth in his temper and conduct. Even
towards those from whom he had suffered the most virulent reproach and abuse, he discovered an exemplary
spirit of meekness. It was observed, that he either
made no mention of them, or repaid their calumnies by
giving them those commendations, of which, on other
accounts, he considered them deserving. Under all
the diversified sufferings of life he displayed admirable
fortitude and patience; and such was his contentment
with his lot, that he often declared to his friends
he would not exchange his place in the Church and
University, for all the power and splendour of which
kings and emperors can boast. Those habits of activity
which he formed in youth, he retained to the last. In
the prime of life, he spent many nights totally without
sleep, and spared no effort or fatigue by which he might
advance the interests of literature and piety. His great
labours and frequent watchings, indeed, ill suited to a
feeble constitution, were probably carried to an injudicious excess. Amidst all his attainments and exertions,
unaffected humility and modesty adorned him. It was
evident that he indulged no vain conceit of his own capacities or performances; and when his most intimate
friends began to address him in the language of praise,
he immediately checked them. He was a real Christian, in short, as well as a great Divine. Sincere and
exalted piety was the foundation of all his virtues.

Animated by that " faith which worketh by love," he delighted in the various exercises of religion. To a regular and devout attendance on public worship, he added a conscientious performance of the more retired duties of the family and the closet. He never was happier than when he enjoyed fellowship with Heaven in spiritual meditation, and in stated and ejaculatory prayer. In singing praises to his Saviour and his God, he found a similar pleasure; and with a view to assist himself and his friends in that noble exercise, he composed several beautiful Hymns. The objects of eternity, in fact, were habitually present to his mind; and it was the wish of his heart to promote the highest interests of his pupils, and the people of his charge. The whole tenour of his conduct served to evince, that he was himself " spiritually minded," and that he aspired at nothing less, on behalf of all of whom he had the oversight, than to guide them, by the united influence of precept and example, to " the everlasting kingdom of our Lord and Saviour Jesus Christ." The religion of which Witsius was so able a teacher and so bright a pattern, be it remarked in conclusion, was equally at variance with that of the cold formalist, and the proud self-righteous devotee. With him it was a fundamental maxim, that Christ " in all things must have the pre-eminence;" and free and sovereign grace, reigning through the person and righteousness of the great Immanuel, he cordially regarded as at once the source of all our hope, and the grand incitement to a holy practice.

This extraordinary man, though dead, yet speaks by his writings; most of which, it is hoped, will continue, through many succeeding ages, to give instruction and delight to the lovers of sacred truth. In the year

1660, about three years after his entrance on the ministry, he published a learned and ingenious Treatise in Latin, which is now extremely scarce, entitled "*Judæus* " *Christianizans circa principia fidei et S. S. Trinita-* "*tem,*" i. e. " The Jew resembling the Christian with " regard to the principles of faith and the doctrine of " the Holy Trinity." In the year 1665, he gave to the public, in the vernacular language of Holland, " The practice of Christianity, with a spiritual repre- " sentation, first, of what is laudable in the unregene- " rate, and then, of what is culpable in the regenerate." He afterwards published, in the same language, "The " Lord's Controversy with his vineyard," and a defence of that treatise against some who impugned its tenets. His subsequent works in Latin were first given to the world at different dates, whilst he filled the theological chair successively at Franeker, Utrecht, and Leyden; and were afterwards collected in six Quarto Volumes. The first contains his celebrated work on the Covenants, which was early translated into Dutch by HARLIN- GIUS, a Minister of the Gospel at *Hoorn,* and of which an English Version has for nearly sixty years been in the hands of the public. The second Volume includes the Dissertations on the Creed, and on the Lord's Prayer. Those on the Creed were turned into Dutch soon after their publication, by Mr COSTERUS at Delft. His third Volume consists principally of a very learned treatise entitled *Ægyptiaca.* Its subject is the sacred rites of the Egyptians compared with those of the Hebrews; and the Author's design is to refute the sentiments of those who hold, that the ceremonies of the Mosaic ritual were borrowed from the idolatrous observances of ancient Egypt. The same Volume includes, also, the *Decaphylon,* or an Inquiry into the fortunes of the ten tribes of Israel, and an

Essay on the Thundering Legion under Aurelius Antoninus. The general title of Volumes fourth and
fifth is *Miscellanea Sacra,* " Sacred Miscellanies."
The Prophets and Prophecies of Scripture, the mysteries of the Levitical tabernacle, and the heresy of the
Donatists, form the principal subjects of the fourth.
The fifth, besides twenty-three Dissertations on a vast
variety of topics, biblical, historical, and theological,
comprises several public Orations, and the *Irenicum,*
or " Conciliatory Animadversions" formerly noticed.
A faithful Translation of this excellent little work, followed with judicious Notes, by the late Rev. Thomas
Bell of Glasgow, was published in that city, in the year
1807. The sixth and last Volume contains the most
of those performances of the author which were originally published during his residence at Leyden. It
consists of academical Lectures on the life of the Apostle Paul, twelve Dissertations on various topics, and a
Commentary on the Epistle of Jude.

It would be improper to protract this Memoir by a
more particular account of these instructive Volumes.
The brief sketch of their contents now given will enable the English reader to form some idea of their value
and extent. At their first appearance they were eagerly
sought after in every Protestant country, and under-
went numerous impressions. The lapse of more than
a century has neither consigned them to oblivion nor
impaired their worth; and many learned and good men
have expressed their persuasion, that the Works of
Witsius are immortal, and that they will never cease
to be admired for the classical elegance with which they
are written, the profound and varied erudition they discover, and the spirit of ardent and evangelical piety
which they uniformly breathe.

———

EVER since I entered on academical employments, FATHERS OF THE SENATE, I have considered it as the principal part of the business assigned me, to exert my best endeavours, with purity, perspicuity, accuracy, moderation, and gravity, to inculcate the sacred truth of the Gospel on the Students committed to my care, and to refer it, in its whole extent, to the practice of undissembled piety. As there is nothing more excellent, nothing more deserving of diligent study, and nothing which it is more profitable or pleasant to know, than that divine doctrine; so it is a subject, which, above all others, requires to be treated with pure and

holy dispositions. The man who does not bring to it
a candid, peaceable, and tranquil temper, and a mind
assiduously devoted to genuine piety, is not merely unworthy to teach, but even incapable of learning to advantage, this heavenly wisdom. Wherever an unhappy
zeal for innovation, a love of debate, an acrimonious
spirit of wrangling, a frantic spirit of party, an arrogant
self-exaltation joined with contempt of others,—where-
ever these and the like mischievous tempers prevail, it
is difficult to believe that a pure love of truth dwells
in the same breast, whatever fair pretences to it may
be assumed. That person, in reality, doth not yet
know and discern the truth as it is in Christ Jesus,
who knows it, merely to exercise the volubility of his
tongue in vain talking, to employ the dexterity of his
pen in litigious disputation, or to render it, in any other
way, subservient to his own ambition. The Gospel
will only unfold its treasures, and fill the mind with a
sense of its sacred sweetness, when it irradiates the understanding with the native light of its simplicity, and
thus inflames the will and affections with the ardours
of a pure love,—when it consumes the noxious tares
and destructive weeds of vice,—and when, elevating
the whole man above the transitory vanities of this
world, and causing his heart to burn with the desire of
heaven, it transforms him into the image of the divine
purity.

Impressed with these sentiments respecting the manner and the object of teaching and learning divine
truth, I formed the resolution of giving some specimen
of my design to the young men attending the University. With this view, I selected the principal articles
of our Religion, as they are contained in the Catholic
Creed, for the subject of lectures to my Pupils; that I

might explain to them the nature of those doctrines; assert, demonstrate, and vindicate their truth; and, what was chiefly intended, illustrate and enforce their application to holy practice. Such was the origin of these Dissertations; which I began at the very commencement of my professional labours in the celebrated School of FRIESLAND, and finished in your Academy, FATHERS OF THE SENATE; to whom, conformably to the dictates of reason and justice, they are now cheerfully DEDICATED.

Since you have already befriended the Author by the generous invitation with which you honoured him, by the favourable reception which you gave him at the first, and by the remarkable kindness and liberality which you continue to show him; have the goodness to accept of this small literary gift in the same obliging manner.—Accept of it, not as a price by which I exempt myself from all obligations, but as a pledge, by which I bind myself to serve you; for, by these discourses, which are of inconsiderable value, and written solely for the benefit of my pupils, I by no means propose to pay, but only to acknowledge, the debt of gratitude I owe you. Let me request you, in addition to all your other favours, to form your estimate of the gift which I now present, not so much from its intrinsic worth, as from the disposition of him that offers it; who, whilst he holds himself bound to render to you the most valuable offerings, was able to find nothing else, at present, in the whole circle of literature, by which he could give any proof of his regard and fidelity.

I conclude with my prayer on your behalf. May that ALMIGHTY GOD, who has rescued your Republic, and together with it, your Church and University from so many dangers,—who, with his powerful right hand has defended, protected, and prospered it,—who, in these times of extraordinary peril and difficulty, whilst one tempest followed another in close succession, and the Republic seemed on the verge of ruin, caused you to remain at the helm—May the same GOD still preserve the Republic to you, and you to the Republic! Under your benign and auspicious government, " may concord and virtue return! may religion and integrity prevail!"*

FATHERS OF THE SENATE, farewell; and, after having prosperously exercised the magistracy for many years, may you transmit it hereafter to your sons, and to your descendants in the remotest times!

In these terms I wrote, in your City, on the 2d of May, in the year 1681, during the Consulship of ALBERT VAN BENTHEM, and PAUL VOET VAN WINSSEN. I repeated the writing on the 6th of July, in the year 1689, during the Consulship of JOHN BORRE VAN AMERONGEN II. and ARNOLD SPOOR. And, now, for the third, and, possibly, the last time, I write in the same terms, on this 1st day of April, in the year 1697, during the Consulship of CORNELIUS VAN LIDT DE JEUDE, and EVERARD VAN ZYPES-TEIN II.;—the year, in which, from your distinguished friendship for me, for which I can never be sufficiently grateful, you have been pleased, FATHERS, to appoint me, for the second time, Rector of your University.

---

* ——— Redeat concordia virtus,
    Cumque fide, pietas alta cervice vagetur.

AUTHOR'S PREFACE

THE THIRD EDITION.

———

I SHALL not trespass on your patience, CANDID READER, by a tedious preamble, but will show you, in a few words, the design and scope of the following work. It seems proper to apprize you, first of all, that it is not intended for the learned, or for such as have been long engaged in sacred studies, but only for learners, and my own Pupils, whom I wished to furnish with a light to direct them to the proper improvement of our holy Religion. It appeared to me extremely undesirable, that those with whose education for the sacred office we are intrusted, should at length ascend the pulpit to entertain the Christian people with frigid, though perhaps sublime, discourses, or with unprofitable, though sufficiently warm, discussions; neglecting, in the mean time, to inspire their minds with any relish for heavenly objects, with any desire for divine consolations, with any love for genuine piety. I daily urged them to consider that Religion is not seated in the tongue, but in the mind; that it consists not in words, but in deeds; not in the subtlety of specula-

tions, but in purity of heart; not in the affectation of
new discoveries, but in the prosecution of a new life.
They were frequently reminded, that he alone is a true
Theologian, who adds the practical to the theoretical
part of Religion—who combines exhortation to duty
with the elucidation of doctrine.   They were told, also,
that this is not to be done merely in a superficial, formal, and customary manner, at the conclusion of a sermon; but that the whole discourse should be so framed,
that the soul, fixed in earnest and adoring contemplation of astonishing truths, may feel itself inflamed with
a heavenly zeal to regulate the life in a manner becoming the knowledge and the faith of those glorious reali-
ties.   I inculcated, further, that the minds of the
hearers must be so instructed, that they may attempt a
careful examination of themselves, and be able to ascertain by infallible marks, whether they have a personal interest in the promises of the Gospel :—and that
this must be so strongly and pathetically urged, that
the most secure may be roused from their fatal lethargy,
and every hearer induced to inquire, with eager solicitude, into the state of his own soul.   I added, that
there is not a single article of our Religion which is
not mightily adapted to accomplish this purpose, and
proceeded to confirm the truth of this remark by several
examples.   Some of my Students then began most
earnestly to request me to favour them with my thoughts
in writing; and such is the origin of these Dissertations.

I intended, in the first instance, that what relates to
the Theory should be supposed to be sufficiently known
already, from Catechetical Institutes, Systems of Theology, and what are called Common-place books; and
that my only business should be to point out the application of the doctrines of faith to Christian practice.

But at the very commencement of the undertaking, my Pupils expressed a strong desire to learn, also, what appeared to me to be the best method of illustrating, and the most eligible arguments for defending, the doctrines themselves; and this part of their request, too, I was unwilling to refuse. Hence I have sometimes stated those doctrines, from the Scriptures, at considerable length; and when the occasion required, have refuted the objections and cavils of adversaries.

In the selection of the arguments, however, and in the manner of treating them, I have used my own liberty;—a liberty of which I think no one ought to be deprived, who is sincerely desirous that all those truths, by the profession of which the Church of Christ is distinguished from erroneous societies of every sort, may be preserved pure and entire; and to whom nothing in his whole life affords greater pleasure than exerting his utmost efforts to illustrate and confirm these doctrines, and to apply them to their legitimate use. We are Christians. We have one infallible Master and Teacher, Jesus Christ. When we recur to men, " to " follow constantly the sentiments of one individual," as *Seneca* somewhere elegantly says, " is to act not as " a member of the commonwealth, but as an abettor of " a party."* Such conduct I utterly detest, and trust that I shall always avoid. " I am the servile follower " of no man; I bear no man's name; I show great re- " spect for the judgment of eminent men; I claim per- " mission, also, in some degree, to respect my own."

As I grudge no one this innocent liberty, so I supposed that no one would have grudged it to me. There were not wanting several persons, however, whom it

* Unius semper sententiam sequi, non id curiæ, sed factionis est.

displeased.   Some apprehend that I have not every
where expressed myself in a manner sufficiently conformable to old opinions; whilst others are still more
highly offended, because I have not always acquiesced
in new doctrines, and in periodical interpretations of
the prophecies.   To make no mention of others, with
whom I shall never be disposed to have any altercation;
—the celebrated JOHN VAN DER WAEYEN, once my
Colleague, friend, and familiar acquaintance, after
he began to differ from himself, also deserted and
opposed his friends.   Although, formerly, his opinion
of me was not very unfavourable; yet, having altered his
procedure, he has thought proper, in most of his writings, both in the Latin and in our vernacular tongue,
not only to censure and expose my publications; but,
likewise, to attack and traduce my character, with such
violence, haughtiness, and arrogance, with such daring
falsehood, such unbounded licentiousness of calumny,
and such wanton scurrility; that he seems either not
to have known, or, at least, to have, in this instance,
forgotten alike all the rules of politeness, and all the
laws of equity and probity.

What, after all, is the crime of which I have been
guilty?   None whatever, except that, in conformity
to my duty as a Professor of Theology, neither attach-
ing myself to parties nor indulging in invectives, I have
calmly expressed my sentiments in relation to those
topics, which, during these years, have been disputed
among the learned; and that, being a person of a weak
capacity and timid disposition, I entertained apprehensions in my own mind, and gave warning to several
men of distinction, of those disorders by which the
peace of the Churches of Friesland has now, for some
time past, been disturbed.

This obloquy would have given me more uneasiness, had I not seen others treated in the same manner, whose names are venerable in the Church; and, in particular, that eminent individual, who is so distinguished for his extensive and correct acquaintance with every department of sacred learning, that he has, perhaps, no superior in the Reformed Churches; and whose hearer, pupil, and admirer, not his colleague, VAN DER WAEYEN himself once was.

If the great man thinks proper to treat his Brethren in this manner, he shall gratify his inclination without any interruption from me, provided he can justify his conduct to God and to the Churches. Far be it from me, ever to follow his example. I leave his expressions with himself, determined to answer his revilings with perpetual silence; and to endeavour, through the grace of God, to refute them, not by words, but by actions. I do not think so highly of him, or so meanly of myself, or so unjustly of his readers, as to fear that prudent and impartial men will form their judgment respecting me, according to his reproaches. If, in the mean time, he shall throw out any suggestion which may prove conducive to a more clear and distinct knowledge of divine truth, whatever be the manner in which it is propounded, I will accept of it with gratitude. I am one of those who are solicitous to make daily advances, and who refuse sound and salutary instruction from no man. It would have sincerely rejoiced me, to have been able to receive information from the SUMMARY OF CHRISTIAN THEOLOGY which he published lately: nor, although I found myself repeatedly censured in it at great length, should I have thought that any cause of displeasure was given me, if the censure had been accompanied with arguments sufficient to establish the charge of inaccurate conceptions or unfair reasoning. I now clearly perceive, that, owing either to multiplicity of business, or to precipitation, he has not sufficiently understood me in some places, and has, consequently, imputed to me absurdities, which I am far from maintaining. In other points, it is a great consolation to me, that if I do err, I hold errors in common with the most excellent, and even the greater part of the doctors of our Church; nor can I be accused of any fault, but that of defending sentiments which are generally received. Whether I act considerately or otherwise, this celebrated man must forgive me, if I prefer the sentiments of others, who apply to these sacred studies with a more calm and unbiassed mind, and give less indulgence to their passions. " A violent spirit conducts every thing improperly."*

As, however, I do not consider myself faultless, so I would not have my mistakes to prove injurious to the truth. With respect to that want of candour with which he often upbraids me, I know not in what way it is possible for any man to vindicate himself from this aspersion, except by a confident protestation of sincerity, and by discovering it in his conduct when he is convinced of an error. To judge the inward disposition, is the prerogative of Him who alone searches the reins and the hearts. The God of heaven has reserved to himself, the secrets of all minds; and he only who formed the recesses of the breast, is able to unlock and disclose them. Yet I aver that I have never attributed any sentiment to any person, but what I believed he had expressed by word or writing. If I have misrepresented any one's opinion, I have not done this in-

* Malè cuncta ministrat Impetus.

tentionally, but inadvertently; and when informed of my mistake, I will so correct it that no further cause of complaint shall remain. I cheerfully offer " the sponge, to rectify the slips of the pen."*

I have only to request, that others would exercise the same candour, and that they would not conceal, by a studied obscurity of language, sentiments, which, when they have a convenient opportunity, they deliver more explicitly to their friends. My manner of teaching was never of that kind; but, neither courting the favour, nor dreading the displeasure of any man, I have always expressed, as distinctly as I could, what appeared to me, to be true and just, and consonant to the word of God.

I must beware, however, of exhausting the patience of the reader, by an odious dispute about what does not immediately belong to the present design. The topic to which I refer, will be discussed in its proper place in the third Edition of the books which I have written on the *Economy of the Divine Covenants;* where, having examined the whole subject with great care, and in the fear of God, I will show that I have received further instruction, and mention those to whom I am indebted, and at the same time discreetly defend what had been justly expressed.

In compliance with the solicitations of my friends, I wrote thus in the year 1689, lest, as usually happens, a wrong interpretation should be put on my silence. Agreeably to my expectation, the third Edition of the Treatise on the Economy of the Covenants, was subsequently published: and in that Edition I have performed what I had intended, with all that reverence for

---

* Σπογγον, ἀκεστορίην πλαζομένης γραφίδος.

holy writ, with all that candour, moderation, and gentleness, and with all that mildness towards persons of opposite sentiments, which it was possible for me. to manifest. Let the pious, judicious, and impartial reader judge; and let him unite with me in prayer to God, that his good Spirit may lead us in the paths of righteousness and truth.

DISSERTATION I.

ON THE AUTHORS, AND THE AUTHORITY,
OF THE APOSTLES' CREED.

_____

I. As it is my design to illustrate, in a course of academical Dissertations, the doctrine which is briefly
comprised in the Apostles' Creed,[1] the subject seems
to require that I should begin with some account of the
Authors, and the Authority of that Creed. This
branch of theological learning, however, has already
been amply discussed by *James Usher, Gisbert Voetius,
Gerard John Vossius,* and *John Henry Heidegger,*
all of them men of great eminence and most extensive
reading, who may be justly thought to have superseded
the necessity of much labour on the part of their successors. To me, at least, nothing remains, but to exhibit, in this discourse, for the benefit of those who
shall favour me with their attention, a concise abridgment of what these writers have stated at large, and
have confirmed by luminous and satisfactory testimonies from all antiquity.

II. That the Apostles are the real Authors of the
Creed which commonly bears their name, is in general

[1] See Note I.

maintained by the Doctors of the church of Rome, as so indubitable a fact, that they deem it an instance of the most daring temerity to call it in question. They tell us, that the Apostles, after they were filled with the Holy Ghost, and before they departed from Jerusalem to preach the Gospel in the various regions of the earth, judged a form of sound words requisite both for their own sake, lest they should teach discordant doctrines and become alienated from one another in affection, and for the sake of the church, that she might have an authorized formulary for the instruction of those that were to be baptized;—that they, therefore, composed such a form, consisting of a few simple but comprehensive sentences, and containing a summary of whatever it is necessary to believe with the heart unto righteousness, and to confess with the mouth unto salvation;—and that this is the origin of the Creed which we now have. At what time, however, this was done, they cannot certainly determine. Some are of opinion that it took place immediately after the effusion of the Spirit upon the Apostles on the day of Pentecost; while others refer it to the time when, as we are informed in the twelfth chapter of the Acts, Herod Agrippa, (not *Antipas*, as the celebrated *Vossius*, in his sixth *Thesis*, has inadvertently said,) in order to gratify the Jews, stretched forth his hands to persecute the Christians.

III. Another circumstance, too, is added to the story. They say that this formulary was not prepared by any one Apostle, appointed to perform the service in the name of the whole college of Apostles; but that each of them pronounced his own particular article, and that the matter was so adjusted that the number of articles exactly corresponded to the number of Apostles. Thus, whilst the different articles were dictated by different Apostles, the entire Creed received the stamp of their united approbation.

IV. That we might remain ignorant of nothing relative to so momentous an affair, *Baronius,** the Author of *Ecclesiastical Annals,* has even informed us, to which of the Apostles we are indebted for each of the articles. Quoting *St Augustine,* he tells us that this celebrated Father, in his hundred and fifteenth sermon,† wrote as follows. " PETER said, I believe in " God the Father Almighty : JOHN,—Maker of hea- " ven and earth : JAMES,—and in Jesus Christ, his " only Son, our Lord : ANDREW,—who was conceived " by the Holy Ghost, born of the Virgin Mary : PHI- " LIP,—suffered under Pontius Pilate, was crucified, " dead, and buried : THOMAS,—he descended into " hell, the third day he rose again from the dead : " BARTHOLOMEW,—he ascended into heaven, and sit- " teth on the right hand of God the Father Almighty : " MATTHEW,—from thence he shall come again to " judge the quick and the dead : JAMES, the son of " Alpheus,—I believe in the Holy Ghost, the holy " catholic Church : SIMON ZELOTES,—the commu- " nion of saints, the forgiveness of sins : JUDE, the " brother of James,—the resurrection of the body : " and MATTHIAS completed the work, saying,—and " the life everlasting. Amen."

V. To obviate the charge of credulity to which they manifestly expose themselves by giving credit to such traditions, the Roman Catholic Doctors endeavour to establish all these points by a variety of arguments. Why, say they, in the *first* place, should this be deno-

---

* *Ad An.* xliv.   † *De Tempore.*

minated *the Apostles' Creed* by the whole Christian
Church, unless the Apostles were its real authors?
Secondly, They derive an argument from the term
*Symbolum,** which they suppose to denote a *collation,*
resembling that kind of social feast among the ancients,
to which the guests contributed by bringing each his
own share. They affirm that this title was given to
these articles of faith, because each of the Apostles
contributed some undeniable article of the Christian
doctrine to this spiritual banquet. To hear their own
language; " *Symbolum,* says *Gabriel Biel,*† is a word
" derived from *syn,* that is, together, and *bolos,* a par-
" ticle or morsel; signifying, so to speak, a collection
" of particles; for each of the Apostles furnished his
" own particle—his own morsel." *Thirdly,* they produce a cloud of witnesses from antiquity, on the vast
number of whom *Genebrard* lays a mighty stress.‡
Nay, if we believe *Sixtus* of *Sienna,*§ " All the or-
" thodox Fathers affirm that the Creed was composed
" by the Apostles themselves." They avail themselves,
in particular, of the testimony of *Rufinus,* who has
treated the history of the compilation of the Creed at
great length. *Fourthly,* They reason from utility, as
suggesting, or even demanding, this measure. It was
expedient that the Apostles, " when about to separate
" from each other, should conjunctly frame a rule for
" directing them in their subsequent preaching of the
" Gospel; lest, perhaps, when at a distance from
" one another, they should teach mankind jarring doc-
" trines." These are the words of *Rufinus.* So then,

---

* *Symbolum* is the Latin word for *Creed.* T.

† *In distinct.* xxiii. *quæst. unica art.* i. *lib. 3.*

‡ *In* iii. *de Trinitate.*

§ *Bibliothecæ Sanctæ,* Lib. ii.

some form of agreement in doctrine was, from the beginning, useful, if not indispensable, with respect to the Apostles themselves. Still less could the church remain without such a Creed. It was requisite that those who were to be baptized should make a confession of their faith : such a confession must be at once brief, comprehensive, and perspicuous : and we see that the Apostles' Creed is exactly of this description.

vi. But, though these considerations are brought forward with very great confidence, and though they find several abettors even among the Protestants; they are not sufficient to deter us from adopting the language of the excellent *Chamier:** " If it is not abso-
" lutely false that the Creed was composed in this man-
" ner by the Apostles, it is, at the least, what must be
" universally allowed to make the nearest approach to
" falsehood,—utterly uncertain." As it may not be unprofitable to eradicate prejudices of this sort out of the minds of men, let us proceed to examine the force of each of these arguments.

vii. In reply to the *first* argument, we admit that this summary of doctrine is commonly called the *Apostles' Creed;* but we ask, by what authority, and also, in what sense, it is so called ? It is possible that it may have obtained this title, from a general and established opinion that they were its authors. From this, however, no certain conclusion can be formed. Learned men have remarked that not even all the titles of the Sacred Books, nor all the short notices subjoined to the Epistles of Paul, are authentic and certain.[2] And who ever ventured to assert the authen-

---

* *Panstr. Lib.* ix. *de Canone, Cap.* 10.
[2] See NOTE II.

ticity of the title of the Creed? Or, if any man should assert, how could he prove it? Allowing, however, that it was no sooner composed than it received the name of the Apostolic Creed, and even that it was rightly so called; still the opinion for which our opponents contend, will not be satisfactorily confirmed. It is highly probable, that it received this denomination, in reference, not to the authors, but to the matter;—as it contains those principles of faith, which are collected from the Apostolic writings. The Creed of the church of Jerusalem, which differs from ours both in sense and in words, was certainly not composed by the Apostles; yet it is denominated by *Cyril*, " A " profession of the holy and APOSTOLIC faith."* Nor do I suppose the Apostles to have been the authors of the decrees of the council of Nice; yet referring to those decrees, *Athanasius* says, " The councils of our own times write APOSTOLICALLY," that is, conformably to the apostolical writings.

VIII. There is still less force in the *second* argument; for, though we should admit that *Symbolum* means a collection, or a *collation*, the Creed might be so called on account of the plurality, not of the persons collecting, but of the articles collected. As *Cajetan* has ingeniously observed,† we have an instance of this in *Athanasius*, who alone compiled a *Symbolum;* if indeed he be the Author of the Creed commonly ascribed to him. But we do not admit that the word *Symbolum* signifies a collation, or a feast prepared by the contributions of the company. A feast of this sort is called by the Greeks, not σύμϐολον, but συμϐολὴ. It

---

* *Catechesi.* xviii.
† *Ad Thomæ secundam secundæ. Quæst.* i, *Art.* 8.

is certain that, according to the definition which *Aristophanes* gives of the term, " συμβολὴ is a feast upon what is jointly contributed by several persons." Before *Vossius* took notice of this, it was observed by *Casaubon*,* and also by *Matthias Martinius*.† I will not deny, however, that *Hesychius* explains σύμβολον, *symbolum*, as signifying, besides other things, συμπόσιον, *a feast*. But as to the trifling remarks of *Biel*, and other such scholastic writers, respecting the contribution of different morsels, they are unworthy of a serious refutation in the present enlightened age. This formulary is denominated a *Symbolum*, because it is, as it were, a sign of the covenant with God, into which we enter at baptism ; and a sort of military oath, by which faithful soldiers of Christ may be easily distinguished from perfidious deserters. In this sense of the word, *Herodian* speaks of *a military symbolum*.‡ *Maximus* of *Turin*§ has also well observed, that " *Symbolum* is a sign and seal, by which a distinction " is made betwixt the faithful and the perfidious."[3]

IX. The *third* argument, which is derived from the authority of the Fathers, is obviously of little weight; for, 1st, the learned *Vossius* has remarked, that what the Papists now so strenuously urge, was affirmed by no writer prior to the beginning of the fifth century, and that even after that period some time elapsed, before it was asserted by any one that did not belong to the Roman, the Italian, or at least the Western Church. But men who flourished at so great a distance from the apostolic age, cannot, with propriety, be esteemed authors of the highest antiquity. 2dly, Some

---

* *Ad Athenæum*, lib. iii. cap. 31.   † *In Etymologico*.

‡ Lib. ii. cap. 13.   § *De Tradit. Symb.*

[5] See NOTE III.

passages to this effect appear to be forged. It is certain that the hundred and fifteenth discourse of *Augustine*, from which *Baronius* shows what part of the Creed was dictated by each of the Apostles, is not accounted genuine by others;—a circumstance which *Baronius* himself hath not presumed to dissemble. 3dly, Even *Rufinus*, whose testimony on this point is usually placed in the front, is not, in the estimation of Popish writers themselves, an unexceptionable witness. " According to the testimony of *Jerome*," says *Bellarmine*, " he is guilty of many falsehoods in his apology " for *Origen*."* *Possevino* also, calls the writings of *Rufinus* " a labyrinth ;" and adds, " what sort of ca-" pacity or integrity *Rufinus* possessed, it is not easy " to determine."† 4thly, *Rufinus* himself does not positively assert that the Creed was composed by the Apostles. He says merely, that " such was the tradition of the Fathers," intimating that he embraced the opinion which generally prevailed, not that he regarded it as a certain historical fact. *Erasmus*, too, in his Reply to the Censure of the *Parisians*, has remarked, " He does not say, in the course of his narration, *the* " *Apostles*, but *they who compiled the Creed*; as if he " were uncertain by whom it was composed." 5thly, In some instances, even the most ancient Fathers were wretchedly deceived by pretended tradition, though they received it from the lips of those who were believed to be hearers of Apostles. On whom has not *Papias*, that zealous but too credulous and superstitious Father, imposed, by his passion for retailing apostolical traditions ? Who does not know that *Cyprian*, with his

---

* *Libro de Scriptor. Eccles. Num.* 390.
† *In Apparatu Sacro*, tom. ii. p. 358.

followers, alleged apostolical tradition in defence of their Anabaptism; which however, the church of Rome, in common with us, do not acknowledge to be genuine? The marks by which genuine may be distinguished from spurious traditions are so obscure, and the whole subject of traditions is so involved in the thickest shades of darkness, that they are incapable of proving any thing, and furnish no evidence sufficient to command assent. Thus the third argument also falls to the ground.

x. The *fourth* argument exposes to just suspicion, the opinion which it is produced to support. The Apostles, being full of the Holy Ghost, who guided them into all truth, stood in need of no such rule or bond of union for their direction in preaching the Gospel. Nor at the beginning of Christianity was any profession of faith required from those to whom baptism was about to be administered, except a simple declaration that they believed in Christ, or in the Father, the Son, and the Holy Ghost; as appears from the baptism of the converts mentioned in the Acts of the Apostles. Thus, from an examination of the arguments, it is manifest, that they are insufficient to demonstrate that the Apostles are the Authors of that Creed which commonly bears their name.

xi. What has been said might suffice to destroy this hypothesis; which ought not to be believed, because it cannot be proved. To complete its overthrow, however, we shall produce several arguments, calculated to show that it is extremely improbable. 1st, If the Apostles had, by mutual consultation, compiled any such Creed as was intended to be a bond of union between themselves and a compendious rule of faith to the whole Church, it is not probable that St Luke, who

has accurately detailed the acts of the Apostles, and
even some of their transactions that are of far less importance, would have passed over so momentous a matter in so profound silence; or that the Apostles
themselves would have taken no notice of it in their
Epistles.[4] 2dly, The ancient Fathers also, when engaged in controversy with the heretics, would not have
neglected to appeal to this Creed; of which they could
and ought to have availed themselves, as a most useful
compend and a most effectual weapon; if any such
Creed prepared by the Apostles had existed. 3dly,
The holy Fathers, had they possessed such a Creed,
would never have thought of composing so many other
Creeds and Confessions, which are much less plain,
comprehensive, and perfect, than that which is styled
the Apostles' Creed. Their numerous attempts of this
kind can be accounted for on no other supposition, than
that the Creed which is so indisputably superior to all
of them, was not yet compiled and known. 4thly, If
the Apostles had delivered, to the Church Universal, a
particular Creed, consisting of certain sentences, arranged in a certain order, and expressed in certain
words, it is reasonable to suppose that there would not
have been much diversity in the Creeds of different
churches. The Creed of Jerusalem, however, which
Cyril has explained, varies not a little from the common one, in the sentences, in the arrangement, and in
the words; as *Vossius* has shown by an accurate collation. But is it credible that any Church would have
preserved the Creed with stricter fidelity, than that
Church, in the bosom of which it is pretended that the
Creed was formed?

[4] See Note IV.

XII. Further, that the Apostles delivered each his own sentence, is so far from being a probable circumstance, that it appears almost ridiculous, and tends to transform this venerable summary of faith into a strangely incoherent rhapsody. Who can bring himself to believe, that Peter said, " I believe in God the " Father Almighty ;" that John added, "the Maker of " heaven and earth," and so forth ;—the articles sometimes improperly severed, sometimes improperly joined ? What has not temerity attempted, in order to make out the precise number of twelve articles, corresponding to the number of Apostles ? Are these two expressions distinct articles,—first, " I believe in God the Father " Almighty," secondly, " the Maker of heaven and " earth ?" These, however, they so disjoin, as to attribute the former to Peter, the latter to John.—Do the following sentences make only one article, " He de- " scended to hell: the third day he rose again from " the dead ?" Yet these two sentences, which are quite distinct from each other, the one relating to the humiliation, the other to the exaltation of Christ, they reduce to one; which they ascribe to Thomas.—In fine, is this, which they attribute to James the son of Alpheus, no more than a single article, " I believe in " the Holy Ghost, in the holy catholic Church ?" These notions are too puerile, to deserve the least credit among men of sense.

XIII. What opinion then are we to hold respecting this Creed ? We will state in a few words what appears to us to come nearest the truth. In the original simplicity of the Christian Religion, no Creed existed, excepting that which our Lord delivered, Matthew xxviii. 19. " Go ye, therefore, and teach all nations, " baptizing them in the name of the Father, and of the

" Son, and of the Holy Ghost." This short and simple Creed is the foundation, to which the ancient Fathers very frequently appealed. The venerable *Voetius*, a preceptor for whom it becomes me to entertain the greatest respect, has selected from their writings several passages to this effect, two of which I will here cite. " *Athanasius*, in his *Epistle to all every where that* " *are sound in the faith*, and in his *Oration against* " *Sabellius, and against the Arians*, says; ' The whole " sum and body of our faith is comprised in the words " of our baptism, and is founded on that scripture, Go " and baptize all nations in the name of the Father, " and of the Son, and of the Holy Ghost.' *Augustine*, " in his discourse on the Creed, says in like manner, " ' Our Lord Jesus Christ himself hath furnished us " with this standard of doctrine, and no man of piety " entertains any doubt respecting that canon of the " catholic faith, which was dictated by him, who is him- " self the object of faith. Our Lord Jesus Christ, I " say, after his glorious resurrection from the dead, " and shortly before his ascension to the Father, be- " queathed to the disciples these mysteries of faith, " saying, Go and teach all nations, baptizing them in " the name of the Father, of the Son, and of the Holy " Ghost."

XIV. Heresies, however, increasing with the lapse of time, the church was no longer permitted to continue in that state of primitive simplicity. In order to distinguish the doctrine of the church from heresy, and the true sons of the church from heretics and their followers, several articles were gradually added, and reared as a superstructure on this simple foundation. Of this there is abundant evidence. 1st, The most ancient writers, as *Martial, Ignatius, Justin, Irenæus*,

and *Tertullian,* when they propose to give a summary
of the faith, proceed no farther than the doctrine of the
Trinity. *Hilary* contends at great length, that the profession of the Trinity ought alone to suffice, and should
be held sufficient for the exclusion of heretics.* The
same opinion is expressed by *Paschasius.*† 2dly, It
is manifest that there were many copies of the Creed,
in which the article respecting Christ's *descent into
hell,* did not appear. *Rufinus* himself asserts, that, in
his time, it was wanting in the Creed of the Roman,
and of the Eastern churches.‡ It is conjectured by
Moulin, that that article was borrowed from the Creed
of *Athanasius,* and inserted in the Apostles' Creed, by
persons who did not observe that, in the former, the articles concerning Christ's death and burial are wanting.§ But, on this subject, we shall have occasion to
speak more fully and particularly, in its proper place.
3dly, The epithet *Catholic,* given to the church, was
unknown in the age of the Apostles; nor did *Rufinus*
know it. It is probable that the purpose for which
this title was originally assumed, was to distinguish
the church which existed everywhere from the conven-
ticles of heretics and schismatics, such as those of the
Novatians, and afterwards of the *Donatists.* From
these arguments we conclude, that the Creed was not
the production of one author, or of one council, but was
gradually enriched by numerous additions, in successive
ages, on various occasions, by different hands;—traces,
however, still remaining, of the old foundation upon
which the rest of the articles were built.

* *De Trinitate,* Lib. ii. *initio.*
† *Præfat. ad Libros de Spiritu Sancto.*
‡ *Expositio Symboli,* Cap. xx.
§ *Thesi. Sedanens.* Tom. i. p. 581.

xv. Thus far of the Authors of the Creed; let us now consider its Authority. We hold then, 1st, That greater authority is justly allowed to this Creed than to all other compositions of the kind that are extant; for it is at once comprehensive in doctrine, perspicuous in language, and neat in arrangement; and it is now so generally received in Christendom, that the man who wantonly rejects it, ought not to be esteemed a Christian. 2dly, Since it exactly agrees in sense with the Holy Scriptures, and is almost entirely expressed in the words of Scripture, we do not deny that, with regard to its matter, it may be denominated Divine and Authentic. 3dly, With respect to the form, however, and the disposition of the several articles, it is merely a human writing; and, in consequence, has a claim to our faith, not independently or of itself, but purely because it is derived from canonical Scripture, and entirely accords with it. 4thly, We do not admit, therefore, that, formally considered, it is to be accounted no less authentic than the written word of God, as the Papists contend; or *almost* authentic, as some of the Protestants have incautiously said: for the divine authority, being always supreme, admits of no degrees. If the Creed was delivered by Apostles under inspiration of the Spirit of God, it is not almost, but altogether authentic. If it was not dictated by Apostles, or by Apostolical men, from an impulse of the infallible Spirit, (and we have shown above that it has no claim to so high an origin,) it is neither *altogether* nor *almost* authentic. In this matter, an intermediate degree, or a qualifying phrase, can have no place.[5]

xvi. For the direction of young people, one thing

[5] See NOTE V.

still remains to be noticed. In the Church of Rome, the Apostles' Creed is most improperly considered as a kind of form of prayer; and to this childish error their Doctors themselves have given occasion or encouragement, by calling it " a Catholic Hymn, and a Sacred Thanksgiving."* Let it be observed, that these three well known forms, the Decalogue, the Lord's Prayer, and the Creed are to be thus distinguished from each other. In the Decalogue, or ten Commandments, God speaks to men; in the Lord's Prayer, man speaks to God; in the Creed, man speaks both to God and to men. As the Prayer is distinct from the Law, so the Creed is perfectly distinct from the Prayer.

* *Hymnologia Catholica, et Hierarchica Eucharistia.*

DISSERTATION II.

I. SINCE we have more than once affirmed that the Creed is the distinguishing badge of Christianity, it seems not improper to inquire, whether it contains all those articles which are necessary and fundamental; and whether all that it does contain are to be considered in this light. To return a satisfactory answer to these questions, it will be requisite, first of all, to show what we are to understand by necessary and fundamental articles, and to point out their distinguishing marks. This, indeed, is so abstruse a topic, that it has very much embarrassed even the most judicious and acute Theologians who have attempted to explain it; and scarcely any one has given full satisfaction to himself, much less to others. Let us endeavour, however, in common with other writers, and agreeably to their example, to make a few remarks on this point.

II. To enable us to understand the subject the more completely, several distinctions must be premised. *First,* we observe that doctrines may be said to be necessary,—to Salvation,—or to Religion,—or to the Church. A doctrine, without the knowledge and faith of which, God does not save grown-up persons, is necessary to Salvation ;[6] that, without the profession and practice of which, no one can be considered religious, is necessary to Religion; and that, without which none is admitted to the communion of the visible church, is necessary to the Church. There may be articles without which persons ought not to be admitted to the fellowship of the Church, that should not, for that reason, be straightway regarded as absolutely essential to Religion, or to Salvation. Although we dare not pronounce a sentence of condemnation against a man, we ought not, in defiance of order and discretion, to receive him forthwith into the bosom of our church, whatever sentiments he may hold, and to whatever sect he may belong. And with respect to Religion, what falls within the sphere of duty is manifest; but how far it may please a gracious God, or how far it may be possible for him, in consistency with his perfections and character, to extend his forbearance to any one, and save his soul, notwithstanding his errors and sins; or, in short, what are the lowest attainments, without which no man is saved,—who can tell? For this distinction I am indebted to the celebrated *Hoornbeeck.**

III. *Secondly,* The knowledge of those doctrines which are necessary to salvation, admits of various degrees. It is in different measures of clearness, abundance, and efficacy that divine revelation, the means of grace, and the communications of the Spirit are enjoyed; and a corresponding diversity takes place in the degrees of knowledge which the saints attain. In some, it is clear, distinct, steady, and accompanied with a very firm and decided assent; in others, it is more con-

---

* *Socin. Confut.* Tom. i. p. 209.
[6] See Note VI.

fused, more implicit, subject to occasional wavering,
and attended with an assent that is yielded with difficulty.　The command of God, indeed, lays an indispensable obligation upon all men, to make every possible effort to attain a most clear, distinct, and assured
knowledge of divine truth.　It cannot, however, be
questioned that the Deity, in his unbounded goodness,
receives many to the abodes of bliss, whose knowledge
even of the principal articles is very indistinct, and such
as they are hardly capable of expressing in their own
words.　The smallest measure of the requisite knowledge appears to be this, that, when an article of faith
is explained, the mind so far at least apprehends it, as
to recognise and embrace it as true.

　iv. *Thirdly*, Times also must be distinguished.　It
admits of no doubt, that under the bright dispensation
of the Gospel, a more extensive and more explicit knowledge is necessary to salvation, than was required under
the Old Testament economy ; for it is reasonable that
both knowledge, and the necessity of knowledge, should
increase in proportion to the measure of revelation afforded.　Under the Old dispensation, nay, during the
time of our Saviour's abode on the earth, it was possible for a man to be a true believer and in a state of
grace, who was ignorant of the sufferings, the death,
and the resurrection of Christ, and who even presumed
to object to the testimony of Christ himself respecting
those momentous topics, as is clear from the instance
of Peter ;[a]—or who, though he believed in general
in the Messiah, yet knew not that Jesus is the Christ,
as appears from the history of Cornelius the Centurion. [b]
No one, however, I suppose, would now acknowledge

---

[a] Matth. xvi. 21, 22.　　　　[b] Acts x. 2—4.

any person as a true believer, who should discover ignorance of these truths respecting the Lord Jesus; and still less a person who should contradict them when represented to him. On this subject, the expressions of *Thomas Aquinas* deserve to be quoted: " The articles " of faith," says he, " have increased with the lapse of " time, not indeed with respect to the faith itself, but " with respect to explicit and express profession. The " same things which are believed explicitly, and under " a greater number of articles, by the saints in latter " days, were all believed implicitly, and under a smaller " number, by the fathers in ancient times."*

v. Having premised these distinctions, let us now, in the first place, inquire, in general, into the marks of fundamental articles; and then examine, more particularly, whether the number of such articles can be determined with certainty. To entitle an article to be considered fundamental, it must be distinguished by the following characters. 1st, It is requisite that it be contained in Scripture; for the Scriptures " are able to make us wise unto salvation."ᶜ They are the perfect rule of all things necessary to be known, believed, and done, in order to eternal life. This criterion we lay down, in opposition to Papists, and to Enthusiasts.

vi. 2dly, It is necessary that it be so clearly contained in the sacred volume, that any person, even the most simple and illiterate, provided he give attention, may easily perceive that it is a doctrine of Scripture. The reason of this criterion is, that salvation is intended not merely for the learned and for those endowed with great perspicacity of mind, but also for children and

---

* *Secunda Secundæ,* Quæst. i. Art. 7.
ᶜ 2 Tim. iii. 15.

babes in Christ.[d] Among articles clearly contained in
the Scriptures, however, we must include not only
those which they teach in express words, but also those
which, to all who apply their minds to the subject, are
obviously deducible from them by necessary consequence. Our Lord and his Apostles very frequently
confirmed even fundamental articles of faith by consequences deduced from Scripture.—This criterion, too,
must not be understood to intimate, that fundamental
articles are propounded wherever they are taught in
holy writ, in words thus clear and intelligible to all; or
that nothing is to be deemed fundamental, which is
exhibited in any passage in a manner calculated to exercise the industry even of the learned.   It has pleased
God to reveal the same truth in the Scriptures " at
sundry times and in divers manners."[e] Sometimes he
propounds a doctrine, the faith of which is necessary to
salvation, so clearly, that no reader that is attentive, and
is enlightened by the Holy Spirit, can be ignorant of it,
and none but a contentious person can call it in question;
and sometimes he so involves the same doctrine in obscurity, that it becomes necessary for the studious to
compare the more obscure with the more perspicuous
passages.   The knowledge of a fundamental article
consists not in understanding this or the other passage
of the Bible; but in an acquaintance with the truth,
which in one passage, perhaps, is more obscurely traced,
but is exhibited in other places in a clear, nay, in the
clearest possible light.   In fine, we do not concur with
the *Remonstrants*,[7] in requiring so high a degree of

---

[d] 1 Cor. i. 26.   Matth. xi. 25.

[e] Πολυμερῶς καὶ πολυτρόπως.   Heb. i. 1.

[7] See NOTE VII.

clearness, as to consider those articles alone fundamental, which are acknowledged and maintained amongst all Christians as of the most unquestionable authority, and which neither are, nor can be controverted. According to this rule, hardly any thing will remain to distinguish the Christian Religion, from the Pagan morality, and the Mahometan theology. There is much truth in the remark of *Clement* of *Alexandria*; " No Scripture, I apprehend, is so favourably treated, " as to be contradicted by no one."*

VII. 3dly, Another mark of a fundamental article is, that it be of such a nature, that neither faith in Christ, nor true repentance, can subsist without it; for, as without faith it is impossible to please God, so without holiness no man shall see the Lord.[f] For example; since it is impossible for any one to believe in God, unless he know that he is, and that he is faithful in all his sayings; and since it is impossible also for any one to love and serve him, unless he believe that he is the Rewarder of those that seek him,—it must be confidently affirmed, that the articles which respect the existence and the veracity of God, and also the gracious rewards which he confers on his people, are clearly fundamental. Further, as salvation is unattainable without Christ;[g] as no grown-up person can be saved through Christ, but by faith;[h] and as faith supposes knowledge;[i]—the knowledge of Christ is necessary to salvation.[k] Besides, since God will honour them only that honour him,[l] and he who honours not the Son, honours

* *Stromat.* Lib. i.
[f] Heb. xi. 6. xii. 14.   [g] Acts iv. 12.
[h] Mark xvi. 16.   [i] Rom. x. 14.
[k] John xvii. 3. xx. 31.   [l] 1 Sam. ii. 30.

not the Father;[m] and since the Son cannot be rightly
honoured, unless he be recognised as, what he really is,
the true God, *of the same substance** with the Father,[n] and on that account, *of equal dignity*† with the
Father;—we boldly maintain that the article respecting the true Divinity of Christ, is fundamental.

VIII. 4thly, It cannot be doubted that every article
is fundamental, to the denial of which, God, notwithstanding the *grace and benignity* of the Gospel, has
annexed a threatening of destruction. I say, notwithstanding the grace of the Gospel; for according to the
rigour of the law, all culpable ignorance of any truth
which God has revealed, is damnable. In conformity
to this rule, we conclude that the article relating to the
incarnation of Christ is fundamental; for John says,
" Every spirit that confesseth not that Jesus Christ is
" come in the flesh, is not of God."[o] The reason of
this rule is, that no person is saved, in whom any thing
is found, for which, notwithstanding the intervention
of the Gospel, God declares that he excludes men
from the kingdom of heaven.

IX. Some have added, that an article, to which a promise of eternal life is annexed, is fundamental. But
this rule does not hold universally. For instance; it
is said in reference to the prophecies of the Apocalypse,
" Blessed is he that readeth, and blessed are they that
" hear, the words of this prophecy."[p] It would be rash,
however, to conclude from these words, that the prophecies of the Apocalypse are fundamental articles.
The reason is, that those attainments, with which the

---

* Ὁμοούσιος.   † Ἰσότιμος.
[m] John v. 23.   [n] John x. 30.
[o] 1 John iv. 2, 3.   [p] Revel. i. 3.

promise of salvation is connected, are not universally so momentous and indispensable, that the absence of any one of them, inevitably subjects a person to a state of condemnation. Such attainments always suppose that which is essential to salvation, though they are not its necessary or inseparable concomitants. " He that believeth and is baptized," says our Lord, " shall be saved."[q] Yet from this it by no means follows, that baptism is so essential, that without it none can obtain salvation. Our Lord himself, when he converts this affirmative into a negative proposition, drops the mention of baptism, saying only, " he that believeth not, shall be damned;" for it is impossible that an adult can be rightly baptized, unless he is a believer; although it is very possible that a true believer may not be baptized.

x. 5thly, That also is to be regarded as a fundamental article, which the Scriptures call a *foundation;*—whether this be done in express terms, or in words of equal force. Thus the doctrine respecting the Lord Jesus, his person and offices, is denominated by Paul a foundation. " Other foundation can no man lay than " that is laid, which is Jesus Christ."[r] The meaning is, that no man can teach another fundamental doctrine, separate from the doctrine concerning Christ. To this, also, may be referred the following words of our Saviour to Peter, " Upon this Rock, will I build my church :"[s] that is, either upon myself, whom thou hast confessed; or upon this doctrine of which thou hast made a profession, by declaring that I am the Son of God. The learned *Cameron*, an ingenious inter-

q Mark xvi. 16.   r 1 Cor. iii. 11.
s Matth. xvi. 18.

preter of Scripture, remarks, that the words of Paul in
1 Tim. iii. 15, 16. may be connected thus : " The pil-
" lar and ground of the truth, and without controversy
" great, is the mystery of godliness ; God was mani-
" fested in the flesh, justified in the Spirit," &c. With
this passage, he also compares the following sentence,
which occurs at the beginning of a certain celebrated
work of *Maimonides*; " *The foundation of the foun-*
" *dation, and the pillar of wisdom** is, to know that
" there is some First Being." *James Cappel*, a man of
profound erudition, approves of this construction, and
affirms that it also met the approbation of *Andrew
Melville*, and of *John Fabricius*. He adds a quotation from *Irenæus*, from which he gathers, that that
Father, too, seems to have read the passage in this
manner. The third book of *Irenæus* begins thus ;
" We have learned the method of our salvation, from
" no other persons than those who imparted to us the
" Gospel ; which, in the first instance, they preached,
" and afterwards delivered down to us in writing ac-
" cording to the will of God, to be the FOUNDATION
" AND PILLAR of our faith." Much to the same effect, is the following expression of *Basil* of *Seleucia*,
in a discourse on Matth. xvi. 16. respecting the confession of Peter : " This is, indeed, the Rock of religion ;
" this, the basis of salvation ; this, the bulwark of
" faith ; this, the foundation of the truth." *Schultet*
acknowledges, in his *Notes*, that these observations are
equally pious and learned : nor is *John Henry Ursin*
of a different opinion.† And truly, provided these
writers were supported by the authority of ancient co-

---

* יסוד היסוד ועמוד החכמות:
† *Analect*. Lib. vi. cap. 35.

pies, no exposition would appear to me more probable.
Were this exposition admitted, we should possess a
concise summary of fundamental articles, which might
well put Socinians to shame, who blasphemously assert, that scarcely any thing at all relating to the person of Christ is necessary to be known.[8]

XI. 6thly, It must not be omitted, that if any article is stated as necessary to be known, which cannot be
understood, unless some other article shall have been
previously understood and believed; that other article
must also rank among those which are necessary. For
example; it is necessary to know that we are saved
only by the grace of our Lord Jesus Christ; for the
Apostle Paul says, " If any man preach any other gos-
" pel unto you than that which we have preached unto
" you, let him be accursed."[t] But this can be neither
understood nor believed, unless we know that sin
has plunged us into so deep an abyss of misery, that
our deliverance surpassed our own power, and even the
united exertions of all creatures. Thus, from the necessity of the article respecting our deliverance, we
strongly infer the necessity of the article respecting our
misery.

XII. 7thly, When any thing, in fine, the necessity
of which must have been more doubtful, is expressly
represented as necessary to be known; it follows, that
a doctrine will also be necessary, the necessity of which
we should have been less, or at least not more, disposed
to question. To give an instance of this: the Apostle
teaches that the article regarding justification by faith
in Christ without the works of the law, is necessary,

[t] Gal. i. 8, 9.
[5] See NOTE VIII.

when he asserts that they who are "ignorant of God's "righteousness, and going about to establish their own "righteousness, have not submitted themselves to the "righteousness of God."[u] The necessity of this article being thus demonstrated; it unavoidably follows, that it is necessary for us to know also, that, considered in ourselves, we are obnoxious to condemnation and wrath: for this last article is much more evident than the former, and more obvious to every one that is willing to examine himself; nor, without the knowledge of it, can we be induced to seek that righteousness which is in Christ.

XIII. There neither occur to ourselves, nor do we recollect to have seen elsewhere, any marks more certain than those which have now been particularized. Let it be observed, however, that, according to the order in which we have arranged them, the two first serve to show what are not to be accounted fundamental articles; and the others are intended to point out those which, by all means, are entitled to that place. Though every necessary article ought to be contained, and even plainly contained in Scripture; yet every thing that is plainly and expressly delivered in Scripture, is not for this precise reason to be deemed necessary. For instance; it is not necessary to know that Aaron was older than Moses, or that Paul had a cloak. But an article without which neither faith, nor repentance, can be exercised;—that respecting which God himself assures us he admits none who denies it to heaven;—that which the Scripture calls a foundation;—that without which a truth clearly fundamental can be neither understood nor believed;—or that which appears from the very nature of the thing, to be

[u] Rom. x. 3.

no less, or even more necessary, than what the Scripture affirms to be necessary,—every such article, I say, sound reason imperiously requires us to consider necessary.

XIV. Farther, those articles which are thus fundamental, ought to be known and believed by every Christian that has reached the years of discretion, by the learned and the unlearned, by the humblest mechanic no less than the Professor of Theology. We concede, however, that, in men whose capacity is slow, whose memory is weak, and to whom an obscure revelation, or a cold and inefficient ministry are afforded, God tolerates a less distinct and less explicit knowledge than in persons who, in all those respects, are favoured with superior advantages. It is possible, too, that a man who holds the foundation, may embrace some error inconsistent with a fundamental article; whilst, either from the dulness of his capacity, or from some defect in his education, and from prejudices early imbibed, he does not perceive it to be an error at all, much less, an error at variance with the foundation. In such circumstances, the error does not exclude from salvation. Thus amidst the darkness of Popery, the elect, holding the fundamental articles, were saved; though they did not escape a number of prevailing errors,—such as the communion of the mass, respecting which our Catechism has justly said that it is a virtual renunciation of the alone sacrifice of Jesus Christ, and horrible idolatry.

XV. To point out the articles necessary to salvation, and precisely to determine their number, is a task, if not utterly impossible, at least extremely difficult. There are, doubtless, more articles fundamental, than those to which the Scriptures have appended an express threatening of destruction. None of the writers on this subject, however,—none at least whom we have had an opportunity of consulting, how small soever the number to which they reduce the fundamental articles, have even attempted to prove from Scripture, in the manner we have done, the necessity of all the articles which they particularize. Every one has reasoned according to his own inclination; and who does not see that this is a mode of proceeding quite precarious? It should be considered, also, that, in some instances, Divine grace unites the elect to Christ by a very slender bond; and that the most ardent flames of love, the sincerest concern to please God, and an earnest desire of salvation, may be found in persons, whose knowledge of the articles of faith is exceedingly circumscribed. Who then, without instruction and authority from God himself, can, in the present state, exactly ascertain the smallest measure of knowledge in reference to each of the articles, which is indispensably necessary at the tribunal of the supreme and omniscient Judge?

XVI. Nor is it absolutely necessary that we should possess an exact list of the number of fundamental articles. It is incumbent on each of us to labour with the utmost diligence to obtain an enlargement of saving knowledge, lest, perhaps, we should be found ignorant of truths that are necessary. The man who is not solicitous to receive every possible accession to his knowledge, knows nothing yet of the ways of the Lord, as he ought to know. Pope *Leo* has expressed himself with great propriety in the following terms; " Who- " ever is able to attain clearer conceptions of this sub- " ject," referring to the topic which he was then discussing, " and is unwilling to know, or having thus " known, is unwilling to believe it, cannot be saved.

" There are many of the profound mysteries of our holy
" faith, to which not a few are able to extend their re-
" searches ; but into which a considerable number, ow-
" ing either to their youth or to the imbecility of their
" understanding, are unable to inquire. And, there-
" fore, as we have just said, he who is able, but unwil-
" ling, cannot be saved."* It is evident, then, that to
ascertain precisely the number of necessary articles, is
not requisite to our spiritual comfort. It is sufficient
to know in general, that he who has learned cordially
to love God as reconciled in Christ, and to place his
confidence in him, holds what is necessary ; and that,
mean time, it is the incumbent duty of all Christians,
to make progress in the knowledge of the mystery of
God, and of Christ.[v]

XVII. It is of no great importance, besides, to the
Church at large, to know quite correctly the precise
number of fundamental articles. It does not become
us to ascend into the tribunal of God, and to pronounce
concerning our neighbour, for how small a defect of
knowledge, or for how inconsiderable an error, he must
be excluded from heaven. It is much safer to leave
that to God : and even supposing we had succeeded in
discovering it, still we should possess no clear and positive rule of admission to the communion of the Church.
It may not be safe and expedient for us to receive into
church-fellowship, a person chargeable with some error
or sin ; whom, however, we should not dare, on account
of that error or sin, to exclude from heaven. Nor,
were even this point once determined, would the way
be prepared for perfect peace and harmony in the

* *Concili: Gallic: a Sermondo edit.* Tom. ii. p. 257.
[v] 1 Cor. xiv. 20. Ephes. iv. 13.

churches of Christ; as if, provided the necessary articles are maintained, no great solicitude ought to be discovered with respect to the rest. Though one article be of greater importance than another, none of the truths of God ought to be esteemed so trivial and contemptible, that it is of very little consequence whether our sentiments concerning them be right or wrong.[9] Had it been an object of high utility, in short, to have the number of necessary articles fixed and determined, that God who is unbounded at once in wisdom and in goodness, would not have neglected to consult the welfare of his Church in this instance, and would have defined the number in the Sacred Volume. Since he has not been pleased to do this, we may rest assured that it was not necessary.

XVIII. After what has been said, we are now prepared to return the following answer to the question proposed in the first section; to wit, that, if you consider only the truths expressly mentioned in the Creed, all the necessary articles of our Religion are not contained in this summary. For it contains nothing about the Word of God, which is the immediate object, the rule, and the source of our faith; and which is therefore denominated " the Foundation of the Apostles and Prophets;" that is, the Foundation which was laid by the Apostles and Prophets, and on which our faith ought to be built :[w]—Nothing respecting our sin and misery, the knowledge of which is inculcated in Scripture as particularly necessary :[x]—Nothing relative to justification by faith without the works of the law, the knowledge of which article, however, the

---

[w] Ephes. ii. 20.   . [x] Jerem. iii. 13.
[9] See NOTE IX.

Apostle valued so highly, that in comparison of it he accounted all other things but loss and dung[y]—so highly, that he declares that whosoever desire to be justified by the law, have no part in Christ, and are fallen from grace:[z]—Nothing even regarding the worship and service of God, and the leading of a holy life; which cannot be rightly performed, unless they are both known, and believed to be necessary.

xix. If any of the Protestant Divines have affirmed that all fundamental articles are contained in the Creed, they did not intend by this expression, that they considered the mere repetition of the words of the Creed, a sufficient sign of Christianity. Our faith consists not in words, but in sense; not in the surface, but in the substance; not in the leaves of a profession, but in the root of reason. All the heretics of the present day, that claim the name of Christians, are willing enough to subscribe the words of the Creed; each however affixing to them whatever sense he pleases, though diametrically opposite to sound doctrine. It must be remarked, also, that such of the Protestants as have held this language with regard to the Creed, have included under the articles expressed in it, those which are necessarily supposed or deduced, and without which the articles expressed can be neither thoroughly understood, nor sincerely acknowledged.

xx. As all necessary points are not expressly contained in the Creed; so all that it doth contain, are not indispensably necessary. Who would presume to question the salvation of all those, who perhaps know not that Christ suffered *under Pontius Pilate,* or who are ignorant of the precise *time* of his resurrection?

[y] Philip. iii. 8, 9.　　　　[z] Gal. v. 4.

Who would pronounce it impossible for any man to be saved, that does not understand the article respecting Christ's descent into hell, or that concerning the Catholic Church, or the Communion of saints? As for us, we dare not act so rigorous a part, lest we should be found false witnesses against the generation of God's children.

XXI. Neither the ancient Fathers, however, nor the chief men of the Reformed churches, can be justly accused of having done wrong, when they inserted in Creeds and Confessions articles not absolutely necessary, and even when they sometimes expressed those articles in other terms than those of Scripture. Since all the truths of our holy faith are exceedingly precious, and are at the same time intimately connected together, prudence requires us to provide for the security of such as are necessary, by maintaining those which, although less necessary, are yet worthy of all acceptation. It is expedient, also, for the Church, solicitously to distinguish and separate herself from all who pervert the truth : and her safety is ill consulted by those who, under the specious pretext of peace and toleration, would have her to embrace with open arms, all that hold errors not entirely fundamental. Conduct of this sort would be utterly unworthy of the chaste Spouse of Jesus. As heretics, too, are accustomed to use general expressions with a view to deceive, and while they retain the words of Scripture, impose on them a foreign and unnatural sense ; necessity sometimes indispensably requires us, for the purpose of detecting the wiles of seducers with the greater facility, to express the genuine meaning of Scripture in our own language. Thus the Orthodox, long ago, wisely distinguished themselves from the Arians by the term *Consubstantial.** The experience of all ages clearly shows, that persons who calumniate forms of that kind, and are pleased with none excepting such as are extremely brief, and composed entirely of the mere words of Scripture, are secretly entertaining some mischievous design.[10]

---

* ʽΟμοουσιος.
[10] See Note X.

DISSERTATION III.

ON SAVING FAITH.

I. HAVING introduced ourselves to the subject, by saying as much as seemed necessary to our purpose, respecting the Authors and the Authority of the Creed, and also respecting Fundamental Articles in general, let us now proceed to take a nearer view of the several articles which this summary contains; beginning in this Dissertation with the expression, I BELIEVE. This single phrase supplies a copious subject of discourse. It comprises four topics, and those, too, of very great moment. 1st, The ACT of believing itself, or SAVING FAITH. 2dly, The special APPROPRIATION of that act to the mind of every Christian, so that each believer believes for himself. It is not said, WE BELIEVE, but I BELIEVE. 3dly, The CONSCIOUSNESS of that act, by which every believer may and ought to be conscious and assured of his own faith. 4thly, The PROFESSION with the mouth, of that faith which dwells and operates in the heart. We shall illustrate each of these in order.

II. SAVING FAITH, the nature of which we are now about to explain, is not any one particular act or habit of the soul; nor ought it to be limited to any one faculty of the human mind. It is complex, and consists of various acts; which, without the least confusion, pervade one another, and, by a delightful co-operation, mutually promote and assist each other. It implies a change of the whole man. It is the source of every part of the spiritual life. It is, in fine, the holy energy and activity of the whole soul, exercising itself towards God in Christ. The entire extent of this principle, therefore, can hardly be distinctly comprehended under any one conception.

III. Let none consider it strange, that we include so many ingredients under the name of one Christian grace. As when men speak of life, they intend by that word a principle, which, diffusing itself through the whole soul and its various faculties, communicates its virtue also to the body, and extends its influence to all the actions of the living person; so when we speak of faith, which is a most fertile source of every part of the spiritual life, we understand by this term, a principle which pervades all the faculties of the soul, and is the proper mean of uniting them to Christ, and of thus quickening, and making them holy, and happy.

IV. Many things, both *natural* and *moral*, are almost universally allowed to extend themselves through the whole soul, and not to admit of being restricted to any one faculty. In things *natural*, we have an instance in *Free-will*, or *Free-choice;** which, as *choice* is referred principally to the understanding, as *free*, rather to the will: so that, as *Bernard* somewhere speaks, " man is his own free-man, with respect to his " will; his own judge, with respect to his reason." In things *moral*, we may mention the divine image and original righteousness; which are to be viewed as re-

* *Liberum arbitrium.*

siding neither in the understanding only, nor in the will only, but as adorning each of these faculties.

v. Would not every difficulty be removed, and would not the whole controversy which is agitated among Divines with regard to the seat of faith, be settled, were we to deny, as we can justly do, that the understanding and the will are really distinct, either from the soul, or from one another? What else is the understanding, but the soul understanding and knowing? What is the will, but the soul willing and desiring? We must by no means consider the soul as a substance which is brutish and irrational in itself, and becomes intelligent and rational only in consequence of some other thing being superadded to it. As to the notion of those who allege that the understanding is derived from the soul by a kind of emanation, it is scarcely possible to conceive how this can take place. If the soul, in its own proper and formal nature, does not include the power of reasoning, it cannot produce it; for it is vain to expect from a cause, that which it neither formally nor eminently contains. But if the soul possesses, of itself, the power of reasoning, there is no necessity for some other faculty being superadded to that power, of which the soul is thus already possessed. The same remarks apply to the will. It is not really distinct from the soul, any more than the understanding. The will is the soul itself, so far as the soul is a substance which God has endowed with an original capacity to desire what is good.

As both these faculties are formally, not really or essentially, distinct from the soul, so they are only formally distinct from one another. If the will be so separate from the understanding as, considered in itself, to be blind, it is impossible to show in what manner it can perceive, and thus rationally desire, an object which the understanding exhibits as good. For what reason, let me ask, should we make a real difference betwixt these two powers? Is it because their objects are different? The object of both is, in fact, the same, namely, a *true good;* though in the manner of considering it there is a diversity,—while the understanding contemplates the good as true, and the will desires the same true object, as it is good. And is there not a far greater difference betwixt the objects of the understanding, as a speculative and as a practical faculty; which, however, philosophers generally agree in regarding as one and the same power of the mind?—Is it because their acts are different? But every diversity of acts does not infer a diversity of power. Simple apprehension, surely, differs from judging and reasoning; which are, nevertheless, acts of the same faculty. Since it appears, then, that the faculties of understanding and will cannot be separated from each other, let it not be thought strange, that we should consider faith as subsisting in both.[11]

vi. It seems proper, in the mean time, to remark that, amongst the various acts of faith which we are about to describe, there is one which holds the principal place, and in which, as it unites us to Christ and justifies us, we apprehend the essence and formal nature of faith to consist. This must be carefully attended to, particularly in the matter of justification; lest several expressions of love which, in different ways, are involved in the exercise of faith, should be rashly numbered among the causes of our justification.

vii. It must also be kept in view, that several things which, for the sake of accuracy, we shall distinctly and

[11] See NOTE XI.

particularly explain, are, in various forms, mutually interwoven in the exercise of faith. Whilst the whole
soul is exerting itself in this work of God, many operations are, conjunctly, and without an adherence to
any certain method, directed towards God and Christ;
which the believer earnestly engaged in the work itself, has neither leisure, nor in many instances inclination, nor sometimes even the power, to arrange distinctly in their proper order. That we may understand, however, the more thoroughly, the whole nature
and exercise of faith, it is proper for us to attend to its
natural progress.

VIII. The *first* attainment which faith includes or supposes, is the KNOWLEDGE of the truths believed. This
appears, in opposition to the absurd doctrine of Popish
doctors, 1st, From express passages of holy writ, which
make mention of faith in such terms as manifestly intimate, that knowledge is involved in its nature and
exercise.[a] 2dly, From the very nature of faith itself,
which unquestionably signifies an assent given to truth
which God has revealed, and therefore necessarily
presupposes the knowledge of these two things: 1. That
God has revealed some truth: 2. What it is, to which
it assents, as a truth divinely revealed. It is absurd to
say, that a person assents to any truth of which he is
utterly ignorant, and respecting which he does not
know that any testimony worthy of credit exists. 3dly,
From the manner in which faith is produced in the
elect. This is done, *externally*, by the preaching and
hearing of the Gospel,[b] which reveals what ought to be
believed, and manifests the truth to every man's con-

[a] Isaiah liii. 11.   John xvii. 3. compared with Hab. ii. 4.   John
vi. 69.   2 Tim. i. 12.

[b] Rom. x. 17.

science;[c] and, *internally*, by the teaching of God the Father.[d] If faith, then, is generated in the heart by means of instruction, both external and internal, it must certainly be founded in knowledge; for knowledge is the proper and immediate effect of instruction. 4thly, From the natural consequence of faith, to wit, the confession and vindication of the truth.[e] It is impossible that this can take place without knowledge. *Hilary* has well said, " No one can either express " what he knows not, or believe what he cannot ex- " press."

IX. It must indeed be acknowledged, that, owing to the darkness of our minds in the present state, many truths are unknown even to the most enlightened; and many are believed with an implicit faith, by those, in particular, that are babes in Christ, young and inexperienced. Christians of this description, hold, in general, the whole Scripture as the infallible standard of all truth, while it contains many points of which they are ignorant; and they embrace the leading doctrines of Christianity, in which many truths are concentrated, that are evidently deducible from them, and which, at least in their foundation, they believe. The Apostle John, accordingly, affirms concerning the faithful, that they " know all things,"[f] because, through the teachings of the Spirit, they have learned that foundation of foundations, to which all saving truths are referred, and from which they are deduced. I will go further. It is possible that one, to whom God, who is sovereign in the distribution of his blessings, has allotted a scanty portion of knowledge, may yet be remarkably strong

[c] 2 Cor. iv. 2.   [d] John vi. 45.
[e] Rom. x. 9, 10.   1 Pet. iii. 15.   [f] 1 John ii. 20.

in faith, and even prepared to suffer martyrdom. From this, however, it by no means follows, that faith is better defined by ignorance than by knowledge; or that those act a laudable part, who, contrary to the injunction of Scripture,[g] cherish ignorance, among the people, as the mother of faith and of devotion. No one can at all believe a doctrine, of which he is entirely ignorant; and all are bound to exert their best endeavours, that their faith may not be implicit, but as distinct as possible; which becometh those who are " filled with all knowledge."[h] The more distinctly any person perceives, in the light of the Spirit, a truth which God has revealed, and the more clearly he discerns the rays of divinity shining in it, the more firmly will he give credit to that truth. Those very martyrs, who were uninformed respecting other matters, saw most clearly and distinctly, that the truths for which they did not hesitate to sacrifice their lives, were most certain and divine; though possibly they were incapable of reasoning at great length in their defence.

x. Further, the things which it is necessary for a man to know in order to his becoming a believer, are, in general, the divinity of the Scriptures, into which faith must ultimately be resolved; more especially, those points that relate to the obtaining of salvation in Christ; which may be summarily reduced to these three heads. 1st, That you know that by sin you have become alienated from the life of God, and have come short of his glory;[i] and that it is impossible that either yourself, or an angel from heaven, or any creature in the universe, nay, that even all creatures united, can

g Col. iii. 16.   h Rom. xv. 14.
i Rom. iii. 23.

extricate you from this abyss of misery, and restore you to a state of felicity.[12] 2dly, That you know the Lord Jesus Christ as " full of grace and truth;"[k] besides whom there is no other name given under heaven, by which we can be saved;[l] and in the knowledge of whom, consists eternal life.[m] 3dly, That you know that, in order to your obtaining salvation in Christ, it is necessary for you to be united to Christ by the Spirit and by faith; and to surrender yourself to him, not only to be justified, but also to be sanctified, and to be governed by his sovereign authority, " proving what is that good, and acceptable, and perfect will of God."[n]

XI. To knowledge must be added, in the *second* place, ASSENT; which is that act of faith, by which a man receives and acknowledges as true, those doctrines which he knows; receiving the testimony of God, and thus setting to his seal that God is true.[o] Assent is principally founded on the infallible veracity of God, testifying concerning himself and his Son. [p] On this testimony, delivered in the Scriptures, and diffusing all around the rays of its divinity, the believer no less firmly relies, than if he had been immediately present at the revelation of all those doctrines. When the soul, enlightened by the Spirit, beholds those divine truths, and discerns in them a certain *God-like excellency*,* and a most beautiful harmony and inseparable connexion, she cannot withhold her assent from truth recommending itself by so invincible evidence; but embraces for certain that which she thus knows, with

* Θεοπρεπεια.

k John i. 14.   l Acts iv. 12.
m John xvii. 3.   n Rom. xii. 2.
o John iii. 33.   p 1 John v. 9, 10.
         12 See NOTE XII.

as little doubt or hesitation as if she had seen it with
her own eyes, or handled it with her own hands, or had
been caught up to the third heaven and heard it immediately from the mouth of God himself.[13] Whatever may be the murmurings of the carnal mind, or
whatever cavils vain sophists may urge, the soul, though
perhaps she may not be prepared for refuting every
objection, persists, however, in embracing and confessing the truth; which she has seen too clearly, and
heard too certainly from the mouth of God, ever to allow herself to be drawn away from it, by any sophisti-
cal arguments whatever. *I have not followed after
cunningly devised fables*, says the soul, *when I believed the power and coming of our Lord Jesus
Christ; but, in the Spirit, was an eye-witness of his
majesty, and heard his voice from heaven*.[q] Thus faith
is accompanied with ὑποστασις, *substance*, ἐλεγχος, *evidence*,[r] and πληροφορια, *full assurance*.[s] It will not be
unprofitable, to offer a few remarks on the meaning of
each of these words.

XII. Πληροφορια, *full assurance*, is an expression
which occurs more than once in the writings of the
Apostle Paul. He speaks of πληροφορια συνεσεως, " the
full assurance of understanding;"[t] πληροφορια της ἐλπιδος,
" the full assurance of hope;"[u] and πληροφορια πιστεως,
" the full assurance of faith."[v] According to its etymology, this word denotes *a carrying with full sail;*
the metaphor being taken, probably, from ships when
their sails are filled with favourable gales. Thus it
may here signify the vehement inclination of the mind,

q 2 Pet. i. 16, 18.　　　　r Heb. xi. 1.
s Rom. iv. 21.　　　　　　t Col. ii. 2.
u Heb. vi. 11.　　　　　　v Heb. x. 22.
[13] See Note XIII.

impelled by the Holy Spirit, towards an assent to the truth perceived. *Hesychius,* a most excellent master of the Greek language, explains it by βεϐαιοτης, *stability.* In this sense, πληροφορια πιστεως, " the full assurance of faith," is precisely of the same import with στερεωμα της εις χριστον πιστεως, " the stedfastness of faith in Christ."[w] The Apostle seems to use these two expressions as synonymous; and, in the gospel of Luke, πεπληροφορημενα πραγματα, are[14] " things which are most surely believed."[x] So firm is the assent which the believer ought to give to divine truth.

XIII. Most emphatical, also, is the term ὑποστασις, *hypostasis,* or *substance,* which the Apostle employs when speaking of faith.[y] The Latin language furnishes no word that can sufficiently express its whole energy. 1st, It denotes the *existence,* or, as some of the ancients expressed it, the *extantia,* the *standing out* of a thing ; in which sense philosophers say that the properties and circumstances of things have a *hypostasis,* that is, really exist, and are not mere figments of our own imagination. Accordingly, faith causes the thing hoped for, though not yet actually existing, to exist in the mind of the believer ; who assents as firmly to the promises of God, as if he saw the blessings promised already present. *Chrysostome* had this idea in his mind, when he explained the words of the Apostle thus ; " The resurrection has not yet taken place, " nor doth it yet exist in itself; but hope," (we may say *faith,*) " gives it a place and an existence in our " mind."[*] The Greek Scholiast, whose words are

---

* Ἡ ἀναστασις ἐ παραγεγονεν, ὐδε ἐστιν ἐν ὑποστασι. αλλ ἡ ἐλπις ὑφιστησεν ἀυτην ἐν ἡμετερα ψυχῆ.

[w] Col. ii. 2, 5.   [x] Luke i. 1.   [y] Heb. xi. 1.

14 See NOTE XIV.

quoted by *Beza*, has very happily expressed the same idea, thus: "Since those things which are the objects "of hope, have as yet no existence, and are not yet "present; faith, so to speak, becomes their substance "and essence, because it makes them, in some sense, to "exist and to be present, by believing that they are." 2dly, Ὑπόστασις signifies also a *basis* or foundation; in which sense, *Diodorus Siculus*, cited by *Gomar*, speaks of "the foundation of the sepulchre."* *Calvin* seems also to favour this signification of the word, when he says, "Faith is the *hypostasis*, that is, the support "or possession, on which we fix our foot."† 3dly, It denotes *continuance*, or that constancy which will in no degree yield to the attack of an enemy. Thus *Plutarch* says,—"None of the enemy keeping the field, but all ' betaking themselves to flight;"‡ and *Polybius*, in his description of *Horatius Cocles*, "They feared not so "much his strength, as his resolution and constancy," which scorned to give way.§ And, indeed, there is something in faith, which nobly withstands all the assaults of temptation, and preserves it from being moved away from its assent to the truth which it has once discerned. Now, if we join all these ideas together, we shall assert, that faith is so firm an assent to divine truth, that it sets before us the objects of a far distant futurity, as if they were present; and becomes the support of the soul, upon which it stedfastly fixes its foot, yielding to no assault.

XIV. Nor must we omit to mention that the Apos-

---

* Ὑπόστασις τοῦ ταφοῦ.

† Fides est hypostasis, id est, fultura vel possessio, in qua pedem figimus.

‡ Οὐδενὸς ὑφισταμενῶ των ἐναντιων, ἀλλὰ φευγοντων. *in Demetrio.*

§ Οὐχ οὕτω την δυναμιν, ὡς την ὑποστασιν αυτῦ.

tle calls faith ἐλεγχος, *elenchus*, the *evidence* of things
not seen. This word denotes two things : 1st, A *cer-*
tain demonstration. " An *elenchus*," says Aristotle,
" is that which cannot possibly be otherwise, but must
" necessarily be as we affirm."* 2dly, *Conviction of*
mind, arising from such a demonstration of the truth ;
as *Aristophanes* says, " You cannot convince me of
that."† Faith, therefore, if it is ἐλεγχος, an *elenchus*,
implies a firm conviction of mind, founded on a clear
and infallible demonstration of the truth. This demonstration of the truth, it must be observed, rests
upon the testimony of God, who cannot possibly deceive, from which faith reasons thus ; " Whatever
" God, who is truth itself, reveals, cannot fail to be
" most certain, and *worthy of all acceptation* ; although,
" perhaps, I can neither see it with my eyes, nor fully
" comprehend it in my mind."

xv. All these illustrations serve to show, that the
assent included in faith, has a strength and an assurance, which no certainty of mathematical demonstration
can surpass. Those, therefore, who contend that falsehood may be found in a divine faith, express themselves
in a manner extremely unguarded ; since the proper
object of faith is the testimony of God, which is necessarily true, and superior in certainty to all demonstration ; and since they can specify no passage of holy
writ, in which any thing not true, is proposed to the
faith of mankind.

xvi. Another difficulty, however, must here be removed. If faith is so firm and unwavering an assent,
does it follow that those are destitute of true faith, who

* * *

* *Rhetoricorum ad Alexandrum*, Cap. xiv.
† Συγ' ἐλεγξαι μ' οὔπω δυνασαι περι τȣτȣ, in *Pluto*.

sometimes stagger even with regard to fundamental truths? I answer, 1st, We are now describing faith, considered theoretically, as a Christian grace to the perfection of which we all ought to aspire, not as it is sometimes found in its subject. 2dly, It is possible that waverings, staggerings, doubtings, and even inclinations towards the opposite errors, may at times arise in the minds of the most excellent believers, especially when they are exposed to some violent temptation; as is manifest from the waverings of Asaph, Jeremiah, and others, respecting the providence of God. But these are so many defects of faith, arising from the weakness of the flesh. 3dly, Faith immediately resists those temptations; it assents not to the suggestions of the devil, or the dictates of the carnal mind; nor doth it ever rest, until, having entered the sanctuary of God, and having received instruction from the Spirit of faith, it is established in the contemplation and acknowledgment of those truths with respect to which it was disposed to waver. There, at last, and no where else, it finds rest to the sole of its foot.

XVII. The natural consequence of this assent, is the LOVE of the truth thus known and acknowledged. This is the *third* act of faith, and of this the Apostle speaks when he says; " They received not the love of the truth that they might be saved."[z] Since the saving truths of the Gospel afford a bright manifestation of the glory of God, as not only his veracity in his testimony, but also his wisdom, holiness, righteousness, goodness, power, and other divine perfections, shine forth in them,—the believing soul, contemplating these amiable perfections of the Deity in those truths, cannot fail to burn with an ardent love for them, to exult

[z] 2 Thess. ii. 10.

in them, and to glorify God. Hence the believer is said
to "give glory to God,"[a] and to[15] "love the praise
(the glory) of God."[b] Above all, the soul delights in
the fundamental truth respecting Christ. This it loves
as an inestimable treasure, as a pearl of unparalleled
value. This to believers is *a price,*[c] that is, *most precious.* We admit that, strictly speaking, love is to be
distinguished from faith; yet the workings of these
two graces are so interwoven with each other, that we
can neither explain nor exercise faith, without some
operations of love intermingling, such as that of which
we now treat. This remark has been formerly made
by some of the greatest Divines; as, not to mention
others at present, by *Chamier** and *Wendelin.*† Each
of these writers avails himself of the authority of *Augustine,* and makes the following quotation from him:
" What is it to believe in God? It is by believing to
love him."‡ See, also, *Le Blanc,* that celebrated Divine of *Sedan,* in his learned *Theses.*§ If any one,
however, is disposed, agreeably to the language of the
Schools, to denominate this love, an *imperate*‖ act of
faith, we shall not contend with him; provided it is
understood that the believing soul, while exercising
faith, cannot but sincerely love the doctrines of the
Gospel, known and acknowledged, as they are in Je-

---

* *Panstrat.* tom. iii. lib. 12. cap. 14. num. 16.

† *Theol.* lib. ii. cap. 24. *ad Thes.* 8.

‡ *Quid est credere in Deum ? Credendo amare.*

§ *De Fidei justificantis natura, &c.* Sect. xcv.

‖ This scholastic term literally signifies *governed,* and seems to be
employed to denote what is *subordinate,* or *remote.* T.

      [a] Rom. iv. 20.   [b] John xii. 43.

      [c] Τιμη, 1 Pet. ii. 7.

      [15] See NOTE XV.

sus, rejoicing that such things are true, and delighting in the truth ; and is thus very differently affected from devils and ungodly men, who disrelish those doctrines which they know to be true, and wish that they were false.

XVIII. Hence arises a *fourth* act of faith, A HUNGER AND THIRST AFTER CHRIST. The believer, while he knows, acknowledges, and loves the truths of salvation, cannot but wish that all those doctrines which are true in Christ, may also be true to him, and that, according to these truths, and by means of them, himself may be sanctified and blessed. It is his earnest desire that, having been alienated from the life of God through sin, he may be freely justified, and thus possess a sure title to the glory of God; and that his justification may be sealed by sanctification. This is the hungering and thirsting after righteousness mentioned Matth. v. 6. How is it possible, that the man who believes and feels that in himself he is extremely miserable,—who is fully persuaded that he can be rescued from his misery by no creature either in heaven or on earth,—who sees at the same time a fulness of salvation in Christ,—who is assured that without union to Christ he cannot be saved, who cordially loves the truth concerning the fulness of salvation in Christ alone and in communion with him ;—how is it possible, I say, that such a person should not seriously and ardently desire to have Christ dwelling in him,—that he should not seek and pant after him, and have so vehement a longing as can be satisfied with nothing short of the possession of the object desired ; as hunger and thirst are allayed only by meat and drink ?

XIX. This hunger and thirst is succeeded by A RE-CEIVING OF CHRIST for justification, sanctification, and complete salvation. This is the *fifth* act of faith, and indeed its formal and principal act. Our heavenly Father freely offers his Son, and the Lord Jesus Christ freely offers himself, with all his benefits and the fulness which dwells in him to the sick and weary soul,[16] saying, " Behold me, behold me."[d] The soul, now conscious of her misery, discerning also, with joy and hope, a fulness of salvation in Christ, and earnestly desiring communion with him, cannot fail, with the utmost alacrity, to apprehend and receive the inestimable blessing thus exhibited, and by receiving to appropriate, or make it her own.[17] By this act, Christ becomes, so to speak, the peculiar property of the believing soul. All that belongs to Christ being exhibited together with him, the believer claims to himself whatever is Christ's, and especially his righteousness, which is the foundation of salvation. By apprehending Christ in this manner, he is united to him ; and being united to Christ, he is considered as having done and suffered those very things which Christ, as his Surety, did and suffered in his stead. When this is rightly observed, it is easy to understand how we are justified by faith in Christ.

xx. The Scripture more than once describes this act of faith in express terms. Remarkable is the passage in John i. 12. where " as many as received him," is equivalent to " them that believe on his name ;" and in Coloss. ii. 6. " As ye have, therefore, received Christ Jesus the Lord," &c. To these may be added what the Lord very emphatically says in Isaiah,[e] " Let him take hold (fast hold) of my strength," or of my *tower*, so as not to let it go. The words הַחֲזִיק, *to take*

[d] Isaiah lxv. i.   [e] Ch. xxvii. 5. יַחֲזֵק בְּמָעֻזִּי.
[16] See NOTE XVI.   [17] See NOTE XVII.

fast hold of, and שלח *to let go,* are opposed to each other.[f]

XXI. But, as the soul, while it thus apprehends Christ for salvation, at the same time RESTS and DEPENDS upon him, the exercise of faith is frequently explained by this metaphor also; as in the expression, " By thee have I been holden up ;"[g] and again, " They stay themselves upon the God of Israel,"[h] assuming the appearance of a genuine faith. The same thing is expressed by another Hebrew word, namely, נשען, as in Isaiah l. 10.—" and stay himself upon his God."[i] If you are disposed nicely to distinguish this act of the believing soul, thus resting on Christ and staying itself upon him, from the reception of Christ, and to consider it as posterior to the receiving of him, I shall not vehemently oppose you. We may, therefore, call this the *sixth* act of faith.

XXII. This appears to us to be very significantly expressed by the Hebrew term האמין, which properly signifies *to cast one's self upon* the veracity and power of *another, in order to be carried;* as an infant casts itself, for this purpose, into the arms of its nurse. It is derived from אמן, which is properly *to bear, to carry ;* and from which comes אומן *a bearer, a nursing-father.* " Carry them in thy bosom, as האומן *a nursing-father* " beareth the sucking-child."[k] Hence also האמן, *to be carried :* " Thy daughters תאמנה shall be nursed (car-" ried) at thy side,"[l] in thine arms : for it is said in a parallel passage, " Ye shall be borne upon her sides."[m]

[f] Prov. iv. 13.   [g] עליך נסמכתי Ps. lxxi. 6.

[h] נסמכו Isaiah xlviii. 2.

[i] See also Isaiah. x. 20.   2 Chron. xvi. 7, 8.

[k] Numb. xi. 12.   [l] Isaiah lx. 4.

[m] על צד תנשאו Is. lxvi. 12.

Christ carries believers, as nurslings,* in his bosom ;[n] and Moses, too, makes use of this figure : " The Lord " thy God bare thee, as a man doth bear his son ;"[o] " underneath are the everlasting arms."[p]   According to the natural signification of the word, then, האמין is *to give one's self* to Christ *to be carried,* and so to throw one's self into his bosom and his arms ; by which similitude the activity of the believing soul towards Christ is most elegantly expressed.

XXIII. Farther, when the believer thus receives Christ and rests upon him, he considers him not merely as a SAVIOUR, but also as a LORD.   He receives a whole Christ, and acquiesces in him in all those characters which he sustains : but he is not less a Lord than a Saviour ; nay, he cannot be a Saviour, unless he be also a Lord.   Our salvation consists in this, that we belong not to the devil, nor to ourselves, nor to any other creature, but are the property of Christ the Lord. Faith, therefore, receives " Christ Jesus, the LORD."[q] Christ offers himself as a Husband to the soul, only upon this condition, that she acknowledge him likewise as her Lord.[r]   The soul, accordingly, when she throws herself into the arms of Jesus, renounces her own will, and yields herself up to the sovereign will of Jesus, to be carried whithersoever he pleases.   Hence faith includes an humble surrender and giving up of one's self, by which the believer, suitably to the sacred obligations under which he is laid, yields himself wholly to Christ, who is freely given him, saying, " I am my beloved's, and my beloved is mine."[s]   It is said of the

---

* אמונים, 'εγκολπιοι.

[n] Isaiah xl. ii.   [o] Deut. i. 31.
[p] Deut. xxxiii. 27.   [q] Coloss. ii. 6.
[r] Psalm xlv. 10, 11.   [s] Song vi. 3.

Christians of Macedonia, that " they gave themselves to the Lord ;"[t] which they seem to have done nearly in the same form with Amasai and his companions, when they gave themselves to David, saying, " Thine are we, O David, and on thy side, thou son of Jesse."[u] This surrender that we make of ourselves to Christ, which we number as the *seventh* act of faith, is a fruitful and permanent source of all true obedience ; which, on this account, is denominated " the obedience of faith,"[v] that is, an obedience flowing from faith.

XXIV. After the believer has thus received Christ, and surrendered himself to him, he may and ought to conclude, that Christ, with all his saving benefits, is his, and that he will surely bless him ; for faith reasons infallibly in this manner : " Christ offers himself as a " complete Saviour to all that are labouring and heavy- " laden, hungering and thirsting, to all that receive " him, and are disposed to surrender themselves to " him : But I am labouring and heavy-laden, hunger- " ing and thirsting, &c. Therefore, Christ hath offered " himself to me ; he is now mine, and I am his, nor " shall any thing ever separate me from his love." This is the *eighth* act of faith, a *reflex* act, arising from the consciousness of justifying faith.[w]

XXV. Hence arises, in fine, the holy CONFIDENCE of a soul conscious of its union to Christ by faith, a confidence accompanied with tranquillity, joy, peace, a bold defiance of every enemy and every danger, glorying in the Lord, and glorying in adversity. Whilst the soul leans with pleasure upon her beloved,[x] with

[t] 2 Corinth. viii. 5.   [u] 1 Chron. xii. 18.

[v] Rom. i. 5.

[w] Gal. ii. 20.   2 Tim. i. 12.   Rom. viii. 38.

[x] Song viii. 5.

stretched out arms casting herself upon him, or with her elbow sweetly reclining upon him, (for, according to the Talmudists,[18] מרפק signifies the *arm-pit*,) assured of mutual communion and mutual love, whilst she sings, " I am my beloved's, and his desire is towards me;"[y]—she piously exults and delights in her Lord, is filled with his love, " rejoices with joy unspeakable and full of glory,"[z] sweetly melts by the glowing flames of reciprocal love, and, in fine, triumphs in hope of the glory of God.[a]

XXVI. Let us now briefly recapitulate, and exhibit in one view, the particulars which have thus been stated at large.   Faith includes the knowledge of the mystery of God and of Christ in the light of grace, and the full assent of the mind to the truth of this mystery on account of the authority of God by whom it is attested. Nor is this all ; the believer also loves the truth, exults in it and glorifies God ; he is ardently desirous of fellowship with the Saviour, that those doctrines which are true in Christ may be true to himself for his salvation ; consequently, when Christ is offered to him by the word and Spirit, he receives him with the greatest alacrity of soul, rests and leans upon him, surrenders and yields up himself to him ; after which, he now glories in him as his own, and delights in him exceedingly, reclining under the shadow of the tree of life, and satiating himself with its delicious fruits.   This is " the faith of God's elect,"[b] an invaluable gift, the bond of our union to Christ, the scale of Paradise, the key of the ark of the Covenant by which its treasures are un-

[y] Song vii. 10.   [z] 1 Pet. i. 8.
[a] Rom. v. 2.   [b] Tit. i. 1.
          [18] See NOTE XVIII.

locked, the permanent spring of a holy, tranquil, and blessed life.

XXVII. If any one apprehends that he speaks more correctly, when he so distinguishes these acts of faith as to say, that some of them precede faith strictly so called, as the knowledge of revealed truth, to which some excellent Divines add the pious inclination of the will towards God; that others pertain to the very form and essence of faith, as assent, a hunger and thirst after righteousness, the reception of Christ as a Saviour and Lord, and the flight of the soul to him for refuge; and that others are accidental, and belong only to a strong and established faith, to wit, the assurance that Christ is now mine, and a most delightful leaning upon him as mine, joined with exultation and glorying in him;— we see no reason why such a person may not enjoy the accuracy to which he is partial. It is by no means displeasing to us; we only intended to show that all these acts concur in the full exercise of faith.

XXVIII. From what has been said, it is evident, that the faith which is commonly called *Historical* and *Temporary*, differs very widely from that saving faith which we have just described. I question, however, the propriety of those terms. *A naked assent given to those truths which are contained in the word of God, founded on the authority of God who declares them, without any pious motion of the will*, is styled a *historical* faith. But, since this assent may not only be given to the historical parts of the sacred volume, but extends also to the precepts, doctrines, promises, and threatenings, the character *historical* applied to this faith, seems to be too confined. Possibly, however, it may be so denominated, in reference to the manner in which it is conversant with its object; for as a person who reads histories of transactions in which he has no concern, barely contemplates them, and is not inwardly moved or affected with them, so those who have merely the faith in question, satisfy themselves with idle speculation about the doctrines taught in the word of God, and do not reduce them to practice. Yet it is not universally true, that histories, even such of them as relate to the most ancient events, or to the affairs of another world, are read without interest, emotion, and application. It would, therefore, be better to call this a *theoretical*, or *speculative* faith, or the faith of *naked assent*.

XXIX. Our Lord calls that a *temporary* faith, which, besides giving this general assent, rejoices in the truth known and acknowledged, makes profession of it, and gives rise to many emotions in the heart, and actions in the life, which exhibit some appearance of piety; but continues only for a time, while the external circumstances of the church are altogether prosperous, and fails, when the storms of persecution assail her. This is aptly denominated by our Lord *temporary*.[c] But it may possibly happen, and, indeed, it is frequently found, that while the state of the church is tranquil and flourishing, men may persevere to the end of their life in this profession of faith, and imaginary joy, and in such a course of life as they account sufficient for the purposes of piety. The denomination of *temporary* faith, therefore, which our Lord gave to the faith only of apostates, is with less propriety applied to this faith, which, though not saving, is yet abiding. It would be better perhaps to call it a *presumptuous* faith.

XXX. It is of importance, however, to our consola-

[c] Προσκαιρος. Matth. xiii. 21.

tion, to know distinctly, by what means this faith may be distinguished from a true, living, and saving faith, which it boldly counterfeits. *First*, there is no small difference as to the ACKNOWLEDGMENT of revealed truths. This presumptuous faith assents to them as truths: but, being destitute of the true light of the Spirit, it does not see the native beauty of those truths, or their excellence as they are in Jesus; it does not discern the perfections of God shining brightly in them ; nor does it form a right estimate of their value. When it first begins to know them, it is affected with their novelty and extraordinary nature ; but it does not burn with an ardent love to them, nor is it much concerned to have them, not merely impressed upon the soul, but also expressed in the disposition and conduct ; and, whenever other objects present themselves to the mind, which flatter it with a fair appearance of pleasure or profit, it easily suffers the ideas of those truths which are hostile to that gratification to be obliterated, and almost wishes that there were no such truths, the certainty of which, however reluctantly, it is compelled to admit. But, in genuine faith, the reverse of all this takes place, as we have shown in the seventeenth Section.

XXXI. *Secondly*, There is a great difference in THE APPLICATION OF THE PROMISES OF THE GOSPEL. A presumptuous faith does not proceed in the right method: it rashly imagines that the salvation promised in the Gospel belongs to itself; and this hasty conclusion is built either upon no foundation at all, or upon a false one. Sometimes the presumptuous, without any self-examination or diligent inquiry into their own character, which they avoid as too irksome and inconvenient an exercise,—foolishly flatter themselves,—arrogantly lay claim to the grace of our Lord, and sleep on securely, indulging this delusive dream, neither inquiring nor disposed to inquire what ground they have for this imagination. Sometimes they lay as a foundation for their confidence, either a preposterous notion respecting the general mercy of God, and some easy method of salvation which they discover in the Gospelcovenant ; or an opinion of the sufficiency of their own holiness, because they are not so extremely vicious as the most daring profligates ; or their external communion with the Church and attendance on the public worship ; or the security of their sleeping conscience, and the soothing fancies of their own dreams, which they regard as the peace of God, and the consolations of the Holy Spirit. By these and the like vanities of their own imagination, they deceive themselves ; as if these were sufficient marks of grace. But true believers, impressed with a deep sense of their own wretchedness, panting after the grace of the Lord Jesus, and laying hold upon it with a trembling humility, dare not, however, boast of it as already their own, till after diligent investigation they have discovered certain and infallible evidences of grace in themselves. With profound humility, with a kind of sacred dread, and with a sincere self-denial, they approach to lay hold on the grace of Christ : nor do they conclude that they have obtained it, till they have inquired carefully, first into the marks of grace, and, then, into their own hearts. It is otherwise with the presumptuous in both these respects ; for they rashly seize that which is not offered to them in any such order, (since God doth not offer security and joy to sinners, before their mind is affected with sorrow for the sins which they have committed, and roused to a due solicitude regarding salvation ;)

and, then, they rashly boast of having attained grace, although they cannot make good their pretensions to a participation of the grace of God, by any one satisfactory proof.

XXXII. A *third* difference consists in the JOY which accompanies or follows both kinds of faith; and this difference is two-fold; 1st, In respect to the *origin;* 2dly, In respect to the *effect* of that joy. In presumptuous faith, joy arises, partly, from the novelty and rarity of the things revealed, (for the knowledge of a rare and profound truth delights the understanding, as the enjoyment of a good, the will;) partly, from the vain imagination that the blessings offered in the Gospel belong to themselves; of which, from the common gifts of the Holy Spirit, they have some kind of taste, though very superficial, and, so to speak, affecting only the extremity of their lips. But in living faith, there is a much nobler and more solid joy, springing from the love of those most precious truths, by the knowledge of which, the soul taught of God, justly considers itself inexpressibly blessed;—from a well-founded hope and a certain persuasion of its own spirit, with which the testimony of the Divine Spirit concurs, respecting the present grace and the future glory of God;—and, finally, from a delightful sense of present grace, and a happy anticipation of future glory.

Since there is so wide a difference betwixt the causes of these two kinds of joy, it is not surprising that the effects are also extremely different. The former makes the soul full of itself, leaves it void of the love of God, and by its vain titillation, lulls it still deeper asleep in carnal security. The latter, on the contrary, fills believers with high admiration of God's astonishing and unmerited " kindness towards man," inflames them with love to the most gracious and compassionate Jesus, and generates a solicitous care, lest they do any thing unworthy of that unbounded favour and goodness of God, or grieve and offend that Spirit of grace, who hath dealt so mercifully with them.

XXXIII. The *fourth* difference consists in their FRUITS. A presumptuous faith either plunges men into a profound sleep of security, which they increase by the indulgence of the flesh; or leads to some reformation in their external conduct, and causes them, in a certain degree, to " escape the pollutions of the world " through the knowledge of the Lord and Saviour Je- " sus Christ ;"[d] or, when it operates in its most excellent manner, it stirs up some slight and vanishing resolutions and endeavours after a stricter piety. But, even then, it doth not purify the heart; it doth not introduce new principles of holiness; and, whenever either the allurements of the world and the flesh, or some disadvantages attending evangelical religion, assault them with more than ordinary force, they soon become weary of that course of goodness on which they had entered, and return to their sins, like " the sow that was washed to her wallowing in the mire."[e] By that superficial knowledge which they have received of evangelical truth, and of the good, no less pleasant and profitable than honourable, which the Gospel exhibits,—by this knowledge, faintly imprinted on their minds, they are, indeed, excited to some amendment of life : but, when the attainment of any present good or the avoidance of any imminent evil is in question, those ideas of what is true and good, which the Gospel had suggested to them, are so obliterated, that they prefer the acquisition of a

[d] 2 Pet. ii. 20.   [e] 2 Pet. ii. 22.

present pleasure or advantage, or an escape from a present impending evil, to all the promises of the Gospel, and to all evangelical piety. A true and living faith produces far more excellent and salutary fruits. It impresses the image of what is good upon the soul in so deep characters, that it esteems nothing more noble or delightful than to make every possible exertion to attain it. It imprints the bright and spotless holiness of the Lord Jesus, in so vivid colours, that the soul, beholding it with the greatest affection, is transformed into its image.[f] It so pathetically represents the love of a dying Saviour, that the believer deems nothing more desirable, than, in return, to live and die to him.[g] It gives so lively a view, and produces so indelible an impression, of the promised bliss, that, for the sake of that bliss, the soul is prepared to face every danger, and to sustain every suffering.[h] Thus it purifies the very heart, and disposes it to the practice of a sincere and stedfast piety; which is always more lively or more languid, in proportion to the vigour or languor of faith.[i]

XXXIV. Having thus illustrated the nature of a living faith, and the manner in which it is distinguished from that which is presumptuous, we shall now accomplish what remains to be done with the greater brevity and ease. Let us proceed, then, to what we promised to speak of in the *second* place, viz. What is intended by the *appropriation* of this faith to every Christian in particular. We do not say, WE BELIEVE, but I BELIEVE. The principal reasons of this, appear to be the three following. 1st, Because the faith of one cannot avail for the salvation of another; but every indi-

---

[f] 2 Cor. iii. 18.　　　　[g] Gal. ii. 20.
[h] 2 Cor. iv. 16, 17, 18.　　[i] Acts xv. 9.

vidual must be justified by his own faith. We do not
deny that the faith of parents is so far profitable to
their children, that, on account of it, they are numbered
among God's covenant-people, so long as they do not
by their conduct give evidence of the contrary. The
faith of the parents, however, is not sufficient for the
salvation of their children, unless the children themselves be regenerated and united to Christ by the Spirit of grace.[k] To this is usually referred that remarkable passage, Habakkuk ii. 4. which some render,
" The just shall live by his (own) faith."[l] But I will
not dissemble that the relative " his" may properly
be applied to Christ, of whom it is said in the preceding verse, " *he* will surely come, *he* will not tarry ;" so
that the meaning may be, *by the faith of him*, that is,
of Christ. This interpretation corresponds with the
expression in Isaiah, " By his knowledge shall my
righteous servant justify many,"[m] where " his knowledge" signifies the knowledge of Christ. This, also,
appears to be a richer sense, and more glorifying to
Christ. It remains, however, a truth, that every man
is justified by his own faith. 2dly, Another reason for
the singular number is, that this Summary of faith was
framed in the primitive church for this purpose, that
they who were about to be baptized, when interrogated
with regard to their faith, might return an answer, every
one for himself. It was usual to examine a person
who was going to receive baptism, in this manner ;
" What do you believe ?" To which he replied, " I
believe in God the Father," &c. 3dly, This reason
also may be added, that we cannot give testimony con-

[k] John iii. 3, 5.　　וצדיק באמונתו יחיה [l]
[m] Ch. liii. 11.　דעתו .

cerning the faith of another with the same certainty as concerning our own faith. *Augustine* has well said, " Faith resides in our innermost parts ; nor does any " man see it in another, but every one may see it in " himself. Hence it is possible, that it may be coun- " terfeited by artifice, and supposed to be in one who, " in reality, is destitute of it. Every one, therefore, " sees his own faith in himself."*

XXXV. To proceed now to the *third* division of the subject ; let us inquire in what manner every one may be conscious of his own faith. That it is possible and usual for believers to have in themselves a conscious- ness of their own faith, Paul teaches us, not only by his example, when he says, " I know whom I have be- lieved,"[n] but also by the following exhortation addressed unto all, " Examine yourselves, whether you be in the faith ; prove your own selves."[o] This exhortation would be quite nugatory, were it impossible for men, by examining and proving themselves, to attain the knowledge of that which they thus investigate. That this is a possible attainment, he intimates in a manner still more express, by adding, " Know ye not your own selves, how that Jesus Christ is in you ?"

XXXVI. Nor is it difficult to understand, how this consciousness of faith may arise in the minds of believ- ers. It is requisite, in the first place, that they be well instructed from the word of God, with respect to the nature of saving faith. Not that it is necessary to bur- den and perplex the minds of the weak with a multi- plicity of marks. Only let the principal and essential acts of a true faith be simply and clearly shown them. Let them be urged to attend to the difference betwixt a

---

* *De Trinit.* Lib. xiii. cap. 2.

[n] 2 Tim. i. 12.   [o] 2 Cor. xiii. 5.

strong and a weak faith; betwixt a lively and a languid faith; betwixt a faith which is calm and tranquil, and that which is shaken by numerous temptations. Let them be taught, not only that the faith which is weak, languid, and shaken, is, yet true and genuine; but also, that, when they examine themselves, a weak faith is not to be tried by the idea* of a strong faith; nor a languid by the idea of a lively faith; nor that which is shaken by the idea of that which is tranquil; but that each is to be compared with its own proper idea. This being well considered, let every one examine himself, and see whether he puts forth such acts of faith as those which we have now described. Of this, no one that attends properly to himself can be ignorant. Every man is immediately conscious to himself of those things which he thinks and wills, for the precise reason that he thinks and wills them. Now, faith is, unquestionably, an exercise of the understanding and will.

XXXVII. Some, perhaps, may object, " If it is re- " presented as so easy for one to possess a consciousness " of his own faith, how does it happen, that a great " number of believers are tormented with harassing " doubts and waverings, with respect to this point?" For this, however, several reasons may be assigned. 1st, It often happens that they have either formed to themselves a wrong idea of saving faith, or rashly adopted a mistaken notion of it, which others have incautiously suggested. Thus we have learned by experience, that a considerable number of afflicted souls, have entertained the opinion, that the essence of faith, consists in a firm persuasion, and delightful sense of the love of God, and a full assurance of their own

* This expression is here used, as synonymous with *model*, or *pattern.*—T.

salvation. When, therefore, they could not discover these attainments in themselves, they proceeded, by a rigorous sentence, to expunge their own names from the roll of the faithful. The same persons, however, when better informed about the nature of faith, and when taught that the attainments which we have just mentioned are rather the glorious fruits of an established, than the essential acts of a genuine faith, have gradually returned to greater composure of mind. 2dly, The minds of believers are sometimes agitated by so many storms of temptation, that they do not give, or are even incapable of giving, that attention, which is necessary to distinguish the proper exercises of their own souls. In this condition, they perform every thing in so irregular and desultory a manner, that, so long as the perturbation continues, they cannot clearly discern the state of their own heart, whilst the various thoughts of their mind and emotions of their will, mutually succeed and oppose one another with surprising rapidity. 3dly, Sometimes, also, it is not easy for believers, especially when their souls are in a disconsolate state, to compare their exercises with the description of a genuine faith ; or, to speak more clearly, to compare the rule with that which is to be tried by the rule. This is particularly the case, when one has proposed to himself the idea of a lively faith, and finds only a languid faith in his heart. In such circumstances, finding little agreement, or rather, the greatest difference between the two, he must almost inevitably form too unfavourable a decision respecting his faith.

xxxviii. It is not, indeed, absolutely necessary to salvation that every one should know that he is himself a believer ; for the promise of salvation is annexed to the sincerity of faith, not to the knowledge which one has of his faith.[p] It is expedient, however, for the following purposes, that, by a careful search, every one should inquire into the truth and sincerity of his faith. 1st, That he may render to God the praise which is due for this inestimable gift. If the Apostle Paul so often rendered thanks to God for the faith of others,[q] how much more is it incumbent on every believer to bless the Lord for his own faith? This, however, he cannot do, unless he know that he has faith. 2dly, That he may enjoy great consolation in himself; for the consciousness of our faith is accompanied with assurance of our salvation. Accordingly, Paul joins these two together, saying; "I know whom I have believed, "and I am persuaded that he is able to keep that "which I have committed to him against that day."[r] 3dly, That, with the greater alacrity, he may run the race of piety. When he is sure that his works proceed from a principle of faith, he is certain, at the same time, that his "labour shall not be in vain in the Lord;" and this assurance so animates the believer, that he becomes "stedfast, unmoveable, always abounding in the work of the Lord."[s]

XXXIX. In fine, we must say something briefly with regard to the PROFESSION of faith; for the Creed is a kind of formulary of such a profession. This, the Apostle Peter, in the name of God, enjoins upon every believer; "Be ye ready always to give to every one that asketh you a reason of the hope that is in you."[t] This, the Spirit of faith dictates, influencing no less the tongues than the hearts of the faithful, as that

[p] Mark xvi. 16. John iii. 16.

[q] Ephes. i. 15, 16. Phil. i. 3. Col. i. 3, 4. 1 Thes. i. 2, 3. 2 Thes. i. 3.

[r] 2 Tim. i. 12.

[s] 1 Cor. xv. 58.

[t] 1 Pet. iii. 15.

mystical " new wine which makes the maids[19] eloquent."[u] " We having the same Spirit of faith, ac-
" cording as it is written, I believed, and therefore have
" I spoken, we also believe, and therefore speak."[v]
This the glory of God requires; to the promotion of
which, by the declaration of the truth, and of the Divine perfections shining in it, our tongue ought to be
subservient; and the magnifying of which, Paul had in
view in that boldness which he discovered.[w]   Love to
our neighbour, also, who may be edified by this means,
demands an open profession of faith.[x]   Such was the
line of conduct observed by those Christian worthies,
who, amidst the fury of the world, the rage of devils,
and the frowns of tyrants; despising death in all its
forms, whether they were cut off by the sword, or nailed
to the cross, or thrown into the midst of the flames;
with undaunted courage, and with a *most clear unfal-
tering voice*, (to adopt the expression of *Eusebius* concerning *Vetius* the Martyr,*)—declared those doctrines
which they knew to be true. *Basil the Great* has
nobly said, " That, rising superior to every emotion of
" fear and shame, we ought to display great boldness
" and courage in confessing our Lord Jesus Christ and
" his words."†   To this, the Lord Jesus himself directs
us by his own example; " he witnessed a good confession before Pontius Pilate."[y]   To this, if it proceed
from a sincere heart, a promise of salvation is annexed;[z] whilst, on the other side, our Lord denounces the

---

* Λαμπροτατη φωνῆ.   *Hist. Eccles.* Lib. v. Cap. 1.
† *Moralium reg. sexta.*

   [u] Zech. ix. 17.   [v] 2 Cor. iv. 13.
   [w] Philip. i. 20.   [x] Philip. ii. 15.
   [y] 1 Tim. vi. 13.   [z] Matth. x. 32.   Rom. x. 10.
          [19] See NOTE XIX.

most dreadful threatenings against those, who, from false modesty and carnal cowardice, are ashamed to confess him before men.[a]

XL. It has, therefore, been a laudable custom, observed from the most ancient times in the Christian Church, to admit no adult to the sacred laver of baptism, unless he has first made a public profession of his faith. Conformably to this practice, the children of Christians, after they had grown up to the years of discretion, were anciently presented to the Bishop,[20] that they might act the same part which was required of adults who offered themselves for baptism. Having been initiated by baptism in infancy, when they were incapable of making a confession of faith to the Church; they were again presented by their Parents, about the end of their childhood, or when entering on youth, and examined by the Bishop, according to the form of a Catechism which was then well known and generally used. From this ancient rite, as *Calvin* observes,[*] the Church of Rome has derived her fictitious Sacrament of Confirmation. The same custom was also observed by the Bohemian Brethren; amongst whom parents presented their children, when about twelve years old, to the Pastor, in the church; that the children might make a public profession of their faith, and that it might appear, whether the parents had faithfully discharged their duty in giving them instruction, agreeably to the engagements under which they had come at their baptism.[†] The manner in which this observance was introduced amongst them, is accurately related in

* *Instit.* Lib. iv. cap. xix. § 4.

† *Lasitius de moribus et Institutis Fratrum Bohemorum*, cap. xii. § 28, 29.

[a] Luke ix. 26.   [20] See NOTE XX.

the *Account of the Discipline of the Bohemian Bre-*
*thren.** Something similar, as *Durel*† shows, is practised in the Church of England.[21] It were to be
wished that the same observance were in use in our
churches also; or, at least, that they who are admitted
to the sacrament of the Lord's Supper made a public
profession of their faith, in the presence and audience
of the whole congregation. As to persons who refuse
to make such a profession, even before the Consistory
or Session, or before the Pastor in private, alleging the
most frivolous apologies for their refusal,—I would
they were admonished to consider, in the most serious
manner, the awful denunciation of our Lord respecting
those who shall be ashamed of him and of his words.

* *Ratio Disciplinæ Ordinis Fratrum Bohemorum,* p. 46.
† *Vindiciæ Eccles. Anglic.* cap. xxiii. p. 253.
[21] See NOTE XXI.

DISSERTATION IV.

ON THE FAITH OF THE EXISTENCE OF GOD.

———

1. God is at once the principal and the ultimate object of faith; " Ye believe in God,"[a] said our Lord to his disciples; and says the Apostle Peter,—" who by Him," that is, Christ, " do believe in God."[b] Believers consider God as the self-existent, uncreated truth,[*] on whom they may rely with the greatest safety; and as the supreme felicity, united to whom by faith, they may become inexpressibly happy. The Creed, accordingly, begins with these words, I BELIEVE IN GOD.

II. Many have supposed that these three phrases, *Credere Deum*, to believe God, *credere Deo*, to believe God,[†] and *credere in Deum*, to believe in God, ought to be thus distinguished; that the first means, to be persuaded of his existence;[‡] the second, to give credit

---

[*] Ἀυτοαληθεια.

[†] The reader will observe that *Deum* is the accusative, or objective, and *Deo* the dative case, of the Latin word *Deus*, God: but if *credere* is rendered *to believe*, the English idiom requires us to translate *credere Deo*, as well as *credere Deum*, *to believe God*. We may say, *to give credit to God ;* but we cannot say, *to believe to him.* T.

[‡] *Existentia*, or, as Macrobius expresses it, *extantia*.

[a] John xiv. 1.   [b] 1 Pet. i. 21.

to God when he testifies any thing; the third, to rely upon God with a saving confidence of soul.

III. But as this distinction has no foundation in the Scriptures, so it takes its rise from total ignorance of the Hebrew idiom. The expression *Credere Deum, to believe God,* no where occurs in holy writ. Paul says, " he that cometh unto God, must *believe that he is :*[c] and *in Deum credere, to believe in God,* is a Hebraism, contrary to the ancient purity both of the Greek and the Latin tongue.—The Hebrews use indifferently, ל, or ב, in connexion with האמין; as in the expression ויאמינו בדבריו " Then believed they his words,"[d] and, לא האמינו לדברו " They believed not his word."[e] This Hebraism, in common with many others, was imitated by the Hellenists,[22] and by the sacred writers of the New Testament. Let the following instance suffice. In John viii. 30. it is said, πολλοι ἐπιστευσαν ʼεἰς αὐτον, " many believed on him ;" and verse 31. the same persons are called πεπιστευκοτας αὐτω, " those who believed him." Hence it appears that they are greatly mistaken, who assert that the expression *to believe in one,* signifies that devout affection of mind which is an homage due to God alone; for it is expressly said, ויאמינו ביהוה ובמשה עבדו, " and believed (*in*) the LORD, and (*in*) his servant Moses."[f] Those, also, are mistaken, who suppose that the phrase *to believe in God* or *in Christ,* is always descriptive of a living faith; since it is said of the Ninevites that they believed in God,[g] and of the Jews, that they " believed in his," to wit, Christ's " name," to whom " Jesus did

[c] Heb. xi. 6.   [d] Ps. cvi. 12.   [e] Ver. 24.

[f] Exod. xiv. 31.   See also 2 Chron. xx. 20.

[g] ויאמיבו באלהים   Jon. iii. 5.

[22] See NOTE XXII.

not commit himself ;"ₕ—whilst, on the contrary, a different expression is made use of, to denote a living and saving faith, in John v. 24. πιστευων τω πεμψαντι με, " he that believeth him that sent me ;" and in the account of the Jailor, πεπιστευκως τῳ Θεῷ, "who believed God,"ⁱ both phrases are used indiscriminately.*

iv. When we speak of GOD, we understand *a Being who is infinitely perfect, since he is the Creator and Lord of all other beings.* This is the idea common to all nations, which they express, each in their own language, whenever they make mention of God. Now, in order to a man's believing in God, it is necessary, first of all, that he be firmly persuaded in his mind that such an infinitely perfect Being doth really exist. " For he that cometh unto God, must believe that he is."ʲ But, since this persuasion lays a foundation for itself in NATURE, upon which GRACE rears the superstructure of Divine revelation, it will be proper to see, first, what nature can teach us on this topic, and then, what the Christian faith superadds to the persuasion derived from nature.

v. The existence of God is so necessary and so evident a truth, that to one rightly attending to the subject, scarcely any thing can appear more certain, more obvious, or more manifest. It is clear even from that notion of a Deity which is common to all nations. Whoever speaks of God, speaks of a Being infinitely perfect. Such a Being, however, cannot even be conceived of in thought, without including in our conception the necessity of his existence. For, since it is

---

* See the learned observations of *Gomar* on John ii. 23. xiii. 42.

ʰ John ii. 23, 24.   ⁱ Acts xvi. 31, 34.

ʲ Heb. xi. 6.

a greater perfection to exist than not to exist ; to exist
necessarily than to exist contingently and according to
the pleasure of another ; to exist from eternity and to
eternity, than to exist at one time and not to exist at
another time ;—it follows that existence, even a necessary and eternal existence, is implied in the essence of
a most perfect Being.   It is as impossible to form an
idea of a most perfect Being without necessary existence, as an idea of a mountain without a valley.

Besides, the man who denies that there is a God,
denies, at the same time, that it is possible for an absolutely perfect and eternal Being to exist.   For if he
at any time begin to exist, he will not be eternal, and
therefore not absolutely perfect, and consequently not
God.   But it is impossible that a being who neither
is, nor can begin to be, can ever exist.   According to
this supposition, then, the impossibility of existence
will be included in the conception of a Deity ; which
is no less contradictory, than if one should say, that the
want of eminent perfection is necessarily included in
the conception of that which is infinitely perfect.[23]

VI. The Creator has so deeply impressed the idea of
his own existence on the human mind, that all may receive this knowledge from nature.   " That which may
" be known of God is manifest in them ; for God hath
" showed it unto them."[k]   This is what is usually
termed *the innate knowledge of God. Eusebius*
speaks, not improperly, of the " notions which every
" one learns from himself, or rather from God."[*]   It
is not intended, that infants possess an actual know-

* 'Αυτοδιδακτȣς εννοιας, μαλλον δε Θεοδιδακτȣς.   *Præparat. Evang.*
lib. ii. c. 5.

k Το γνωστον τȣ Θεȣ.   Rom. i. 19.
[25] See NOTE XXIII.

ledge of God even from the womb; which is equally contrary to universal experience, and to the word of God, which testifies that they " cannot discern between their right hand and their left."[1] Nor is the above expression to be so loosely understood, as if God merely endowed men with a capacity of knowing himself, provided the proofs of his existence be clearly proposed and set before them, or provided every one make a right use of his capacity in the investigation of those proofs; —as if the knowledge of God's existence could not be attained without laborious exertion. But we intend, that God has so deeply impressed the traces of himself upon the innermost parts of the mind, that man, after having arrived at the use of reason, cannot but often think of a God, and it is only by doing violence to himself that he can expel such thoughts from his breast.

VII. *Maximus Tyrius*, the Platonic philosopher, has the following beautiful sentence in his first Dissertation.* " But if, since the beginning of time, two or " three men have existed, that have lived in an atheis- " tical, degraded and senseless state, deceived by their " own eyes and ears, maimed in their very soul,—a " brutish and unprofitable kind of men, no less desti- " tute of the distinguishing glory of their species, than " a lion without courage, an ox without horns, or a bird " without wings;—from even these men you will learn " something concerning a Deity; for, in spite of them- " selves, they both know and express something on this " subject." *Julian*, too, ungodly as he was, expresses himself equally well, as follows: " All of us, previously

---

* *Dissert.* i. *cujus inscriptio est,* Quid sit Deus secundum Platonem ?
[1] Jonah iv. 11.

" to our receiving instruction, are persuaded that there
" is a Deity ; and that to him we should look, to him
" we should hasten. Our minds are inclined towards
" him in the same manner, I think, as our eyes to-
" wards light."

VIII. This argument is illustrated by the operations
of Conscience, which, in a variety of ways, convinces
men of the existence of God. 1st, As it is the deputy
of God, and the depository of his laws in the human
breast, it inculcates, in the name of God, what ought
to be done, and what ought to be avoided. So great,
too, is the authority with which it speaks, that though
the lords of the earth, and dreaded tyrants, should establish a thousand decrees in opposition to its dictates,
it would, nevertheless, incessantly urge by its secret
whispers, that obedience must be rendered to itself, and
to God, in whose name it speaks, rather than to any
mortal whatever. It says concisely, and with a dignity
worthy of a Lawgiver, " Universal submission is due
to me, and to God."* This is what David intends
when he says, " My heart said unto thee,"m that is,
for thee, in thy behalf, in thy place.[24] 2dly, While it
is acquainted with the most hidden secrets of men, and
while neither the least imagination, nor the slightest
motion of the mind, can be concealed from its view, it
testifies, at the same time, that there is another besides
itself, who is thoroughly acquainted with all our actions, words and thoughts. It is for this reason it is
called Conscience,† that is, a witness associated with
another in perceiving the secrets of man ; and who

* Πάντα ἐμοὶ καὶ τῷ Θιῷ. *Arri. Epictet.* lib. iv. cap. 8.
† Συνειδησις, *conscientia.*

m Psalm xxvii. 8.
[24] See NOTE XXIV.

can that other be but God? On this account, also, it
may be denominated " Conscience towards God."[n] 3dly,
When it judges the state and the actions of men, it
performs this office under God, and with reference to
God. Whilst it commends good works, even though
performed in secret, and though disapproved by others,
it gives us to know that the praise of the upright " is
not of men, but of God."[o] When it rewards the good
man with a most delightful tranquillity, and, in particular, when it causes his peace to abound in dying moments, it shows that God is the Rewarder of those
who serve him.[p] When it reproves, accuses, condemns,
punishes, and scourges a man without mercy for his
wicked deeds, although it is within the man, and indeed a part of him, it stands, however, on God's side ;
nor doth it regard the degree of torment which the man
may suffer from its testimony. Nay, though it be a
thousand times enjoined to keep silence, though it be
treated with violence, though it be almost stiffled,
and seared as with a hot iron, yet it rises again,
and sharply presses its testimony, in defiance of the
struggles of the guilty. 4thly, Amidst all these operations, it summons man to the tribunal of God, and
intimates that there all things are to be re-examined,
and a more exact judgment to be passed on every action ; and, according to the sentence which it has pronounced here, it causes him either to come into the presence of God with confidence, or to tremble at the
thought of appearing before him. Such, also, is the
energy which it displays, that it will not suffer itself
to be hindered in these operations by any created

[n] Συνείδησις Θεῶ. 1 Pet. ii. 19.   [o] Rom. ii. 29.
[p] Heb. xi. 6.

power. " If our heart condemn us, God is greater
" than our heart, and knoweth all things. Beloved, if
" our heart condemn us not, then have we confidence
" towards God."q Paul gives us a concise summary of
the greater part of these operations, when he says of the
Gentiles, " These, having not the law, are a law unto
" themselves; which show the work of the law written
" in their hearts, their conscience also bearing witness,
" and their thoughts the mean while accusing or else
" excusing one another."r Nor are these the terrors of
weak minds, which the stronger can easily elude. Conscience often restrains and overawes the boldest; and
the most daring profligate, though he may assume the
semblance of hope in his countenance, only conceals the
pain which deeply pierces his heart. The laughter of
such audacious transgressors is merely constrained,
while they feel the smart of the sting within.

IX. This faculty of Conscience, because it so powerfully manifests God to man, doth all in his name, refers all to him, and, in short, acts the part of his vicegerent in the soul, was called *God* by the Heathen.
Hence *Menander* says, " Our mind is God."* *Euri-
pides*, in like manner, quoted by *Gataker*, says, " Our
own mind is to each of us God."† By this, they intended nothing else, probably, than what that old
writer expresses more clearly thus, " In all men, conscience stands in the place of God."‡ But the following
passage of *Epictetus* is particularly worthy of notice:
" Knowest thou not that thou nourishest a God? That
" thou givest exercise to a God? Dost thou not carry

---

* Ὁ νῦς γαρ ἡμων ὁ θεος. *Apud Plutarch in Platon.* Quæst. i.
† *Gat. in notis ad Marc. Anton.* p. 432.
‡ Βροτοῖς ἁπασιν ἡ συνειδησις θεος.
q 1 John iii. 20, 21.   r Rom. ii. 14, 15.

" God about with thee, thou wretch, and art not aware
" of this? You imagine, perhaps, that I refer to
" something external, formed of gold or silver. Let
" me tell you that you carry him within your breast.
" - - - - But whilst God himself is present within,
" and sees and hears all things, art thou not ashamed,
" as if insensible to thine own nature, and hostile to
" God, to think and to do these things?"* For the
same reason, *Plato* says, " He mystically called those
" Atheists, who corrupt the God who dwelleth in
" them, that is, Reason."†

x. The mind, also, which attends to itself, cannot be
ignorant that as it was made by God, so it was made for
God. Since it is clear and evident to the mind, that
it did not consent of its own accord and by deliberate
counsel to inhabit this body which it carries about;
nor form the body for itself; nor subject it to its authority; nor even knows how the bodily members in
subjection to it, are moved according to its will; nor
existed any where else before it lodged in the body;
nor became what it is by the contrivance or power of
parents; nor is able to furnish itself with what it perceives to be necessary to its welfare; nor can find in
itself the cause of its existence;—it is forced to acknowledge that it was created, and that, therefore, it is
the property of him who created it. This can be no
other than God; and, as it was made by him, it necessarily follows that it was also made for him. The eye
is adapted for light, the ear for sounds, the tongue for
speech, and speech for the interpretation of the mind.
For what is the mind itself adapted? For an object,

* *Epict. apud Arrianum,* lib. ii. cap. 8.
† *In Philebo.*

certainly, which can fill it—an object, the knowledge of which can make it wise, the love of which can make it holy, the enjoyment of which can make it happy. For an object, better than itself, nobler than all created things, and most amply sufficient to satisfy its boundless capacities. For an object, in short, which is nothing less than God. The human mind, provided it only give attention to the subject, must clearly perceive, that if no such object as this existed, it could never have itself existed, or if it had, must have existed in vain, and for no proper purpose. That man offers violence to his own mind, who does not say, " Where is God my Maker, that giveth songs in the night?"[s]

XI. But, besides that *innate* knowledge of God, of which man has the principles in his own mind, there is another argument arising from the consideration of the various other creatures around him. Since these are unable to secure the continuance of their own existence, it is manifest that they were not made by themselves : and if we trace them particularly, through the second causes of their being, as far backwards as our mind is able to conduct us, we must arrive, at length, at the First Cause, to whom those that are supposed to be the first of creatures owe the beginning of their existence, and in whose eternity, (as he exists necessarily, of himself, and without beginning,) all our thoughts are swallowed up, as in an immeasurable abyss. The sacred writings instruct us in numberless passages, that the existence of the Supreme Being may be inferred, by incontrovertible arguments, from the contemplation of the creatures.[25]

XII. A very emphatical passage to this effect occurs

[s] Job xxxv. 10.
[25] See NOTE XXV.

in Job xii. 7, 8, 9. " But ask now the beasts, and
" they shall teach thee; and the fowls of the air, and
" they shall tell thee ; or speak to the earth, and it
" shall teach thee; and the fishes of the sea shall de-
" clare unto thee. Who knoweth not in all these, that
" the hand of the Lord hath wrought this ?" Here
we are directed to hold a conference with the creatures,
that they may instruct us concerning the Creator.
That conference can mean nothing but an attentive
consideration of the creatures, in their origin, in their
nature, in their capacities, in their operations, in their
order and mutual subserviency to each other, in the
law to which they are subject, and which is inviolably
observed for the preservation of the whole. The response which they give, the doctrine which they unfold, is the demonstration of the Deity. They had no
power to produce themselves, and even now they have
no power to uphold themselves in being, far less to govern themselves with so much wisdom, that every one,
in its own sphere, should both possess what is sufficient
for the continuation of its own existence, and be adapted
for assisting others and for serving the whole universe,
as if most judiciously ranged in a family and state.
Notwithstanding, therefore, the profound silence which
they observe, they proclaim to every reflecting mind,
that, as they were originally created, so they are still
directed, by the hand of an infinitely wise, as well as
infinitely powerful God. Let it be remarked, also,
that this conclusion is not ascribed to any tradition received from the fathers, but to that very instruction
which the creatures themselves afford, independently
of all human tradition.

XIII. No less forcible is the testimony which we have,

Psalm xix. 1, 2, 3, 4. which I shall explain by a short paraphrase. " The heavens declare the glory of God ;" for they are his throne, which he has curiously fashioned, and which testify his power, majesty, and magnificence. " And the firmament showeth his handy-work ;" proclaiming that it was adjusted by his word alone, that things below might be aptly and commodiously united with things above, and that things terrestrial might be maintained by the influence of things celestial, communicating itself through the medium of the firmament. "Day unto day uttereth speech, and night unto night teacheth knowledge." The vicissitudes of light and darkness, succeeding one another in so exact and so uniform an order ; and, (which is the cause of these appointed vicissitudes,) the revolution of the sun and the stars, neither moving more slowly than at the first, nor revolving with a more rapid motion, but still preserving the original measure of their course,—clearly manifest a Ruler of unbounded wisdom. Nor is there a single day, or single night, which doth not at once utter something for itself respecting God, and bear witness to another ; as if it were the scholar of the preceding, and the teacher of the following. No word is uttered, no speeches are made, their voice " is not heard." They do not teach by *words ;* because, were this their manner of giving instruction, it would cease with the utterance of the words. They do not instruct by *speeches*, or discourses, which consist of a train of arguments artfully connected ; for, in such discourses, some degree of obscurity could hardly be avoided. Nor do they utter an audible *voice* in our ears, the sound of which might dun us by its excessive noise. But the heavens instruct us, *constantly*, *clearly*, and *pleasantly*, whilst they exhibit the perfections of their Creator to view, as

in a mirror. Some, however, choose to translate the
words thus, (of which we do not disapprove :) " There
" is no speech, nor language where their voice is not
" heard." Though the nations differ from one another in their languages, and though the Greek may
not be able to understand the Barbarian, yet the language of the heavens is common to all, and equally capable of imparting instruction to all. Nothing but
listlessness hinders those, whose tongues and customs
are the most opposite to each other, from receiving
knowledge, so to speak, from the mouth of one and the
same teacher. " Their line is gone out to all the
earth."* The manner in which the heavens give instruction, bears a resemblance to the method of teachers, who instruct boys in the first principles of literature
by means of figures which they draw for their use:
For the luminaries of heaven, by the beams which they
shed, form lines, and, as it were, first principles;
which, being mutually combined, and variously connected, compose one entire book of wisdom. This idea
is suggested by the word קו *line;* as in the expression
קו לקו *line upon line.*[t] It may be observed, also, that
there is but little difference betwixt this Hebrew term,
and the Greek φθογγος, made use of by the Apostle ;[u]
for φθογγος signifies not only a *sound,* but likewise a
letter; as in *Plutarch* on *Fabius;* of which *Scapula*
has taken notice in his *Lexicon.* This line, then, has
" gone out to all the earth, and their words to the end
" of the world." All mankind, whether they inhabit
cultivated regions, or the most desert and uncultivated
parts of the earth, are instructed by this preceptor.

* בכל הארץ יצא קום
[t] Is. xxviii. 13.   [u] Rom. x. 18.

There is no quarter of the world in which the figures of heaven, which are so many proofs of the divine perfections, are not beheld.

xiv. Though this exposition of the passage is at once simple, consonant to the words, and worthy of the divine perfections, *Socinus* most perversely contends, that it is here taken for granted, that it is *not* evident from the contemplation of the heavens, that they were created by God. He denies that they proclaim the glory of God to any but those who have been previously persuaded, by other means, of the existence of God, and of the creation of the world. What is said, too, about their line going out to all the earth, he restrains to Judea alone, adducing in confirmation of this sense, Psalm xlv. 16. cv. 7. ii. 8. This, however, is a daring perversion of the Scriptures; for, 1st, It is clear to any one who looks into the Psalm, that the Psalmist points out two ways of knowing God; the one by nature, which he describes from the beginning to the seventh verse; the other by revelation, which he then illustrates, and extols as far more perfect. Nor does he represent the latter as the foundation of the former, but the former as the foundation of the latter. 2dly, The words of the Psalm, cannot bear the interpretation which *Socinus* puts upon them, to wit, " The firmament show-" eth the nature and kind of the work, or celebrates " the work :"* But they must be interpreted thus, " The firmament showeth the work of his hands;" that is, proclaims itself to be the work of divine omnipotence. In this sense the heavens, the sun, the moon, and all the sparkling stars, are said to praise God; because, since they were all created at his command, they

---

* *Firmamentum indicat quale sit opus,* seu *celebrat opus.*

furnish men with the most abundant matter and ground for the celebration of his praise.[v] 3dly, Nor is this proclamation made to the Jews only : it is published in a language equally intelligible to Israelites, Greeks, and Barbarians ; for he never left himself " without witness," even to the Gentiles.[w] 4thly, It is published through the whole earth, even to the uttermost parts of the habitable globe; which are by no means comprehended within the narrow circuit of Judea : unless one chose also to confine within the limits of Judea, what the Apostle expresses in the same words,[x] concerning that Gospel which is preached " to every creature."[y] 5thly, Nor is the heretic able to point out any passage of Scripture, where these expressions, *the whole earth,* and *the uttermost parts of the world,* signify only the land of Judea; for the testimonies which he produces, are foreign to the purpose. Psalm xlv. 16. is a prophecy respecting the calling of the Gentiles; as appears from verse 17th. Psalm cv. 7, " His judgments are in all the earth," is with no appearance of reason confined to Judea; since God executes judgments in the whole world, and those which he executed among his people, were published to the Gentiles. The heretic erroneously confounds the judgments of God's *works* with the judgments of his *law;* which, under the old dispensation, were made known to the Israelites alone.[z] Though we should grant that Judea is sometimes called the whole earth, yet *the ends of the* habitable *world,* are never limited to so inconsiderable a spot of earth. The words in Psalm ii. 8. refer not to the kingdom of David, but to the kingdom of Christ; to

[v] Ps. cxlviii. 1, 3, 5.   [w] Acts xiv. 17.

[x] Rom. x. 18.   [y] Mark xvi. 15.

[z] Ps. cxlvii. 20.

whom " all power is given in heaven and on earth ;" [a] and whose " dominion shall be from sea to sea, and from the river to the ends of the earth."[b] 6thly, Though this were the meaning of the expression in some other passages, yet it cannot be so understood here ; since the subject treated in this passage, is the whole of that earth, where the line of the sun is beheld,— where his glorious beams are seen, where his all-maturing heat is felt.

xv. We may add, that, in reality, had it not been long ago ascertained that these most audacious perverters of the Scriptures are lost to every emotion of shame, they must have been put out of countenance, on this occasion, by the more intelligent among the heathen ; a great number of whom avow, that they were excited and compelled to acknowledge a Deity, purely by the consideration of the heavens, and the stars, and of the order which is observed in the universe. *Plato's* expression is well known : " The heavens never cease to give instruction to mankind."* To the same effect are the following words of *Lucilius* in *Cicero :*† " What " can be so obvious, and so clear, when we have beheld " the heavens and contemplated the celestial bodies, as " that there is a Deity possessed of the most consum- " mate wisdom, by whom they are governed ?" And again, a little after ; " If any one doubts of this, I know " no reason why he may not also doubt of the existence " of the Sun ; for what can be more evident ?" I shall quote another passage from *Cicero.* " Who is so stu- " pid and infatuated," says he, " as not to perceive, " after having looked up to the heavens, that there are

* Ὀυρανος ουδεποτε παυεται διδασκων ανθρωπους.

† *De Natura Deorum,* lib. ii.

[a] Matth. xxviii. 18. 　　　[b] Ps. lxxii. 8.

" Gods ; or to ascribe to the operation of chance, works
" which discover so great intelligence, that scarcely any
" one is able, by any art, to trace their order, and their
" revolutions."* But why do I insist on the convic-
tions and declarations of individuals? *Zaleucus*, the
lawgiver of the *Locrians,* by a law which he enacted,
bound all his fellow-citizens to acknowledge a Divinity,
from the contemplation of the heavens.[26] According
to the testimony of *Diodorus Siculus,* " *Zaleucus,*
" having been chosen by the people to frame laws, and
" attempting to confirm them by new sanctions, began
" by directing their attention to the celestial Gods. At
" the beginning of the preamble to the whole code he
" says; that the inhabitants of the city are required,
" first of all, to believe and to be firmly persuaded that
" there are Gods, and having attentively considered the
" heavens and their astonishing magnificence and order,
" to conclude that they are neither the production of
" chance, nor the workmanship of man."†

XVI. Further, where can we find a more striking
confirmation of the doctrine we are now illustrating,
than the following remarkable expression of Paul?
" For the invisible things of him, from the creation of
" the world are clearly seen, being understood by the
" things which are made, even his eternal power and
" godhead."[c] Here notice, 1st, What respecting God
the Apostle affirms to be known. 2dly, In what manner it is known. 3dly, From what time. 4thly,
Whence this knowledge is derived.

XVII. 1st, *What* is it that is known respecting God? .
The Apostle, in the first place, shows, in general, that

---

* *Orat. de Haruspic. Respo.* † *Diod. Sic.* lib. xii.

c Rom. i. 20.

26 See NOTE XXVI.

it is his " invisible things;" for it is one of the fundamental principles of religion, that God is a Spirit, quite
distinct from the whole mass of matter, and invisible
to every eye.   He then takes particular notice of what
is included in these "invisible things."   1. His POWER ;
which, by his own simple fiat, with no assistance
whatever, with no advantage arising from pre-existent matter—by his mere good pleasure—causes all
things to exist, and to continue in existence so long as
he pleases.   2. His ETERNITY ; which has neither
beginning nor end of days, nor any thing corresponding
to the succession of time.   Unless God had existed
from eternity, he could not have existed at all ; for that
which neither existed from eternity, nor is capable of
being produced, has no existence ; but that God is produced, is an idea utterly repugnant to every dictate of
reason.   A Being, too, who had no beginning, can
have no end ; for he possesses, in his own perfections,
the cause of a necessary existence.   *Aristotle* has,
somewhere, finely said :   " Necessary existence and
eternity are inseparable from each other."*   Unless
God were eternal, besides, he could not be the lord
of time, and the disposer of seasons.   *Synesius*, accordingly, has the following elegant expression in his
third Hymn, " Thou, who art the Eternal Mind, art
the Root of the world."†   3. His GODHEAD ; which
here means the perfections and excellencies of God ;
in particular, his self-sufficiency and absolute independence,[d] and also the relation in which he stands
to the creatures, as the Lord of all, and therefore entitled to the love and the service of all.

* Το 'εξ 'αναγκης, καὶ ἀει ἅμα.
† Προουσιε νοῦ, Κοσμοῦ ρίζα.
[d] Acts xvii. 25.

xviii. 2dly, *In what manner* are these things known? They are " clearly seen by the mind."* 1. Though not perceptible to the eye of the body, they are perceptible to the mind and soul : To the mind, however, that *gives attention*,† and considers them ; not to the mind that either resigns itself to stupidity and torpor, or that impiously excludes the light, and surrenders itself to a voluntary blindness. 2. By the attentive mind, they are " clearly seen :" For this knowledge, like the knowledge of those objects that are presented to the faithful eye, (as the sun, who enlightens the world, or the moon, or the stars,) is so prompt and easy, that men cannot reasonably demand a more ample or obvious demonstration.

xix. 3dly, *From what time* are these things thus clearly seen? " From the creation of the world."‡ Some construe this clause in connexion with the words preceding, and give the sense thus, *Those things which have been invisible ever since the creation of the world.* But as the properties of the divine nature are necessarily and eternally invisible, it is better to refer the expression to what follows : *They are clearly seen from the creation of the world.* This, again, is susceptible of two senses. 1. It may denote the *source* of knowledge ; as if the Apostle had said, " from the consideration of the creation of the world :" as in these words, " By their fruits ye shall know them."ᵉ 2. It may respect the *time* ; the Apostle may intimate, that those perfections of God have been displayed to mankind, as long as the world has existed, and been inhabited by the human race.

* Νοούμενα καθορᾶται.   † Νοοῦντι.

‡ Απο κτισεως κοσμȣ.

ᵉ Ἀπὸ τῶν καρπῶν αὐτῶν. Mat. vii. 16.

xx. 4thly, *Whence*, in fine, can men derive the knowledge of these perfections?—From " the things that are made." The works of nature, which our eyes behold, testify concerning themselves, that they are " things made,"* that is, that they have a Cause, a Maker, an Architect. Thus they lead us to the Maker of all, who, whilst he is entirely free from the imperfections of the creatures, possesses all their excellencies in a supereminent degree.

xxi. The way in which *Socinus* perverts the Apostle's expressions in this passage, is truly surprising. By " the invisible things of God," he understands the mysteries of the Gospel, which are said to " have been kept " secret from the foundation of the world."[f] " His " eternal godhead," he affirms to be " that which God " would constantly have us to do ;" in which sense, he says, the term " godhead" is employed in Col. ii. 9. " His eternal power," he would have to be, " the promises which shall never fail ;" in which sense Paul had said, in a preceding verse of the chapter, that the Gospel is " the power of God."[g] Finally, he refers " the things that are made," to the miracles performed by God, and Christ, and the Apostles.

xxii. On this strange exposition, we offer the following remarks. 1st, The heretic perverts the *scope* of the Apostle; which is to convince the Gentiles, who were destitute of the written word of God, of their having sinned and merited the curse; in the same manner as he convinces of their guilt and danger, the Jews who possessed the written word ;[h]—that thus he may establish the conclusion, that both of them must be justi-

* Ποιήματα.

[f] Matth. xiii. 35.   [g] Verse 16.
[h] Ch. ii. 17.

fied solely by the grace of God through faith in Christ. [i]
It is manifest, therefore, that the Apostle here considers the Gentiles, as in a state of nature, in the darkness
of Paganism, not yet enlightened by the preaching of
the Gospel.

XXIII. 2dly, He perverts, also, the *words* of the
Apostle; for, 1. "The invisible things of God," are
quite distinct from the mysteries of the Gospel, which
he does not even attempt to prove to be any where intended by that expression. The Apostle here opposes
the eyes of the body to the eyes of the mind, and the
things which he represents as invisible to the former,
he asserts to be visible to the latter; as elsewhere he
speaks of " the invisible God." [j] With regard to
Matth. xiii. 35. we have there another expression, and
an extremely different subject; and that saying of
Christ, therefore, is improperly adduced to illustrate
this passage of Paul. 2. "Eternal godhead," and
" that which God would constantly have us to do," are
totally different from each other. To endeavour to pass
them for the same, is worthy of a man, who, " having
his conscience seared as with a hot iron," scruples not
to confound things which are diametrically opposite to
each other. By what authority, by what example, I
say not from the sacred volume, but from any writer
whatever, will he prove, that " godhead" is that which
God would have us to do? That which he produces
for this purpose from Col. ii. 9. discovers only the rage
of a furious mind. The expression there, is not θειότης,
but θεότης. Nor does the word in that passage, denote
that which God wills to be done by us; for how doth
this dwell in Christ, and dwell bodily in him ? But it

[i] Chap. iii. 9, 23, 24.   [j] 1 Tim. i. 17.

signifies the divine nature itself, which resides in Christ,
not typically and symbolically, as in the temple of old,
but truly and really. 3. The " eternal power" of God,
nowhere denotes his promises. The Gospel is called
" the power of God," because it is an efficacious mean
of salvation; the word " power" being taken in its native sense. The Apostle does not intend to intimate,
that the Gospel is the promise of God; but that, in
converting his elect by the preaching of the Gospel,
accompanied with the energy of the Holy Spirit, God
displays " the exceeding greatness of his power, according to the working of his mighty power."[k] 4. Miracles
are not usually called " things that are made,"[*] but
" mighty deeds, signs, wonders."[†] Ποίημα signifies *a
thing created* by God, as in Ephes. ii. 10. " For we
are his workmanship, created," &c.[‡] Ποίημα and κτισμα
are words of the same import; and, accordingly, the
Arians of old, blasphemously styled Christ, Ποίημα καὶ
κτίσμα, *a made being, and a creature.*

XXIV. It is disgraceful for those who wish to be called Christians to wrest to another meaning, such clear
and satisfactory testimonies of Scripture; since even
heathens ascended from the consideration of the world
to God its Creator. *Aristotle,* or whoever else is the
Author of the *Book concerning the world,*[§] says: " It
" is, therefore, an ancient doctrine, and a sentiment
" congenial to all mankind, that of God, and through
" God, all things were framed and established." This
doctrine, however, doth not rest upon ancient tradition

---

[*] Ποιήματα.

[†] Δυνάμεις, σημεῖα, τέρατα.

[‡] ᾿Αυτῦ γαρ ἐσμεν ποίημα, κτισθέντες.

[§] *Liber de Mundo,* cap. xi.

[k] Ephes. i. 19.

alone ; it is strongly inferred from the imperfection of all the creatures. Hence it is added by that Author, " For no creature, deprived of that support which He " affords, is sufficient for its own subsistence." This is fair reasoning. It is highly proper to rise from the imperfection and insufficiency of the creatures, to the absolutely perfect and all-sufficient Creator. Whatever is called imperfect, is accounted such, because it falls short of what is perfect. Take away that which is perfect, as *Boethius* reasons ;* and it becomes impossible even to conceive, whence that which is deemed imperfect, derived its existence. *Cicero* also says, " The " beauty of the world, and the order of the heavenly " bodies, oblige us to acknowledge the existence of " some glorious and eternal Being, whom mankind are " bound to admire and adore."†

xxv. This truth is confirmed by the admirable predictions of astonishing events which were yet in the womb of futurity, by the fatal periods of monarchies, and by several other considerations of this sort. But as those arguments have been copiously illustrated by others, let it suffice that we have merely alluded to them here.[1]

xxvi. Since the doctrine of the existence of God is established by so many, and by so clear and incontrovertible evidences, it ought to receive the firm assent of every individual. Doubts of it should not be entertained, at any time, or upon any pretext ;—not even for the purpose of attaining, in consequence of doubting, a more certain knowledge and a stronger faith. This truth is so manifest, that no man who seriously attends,

* Lib. iii. *Prosa.* 10.
† *De Divinatione,* lib. ii.
[1] See Dan. iii. 26, &c. iv. 34. vi. 27.

can seriously doubt of it. Those who were anciently called Atheists, were at once very few, and generally men of a profligate character, whose interest it was that there should be no God. They were actuated, too, in their reasonings, rather by a love of contradiction, than by any sincere conviction of mind ; like the man who contended that snow is black. Besides, as *Vossius* has shown,* persons were sometimes stigmatized as Atheists, merely because they renounced the false gods of the Gentiles. Whatever be the purpose in view, to plunge into doubts of the existence of God, is always contrary to piety. It is never right to say, " Perhaps " there is no God ; perhaps, in all the thoughts which " we have of a Deity, we are deceived by some malig- " nant and powerful spirit." This truth, however, must not be negligently passed over ; nor are we rashly to presume that we already possess a competent knowledge of so noble a subject, lest, possibly, we may not duly love or adore a God whom we do not sufficiently know. To attend carefully and deliberately to this matter, is not to doubt of the existence of God, but to doubt concerning ourselves, whether we have discharged our duty in this respect with becoming diligence.

xxvii. Nature and Reason are able to teach man, though a sinner, all that we have hitherto said respecting the existence of God. Of all this, faith avails itself, as a groundwork ; not overthrowing nature, but ascending by it, and above it. *Tertullian,* accordingly, well observes ; " God has, in the first instance, ap- " pointed nature your teacher, intending to follow up " her instructions with prophecy ; that, having been " the disciple of nature, you may the more readily give

* *De Idololatria*, lib. i. cap. 1.

" credit to prophecy."* *Clement* of *Alexandria* says, also, to the same effect : " The Greek philosophy, as " it were, purifies and prepares the mind for the recep- " tion of faith ; upon which, truth raises the super- " structure of knowledge."† In this sense we may ex- cuse his expression in another place, where he calls Na- tural Philosophy, " the groundwork of Christian Phi- losophy."‡ Let us now see what Christian Faith su- peradds to this natural persuasion concerning the ex- istence of God.

XXVIII. 1st, It disposes one to observe with attention, those proofs of a Deity which every part of the crea- tion affords. " By faith we understand," observe, and consider.ᵐ Many things " which may be known of God," and which are placed in the clearest light, are neglected by the generality of men, their eyes being blinded. In this concern, the greater part of mankind are cold, languid, and torpid : and, hence, they either rest in a bare notion of the Divinity, or if they descend a little deeper into the contemplation of his character, are satisfied with meagre elements of truth, which they pollute by a large mixture of error ; so that, while they seem to be wise, and give indulgence to their own rea- sonings, they are, in reality, fools. Those, in particu- lar, who, instigated by the fury of a wicked mind, wish that there were no God, (of whose character, as the avenger of crimes, they cannot be ignorant,) exert themselves to suppress all thoughts of a Deity, which are never welcome to their hearts. Of such persons, the Apostle says, " they did not like to retain God in

* *De Resur. Carnis.*
† *Strom.* lib. vii. p. 710. edit. *Parisiensis,* anno 1641.
‡ Ὑποβαθραν της κατα Χριστον φιλοσοφιας. Lib. vi. p. 648.
ᵐ Πιστει νοουμεν. Heb. xi. 3.

their knowledge :"[n] that is, as *Theophylact* explains it, " they rejected the knowledge of God." This, as *Chrysostom* observes, was, on their part, " not a sin of ignorance, but a wilful sin." It was of the same nature with the sin of those who say to God, " Depart " from us, for we desire not the knowledge of thy " ways."[o] But Christian faith causes one to love the truth relating to God, and, consequently, to attend with care to the evidences by which the beloved truth is confirmed, and to take pleasure in the contemplation of them; singing to God, " My meditation of thee shall be sweet ; I will be glad in the Lord."[p] It keeps at a distance, at the same time, all pretended wisdom and vain conceit of science, and determines a man to become an humble disciple of God, to hang upon his lips alone, and to desire instruction from him, in other matters relating to the Deity; saying, " Who teacheth like him ?"[q]

XXIX. 2dly, It is not satisfied with knowing the Divinity by those evidences which nature supplies ; but depends, also, on the testimony of God, who testifies concerning himself, as well externally by the word of divine revelation, as internally by the secret voice of the Spirit. He BELIEVES that God is, because he hears his word, and finds it so wise, so pure, so sweet, so efficacious, and so full of majesty, that it can be nothing else than the word of God. As one believes that his father is present, because he hears his well known voice, so faith believes that God is present in the world, because with her own ears she hears that divine voice, which, with incredible power and sweetness, penetrates

[n] Οὐκ ἐδοκιμασαν τον Θεὸν ἔχειν ἐν ἐπιγνωσιι Rom. i. 28.

[o] Job. xxi. 14.   [p] Psalm civ. 34.

[q] Job xxxvi. 22.

to the inmost soul, and widely differs from all the illusions of deceiving spirits. As the spouse no sooner hears the familiar accents of her beloved Husband than straightway she cries out, " The voice of my Beloved! behold, he cometh;"[r] so the believer, when he hears the voice of God in the world, knows and discerns it,[s] and exclaims; " My Lord, and my God!"[t]

xxx. 3dly, Nature teaches merely, in an indistinct and general manner, that there is a God; but doth not expressly and particularly declare WHAT he is. *Maximus Tyrius*, whom we formerly quoted, after having, in his *first Dissertation*, made some general remarks respecting the Deity, adds: " That distinguished " Master of the Academy," (he intends Plato,) "shows " that such a Father and Author of the Universe " exists: but he does not mention his name, for " he did not know it." *Clement* of *Alexandria*, not unjustly, represents the Gentiles as guilty of Atheism, and that twofold; first, " as they knew not him " who is truly God;" and, secondly, as "they regarded " those who are not, as though they were; and call- " ed those Gods, who, in reality, are not so."[*] *Vossius*, also, says with great elegance: " The same thing " happened to them as to the blind man of whom " we read in the Gospel of St John.[u] When this man " saw the Son of God, from whom he had received " sight, he inquired, nevertheless, who was the Son of " God: for he did not know that he whom he saw, was " the person whom he saw; as if you should see the " King, and not be aware that the man whom you see

* *Admonitio ad Gentes,* pag. 14.

[r] Song ii. 8. [s] John x. 4.
[t] John xx. 28. [u] Ch. ix.

" is the King. Almost all the Gentiles, in like manner,
" saw him who is invisible displaying himself in his
" works, and heard him declaring by expressive silence,
" that he is the Creator and Ruler of the universe, and
" that he demands and is entitled to our worship : But
" they shut their eyes against the sight, they stopped
" their ears against the voice ; as if overpowered by a
" deep sleep, they imagined that he resembles those
" objects which daily presented themselves to their
" eyes ; and, giving easy credit to their own dream,
" they adored the work instead of the Artificer, and
" rendered divine honours, not to God, but to that
" which is not God. This was, certainly, to change the
" truth into a lie."* The same writer expresses himself elsewhere in a manner equally excellent ; and, although the passage is somewhat long, it illustrates the
subject so well, that I shall not hesitate to quote it. It
is as follows :† " Though we know something of God
" by nature, yet we do not know the true God but by
" divine revelation. - - - Nor let it be objected, that it
" is wrong to affirm that the Gentiles knew not the
" true God, since the Apostle himself says of them that
" *they knew God.*ᵛ For, as *Oedipus,* when, as the
" Poets tell us, he knew that he had a father, was yet
" ignorant that *Laius* was his father ; so the Gentiles,
" whilst they were enabled by the light of nature to
" know that there is one God, and that he is the Foun-
" tain of all good, knew not, however, who is that
" God. Hence, as the Apostle testifies, it was necessary
" that this UNKNOWN GOD should be declared unto
" them."ʷ The knowledge of God, then, is of two

---

* *De Idololatria,* lib. i. cap. 4.

† *Hist. Pel.* lib. iii. part iii. thes. 6.

ᵛ Rom. i. 21.　　　　ʷ Acts xvii. 23.

" kinds; the one, simple, by which it is understood, in
" general, that there is a God, and that he is a wise,
" good, and powerful Being, the rewarder of righteous-
" ness, and the avenger of wickedness; the other, de-
" terminate, and applied to a certain object, namely,
" the God of Israel. The Gentiles, we admit, possess-
" ed the former, but they were destitute of the latter;
" for they imprisoned in falsehood and unrighteousness,
" those bright conceptions which they had of God, and
" ascribed them, not to the true, but to a false Deity.
" Hence, in many passages of Scripture, they are said
" not to have known God."

xxxi. Christian faith, on the contrary, being instructed by the doctrine of Christ,[x] is acquainted with
the name of God; and makes mention of that name,
saying, " Thou, whose name alone is JEHOVAH, art
the Most High over all the earth."[y] Faith recognises
Divinity in God himself, and doth not ascribe his pre-
rogatives to one who is not God. It doth not say,
" JEHOVAH hath not done all this ;"[z] which would be
to alienate from God the glory of his godhead, and of
his works. Faith knows *distinctly*, that he alone is
God, who manifested himself to our first parents in
paradise, and afterwards, " at sundry times and in divers manners," to patriarchs and prophets; and at last
condescended to make a visible appearance in the person of the Son, clothed with human flesh. As he proclaims himself in his word, saying, " I, even I, am JE-
HOVAH, and besides me there is no Saviour ;"[a] so faith
assents to this declaration, and replies, " Thou, even
" thou, art JEHOVAH alone ; thou hast made heaven,

---

[x] John xvii. 6.   [y] Ps. lxxxiii. 18.

[z] Deut. xxxii. 27.   [a] Isaiah xliii. 11.

" the heaven of heavens with all their host," &c.[b]   It belongs to the sincere Christian to say in truth, what was vauntingly said by *Tryphon* in *Lucian*, or the author, whoever he be, of the Dialogue entitled *Philopatris:* " Having discovered the Unknown God of Athens, we " will adore him, and, with hands stretched forth to- " wards heaven, render thanks to his name."

[b] Nehem. ix. 6.

DISSERTATION V.

ON FAITH *IN GOD.* *

————

1. In the preceding Dissertation, we have shown what the Christian believes with respect to the existence of God. It must, by no means, however, be supposed, that this weighty expression, I BELIEVE IN GOD, includes nothing further. These words imply, without doubt, the whole exercise of the pious soul, who relies on God as her salvation; of which a more particular account must now be submitted to the consideration of our pupils. Faith in God, considered in its full extent, comprises, 1st, The knowledge and acknowledgment of those perfections of God, from which a sinner may derive salvation and happiness: 2dly, The desire of union and fellowship with Him who is at once blessed for ever, and the fountain of blessedness: 3dly, A cheerful acceptance of God as exhibiting himself for our salvation: 4thly, The soul's diligent self-investigation, to see whether it possesses the evidences of God's dwelling in it: 5thly, Unutterable joy arising from the consciousness of such evidences. 6thly, A holy solici-

* The title of this Dissertation, more literally translated, is— " An explanation of what it is TO BELIEVE IN GOD." T.

tude of mind to walk worthy of God. We shall consider each of these in order.

II. Every one who employs himself assiduously in the contemplation of the Deity, will be able to discover, even by the light of nature, that God is the best, and the happiest of beings, and possessed of unbounded fulness and sufficiency; and that from this it follows, of necessity, that the chief good consists in his image and fellowship. *Boethius* has ingeniously demonstrated this truth, by philosophical arguments.* " It appears," says he, " from the universal conceptions of the " minds of men, that God, who is the *First* and the " *Greatest*† of all, is good; for, as nothing better than " God can be imagined, who can doubt, that he, who " is surpassed by none, is good? Reason, indeed, shows " that God is not only good, but possessed of perfect " goodness; for, unless he be so, he cannot be the " greatest of all beings; but there will be something " better than he, which, possessing perfect goodness, " will appear to be superior and more excellent. What- " ever is perfect, is unquestionably superior to that " which falls short of perfection. Not to protract this " reasoning beyond bounds,—it must be acknowledged " that the Most High God possesses, in the amplest mea- " sure possible, the highest and most perfect goodness. " Now we hold, that perfect goodness is true happiness; " it necessarily follows, therefore, that true happiness re- " sides in the Most High God." From these principles, he deduces the following conclusion: "Since men become

---

* *De Consolatione Philosophiæ,* lib. iii. pros. 10.

† When *Boethius* employs the terms *princeps, prior,* and *antiquius* in this quotation, he has perhaps some reference to priority of existence; but he obviously refers, at least chiefly, to superiority in excellence and dignity. **T.**

" happy by attaining happiness, and since Divinity itself
" is happiness, it is manifest that they become happy by
" attaining Divinity. But as by the acquisition of jus-
" tice men become just, and by the acquisition of wis-
" dom they become wise, so, by parity of reason, it un-
" questionably follows, that by the attainment of Divini-
" ty they become Gods. Every happy person, therefore,
" is a God. By nature, indeed, there is only one God;
" but, by participation, there is nothing to prevent the
" existence of a great number of Gods." Thus far
Boethius; with whose last words, you may compare the
expression of the Apostle Peter,—" that ye might be
PARTAKERS OF THE DIVINE NATURE."[a]

III. But, however evident and certain this inference
may be, and how impossible soever it is to deduce any
conclusion, more just in itself, more strongly supported
by arguments, or more worthy of God, very few of those
who had nature alone for their guide seriously thought
of this truth. It may reasonably be doubted if these
ideas would ever have occurred to *Boethius* himself,
unless his philosophy had borrowed lights from a more
spiritual teacher. *Plato* having defined the sum of
happiness to be " the nearest possible resemblance to
God,"* *Clement* of *Alexandria,* when quoting this expression, not unjustly questions, whether it is to be attributed to the sublimity of *Plato's* genius that he discovered a truth so congenial with the sacred doctrines
of Christianity, or whether he did not rather derive it
from some of those inspired writings which were then
extant.† But, while this manifest truth was very imperfectly perceived by the minds of the heathen philo-

* Ὁμοίωσιν θεῷ κατα το δυνατον.
† *Strom.* lib. ii. p. 403.
[a] 2 Pet. i. 4.

sophers, they were equally ignorant with the most illiterate of the way by which communion with God may be obtained. The thoughts of the natural man are, in consequence, easily diverted from meditation on this truth; the will is not duly inclined to desire the Chief good; and the mind, weighed down by the power of the passions, at last becomes vain, and loses itself in the sublimity and subtlety of its own speculations; and, forgetting God,[b] meanly grovels among corporeal, earthly, and transitory enjoyments.

IV. But Christian faith irradiates the mind with a more abundant light, and enables us to know, distinctly, the following truths relative to God. 1st, That he is "the blessed and the only Potentate,"[c] who finds in the possession, knowledge, and enjoyment of his own unbounded perfections, blessedness the most perfect, and most worthy of himself. 2dly, That he is infinitely able not merely to secure his own happiness, but also to communicate happiness to such of his rational creatures as he may deign to admit to fellowship with himself: for he is "the almighty (all-sufficient) God,"[d] and "all in all;"[e] and "in his presence is fulness of joy,"[f]—joy which so completely fills and satisfies the soul, that it neither knows, nor wishes to know, any thing desirable besides him.[g] 3dly, That the riches of the all-sufficiency of God are so great, that, what appears almost incredible, he can, and even will be, the God and the salvation of guilty and ruined men, in a manner fully consistent with his majesty, holiness, righteousness, veracity, and other perfections; so that the sinner is permitted to say and to sing, "Lo, this is

[b] Ps. ix. 17.

[d] אל שדי　Gen. xvii. 1.

[f] Ps. xvii. 11.

[c] 1 Tim. vi. 15.

[e] 1 Cor. xv. 28.

[g] Ps. lxxiii. 25.

" our God; we have waited for him, and he will save
" us : this is the LORD; we have waited for him, we
" will be glad and rejoice in his salvation."[h]   4thly,
That a salvation already purchased by the Son, and to
be applied by the Spirit, is freely offered in the Gospel
to all who desire it, and that God kindly and graciously
invites men of every description to partake of it; crying with a loud voice, " Who hath declared this from
" ancient time ? who hath told it from that time ? have
" not I the LORD ? and there is no God else besides
" me; a just God and a Saviour; there is none besides
" me.   Look unto me, and be ye saved, all the ends of
" the earth : for I am God, and there is none else."[i]
5thly, That a salvation so great is on no account to be
neglected; but that, preferring it to every thing else,
we must strive to become partakers of it; embracing
with great alacrity and cordial delight, that God who
graciously exhibits himself to us, and yielding ourselves
to him in return, with ardent affection.[j]

v. All these truths are contained in the following
words of the Apostle, Heb. xi. 6. - - - " He that com-
" eth unto God must believe that he is, and that he is
" the rewarder of them that diligently seek him."   In
these expressions something nobler is exhibited, than
any instructions which nature can impart to a sinner;
for, 1st, TO BELIEVE THAT GOD IS, is to give credit
to the testimony, in which God has revealed his name
and attributes, and the riches of his all-sufficiency.
Faith is knowledge founded on the divine testimony ;
and since God, as revealed by himself in his word, is

[h] Is. xxv. 9.   [i] Is. xlv. 21, 22.
[j] Heb. ii. 1, 2, 3.

such and so great a God that he can be the salvation
of a sinner, that man does not truly believe that God
is, who does not believe the Gospel, when it ascribes to
Jehovah this illustrious character, that he can justify
the ungodly: for this is included in the representation
which God has made of himself in his word. 2dly, It
is possible, however, that God might be God, even
though he were *unwilling* to become that, which, from
his all-sufficiency, he *can* become, to wit, the God and
the salvation of a sinner. Christian faith, therefore,
proceeds further, and, agreeably to that divine declaration, " I said not unto the seed of Jacob, Seek ye me
" in vain,"[k] believes that God is, in fact, THE RE-
WARDER of those who diligently seek him. 3dly,
Faith teaches, that this good ought to be earnestly
SOUGHT, and that it is incumbent on us to COME to
him; which supposes that, on the part of God, there is
a testimony which points out the way in which he is
pleased to be sought, and to be approached unto by sinners. It must, by all means, be maintained, that a sinner cannot seek God, unless he seek, also, the righteousness of God, which, of necessity, must be declared
in the salvation of a sinner;[l] and that it doth not become a sinner to draw near to God without a priest,[m]
as without a priest he cannot approach with confidence.
We read accordingly in Jeremiah, " Who is this that
" engaged his heart to approach unto me? saith the
" LORD;"[n]—for these words have a relation to the doctrine concerning Christ, and that satisfaction which he
made to divine justice.

From these remarks it appears, that this passage of

[k] Is. xlv. 19.   [l] Rom. iii. 26.
[m] Rom. iii. 26.   [n] Ch. xxx. 21.

the Apostle's writings, is interpreted too loosely, by those who would have it to include nothing more, than that knowledge of God, which is taught by natural theology. Not to mention that this knowledge, of whatever sort it is, cannot with propriety be denominated faith; this *natural* faith, if we may be allowed to call it so, was never sufficient for salvation, and never enabled any man to please God.

VI. The distinct knowledge of those truths concerning God, which are embraced by Christian faith, excites in the mind a vehement DESIRE of God and of communion with him. It is not merely carried towards him for a short time by a kind of sudden impulse of affection, but enjoys no rest or tranquillity, till it become actually a partaker of that chief good, for which it fervently longs. The conscience, enlightened by faith, or, as the Psalmist speaks, the *heart* of the believer, discerning that perfection of beauty, and that assemblage of all possible excellencies, which are to be seen in the face of God, says in God's stead, "Seek ye my face." To this invitation, faith causes it immediately to answer, "Thy face, LORD, will I seek;[o] O "God, thou art my God, early will I seek thee; my "soul thirsteth for thee, my flesh longeth for thee, in "a dry and thirsty land, where no water is."[p] Hence that holy wish which is opposed to the confused wishes of the men of the world: "There be many that say, "Who will show us any good?" But I say, "LORD, "lift thou up the light of thy countenance upon us."[q] Hence the complaints of the soul which can find no rest, so long as she remains uncertain of her having fel-

[o] Ps. xxvii. 8. [p] Ps. lxiii. 1.
[q] Ps. iv. 6.

lowship with God, and which incessantly exclaims, *What doth it avail me that there is a* GOD, *unless he be* MY GOD? Hence the firm and resolute purpose of not ceasing to seek after God, until she find him as her God, and her exceeding joy.[r]

VII. When, amidst this solicitude of the mind inquiring after God, the Deity graciously exhibits himself, saying, " Behold me, behold me;" faith, without delay, EMBRACES him with open arms. She " takes hold of his strength," (takes possession of the tower of his strength;)[s] and, as the mariner, in a tempestuous sea, while in imminent danger of being swallowed up by the deep, no sooner finds some fragment of the shipwrecked vessel than he casts himself upon it with the whole weight of his body; so the soul, concerned for her own salvation, relies upon that God who offers himself in the Gospel, and falls, so to speak, with her whole force, into his arms and his bosom. God lifts up his voice in the Gospel, saying, *Who is the man that is desirous of me, and of salvation in me? It is I,* replies the believer. *As the hart panteth after the water-brooks, so panteth my soul after thee, O God.*[t] *Behold me, then,* replies God by the Spirit, *able and willing to satisfy thy thirst. I accept of thee,* rejoins the believer immediately; *condescend thou then to be mine, let me be thine, and henceforth let none ever separate betwixt thee and me.* This is to believe in God, so as cordially to receive him.

VIII. But the more excellent the good in question, and the more vehement the desire that is cherished for it, the believing soul becomes, in the same proportion,

[r] Song iii. 1, 2, 3.   Is. viii. 17.   [s] Is. xxvii. 5.
[t] Ps. xlii. 1.

the more solicitous that it do not falsely and rashly claim it as its own. True faith in God, while it generates and promotes a well-founded confidence, detests and expels all temerity and arrogance. It does not teach a man to say boldly to God, on slight grounds, *Thou art mine.* It is by degrees, that it reaches this height; and it is after having accomplished a thorough search, that, at last, it forms this conclusion, which is the foundation of all comfort.[27] The marks, by which the believer is persuaded that the God in whom he believes, has become his own, are, principally, the following.

IX. 1st, This sincere desire of God, and of the most intimate union with him, is never found, but where God has begun to communicate himself, in a saving manner, to the soul. Unless he first draw near to the soul to enlighten it with the glorious beams of his reconciled countenance, and to draw it to himself with the cords of his preventing love, it can neither know, nor desire, nor seek him. The desire of the soul panting after communion with God is not felt, where communion with God is not already, in some degree, enjoyed. Hence David joins these together, saying, " O God, thou art MY GOD, early will I seek thee."[u] The man who so earnestly seeks God that he regards all other things, in comparison of him, as nothing better than dung, gives evidence that he is already apprehended of God.[v] He does not run, till he is drawn.[w] He does not love, till he is loved.[x]

X. 2dly, When God communicates himself to the soul, he not only makes it happy, but also holy. He communicates himself in a manner suitable to his real character :

[u] Ps. lxiii. 1. [v] Philip. iii. 8, 12.
[w] Song i. 4. [x] 1 John iv. 10, 19.
[27] See NOTE XXVII.

But he is the Holy One,[y] and he is the LORD that sanc-
tifieth Israel.[z] He puts his law in the minds of his people, and writes it on the hearts of those whose God he is; [a]
and he gives them one heart and one way, that they may
fear him for ever.[b] Whilst he is pleased to become the
Portion of his people,[c] he still remains their Lord.
The more intimate the fellowship with himself to which
he condescends to admit them, the stronger, in proportion, are the obligations under which they are laid, re-
verently to adore his majesty, carefully to imitate his
holiness, humbly to proclaim his goodness, and assiduously to cultivate his friendship.   Nay, as, in the beginning, the Spirit of God, by moving on the face of
the waters, rendered them wonderfully productive of
life; so, when God takes up his residence in the soul,
he makes it a partaker of his own life.   The old and
natural life of the soul is now gradually absorbed by the
more excellent life of God; and it is not so much the
man himself that lives, as God that lives in him.[d]
This communication of vital holiness, is so inseparably
connected with fellowship with God, that no man can
truly glory, or sincerely exult in the latter, unless he
is, at the same time, adorned with the former; and
when the holiness of believers declines, the full assurance of their communion with God never fails at the
same time to be impaired.[e]

   XI. 3dly, They who have JEHOVAH for their God,
cannot bear his absence with indifference.   When he
hides his face from them,[28] and withholds those gracious

---

[y] Is. vi. 3.   [z] Ezek. xx. 12.
[a] Jerem. xxxi. 33.   [b] Jerem. xxxii. 38, 39.
[c] Jerem. x. 16.   [d] Gal. ii. 20.
[e] Ps. li. 12, 14.
                [28] See NOTE XXVIII.

influences, which produce a happy serenity of mind, and
an alacrity and vigour in the various exercises of the
spiritual life, they are so troubled that their soul in a
manner fails, [f] they are sick of love,[g] and can receive no
consolation until he return.[h] This sorrow arises, if not
from the sense and experience of former enjoyment, at
least from a great esteem for familiar intercourse with
God. None but one that has enjoyed this privilege,
can form a just estimate of its value. Even those who
are strangers to God can feel a kind of sorrow for their
sins; but none excepting the children of the bride-
chamber lament the absence of the Bridegroom.[i]

XII. 4thly, Those whom God has blessed with a
special interest in himself, are often employed in devout and affectionate meditation upon him. Where the
treasure is, there will the heart be also.[j] Accordingly
they who gloried in God as their own God, have una-
nimously protested, that they thought of nothing with
greater pleasure than of Him. The spouse rejoiced
that her Beloved was her's;[k] but she added, " A bun-
" dle of myrrh is my well-beloved unto me; he shall
" lie all night betwixt my breasts."[l] David struck his
harp and said, " The LORD is the Portion of my inhe-
" ritance and of my cup;"[m] but he added, " I have set
" the LORD always before me."[n] " My mind," says the
pious *Augustine,*[*] " is devoted to thee, inflamed with
" love to thee, breathing for thee, panting after thee,
" desiring to see thee, alone. It accounts nothing de-

---

[*] *Præfatio Manualis.*

[f] Song v. 6.   [g] Song ii. 5.
[h] Ps. lxxvii. 2.   [i] Mat. ix. 15.
[j] Mat. vi. 21.   [k] Song vi. 3.
[l] Song i. 13.   [m] Ps. xvi. 5.
[n] Ps. xvi. 8.

" lightful but to speak of thee, to hear of thee, to write
" of thee, to converse about thee, and often to revolve
" thy glory in my heart; that the sweet remembrance
" of thee, may afford me some respite and refreshment
" amidst these calamities.   Upon thee, therefore, do I
" call, O thou most beloved of all objects; to thee I
" cry aloud with my whole heart.   When I call upon
" thee, too, I call upon thee as a God dwelling in my-
" self; for unless thou wert in me, I could not exist at
" all.   Surely, thou art in me, for thou abidest in my
" memory; by this I recognise thee, and in this I find
" thee, since I have thee in remembrance, and in thee,
" and from thee, enjoy my supreme delight."

From these and similar evidences, it is possible for
the believer to attain assurance, that God has become
his own God.

XIII. When the soul knows this for certain, especially if she hear it from the mouth of God himself ad-
dressing her inwardly by the Spirit, and actually taste
something of the Divine sweetness, she is filled with a
great, an incredible JOY.   Hence Peter says, " In
" whom, though now ye see him not, yet believing, ye
" rejoice with joy unspeakable, and full of glory."[o]
Hence that sweet song of a soul rejoicing in God as
her own :   " The LORD is the Portion of mine inhe-
" ritance and of my cup; thou maintainest my lot.
" The lines are fallen to me in pleasant places; yea, I
" have a goodly heritage.   Therefore my heart is
" glad, and my glory rejoiceth."[p]   In another Psalm
also, the two following expressions are conjoined, as if
by the same stroke of the harp :—" God, my exceeding
joy," and,—" O God, my God."[q]

[o] 1 Pet. i. 8.   [p] Ps. xvi. 5, 6, 9.
[q] Ps. xliii. 4.

XIV. This joy, indeed, is not to be wondered at; for when any one knows that God is his own, he finds in Him the most powerful *protection against all evil.* " In the LORD JEHOVAH, is everlasting strength," (the Rock of ages.)[r] " I will say of the LORD, he is " my refuge, and my fortress, MY GOD; in him will I " trust."[s] He finds in him, also, an inexhaustible *fountain of all desirable good;* not only what equals, but also what infinitely transcends his conceptions and desires. " How excellent is thy loving-kindness, O " God! therefore the children of men put their trust " under the shadow of thy wings. They shall be abun- " dantly satisfied with the fatness of thy house, and " thou shalt make them drink of the river of thy plea- " sures. For with thee is the fountain of life; in thy " light shall we see light."[t] Both of these ideas are briefly, but strikingly, united, in the words of God to Abraham, " I am thy SHIELD, and thy exceeding great REWARD ;"[u] and in the following expression of the Psalmist, " For the LORD God is a SUN and a SHIELD."[v]

XV. The representation and enjoyment of so great a good, cannot fail to be delightful in the highest degree. If separate goods are pleasant, how delightful is that good, which contains the sweetness and quintessence of every good; and not merely such sweetness as we have experienced in created objects, but as widely different from these, as the Creator differs from the creature! All the beauty, all the glory, and all the joy of the material world, are nothing but resplendent beams, emitted

[r] Is. xxvi. 4.
[s] Ps. xci. 2.
[t] Ps. xxxvi. 7, 8, 9.
[u] Gen. xv. 1.
[v] Ps. lxxxiv. 11.

and diffused around, by the King of beauty, of glory, and of joy. Whatever things were made, were made by him ; and, therefore, whatever goodness is found in the creatures, could be derived from him alone, by whom all were made. The borrowed goodness, consequently, of which they are possessed, is darkened and eclipsed, when compared with that uncreated goodness which is its spring and original. God is, doubtless, a Being, in whose light alone, all that is luminous—in whose glory alone, all that is glorious—in whose beauty alone, all that is beautiful—in whose joy alone, all that is joyful, is contained. When he bestowed upon the creatures light, glory, beauty, and joy, he reserved to himself, the source of light, glory, beauty, and joy ; and thus he always retained within himself as the fountain, more than he communicated from himself to the creatures. Ought not, then, the possession of so boundless a good, to produce an almost boundless joy ?

XVI. Further, the sweetness arising from the·gracious communication which God makes of himself, is so great, that it has virtue to sweeten all that is bitter in the bitterest calamities. The smallest drop of this sweetness, distilled into the mouth which pants after it, quickly dispels the greatest sorrows. This rendered torrents of stones pleasant to Stephen, the cross to Andrew, the violent tearing of the skin to Bartholomew, the gridiron to St Laurentius, rods, racks,* wheels, and flames, not to mention prisons and exile, to so many myriads of holy martyrs of Christ ; who, having tasted this sweetness of God, rejoiced and sang when they were led forth to the most dreadful tor-

---

* The Latin term is *equuleos,* which literally signifies instruments of torture resembling a horse.   T.

tures, as if they were conducted to the most splendid entertainments. These things, indeed, seem incredible to the world. But such is the nature of this sweetness of our God, that none can understand it in any other way than by tasting it. Those only who eat of this manna, can conceive how delicious it is.

XVII. In whatever measure, too, this blessedness is imparted to man in the present life, it is nothing more than the first fruits and earnest of greater, and everlasting enjoyment. Hence arises the constancy and permanence of this joy, if not with regard to its effects, and what are called its secondary acts, at least with regard to its foundation and its primary act. " Ever-" lasting joy shall be upon their head ;"ᵂ " Your heart " shall rejoice, and your joy no man taketh from you."ˣ Though, agreeably to the dictates of his infinite wisdom, God is pleased, in this life, to temper the communication of his sweetness with a mixture of bitterness, often very large, but always salutary; there is a principle abiding in believers, which soon gives rise to renewed emotions of joy, and ultimately proves a most abundant source of never-ending delight.

XVIII. Nor has any one cause to be afraid lest he should err by indulging this joy to excess; for God himself invites us not only to cheerfulness, but even to a certain holy and mystic ebriety.ʸ The more liberally a person has drunk of this spiritual nectar, though he may seem to others that are ignorant of these delights to be beside himself, he is, in reality, at once the happier and the wiser. There are spirits in material wine, which serve to exhilarate the animal spirits of the hu-

ᵂ Is. xxxv. 10.   ˣ John xvi. 22.
ʸ Song v. 1.

man body; but when it is too copiously drunk, it disorders the brain, and makes wise men mad. This spiritual wine, however, which is wholly spirit, and spirit in the very height and exuberance of spirituality, and which is newly extracted and imbibed from the first and greatest Spirit,—with what mighty force, and with how surprising an ecstasy does it seize and ravish the soul! Yet it produces no agitation but what is salutary, consistent with discretion, and conducive to holiness; it enables the man, no longer his own master, but full of his God, and on the confines of heaven, both to think and to speak with a dignity and energy more than human. Oftener than once, I recollect, I have observed this, with astonishment, in persons whose minds were, in other respects, endowed with very ordinary faculties. Such is the spiritual and mystical joy of Christian faith, when exulting in God as her own.[29]

XIX. This same faith in God is also the spring of true HOLINESS. It cannot be denied, that even that persuasion of a Deity which the Gentiles derived from nature, was calculated to produce a certain attention to repentance and virtue. *Epictetus,* in his meditations upon this subject, almost rises above heathenism, when he expresses himself in the following terms :* " It is " requisite, first, to learn that GOD IS,—that his provi- " dence extends to all, and that it is impossible to con- " ceal from his penetrating eye, not merely external " actions, but even the thoughts and emotions of the " mind. What sort of nature and character, then, " have the Gods? Whatever perfections they are " found to possess, it is necessary for the man who is

* *Apud Arrian.* lib. ii. cap. 14.
[29] See NOTE XXIX.

" desirous to please and obey them, to exert his endea-
" vours to resemble them as closely as possible. If the
" Deity is faithful, he, too, must be faithful ; if free,
" he, also, must be free ; if beneficent, he must be be-
" neficent; if magnanimous, he must be magnanimous.
" In short, it is incumbent upon him, in all other re-
" spects, to think and to speak as an imitator of God."
Thus the persuasion of a Deity is the mother of probity.

xx. These expressions, indeed, are equally beautiful
and just. But the truth which they inculcate was
known to very few ; and, in those who knew it, was so
enchained by the fetters of corrupt propensities, that it
was far from elevating the character, or governing the
conduct. Hence the Apostle overthrows their pretensions by the following sentence, as by a thunderbolt :
" When they knew God, they glorified him not as
" God, neither were thankful, but became vain in their
" imaginations, and their foolish heart was darkened." [z]
God caused some of his rays to shine upon them, and,
accordingly, they are said to have known God : but
they did not admit those rays to the secret recesses of
the heart; which is, therefore, said to be darkened.
" In the wisdom of God, the world by wisdom knew
" not God." The fabric of nature displayed the power,
the wisdom, and the goodness of the Most High, and
thus called on mankind to serve him with fidelity, both
on account of his supreme majesty, and his numberless
benefits ; and also because a blessed and glorious reward is reserved for his worshippers in a future state of
existence. But the world chose rather to amuse themselves with idle speculations and frigid discourses respecting the works of God, while, in the mean time,
they rendered no homage to their great Author. Even

[z] Rom. i. 21.

those who were possessed of more sagacity and penetration than others, did not betake themselves to the true God, to whom they ought to have resorted, but had recourse to the creature, in common with the populace—against whom, however, these distinguished masters of wisdom, whenever a convenient opportunity occurred, loudly exclaimed, as in this respect acting the part of madmen.

xxi. A Christian faith in God, on the contrary, does not suffer a man to continue destitute of true piety and holiness. The truth of this assertion may be illustrated in various ways. 1st, While faith elevates the mind to the contemplation of the ever adorable Deity, and holds it fixed in delightful meditation upon him, the mind is insensibly transformed into the image of the divine holiness.[a] After Moses had remained forty days on the holy mount, enjoying familiar intercourse with God, the skin of his face shone with so bright an effulgence, that the eyes of the Israelites were unable to endure the sight of him.[b] The same, in a spiritual sense, is the attainment of those who frequently and attentively contemplate God in the light of faith. The beams of celestial influence, flowing in abundance from the Father of lights, and received by faith, penetrate and pervade the innermost parts of the soul, and adorn them with a new lustre of celestial purity. The more frequently the believer beholds him in the spirit, his knowledge of his perfections, of which holiness is the ornament, becomes the more clear. The more clearly he knows the divine perfections, the more ardently does he love them. The more ardently he loves them, the more solicitous doth he become increasingly to resemble them; for love naturally leads to a resemblance to the

[a] 2 Cor. iii. 18.　　　[b] Exod. xxxiv. 29, 30.

object beloved. The more ardently he loves God, too, he contemplates him the more frequently, and with the greater attention and pleasure : and, whilst he is engaged in performing this endless circuit of contemplation and affection, he obtains, at every repetition of the exercise, some fresh lineament of God's glorious image.

XXII. 2dly, When faith considers the unspotted purity of God, she readily concludes that she must exert her endeavours also to attain eminent holiness, if she wishes to possess, to cultivate, and to retain such communion with God as will prove effectually conducive to her joy. She assents to the voice of reason suggesting this truth. She gives credit to the sacred volume teaching it still more expressly ; " The secret of the LORD is with them " that fear him :"c—and to the Lord himself crying aloud in her ears, " Be ye separate, and touch not the " unclean thing, and I will receive you."d She learns, also, by experience, that she no sooner relaxes her ardour in the pursuit of piety, than the joy of fellowship with God is immediately impaired. But since faith prizes this joy above every thing else, it cannot fail powerfully to stimulate her to a certain distinguished sanctity of life; as she is well assured that, without this, she can neither attain nor preserve that communion with God, which she so earnestly desires.

XXIII. 3dly, That stupendous love of God, by which he gives himself to the soul for its salvation, when it is apprehended by faith, and represented to the believer in its true light,—kindles surprising flames of reciprocal love. No one, I may venture to affirm, truly believes that God has become his own God, who, whilst he believes, is not swallowed up with amazement at that

<hr>

c Ps. xxv. 14.   d 2 Cor. vi. 17.

abyss of divine love, and doth not sincerely wish that
he had a far more capacious soul, that it might be entirely replenished with the love of God,—who so greatly
loves, and is so greatly loved.　In believers themselves,
I am aware, that fervent and unbounded love, with
which they are required to love their God, sometimes
languishes.　But on such occasions, their faith towards
God as their own God, is either scarcely present, or
not lively, or not called forth into exercise.　When
this faith is at once present and vigorously exercised, it
dictates to the man a song of love not unlike the following, in which *Augustine* adored his God:*　" I
" love thee, O my God, and I desire always to love thee
" more; for thou art truly sweeter than all honey, more
" nourishing than all milk, and brighter than all light.
" Thou art dearer to me than all gold, and silver, and
" precious stones.　O my Love, whose heart is ever
" warm, and never waxes cold, be pleased to inflame
" me.　O let me be entirely inflamed by thee, that I
" may entirely love thee; for if one love any other ob-
" ject together with thee, which he does not love for
" thy sake, he loves thee the less.　May I love thee,
" O Lord, since thou hast first loved me!"

xxiv. 4thly, Whoever truly believes that he is now become a partaker of God, as he cannot be his own, so cannot
wish to be his own; but, did he possess any thing more
valuable than himself, he would give it up to his God.
Far from desiring to reserve any thing to himself instead of employing it in the service of God, he is truly
grieved because he himself is not better, and more worthy of being surrendered to the Lord.　On this topic,
nothing can be conceived more elegant and forcible,

---

* *Soliloq.* cap. xix.

than the following expressions of *Bernard*, in his treatise *on loving God*,* which I cannot help quoting.
" If," says he, " I owe my whole self for my creation,
" what can I add for my renovation by means so asto-
" nishing? I have not been renewed so easily as I
" was made. God made me, by merely speaking a sin-
" gle word; in renewing me, he has not only spoken
" much, but endured many grievous and ignominious
" sufferings. In the first work he gave ME to myself;
" in the second he GAVE HIMSELF; and when he thus
" GAVE HIMSELF, he RESTORED ME to myself. Hav-
" ing, then, been both GIVEN and RESTORED, I owe
" MYSELF,—I doubly owe MYSELF for MYSELF. What
" shall I render to God for HIMSELF? for though I
" were able to render MYSELF a thousand times, what
" am I in the presence of GOD!" Christian faith in
God teaches a man thus to reason, and thus to stir up
his soul.

xxv. We remark, in conclusion, that what has been
said must not be understood to intimate, that no person
in whom all the attainments of which we have now
spoken, and these in the degree which we have deli-
neatèd, are not found, can say in sincerity, I BELIEVE
IN GOD. We have described " believing in God,"
not as it subsists in Christians that are weak and " of
little faith," but as it may be conceived, and as it is
sometimes seen in those to whom the Lord has imparted a richer measure of his Spirit. It is proper in this
manner to propose faith in God to ourselves, not that
we may fall into despair, or be unduly discouraged,
when we cannot discern some parts of the description

* *De Diligendo Deo.*

in ourselves; but that captivated with its beauty and excellence, we may cultivate, with all possible zeal and activity, the small beginnings which we have, till we gradually reach that full assurance of faith, which produces so many excellent fruits.   Lord, we believe; help thou our unbelief.   AMEN.

DISSERTATION VI.

ON FAITH IN A *THREE-ONE GOD.*

I. THE Creed is usually divided into three parts; of which the *first* relates to GOD THE FATHER, and the work of CREATION; the *second* to GOD THE SON, and the work of REDEMPTION; the *third* to GOD THE HOLY GHOST, and the work of SANCTIFICATION. The most ancient formulary having consisted of a simple profession of the Trinity, our present Creed, which took its rise from that formulary, and in course of time was completed by the addition of various articles, is still so framed that these may all be referred to the Three Persons in the Godhead. This great doctrine remained as the Foundation of foundations, upon which the other articles were built.

II. When, however, his own distinct actions are ascribed to each of the Persons respectively, this must not be understood to intimate that either the power or the operation of the Persons is divided, or that any one of them accomplishes his work more *immediately* than another. As God is one, so the power and operation of all the Persons are one and undivided; and each person is the immediate and perfect cause of the whole work. The Son and the Holy Ghost created the world by the same power, and by the same act, with the Father. The manner of those works which respect our redemption, is, nevertheless, somewhat different. As a participation of the human nature was requisite to the performance of these, and as the Son alone assumed this nature into personal union with himself, these works, being the works of the God-man, are peculiar to the Son. Yet it is admitted that in so far as the Godhead was concerned, they are the works of the whole Trinity ; and, accordingly, they are, in this view, attributed to the Father and the Holy Spirit equally with the Son.—To the Father: " Believest thou not that I am " in the Father, and the Father in me? The words " that I speak unto you, I speak not of myself, but the " Father that dwelleth in me, he doth the works." [a]— To the Holy Spirit: " I cast out devils by the Spirit " of God."[b] The incarnation itself, and similar acts, though peculiar to the Son in respect that they terminate upon him only, are nevertheless, in regard to the agency by which they are effected, the works of the whole Trinity.[c]

III. But this distinction of the Divine works, has a respect, 1st, To the order of the Persons, which ought to be observed in their operation, as well as their subsistence. Thus, because the Father is the First person of the Godhead, and creation is the first external work of the Deity, as it is the beginning of all those things that are *without God,** it is justly ascribed, by special economy, to the Father, who, on this account, is called " Lord of heaven and earth."[d] Yet the agency of the

---

* *Extra Deum.*

[a] John xiv. 10. [b] Matth. xii. 28.
[c] Heb. x. 5. Luke i. 35. [d] Matth. xi. 25.

Son,[e] and the Holy Ghost,[f] is not excluded from this
work. 2dly, It is necessary, also, to attend to the ter-
minating of an act upon some certain Person. For
this reason, redemption is attributed to the Second
person, for whom alone the human nature was prepared,
in and by which the Godhead performed many acts relating to our salvation.[g] The Father, however, is said
to have " reconciled the world to himself,"[h] and to have
" made peace by the blood of the cross of Christ :"[i] and
we " are washed, sanctified, and justified, by the Spirit
" of our God."[j] Paul, in like manner, says of the living God, essentially considered, that he is " the Saviour
" of all men, especially of them that believe."[k] 3dly,
Some add that the distinction of the Divine works has
a respect to the proximate and immediate principle of
operation, and that, in this view, our sanctification
should be ascribed to the Holy Ghost.[l] We may be
permitted, however, to call in question the solidity of
this sentiment ; for one Divine person doth not act by
another, as an intermediate cause ; and, as the power of
all the persons is one and the same, each of them accomplishes an effect by the same immediate operation.
A holy God, essentially considered, is the sanctifier of
Israel.[m] The Father and the Son perform this work
not less immediately than the Spirit ; for the power
and the operation of all the three are the same. If, indeed, the order of operation amongst the persons be
considered, the Father acts by the Son and the Holy
Ghost. But, in this sense, all the works of God ought

[e] Heb. i. 10.   [f] Gen. i. 2.
[g] Matth. i. 21.   [h] 2 Cor. v. 19.
[i] Col. i. 20.   [j] 1 Cor. vi. 11.
[k] 1 Tim. iv. 10.   [l] 2 Thess. ii. 13.
[m] Ezek. xx. 12.

to be characterised as the immediate works of the Holy Ghost. This, however, is foreign to the purpose; for the Father acts no less immediately by the Son, than the Son himself acts; and the Father and the Son act no less immediately by the Holy Spirit, than the Holy Spirit himself acts. It is only where there is a diversity of essences and of operations, that the distinction betwixt a remote and a proximate, or betwixt a mediate and an immediate cause, can have any place.* Why, then, is sanctification so uniformly ascribed to the third person? No reason occurs to me, at present, more satisfactory than the following. The sanctification of a sinner is the consequence of the grace and the merits of Christ:[30] in the order of subsistence and operation amongst the three Divine persons, the Holy Spirit follows the Son, and hence he is called " the Spirit of the Son :"[n] it appears, therefore, that the application of the merits of the Son, cannot be more properly attributed to any of the persons, than to him who is next the Son, who is sent by him, and who applies those blessings only, which belong to the Son, and which he receives from him.[o]

IV. It is of importance to examine this mystery more distinctly. I shall not now explain the terms made use of by the Church on this subject, which *Gomar*, according to his usual manner,† has treated accurately, and *John Gerhard* more copiously.‡ Nor shall I scholastically define what is intended by essence, existence, *suppositum*, and person. Such definitions may be

---

* *Vid. Forbes. Instruct. Histor. Theol.* lib. i. cap. 10.
† *In Thesibus.*
‡ *In Locis Communibus,* loc. iii. cap. 2.
[n] Gal. iv. 6.   [o] John xvi. 14.
[30] See NOTE XXX.

learned from those systems which are in every one's hand. I shall only state, with great simplicity, and in a manner adapted to the weakest capacities, what we ought to know and believe respecting this tremendous mystery. The true God, who is the Creator of heaven and earth, and the salvation of his chosen people, is one only,* according to the most absolute unity.ᴾ But, in perfect consistency with this unity, there are three *Hypostases*, or Persons distinct from one another ; each of whom is the only true God, and who have the same common form,† nature,‡ or essence :§ for, " according " to the holy Fathers, essence, and nature, and form are " synonymous terms."‖ These three are the FATHER, the WORD or SON, and the HOLY GHOST ; who are not three Gods, nor merely three names, or attributes, or powers of God ; but three distinct Persons in one individual Godhead. It is sufficient for salvation to know what has just been stated, though one remain ignorant of the subtle refinements of the schools, which are often bold, and really presumptuous and unadvised.

v. This doctrine belongs to the number of those mysteries of our religion, which man, particularly in his corrupt state, cannot learn from nature alone, and of which *Justin Martyr* beautifully says : " They surpass " all the understanding, all the language, in short, all " the comprehension of a created nature. If, therefore, " amidst your inquiries into them, any doubt arise in " your mind, avail yourself of that which affords a ready " solution of your doubts respecting the subject of in-

---

* *Unus et unicus.*   † Μορφη.
‡ Φυσις.   § Ὀυσία.
‖ *Damascen. Isag.* cap. 1.
   ᴾ 1 Cor. viii. 6. 1 Tim. ii. 5.

" quiry, to wit, faith."* Christ himself says in reference
to this mystery, " No man knoweth the Son but the
" Father; neither knoweth any man the Father, save
" the Son, and he to whomsoever the Son will reveal
" him."q   It is, therefore, only by the revelation of the
Son, that the relation which exists between him and the
Father is known.   On this account, we cannot subscribe
to the opinion of such of our theologians as have endeavoured to prove, to confirm, and by tedious similitudes to illustrate this mystery, by arguments derived
from nature ; which, after others, *Bisterfeld* has acutely and copiously attempted, in the *Synopsis* prefixed to
his learned work against *Crellius*.   It is much safer to
keep within the bounds of Scripture alone, lest we involve ourselves in unnecessary difficulties.   The testimonies produced from *Orpheus, Zoroaster, Trismegis-
tus,* the *Sibyls,* and similar writers, are not genuine;
and the clearer they are, they are the more to be suspected.   It seems contrary to the sacred oracles, as *Casaubon* well argues,† to imagine, that mysteries so profound
were more clearly propounded to the Heathen, than to
that people whom God Almighty was pleased to favour
as peculiarly his own, and to instruct, by his own immediate voice, and by that of his faithful servants.   The
passages produced from *Plato* and his disciples, whilst
they tally with this doctrine in words, differ from it in
sense, and may be considered as borrowed either from
the sacred writings which were then extant, or from

---

* *Confut. Græcar.* Quæst. p. 304.

† *Exercit.* i. *ad Apparatum Annalium,* Num. xviii. p. 53.   See,
in particular, Amyrault's *Dissert. de Myster. Trinit.* p. 112, 117,
et seq.

q Mat. xi. 27.

tradition; the probability of which has been shown by *Clement* of *Alexandria.**

VI. The Scriptures of the Old Testament, as well as of the New, abound with clear and striking testimonies respecting this mystery. It appears from both, 1st, That there are more Divine Persons than one; 2dly, More particularly, that they are three in number; 3dly, Still more particularly, that they are the Father, the Son, and the Holy Ghost.

The *first* of these assertions is proved, 1. From those passages of Scripture where God either addresses himself, or speaks concerning himself, in the plural number; such as those quoted at the bottom of the page.[r] 2. From those passages in which the LORD speaks of the LORD, or is distinguished from the LORD.[s]

The *second* assertion is confirmed by the places of Scripture where three distinct persons are mentioned.[t]

The *third* is proved from Mat. xxviii. 19. Rom. i. 4. 2 Cor. xiii. 14. 1 John v. 7.

To explain and vindicate all these testimonies might seem somewhat tedious, and it is foreign to our present design.[31]

VII. We have undertaken to show what it is to *be-*

---

* *Strom.* lib. ii. p. 103. See John Gerhard's *Loc. Comm.* p. 329, and Lipsius's *Manuductio ad Philos. Stoic.* lib. ii. diss. 19. This subject has been discussed professedly and at the greatest length by *Christianus Schotanus,* in his *Triumphus Biblicus,* lib. iii. cap. 7.

[r] Gen. i. 26. iii. 22. xi. 7. Isaiah vi. 8.

[s] Gen. xix. 24. Ps. xlv. 6. comp. Heb. i. 8. Ps. cx. 1. comp. Mat. xxii. 43, 44. Dan. ix. 17. Hos. i. 7. Prov. xxx. 4.

[t] Ps. xxxiii. 6. Isaiah lxi. 1. comp. verse 8, from which it appears that JEHOVAH is the speaker in that passage. Isaiah lxiii. 9, 10. Hag. ii. 5, 6, 7. Mat. iii. 16.

[31] See NOTE XXXI.

lieve in a Three-one God. This implies, principally, three things. 1st, The knowledge of this mystery. 2dly, The acknowledgment of it, or an assent to it. 3dly, The calm and holy dependance of the soul upon God as a Three-one God.

VIII. With regard to the KNOWLEDGE of this mystery, we deem it so necessary, that we cannot venture to assure any adult of salvation, without this knowledge. A distinction should be made, we allow, betwixt the degrees of knowledge, as more or less clear and distinct; —times, also, must be distinguished, for it is fit that knowledge should correspond with the measure of revelation afforded ;—the different capacities of men should be distinguished, since some are far more capable of instruction than others;—knowledge existing in the mind, too, must be distinguished from the expression of it with the mouth ;—we ought to take into consideration, in fine, the diversity of the ministry under which individuals live. We do not presume to determine the degree or measure of the knowledge required. This only we state, that it does not appear to us, that the man who is entirely ignorant of this mystery is in the way of salvation. The following arguments tend to confirm this opinion.

IX. 1st, Since our Lord himself makes eternal life to consist in the knowledge of the Father, and of the Son whom he hath sent,[u] who will say that such knowledge is not necessary to eternal life ? This would be equally absurd as if one should affirm, that that in which salvation itself consists, is not necessary to salvation. No one, it must also be remarked, knows the Father, who is ignorant that from eternity he had an only-begotten Son; nor does any one know the Son, who does not

[u] John xvii. 3.

know He is the same God with the Father. " Jesus
" saith unto him, Have I been so long time with you,
" and yet hast thou not known me, Philip? He that
" hath seen me, hath seen the Father. - - - Believest
" thou not that I am in the Father, and the Father in
" me ?"ᵛ These words import a Trinity, at least a plurality, of persons in one godhead.

x. 2dly, It is admitted, that there is no hope of salvation without the knowledge of the true God. But
he only is the true God, who, while he is One in essence, subsists in Three persons. Whoever entertains
any other view of God than this, does not represent to
himself the true God, but a figment of his own imagination, and an idol. " Whoever," says *Augustine,*
" thinks that God is such a being as he is not, enter-
" tains a conception, in reality, of another and a false
" God."* On this account, the heathen, who knew in
general that there is some infinite Deity, but were ignorant of the Trinity, which is the foundation of the
covenant of God with elect sinners, are said to have
been " without God in the world."ʷ The true God,
whom Paul preached, was to them UNKNOWN.ˣ " The
Gentiles," it is said, " knew not God;"ʸ that is, they
did not know him as a Tri-une God. They knew, indeed, that there is some Supreme Being; and thus
far, the same Apostle affirms that " they knew God;" ᶻ
but they were ignorant of what God is; as if one
should know there is a certain King in the realm, but
be unacquainted with the person of the King.

xi. 3dly, When the Trinity is not known, the ne-

---

* *Quæst.* 29. *in Josuam.*

ᵛ John xiv. 9, 10.   ʷ 'Αθεοι 'εν κοσμω. Ephes. ii. 12.
ˣ Acts xvii. 23.   ʸ 1 Thes. iv. 5.
ᶻ Rom. i. 21.

cessary consequence is, that the principal foundations
of our faith and comfort, are unknown.   All the treasures of wisdom and knowledge, are hid in the mystery
of God,[32] and of the Father, and of Christ.[a]   I cannot
know how God can show mercy to a sinner in a manner worthy of himself, unless I know he has a Son
whom he could send to make satisfaction for sin, and a
Spirit who can apply to me the merits of the Son.   If
I know not that the Father is God, I shall be ignorant
that I am a Son of God,—which is the sum of our felicity.   If I know not that the Son is God, I shall not
form a right estimate of the love of the Father who has
given him to me, nor of the grace of the Son, who,
though possessing inconceivable majesty, humbled himself so wonderfully for my sake ;—nor shall I be able
to place a firm dependance upon his satisfaction, which
could not be sufficient unless it were of infinite value,
or to rely securely on his power, which cannot save me
unless it be evidently omnipotent ;—it will be impossible for me, in short, to regard him as my Saviour and
my Chief Good, because none excepting the true God
of Israel is Israel's GOD and Redeemer.[b]   If, in fine, I
am not sure that the Holy Spirit, to whose direction
and government I ought to commit myself, is God, I
shall not be able to esteem my subjection to him as true
liberty, to maintain a holy acquiescence in his protect-
ing care, or to rely on his testimony respecting my salvation as a most ample security.   Christian faith is of
so delicate a character, that it can firmly acquiesce in
none but the Most High God.   It must, then, be
of the first importance and necessity for us to know a
doctrine, on which the knowledge of so many necessary

[a] Col. ii. 3.   [b] Is. liv. 5.
[32] See NOTE XXXII.

points depends. This argument is confirmed by experience; for, as we see in the Socinians, the same men who deny the Trinity, deny, also, the satisfaction of Christ, the invincible power of the Spirit in our regeneration and conservation, the certainty of salvation, and the full assurance of faith. The mystery of our salvation through Christ is so intimately connected with the mystery of the Trinity, that when the latter is unknown or denied, the former cannot be known or acknowledged.

XII. 4thly, It is indisputably manifest, that he who does not honour God the Father cannot be saved; for his own words are as follows: " Them that honour me, " I will honour; and they that despise me shall be " lightly esteemed."[c] No one, however, rightly honours the Father, who does not, also, honour the Son. " The Father hath committed all judgment unto the " Son, that all men should honour the Son, even as " they honour the Father. He that honoureth not the " Son, honoureth not the Father who hath sent him."[d] Further, no man can honour the Son who does not know him, and who does not know him even in his true character as the Only-begotten, of the same substance with the Father, and, therefore, worthy of the same divine honour with the Father. For what is honour but a reverential acknowledgment of the excellency possessed by the person whom we honour? It follows, then, that without the knowledge of Christ as one God with the Father, there is no salvation.

XIII. 5thly, It is necessary to salvation, to know him of whom all that are about to be baptized according to Christ's appointment, ought to make a profession. No one can profess what he does not know. But ever since the commencement of the Christian dispensation, it has

[c] 1 Sam. ii. 30.   [d] John v. 22, 23.

been incumbent on believers to make a profession of
that Trinity, into whose name they are baptized. To
be baptized into the name of any one, is to surrender
ourselves to him, in order to yield him such homage as
is due to God. It, therefore, involves or supposes a
confession of his Divinity. It is not, indeed, expressly
mentioned in Scripture, that a confession to this effect
was demanded in these very terms. But neither is it
explicitly affirmed, that the Apostles baptized in the
name of the Father, the Son, and the Holy Ghost:
yet, without doubt, they observed the institution of our
Lord with the most scrupulous exactness. When the
Apostles, too, baptized in the name of Christ, which
Luke, in his account of their labours,[e] testifies that
they did; the whole Trinity, as *Ambrose* ingeniously
observes,[*] is intended by that name: for when Christ,
that is, the Anointed, is mentioned, the expression includes the Father, by whom he was anointed; Christ
himself, who received the anointing; and the Holy
Ghost, the oil with which he was anointed. In this
remark *Ambrose* has followed *Basil*, whose words are
these: " The naming of Christ is the confession of
" the whole; for this word denotes, at once, him who
" anoints, viz. God; the Anointed, viz. the Son; and
" the unction, viz. the Spirit."[†] Besides, when our
Lord says, " He that believeth and is baptized shall be
" saved; but he that believeth not shall be damned," [f]
what is more consonant to reason than that the object
of faith to which he referred was that very doctrine
which is delivered at baptism? Hence all the ancients,
with hardly any exception, made a solemn recognition

---

[*] Lib. i. *De Sp. S.* cap. 3.
[†] *De Spir. Sanct.* Vide *Vossium de Baptismo,* p. 51.
  [e] Acts ii. 38. viii. 16. xix. 5.   [f] Mark xvi. 16.

of the Trinity at the administration of baptism. " You
" were asked," says Ambrose,* " Do you believe in God
" the Father Almighty? You replied, I believe; and
" you were immersed, that is, you were buried. You
" were asked, in the second place, Do you believe in
" our Lord Jesus Christ? You said, I believe; and
" you were immersed, and thus buried together with
" Christ. - - - - You were asked, in the third place, Do
" you believe in the Holy Ghost? You answered, I
" believe; you were immersed[33] a third time, &c."
" We ought," says Basil, " to be baptized as we have
" learned, to believe as we have been baptized, and to
" honour the Father, the Son, and the Holy Ghost as
" we have believed." See several other testimonies of
the Fathers in *Forbes*;† to which I here add the expressions of *Nazianzen* in the speech which he delivered in the Council of Constantinople, the 6th General
Council, held in the year of our Lord 381. " We be-
" lieve in the Father, and the Son, and the Holy Ghost,
" of the same substance and the same glory; in whom,
" also, baptism has its perfection: for in baptism, AS
" THOU WHO ART INITIATED KNOWEST, there is both
" in word and deed, a renunciation of atheism and a
" confession of the Deity."‡ Thus it appears that the
pious ancients believed, that when a man makes a profession of the Trinity in baptism, he passes from atheism
to an acknowledgment of the true God.

xiv. It will not be unseasonable here to inquire,
WHETHER THE MYSTERY OF THE TRINITY WAS
KNOWN TO ADAM IN THE STATE OF INNOCENCE ?

---

* Lib. ii. *De Sacramentis,* cap. 7.
† *Instruct. Histor. Theol.* lib. i. cap. 17.
‡ *Orat.* xxxii.
[35] See NOTE XXXIII.

Moses Amyrault, a celebrated divine, has thought proper to deny this, and to contend,* that the economy which takes place among the Three persons of the Godhead, so peculiarly respects the redemption of mankind, that " the knowledge of it cannot pertain to the state " of innocence, in which there was no place for salva- " tion or redemption." To us the matter appears in a different light; and we will explain and confirm our opinion by the following arguments.

xv. The doctrine of the Trinity, we confess, is a mystery, which man, how distinguished soever for wisdom and industry, could not discover by the mere consideration of himself and the creatures. We hold it, however, as unquestionably certain, that God revealed several truths to Adam in his original state of integrity, which unassisted nature was incapable of teaching him. Being the confederate, the friend, and a kind of vicegerent of the great God upon earth, it was essential to his happiness to enjoy communion with his God, and from time to time to receive such instruction from his lips as might serve to prepare him more thoroughly for rendering praise to his Creator. Whence, indeed, did he receive the command respecting the tree of knowledge; whence did he learn the signification of the tree of life, —if not by Divine revelation? How else, did he so well know the manner of the creation of his wife, though formed while he was asleep, as to declare that she was bone of his bone and flesh of his flesh?

Zanchius says,† he has no doubt that God sometimes spoke to Adam, in an external and visible form, by his own Son, clothed with the appearance of a human body.

---

* *Dissert. de Mysterio Trinitatis,* p. 121, and at greater length p. 158, *et seq.*

† *De Creatione Hominis,* lib. i. cap. i. sect. 12.

To him it appears altogether improbable, that this privilege which God afterwards granted to a considerable number of men was withheld from the first man, who was the chief friend of God, and created in his perfect image. He affirms, too, that this was the opinion of the Fathers, of *Justin, Irenæus, Tertullian, Eusebius, Ambrose, Augustine,* and others. For my part, as I dare not determine any thing respecting the mode of revelation, beyond what is related in sacred writ, so I am persuaded that, from the instances which we have adduced, it cannot be questioned that several revelations were, in reality, made to Adam.

xvi. That the mystery of the Trinity was included amongst the subjects of divine revelation to our first father, may be proved thus. It is universally admitted, that the understanding of Adam was adorned with the most excellent wisdom. Now it is the principal branch of wisdom, to know God: Not, however, to know him in so general and indistinct a manner that one understands there is some Infinite Deity, from whom all other beings derive their existence; for such knowledge remained among the heathen, who, we all know, were blind and foolish, and destitute of the divine image. It is essential to a true knowledge of God, that you know distinctly what he is. If you apply those general notions which you have of a Deity to any other than to Him, who, while he is One in essence, subsists in Three persons, you must be considered, not as possessing the knowledge of the true God, but rather as substituting an idol, and a figment of your own imagination, in the place of the true God. But, since it is incongruous and almost blasphemous to impute this to Adam in his state of innocence, we must conclude that he had some knowledge of a Three-one God, who alone is the true God. *Epiphanius*,* in the following expressions concerning Adam, employs the same argument: " He was not an idolater, but knew God the " Father, and the Son, and the Holy Ghost; for he " was a prophet, and knew that the Father said to the " Son, Let us make man." We are here taught by this writer, first, that revelations of a prophetical sort were given to Adam; and, then, that the mystery of the Trinity was one of the points revealed to him: which he proves by this consideration, that he was no idolater. He manifestly supposes, that he would have been an idolater, if he had entertained any other conception of the Almighty, than as a Three-one God.

XVII. In these words, too, *Epiphanius* suggests another argument, which we shall more fully illustrate. In the work of creation God evidently showed himself a Three-one God; for the Father made the worlds by the Son;g the Holy Spirit moved upon the waters, and thus rendered them prolific; and the whole Trinity, by mutual excitation, prepared for the creation of man. It is incredible, therefore, that the Trinity was utterly unknown to the first man; unless we can suppose him to have been ignorant of his Creator. Since both the Son and the Holy Spirit created him, he could not have been ignorant of these Divine persons, without being ignorant of his Creator, and unable to praise or adore him aright. Truly it is not without emphasis and meaning, that in a considerable number of passages in which the Scripture speaks of the Creator of man, it makes use of the plural number. Thus where we read, " Thy Ma-" ker is thy Husband," the words in the original literal-

* *In Panario,* p. 8.
g Heb. i. 2.

ly signify, " Thy *Makers* are thy *Husbands.*"[h] Again,
" Let Israel rejoice in him that made him ;" literally,
" in his *Makers.*" [i] Man is enjoined to attend to this,
and even in early years, to engrave it on his mind ;
" Remember, now, thy Creator, *Creators*, in the days
" of thy youth." [j] It is represented as criminal in man
to neglect this, and not to say, " Where is God my
" Maker, *Makers*, who giveth songs in the night ?"[k]
Unless these expressions be referred to the Trinity,
they might seem dangerous. It is absurd, too, to
think that Adam was ignorant of a truth respecting
his Creator, (I say *Creator*, because this is the character now pressed on our attention,) about which his posterity are not permitted to be ignorant. The absurdity
is the more apparent, when it is considered that God created man to be a herald to proclaim himself and his attributes in the new-formed world ; for unquestionably it
tends to the glory of God, that man should particularly
celebrate not only the Divine perfections, but also the
manner in which these perfections are displayed in the
distinct Persons of the Godhead, and in the mode and
order of their operation.

XVIII. Hence it appears that the economy of the
Trinity ought not to be so restricted to the plan of the
redemption of mankind, as not to be observed in the
first creation of the world and of man. The Gospel itself, while it unfolds this admirable economy as it respects the method of our salvation, leads back our
thoughts at the same time to that economy, as it was
discovered in the first formation of the world. It shows

[h] בעליך עשיך   Is. liv. 5.
[i] ישמח ישראל בעשיו   Ps. cxlix. 2.
[j] זכר את בוראיך   Eccles. xii. 1.
[k] איה אלוה עשי   Job xxxv. 9.

us, that in the old creation there was a certain type and figure of the new;[1] and that the Son of God our Saviour is " the Beginning" (viz. in the active sense of the term) " of the creation of God ;"[m] by whom were made thrones, and dominions, things visible and invisible, " that in all things he might have the pre-emi-" nence ;"[n] that is, that he might hold the pre-eminence as well in the works of nature, as in those of grace. It is, therefore, wrong to conclude that Adam had no knowledge of the Trinity, from the supposition that the economy of the Trinity is principally concerned in the work of redeeming sinners ; since this work of redemption, which is a new creation, was shadowed forth by the first creation, in which the economy of the Three persons no less manifested itself.[34]

xix. It is rashly asserted, too, " that in the state of " innocence there was no room for *salvation* * or re-" demption." This, indeed, is true with regard to redemption, but with respect to *salvation*, it is false. The same salvation, the same eternal life, which we obtain through Christ, (as we have shown at large elsewhere,) was promised to Adam upon condition of his persisting in holiness.[35] We have an evidence of this in the tree of life, which was, then, a symbol, though not of the Mediator as such, yet of the Son of God ; for " In him was " life."[o] This symbol would have been nugatory, if its meaning had been unknown to Adam.

---

* The Latin word *salus* cannot, perhaps, be well rendered here by any other English term than *salvation*. Let it be observed, however, that though *salvation* is commonly understood as necessarily including *deliverance from evil, salus* signifies, in general, *health, life, safety*. T.

[1] 2 Cor. iv. 6.　　[m] Ἀρχη της κτίσεως Θεῦ.　Rev. iii. 14.
[n] Col. i. 16, 18.　　[o] John i. 4.
[34] See NOTE XXXIV.　　[35] See NOTE XXXV.

xx. Thus far respecting the KNOWLEDGE of this mystery. An ASSENT to the doctrine, and an ACKNOWLEDGMENT of it, after it has been explained to one from the word of God, are no less necessary. The condition of one who denies and impugns a fundamental truth which he knows, is evidently far worse than that of one who is simply ignorant of it. They who oppose the doctrine of the Trinity, I do not hesitate to declare with confidence, have no part in eternal salvation. The Apostle John expressly warns us, that " Whosoever denieth the Son, the same hath not the " Father."[p]   Now, that man denies the Son, who denies his Divinity, and who denies the Spirit of the Son, —who is of the same substance with the Son, and, without whom, no man can say that Jesus is Lord.[q]

xxi. When, therefore, men deny, oppose, and blaspheme the doctrine of the Trinity, as the modern Socinians do, we cannot acknowledge them as Christians and Brethren ; we cannot offer them any Church communion, nor accept of it, if offered by them. How much soever they may attempt to recommend themselves by a specious appearance of piety, we boldly pronounce them perverters of Christianity, *fighters against God*,* and gross idolaters ; with whom we wish to have no fellowship in our Churches, and to whom, according to the injunction of an Apostle, we will not say, " God speed."[r]   We applaud the zeal of *Christopher Krainscius*, who, when *Smalcius*, a Socinian leader, with his followers, troubled the Orthodox with an unreasonable demand of union, first in the Synod of *Lublin*, in the year 1612, and afterwards in the Synod

---

* Θεομαχοι.

[p] 1 John ii. 23.

[r] 2 John, verse 10.

[q] 1 Cor. xii. 3.

of *Belzo,* honestly replied, " Sirs, begone, give us
" no trouble ; for sooner may heaven enter into an
" agreement with hell, than we, the Evangelical, with
" you.   Let the man who fears God, go out from this
" Church ;" and instantly he himself went out.
When the adversaries complained of *Krainscius,* as
having by this conduct and language pronounced them
unworthy of his company, *Count Leszczinius* rejoined,
" I also fear God, and therefore, I will remove ;" and
no sooner did he utter the word than he went out,
mounted his carriage, and departed.   Thus the union
demanded was refused.*   Whoever wishes to see more
on this topic, may consult the learned *Theses* of the
venerable *Voet, on the necessity and utility of the doctrine of the Holy Trinity.*"†

XXII. But what would a naked and merely speculative knowledge and acknowledgment of this mystery
avail, unless to these were added the pious DEPEN-
DANCE OF THE SOUL UPON A THREE-ONE GOD ? No
sooner is the believer divinely instructed in this truth
than he delights in it ; rejoicing that now he knows
and believes those mysteries relating to his God, which
transcend all sense, all language, all understanding ;—
which are worthy of his incomprehensible infinitude ;—
and by which, in fine, he is distinguished from all the
idols of the nations, and from those false Gods which
every one, by his own perverse conceptions, has formed
for himself.   " I have found thee," says Faith, " I have
" found, and I recognise thee, O my God, the Rock of
" my salvation, of whom the rest of the world are igno-
" rant ; and whom the Athenians, the wisest of mortals,

* *Lœtus in Compendio Hist. Univers.* cap. xxxv. p. mihi 508.
† *De necessitate et utilitate Dogmatis de SS. Trinitate.*

" confessed to be to them UNKNOWN. Thou art He;*
" in the most absolute unity Three; in a distinct Tri-
" nity, One; Father, Son, and Holy Ghost. Thou
" alone art the ' true God and eternal life.'

XXIII. Nor does faith stop here. But, acknowledging the Father as God, she confidently commits herself to his omnipotent power, his unsearchable wisdom, his unbounded goodness, and the inexhaustible
riches of his all-sufficiency. Acknowledging the Son
as God, she rests securely on his satisfaction as most
ample, and as deriving infinite value from the dignity
of his godhead. " Surely shall one say, In JEHOVAH
" have I righteousness and strength; even to him shall
" men come. - - - In JEHOVAH shall all the seed of
" Israel be justified, and shall glory."ˢ Acknowledging
the Holy Ghost as God, she firmly relies on his wise
and holy guidance, and reposes an unsuspecting confidence in his testimony as infallible, and infinitely worthy of credit.† Knowing, too, that these three are
One, faith is not distracted in her operations, but de-
volves her whole weight on this Tri-une God;—assured
from their unity of will, as well as of essence, that all
the three persons harmoniously concur in promoting her
salvation.

XXIV. Nothing is more false than that calumny of
the *Remonstrants,* by which they deny that the article
of the Holy Trinity has any practical use. Every doctrine of "the truth, is according to godliness:"ᵗ and shall
this character not apply to a doctrine so conspicuous, so
fundamental? This article is even the source of all genuine faith, of all true religion. He cannot have
Christian faith, who doth not believe that a person in

---

* אתה הוא   † 'Αυτοπίστος.
ˢ Is. xlv. 24, 25.   ᵗ Tit. i. 1.

the Godhead could have been given, and has been actually given us, to be a successful Mediator with God;
but this would have been impossible, if the Godhead
had subsisted only in one person. He who does not adore
the Father, the Son, and the Holy Ghost, as equal in
divine majesty, worships not the true God, but a creature of his own imagination. Go now, if you will, and
boldly affirm, that this doctrine, which is absolutely essential to Christian faith and piety, is unprofitable in
relation to practice. The *Remonstrants* are guilty of
offending and dishonouring God, when, in order to flatter the *Socinians*, for whom they entertain too great a
regard, they describe them as persons, " who so regu-
" late their lives according to the rule of the Gospel,
" that they worship the Father in his Son, and, by de-
" vout and pious supplications, solicit from both, the
" grace of the Holy Ghost."* What sort of language,
alas! shall we now have the unhappiness to hear? Do
they regulate their lives according to the rule of the
Gospel, who, by denying the satisfaction of Christ,
overthrow the Gospel? Do those worship the Father
in the Son, who slanderously affirm that the eternal Son
of God is a *mere man*,† and who, whilst they adore him
as such, make him an idol? Do those men, by pious
supplications, implore the grace of the Holy Spirit from
the Father and the Son, who blasphemously allege, that
the Spirit is only an attribute of God, or a creature,
or at least, a person of some intermediate dignity betwixt God and a creature? How much more justly
does *Ignatius* say,[36] " Whosoever declares that God is

---

* *Apol.* fol. 53.

† Ψιλὸς ἄνθρωπος.

[36] See NOTE XXXVI.

" one only, in such a sense as to rob Christ of Divinity,
" is a devil, and an enemy of all righteousness."*

xxv. Let us now point out the more special uses of
this article. The doctrine of the Holy Trinity is profitable, in the *first* place, for INSTRUCTION, and that
in a two-fold respect. 1st, Our understanding is informed in what manner it ought to be exercised in its
meditations concerning God. Not confining its views
merely to his One essence with its attributes, it must
ascend to the Wonderful Trinity. Rightly to know
God, is, unquestionably, an important part of piety; [u]
and a more excellent object of contemplation cannot be
presented to the mind, than this tremendous mystery,
the intuitive and perfect knowledge of which, will complete its felicity in the light of glory. 2dly, From this incomprehensible mystery, which surpasses all sense and
reason, we learn that we must renounce our own wisdom
in divine matters, and reduce every thought into cap-
tivity to the obedience of faith. No one is prepared to
form right views of this mystery, who has not risen
above the low sphere of the senses and human reasonings, and soared to the sublimer region of faith; where,
relying solely on God's own testimony respecting himself, he believes what he is able neither to see with his
eyes, nor comprehend with his mind,—stopping at that
precise point, beyond which divine revelation doth not
conduct him. " You hear," says *Gregory Nazianzen,*
" of the generation of the Son; be not inquisitive with
" respect to its mode. You hear that the Spirit pro-
" ceeds from the Father; beware of curiously inquir-
" ing into the manner of this procession." †

XXVI. *Secondly,* This doctrine is conducive to CON-
SOLATION. 1st, O how delightful is it to behold in the
very intimate union, or rather unity, of the Three Divine persons, a pattern and representation of our own
union with Christ, and, through Christ, with God!
This astonishing idea is suggested by our Lord's prayer,
—" That they all may be one, as thou, Father, art in
" me, and I in thee; that they also may be one in us;
" - - - that they may be one, even as we are one; I in
" them, and thou in me."ᵛ 2dly, O how pleasant is it
to believe that the Father, who has adopted me for a
son, is God; who, being himself Lord of all, is able to
make me an heir of all things;—to reflect that the
Son, to whom my soul is betrothed, is, equally with the
Father, God, and the King of glory;—to know that
the Holy Spirit, by whom I am sealed unto the day of
complete salvation, is, in like manner, God, and, consequently, *truth itself!** 3dly, O how delightful is it for
me, when meditating on the mystery of the Sacred Trinity, to behold in the face of the eternal Father, the
kindness of his unbounded love towards me;—in the
face of the co-eternal Son, the endearing familiarity of
the purest *brotherly love;*†—and in the light of the
Holy Spirit, the bonds of my union with God!

XXVI. In the *third* place, it is useful for ADMONI-
TION.³⁷ It serves to admonish us, 1st, That we Christians, who ought to " be followers of God, as dear chil-
" dren,"ʷ should live together in perfect harmony, being " of one accord, of one mind;"ˣ " endeavouring to

---

* Ἀυτοαλήθεια.

† Φιλαδελφία.

ᵛ John xvii. 21, 22, 23.   ʷ Ephes. v. 1.

ˣ Phil. ii. 2.

³⁷ See NOTE XXXVII.

" keep the unity of the Spirit in the bond of peace." [y]
2dly, That we should reverence the divine majesty of
our Father ;—that we should, with alacrity, throw open
the doors of our hearts to the Son, the king of glory ;—
that we should not " grieve,"[z] nor " vex,"[a] nor " quench,"[b]
the Holy Spirit, who is a person of the same divine
dignity with the Father, and the Son; but consecrate
our whole selves to him as temples sacred to his honour,[c]—solicitously avoiding all approaches to that sin
against Him, which shall never be forgiven, neither in
this world, nor in the world to come.[d]

I conclude with the words of *Synesius,* in his third
Hymn.*

" I praise thee as One ; I praise thee as Three.
" While Three, thou art One ; while One, thou art Three."

---

* Ὑμνῶ σε μονάς᾽, Ὑμνῶ σε τριάς᾽.
  Μονάς εἰ τριάς ὤν. Τριάς᾽ εἰ μονάς ὤν.

[y] Ephes. iv. 3.   [z] Ephes. iv. 30.
[a] Isa. lxiii. 10.   [b] 1 Thes. v. 19.
[c] 1 Cor. iii. 16. vi. 19.   [d] Matt. xii. 32.

DISSERTATION VII.

ON FAITH IN *GOD THE FATHER.*

————

I. IT is an approved and well-known observation of Divines, that the term FATHER, when applied to God, is sometimes taken *essentially,** and sometimes *personally.*† Taken *essentially*, it is common to the whole undivided Trinity. In this view, it is employed chiefly with reference to the creatures; for that on account of which God is denominated the Father of mankind and of other creatures, is not peculiar to any one Person, but pertains equally to each. He is called " the Fa- " ther of all," because he created all,[a] and " the Father " of Spirits,"[b] because ." he formeth the spirit of man " within him;"[c] and, also, because he exercises a watchful providence over mankind, extending his care to every individual. " He hath made of one blood," said the Apostle Paul to the Athenians, " all the nations " of men. - - - He is not far from every one of us; for " in him we live, and move, and have our being; as cer- " tain also of your own poets have said, For we are also

* 'Ουσιωδᾶς.   † 'Υποστατικως.
[a] Mal. ii. 10.   [b] Heb. xii. 9.
[c] Zech. xii. 1. comp. Jer. xxxviii. 16.

" his offspring."[d]   Now these expressions are to be deemed no less applicable to the Second and the Third, than to the First Person in the Godhead.

II. The name FATHER, however, now falls to be considered by us *personally,* as the designation of the First Person. We shall observe that he is from himself; that he alone begat the Son, in an incomprehensible manner; and that from him, together with the Son, the Holy Spirit proceeded, in a manner equally ineffable. All that the Scriptures propound as the distinguishing properties of the Father, are comprised in this description.

III. The first of these properties, is the Father's being the FIRST PERSON.*   When we call the Father the first person, let it be observed, we do not understand the expression as relating to the order of DURATION; as if he were before the other persons with regard to age or time. For the " goings forth" of the Son, " have been from of old, even from everlasting."[e] " The LORD possessed," this personal wisdom, " in the " beginning of his way, before his works of old," before all time.[f]   Hence *Athanasius* has justly said; " The " Son is of the Father without beginning, and begotten " of him from eternity."†   The Spirit also, through whose agency Christ was offered up as a spotless sacrifice to God, (which without any inconvenience, and even with great propriety, may be understood of the Third person,)[38] is called " the Eternal Spirit."[g]   Eter-

---

* *Patris Personalis Primitas.*

† Ὑιὸν ἐκ τῦ Πατρὸς ἀναρχως καὶ ἀϊδίως γεγεννημένον. *Exposit. Fidei.*

   [d] Acts xvii. 26, 27, 28.

   [e] מקדם מימי עולם Mic. v. 2.

   [f] Prov. viii. 22.   [g] Heb. ix. 14.

            [38] See NOTE XXXVIII.

nity, indeed, is so essential a property of God, that a person not eternal ought not to be acknowledged as Divine. " Eternal power," is part of that which may be known of God from the suggestions of nature itself.[h] What is eternal, too, could have nothing prior to it, even for a moment. *Athanasius* has, accordingly, well said in his Creed; " The Godhead of the Father, and " the Son, and the Holy Ghost, is one; and their ma-" jesty CO-ETERNAL."*

IV. Again, we do not call the Father the First person, in the order of NATURE or CAUSALITY. This is nowhere affirmed in Scripture, beyond which it is not safe to speak on so awful a mystery. A cause is properly defined, that which gives existence to something else. But this cannot take place among the Divine persons, whose essence is one and the same. It is wrong, too, where the nature is one, as here, to entertain any conception of priority or posteriority of nature. The ancient Greek Christians, I am aware, admitted *the cause and what is caused*,† amongst the Divine persons. But though they thus employed phrases which scarcely merit approbation, their meaning was sound; they explicitly denied all priority and inequality of nature. Let us see how *Damascenus* expresses himself on this topic. "When " we say that the Father is the head of the Son, or " greater than the Son, we by no means affirm that he " is PRIOR IN TIME OR SUPERIOR IN NATURE TO " THE SON, for by him he made the worlds: We in-" tend nothing but this, that the Father is the cause " of the Son; that is, that the Son was begotten of the " Father, not the Father of the Son."‡ We disap-

---

* Καὶ συνδιαιωνίζουσα (*alii legunt* συναΐδιος) ἡ μεγαλειότης.

† Τὸ αἴτιον καὶ τὸ αἰτιατὸν. See *Forbes*, lib. i. cap. 20.

‡ *De Orthodoxa Fide*, lib. i. cap. 9.

[h] Rom. i. 20.

prove of some expressions in this quotation, as inaccurate. To say that " the Father is the cause of the Son," is harsh, indistinct, and unscriptural. Nor is it true that, in that respect, the Father is greater than the Son; since the Son accounts it no robbery " to be equal " with God."[i] Orthodoxy, however, is secured, when it is affirmed, that the Father is not styled the cause of the Son, in any other sense, but as the Son is begotten of him; and when all priority of nature and of time is excluded.

v. In fine, we do not consider the Father as first in DIGNITY or EXCELLENCE. Infinite and supreme excellence is an essential attribute of Deity: and if any person were possessed of greater excellence and dignity than the Son or the Holy Spirit, neither of these persons could be the Most High God. " These three are " one,"[j] in essence, and in all essential attributes; equal in dignity, and equal in glory.*

vi. But the Father is the First person in the following respects. 1st, In the order of SUBSISTENCE. The *hypostasis* is ascribed to the Father. The Son is called " the express image of his person," *the character of his hypostasis*.[k] The Father, therefore, is the *archetype*,† the Son the *resemblance* :‡ But the archetype is prior to that which is conformed to it.§ The Apostle makes use of the same similitude in another place, when he calls the Son " the image of the invisible " God."[l] Whilst this priority deprives the Son of no part of his excellence, it brings no addition to that of

---

* Ἰσότιμοι καὶ ἰσόδοξοι.   † Ἀρχέτυπος.

‡ Ἐκτύπωμα.   § Τῷ ἐκτυπωθέντι.

  [i] Phil. ii. 6.   [j] 1 John. v. 7.

  [k] Χαρακτηρ τῆς ὑποστάσεως αὐτῦ. Heb. i. 3.

  [l] Εἰκων τῦ Θεῦ τῦ ἀορατῦ. Col. i. 15.

the Father. On the contrary, the equality of both is elegantly pointed out by this metaphor. *Theophylact* has the following beautiful remark: " The *charac-* " *ter*, or the form expressed, doth not exceed the *hy-* " *postasis*, or the form expressing; lest, in so far as it " exceeds, it should have no *hypostasis*. Nor is the " *hypostasis* greater than the *character;* otherwise, " some part of it, at least, would not be expressed."

VII. 2dly, In the order of OPERATION. Since the Father works by the Son, it necessarily follows that, in relation to the other persons, he works *originally and from himself*,* and has in himself the principle of operation, as well personally as essentially. The following assertion of our Lord relates to this subject: " The Son " can do nothing of himself, but what he seeth the Fa- " ther do; for what things soever he doeth, these also " doeth the Son likewise."m This declaration holds respecting the Son, considered as well in his Divine, as in his Mediatorial character. As, in his human nature, the Son doth nothing without the incitement, command, and example of the Father, but in all his actions performs the will and displays the holiness of the Father; so as the Son of God, he can do nothing " of himself," † nothing, as the Hebrews would express it לבדו, *separately* from the Father. The essence, the power, and the will of both, are one and the same; yet the Father takes the lead in the order of operation, and the Son " sees" him operating; that is, knows intimately, approves, and executes with perfect exactness, the Father's counsels and decrees,—which are, at the same time, his own.

Thus it is clear that the order of operation begins on

---

* Ἀναρχως.   † Ἀφ᾽ ἑαυτῦ.

m John v. 19. See also Heb. i. 2.

the part of the Father. Nor, again, doth this prerogative of order, derogate in the least from the supreme dignity of the Son; unless one should very absurdly regard it as an evidence of weakness and inferiority that, since the power and will of the Father and the Son are one and the same, the Son can neither do nor will any thing, but in and with the Father. The Son himself hath amply guarded his own dignity, by testifying, that " what things soever the Father doth, these also " doth the Son *likewise*."* The meaning is not, as *Grotius* wrests the expression, that the Son does other works corresponding to these; but that he does the same works, and performs them *in like manner*. This is to be understood, as *Nazianzen* observes, " not with respect " to the likeness of the things done, but with respect " to an equal dignity of power and authority." † The expression intimates too, as *Cyril* of *Alexandria* says on this text, " the absolute identity of the works." ‡ If the words are explained in this manner, they will furnish an incontestable proof, not only that our Lord had done nothing wrong in curing the impotent man, but even that it was utterly impossible for him to do wrong; because, provided only the distinction of the personal order of operation be preserved, the power and the will by which he works miracles, are the same with the power and the will of the Father. Now this was the scope of our Lord's discourse.

VIII. The *second* characteristical property of the Father, is that he is OF HIMSELF. This is to be under-

---

* Ὁμοίως.

† Ου κατα την γινομενων ὁμοιωσιν, ἀλλα κατα την της ἐξουσιας ὁμοτιμιαν.

‡ Την 'εν τοις ἔργοις ἀπαραλλακτον ταυτότητα.

stood, not in relation to the essence, but to the mode of having the essence. With respect to the essence, both the Son and the Holy Spirit are that God who is of himself. That the Deity is of himself—that, owing to the glory of his infinite perfections, he depends on no other, but has his existence and all that he possesseth of himself,—is so necessarily included in the notion of the Deity, that one who, with regard to his essence, is from another, for this precise reason, cannot be God. The ancients, therefore, rightly called Christ, *God of himself*, and *by himself*.* Amongst other instances, *Eusebius*, in a panegyrical Oration on *Paulinus*, Bishop of Tyre, denominates Christ " the proper Son of " the supreme God, and God of himself;" † because being the true God, he possesses that Divine essence, which is from itself, although he has it as a Son from the Father. The Father, then, is from himself with regard to personality; that is, the Divine essence is communicated to him from no other person; for nowhere does the sacred volume intimate that the Father was begotten, or proceeded, or in any manner came forth from another. *Athanasius*, accordingly, has well said : " We believe in one unbegotten God, the Father " Almighty, who hath his subsistence from himself."‡

IX. The *third* distinguishing property of the Father, is that HE ALONE FROM ETERNITY, BEGAT THE SON. He, accordingly, says, " Thou art my Son ; this day " have I begotten thee." These words were addressed to Christ, as the Apostle expressly assures us, in a sense altogether peculiar to himself :[n] but, in what this ge-

---

* 'Αυτοθεός.

† Τῦ καθόλῦ Θεῦ παιδα γνησιον, καὶ 'Αυτοθεόν. *Hist.* lib. x. cap. 4.

‡ *Exposit. Fidei.*

[n] Ps. ii. 7. Heb. i. 5.

neration consists, it is impossible for us weak mortals to understand or explain. *Athanasius,* whom I have just quoted, very properly says, " He was begotten in a man- " ner ineffable and incomprehensible."* The very idea of generation, however, properly so called, namely, that by which one is constituted the son of any person, includes the communication of the same nature.[39] In created persons, the nature is the same only in species ; but in God, owing to his absolute unity, it is the same in re- ference to number. By the generation of the Son, then, we understand that act of God, by which he has com- municated to the Son the same numerical essence which he himself hath, that the Son may have it in like man- ner.

x. We do not hazard these assertions without autho- rity from sacred writ. The Son himself leads the way, saying, " As the Father hath life in himself, so hath " he given to the Son, to have life in himself." ⁰ " To " have life in himself," is, not merely, to have enough for himself for that infinitely happy life, which alone is worthy of God ; but, also, to be a fountain of life, to impart it to those who had no existence, and to restore it to those who are dead. These are essential perfec- tions of God. In this manner, " the Father hath life " in himself." Now the Father hath given to the Son to have the same life in himself, in the same manner ; and this necessarily implies the communication of the same essence, which lives by itself, and is the source of all true life.[40] Several Protestant Divines, I am aware, and some, too, of great eminence, contend that these expressions refer to Christ, not directly in relation to

---

* Ἐγεννήθη δὲ ἀνεκφράστως καὶ ἀπεριvoήτως.

⁰ John v. 26.

[39] See NOTE XXXIX.　　　　[40] See NOTE XL.

his Divine character,* but to his Mediatorial office.† But, although we should grant them this, (which, however, it is not necessary for us to do,) still it could not have been given to Christ, that, as Mediator, he should possess a fountain of life in himself, unless he possessed a nature which lives of itself, and which is even *life from and by itself*:‡ For this is the peculiar prerogative of God, and hence the Psalmist adores him thus: "With thee is the fountain of life;"[p] and this glory he will give to none that is not God.[q]

XI. But we cannot so easily concede to our adversaries, that, by the *generation* of Christ mentioned in the second Psalm, his resurrection from the dead is intended; and that, by *this day*, we are to understand the day on which God, having raised him from the dead, appointed him the King of his church. For, 1st, To beget, signifies nowhere in the sacred volume, to rescue from death; and we are not at liberty to coin new significations of words. 2dly, Though, possibly, it were sometimes used in that metaphorical acceptation, (which, however, is not yet proved,) it cannot be understood in this passage in any other than its proper sense. It is here adduced as a reason for which Christ is called the Son of God. Now Christ is the Son of God, not figuratively, but properly; for the Father is called his *proper Father*,[r] and he himself is denominated the *proper Son* of the Father;[s] by which designation he is distinguished from those who are his sons

* Κατα θεολογιαν. † Κατ' οικονομιαν.

‡ Αυτοζωή.

[p] Ps. xxxvi. 9. [q] Is. xlii. 8.

[r] Πατερα ἴδιον. John v. 18.

[s] Τȣ̃ ἰδίȣ υἱȣ̃. Rom. viii. 32.

in a metaphorical sense. 3dly, These words are spoken to Christ with a certain emphasis, with which they could not have been addressed to any of the angels, much less, to any of mankind.[t] But if they meant nothing more than the raising of him from the dead, they would attribute nothing to Christ, which he doth not possess in common with many others, who, in like manner, are raised up by the power of God to glory and an everlasting kingdom. 4thly, Christ raised himself from the dead, too, by his own power;[u] from which it would follow, according to this interpretation, that he begat himself, and that he is his own Son. 5thly, It is not true, in fine, that Christ was not begotten of the Father, nor called his Son till that very day on which he was raised from the dead; for, as is abundantly manifest from the Gospel history, he often, when yet alive, professed himself the Son of God, and was often acknowledged as such. 6thly, *To-day* refers to time, when human concerns are in question; but this expression, when applied to Divine things, must be understood in a sense suitable to the majesty of the godhead.* And if any word may be transferred from time to denote eternity, which is the complete and perfect possession, at once, of an interminable life; what can be better adapted to express its unsuccessive duration, than the term *to-day?*

XII. Nor can our adversaries derive any support to their cause from the words of Paul, Acts xiii. 32, 33. " And we declare unto you glad tidings, how that the " promise which was made unto the fathers, God hath " fulfilled the same unto us their children, in that *he*

---

* Θεοπρεπῶς.

[t] Heb. i. 5.   [u] John ii. 19. x. 18.

" *hath raised up Jesus ;** as it is also written in the se-
" cond Psalm, Thou art my Son, this day have I be-
" gotten thee." For, 1st, Paul doth not here prove
the resurrection of Jesus from the dead, from this expression in the second Psalm, (which, though it describes him who is raised again, doth not prove his resurrection ;) but from Isaiah lv. 3, and Psalm xvi. 10,
while he adds, verses 34th and 35th, " And, as con-
" cerning that he raised him up from the dead," &c.
2dly, The words, " having raised up Jesus," do not
even relate to the resurrection of Jesus from the dead,
but to the exhibition of him as a Saviour. This raising of him up, is expressly distinguished from the raising of him again from the dead, which is subsequently
spoken of, verse 34th. The meaning is, that God fulfilled the promise made to the fathers, when he exhibited Christ to mankind in the flesh. But what was that
promise ? This appears from the second Psalm, where
God promises to the Church that, in due time, he would
anoint as King over her, his own Son, begotten of himself, TO-DAY ; that is, from eternity to eternity ; for
with God there is a perpetual to-day. *Grotius,* whose
name is not offensive to our opposers, has remarked that
Luke makes use of the same word† to signify *exhibiting* in Acts ii. 30. iii. 26. To these we add another
instance from chap. vii. 37. " A Prophet shall the Lord
" your God raise up unto you." ‡ 3dly, Were we to
admit that the words of the Psalm are applied to the
resurrection of Christ, which seemed proper to *Calvin,*

---

* Ἀναστήσας Ἰησοῦν. The particle *again,* which is added after
Jesus in our English version, is, at all events, unnecessary ; and, if
our author's interpretation be just, it tends, in some degree, to obscure the sense. T.

† Ἀναστήσας.   ‡ Προφήτην ὑμῖν ἀναστήσει κύριος.

Cameron, and several other Protestant Divines; the sense will only be this; that, by his being thus raised up again, it was declared and demonstrated that Christ is the Son of the Father, begotten of him from everlasting. The Jewish Council condemned him for blasphemy, because he had called himself the Son of God. But, by raising him again from the grave, after he had been put to death as a blasphemer, God acquitted him from that charge, and publicly recognised him as his Only-begotten Son.[41]   Thus he was *declared, exhibited, and distinguished as the Son of God with power,* expressly and particularly, to the entire exclusion of all others.[v]   The original word here employed by the Apostle, is remarkably expressive; and, as *Ludovicus de Dieu* has learnedly observed, it signifies that Christ was placed betwixt such bounds, and so separated and discriminated from others, that he neither should nor can be judged to be any one else than the Son of God. The expression, " with power,"[*] may be joined with " declared ;" and then the meaning will be, that he was shown to be the Son of God by a powerful argument. Or it may be connected with " the Son of God ;" and then it will intimate, that he is the Son of God in the most ample and exalted sense of which the term is susceptible; so that this name, when ascribed to him, is " a more excellent name" than any that is given to the noblest of creatures.[w]

XIII. The *fourth* personal property of the Father is, that THE HOLY SPIRIT PROCEEDS FROM HIM, TOGETHER WITH THE SON.[†]   The Spirit is, therefore,

---

* 'Εν δυναμει.   † *Una cum Filio, Spiritum Sanctum spiret.*

v 'Ορίσθη υιος Θεου εν δυναμει. Rom. i. 4.

w Διαφορωτερον ονομα. Heb. i. 4.

41 See NOTE XLI.

styled, " the Spirit of his mouth;"[x] and, again, " the
" Spirit of God," and " the breath of the Almighty."[y]
Thus far our knowledge extends.   But what the mode
of this *breathing* is, and how the communication of the
essence to the Third Person by *breathing* differs from
the communication of the same essence to the Second
Person by generation,—are mysteries, the knowledge
of which, it has seemed good to the great Teacher to
reserve for the celestial state.   We have no complacency
in the boldness of the Scholastic Theologians, who have
asserted, that *generation* pertains to the Understanding, and that the Father, by the contemplation of himself, begat that personal image of himself, who is called
the Son: while they refer *breathing* to the Will, and
say, that the Father, in conjunction with the Son, by
favouring and loving himself, produced the Holy Spirit.
Not only are we afraid of becoming so profoundly wise;
but we have, also, an aversion at such vain refinements
of human ingenuity, presumptuously amusing itself
with Divine topics.   Far better, in our apprehension, is
the discretion of *Gregory Nazianzen*, who satisfies himself with the following simple declaration of the truth :
" The Holy Spirit is truly a Spirit, who proceeds from
" the Father; not, however, by filiation, or generation,
" but by procession."[*]

xiv. This one thing, however, we can safely affirm;
that, while it belongs to the Father alone to beget the
Son, the Spirit proceeds from both the Father and
the Son.[†]   This may be gathered from John xv. 26.
" But when the Comforter is come, whom I will send

---

[*] Orat. xxxix.
[†] *Generatio soli Patri competat, Spiratio autem Patri et Filio.*
[x] רוח פיו Ps. xxxiii. 6.
[y] רוח אל ונשמת שדי Job xxxiii. 4.

" unto you from the Father, even the Spirit of truth,
" which *proceedeth** from the Father, he shall testify
" of me." It is no less certain that the Spirit is sent
by the Son, than it is, that he proceedeth from the Father. Both the sending and the procession here spoken
of, I acknowledge, are not *natural,* or *hypostatical,* but
economical;† and the subjects directly intended, are
the giving of the Holy Spirit, and his going forth, to
men. But these presuppose the eternal mystery; for
it is altogether fit and congruous that the manifestation
of the Divine persons, which is afforded in time, should
correspond with the real manner of their subsistence
from eternity.

xv. I do not, however, dissemble, that to this observation it may be objected, that Christ, who, in respect
to his person, is not from the Holy Spirit, is said to be
sent by the Spirit; for we read in Isaiah xlviii. 16.
" And now the LORD God and his Spirit hath sent
" me." But I reply, 1st, It is not quite certain whether it be Christ that speaks in this passage. Eminent
theologians, as *Jerome, Vatablus, Calvin, Junius,* our
own *Dutch* Divines, and others quoted by *Cornelius a
Lapide,* will have these to be the words of Isaiah himself, by which he vindicates his authority as a Prophet
of God. 2dly, If the words are to be referred to Christ,
which is the opinion of a great number of ancient as
well as modern writers, whom I dare not contradict; it

* Ἐκπορεύεται.

† The author's words are: *Fateor et missionem et* ἐκπορεύσιν *istam
non esse* φυσικην *sive* ὑποστατικην, *sed* οἰκονομικην. The meaning is,
that the mission and the procession spoken of in this verse, *immediately* relate, not to the Divine essence, or to the subsistence of the
Divine persons, but to their respective operations in the work of redemption. T.

may be affirmed that he was sent by the Holy Spirit, as he was man, and sent for the redemption of mankind; for the formation of our Lord's human nature is ascribed to the Holy Spirit.[z] In this manner *A Lapide*, after *Anselm*, answers the objection.   3dly, The Hebrew text may, with propriety, be translated thus; " The LORD God hath sent me, and his Spirit."[*] According to this version, the mission of the Spirit is connected with the mission of the Son; which exactly corresponds with the event. In whatever sense you interpret the passage, it makes nothing against our hypothesis.

XVI. Why, too, should he be called " the Spirit of " the Son,"[a] and be said to " receive of the things of " the Son,"[b] unless he proceeded from the Son? In the economy of redemption, as has been more than once remarked, the Three persons act suitably to the relations in which they stand to each other in the godhead.[†]

XVII. Hence it is evident, what opinion we ought to form respecting the obstinate contention of the Greeks with the Latins relative to this point. There are faults, I doubt not, on both sides. Since the Creed of Constantinople, published in the year of our Lord 381, contained this expression, " the Holy Spirit proceeding " from the Father;"[‡] the Latins did wrong in adding to that Creed these words, " and to the Son."[§] On this addition see *Vossius*,[||] and Heidegger.[¶]   The Latins did wrong, I say, in this matter; for, although what

---

[*] אדני יהוה שלחני ורוחו

[†] 'Οικονομία sequitur την θεολογίαν.

[‡] Τὸ πνεῦμα τὸ ἅγιον, το ἐκ τοῦ πατρὸς ἐκπορευόμενον.

[§] FILIOQUE.

[||] *De Tribus Symbolis,* Disser. iii. Thesi xv. et seq.

[¶] *Dissert.* Sel. tom. ii. p. 728.

[z] Luke i. 35.   [a] Gal. iv. 6.   [b] John xvi. 14.

they added was true, the words of the Creed were the words of Scripture, whilst the addition is not contained in Scripture, in these precise terms. Besides, whoever makes any addition to an ancient Creed, involves himself in the guilt of bearing false witness; for he would have it to be believed that the Fathers who compiled that Creed determined something which they did not determine. The Greeks, also, have done wrong in contending so pertinaciously concerning this point; for the doctrine of the Latins is conformable to truth, and it was delivered in the same manner by ancient Doctors of their own church; as has been long ago shown from the writings of *Athanasius, Epiphanius, Cyril* of *Alexandria, Gregory* of *Nyssa,* and others. Nay, if we are willing to rest satisfied with what is essential, scarcely any real controversy remains. For it is of very little consequence, whether we hold that the Holy Ghost proceeds from the Father and the Son, or " from " the Father through the Son ;"* as *Cyril* of *Constantinople* expresses it in his Confession, written in the year of Christ 1631. As neither of these two expressions occurs in holy writ, so neither of them is improper, or inconsistent with the truth. But let thus much suffice on this subject.

XVIII. We must here take notice of the opinion of *Episcopius* respecting the subordination of the other persons to the Father. He contends " that the Father " is so the First person, that he is, also, the HIGHEST " in ORDER, in DIGNITY, and in POWER.—In OR- " DER, because it was necessary that the Son and the " Holy Spirit should be from him—In DIGNITY, be- " cause the Father is the Fountain and the cause of " their existence; and it is more honourable to derive

* Ἐκ τοῦ Πατρος δι υἱοῦ.

" existence from none than to receive it from another,
" to beget than to be begotten, *to cause to proceed*
" *than to proceed**—In POWER, that is, authority
" or dominion ; because the Father has authority to
" send and to give the Son, and to pour out the
" Holy Spirit; but neither of them has authority over
" the Father ; and accordingly we no where read of
" the Father as sent or given, but always as sending
" or giving." Such is the doctrine of *Episcopius ;*[†] and
similar sentiments are expressed by *Curcellæus.*[‡]

XIX. In reply to these writers, we make the following general remarks. 1st, They depart in this instance from the catholic faith of the Church, which,
as it is expressed by the Emperor,[§] " believes, ac-
" cording to the instructions of Apostles and the doc-
" trine of the Gospel, that the Father, the Son, and
" the Holy Ghost, are one God, subsisting in equal
" majesty, and in an adorable Trinity." [||] *Athanasius,*
in like manner, states the common faith in the following terms: " Where there is an undivided dignity, one
" sovereignty, one power, and will, and energy, peculi-
" arly distinguishing the Trinity from the creatures,—
" there is one God."[¶]   2dly, The majesty of the Father is artfully extolled with a view to disparage the
infinite dignity of the Son and the Holy Spirit. It is
the will of the Father himself, " that all men should

---

* *Spirare, quam spirari,* is the Latin expression ; which literally
signifies, *to breathe than to be breathed.*   T.

† *Instit. Theol.* lib. iv. cap. 32.

‡ *Dissertat. de vocibus Trinitatis,* &c. parag. lx.

§ Lege i. Codi. *De Sum. Trinit. et Fide Catholica.*

|| These expressions are quoted in Justinian's *Corpus Juris Civilis,*
tom. 2. from an Edict relating to the Trinity, issued by the Emperor GRATIAN in the year of our Lord 380.   T.

¶ *Libro de Communi Essentia,* &c. Capite, *Quod non tres Dii sint.*

" honour the Son even as they honour the Father."ᶜ
3dly, All these expressions have a manifest tendency
utterly to deprive the Son and the Spirit of true godhead. A subordinate Deity, is not Deity. Supreme
majesty, dignity, and power, are essential attributes of
godhead ; and he that is not possessed of them, is not
God.

xx. More particularly, 1st, The Scriptures teach a
distinction of *order ;* but, since it is merely a distinction of personal order, it implies no superiority or inferiority attributed to the essence. *Athanasius,* who
has stated this distinction of order with singular accuracy, makes the following excellent observation, in the
Creed which is commonly received by the Church :
" And in this Trinity, nothing is prior or posterior,"
that is, with respect to dignity, " nothing greater or
" less ; but all these Three persons are co-eternal and
" co-equal." 2dly, Begetting and being begotten, *caus-*
*ing to proceed and proceeding,** imply no distinction
of DIGNITY amongst the Divine persons : for the begetting and the causing to proceed are the communication of the same numerical essence, which belongs to
him who begets and causes to proceed ; and which possesses an infinite dignity, than which none greater can
either be allowed, or imagined, without a contradiction.
3dly, The sacred writings nowhere speak of the Father's
having *power, authority,* and *dominion* over the Son
and the Holy Spirit. Nor is it warrantable to infer
any such superiority on the part of the Father, from
the mission of the Son and Spirit ; which is entirely according to the economy in redemption, and founded in
the common council of the whole Trinity.

* *Spirare et spirari.*
ᶜ John v. 23.

xxi. When the Father is denominated absolutely
GOD, or ONE GOD,[d] or THE ONLY TRUE GOD;[e] this
is intended to exclude those who are " called Gods,"[f]
not the other persons in the same individual essence.
Oecumenius has the following remark on 1 Tim. ii. 5.
" When it is affirmed that *there is one God,* this is
" not in contradistinction to the Son or Spirit. Far be
" the thought. But the words refer to those who are not,
" and yet are styled Gods."* The appellation of Father even includes the Son in the same conception of
godhead.   Hence says *Cyril* of *Jerusalem,* " We call
" God Father, that as soon as we have thought of the
" Father, we may also think of the Son; for there
" is an immediate relation between Father and Son."†
Gregory of *Nyssa* expresses the same idea thus : " The
" appellation of Father, by its relative import, shows
" that He hath a Son." †

xxii. When the Son calls the " Father greater than
" himself,"[g] the expression is not to be understood of
him in relation to his Divine nature as the Son.   We
must not suppose that the Father is greater than he,
" as the cause and principle of his existence." ‡   I sincerely wish that this expression had not been used by
Basil, Gregory, Nazianzen, Hilary of *Poitiers,* and
Damascenus, amongst the ancients ; and, amongst the
Protestants, by *Danæus* (who unjustly censures *Lom-
bard* for omitting this reason of Christ's inferiority,) by
Zanchius on Philip. ii. 6, and by *Gomar* on the same
passage.   But the Father is greater than the Son, 1st,

* *Catechesi* vii.
† *Oratio prima contra Eunomium.*
‡ Ὡς αἰτιος και αρχη.

[d] 1 Cor. viii. 6. Ephes. iv. 6.   [f] Λεγομενοι Θεοι. 1 Cor. viii. 5.
[e] John xvii. 3.   [g] John xiv. 28.

With regard to the human nature, which he has assumed. 2dly, With regard to the office of an ambassador, which he has undertaken. 3dly, With respect to the economy of his humiliation, and assuming the form of a servant. Accordingly, *Athanasius*, at the conclusion of his book on *the Incarnation of Christ*,* has the following remark : " And, when he says the Father " who sent me is greater than I, he calls the Father " greater than himself, with regard to his human na- " ture. But, as he is the Word of the Father, he is " his equal." In the *first Dialogue against the Macedonians*, too, he says, " Having assumed the subjec- " tion of a servile form, he is, for our sake, subjected " to the Father ;—not in the Divine nature, but by " the union of that servile form which he assumed."†

XXIII. When the First person is called " the God " and Father of our Lord Jesus Christ," (a title which often occurs at the beginnings of the Epistles,) he is called his Father, *according to the Divinity*,—his God, *according to the Economy*, both in relation to his human nature, and in reference to the covenant which subsists betwixt him as Mediator, and the Father. *Athanasius*, in the Dialogue just quoted, says, " As " to the Divinity, God is his Father ; but, as to the hu- " manity, his God :" which he, afterwards, proves by that expression, " Thou art my God from my mother's " belly."[h] The same remarks are made by *Gregory* of *Nyssa*, *Nazianzen*, *Epiphanius*, and others, whose words are quoted by *Forbes*.‡ We thus answer novices who have dared to pervert our faith, in the lan

---

* *De Humana Natura suscepta a Deo Verbo.*

† *Dialogus i. contra Macedonianos.*

‡ Lib. i. cap. 29.

[h] Ps. xxii. 10.

guage of the Fathers, that they may not boast of these frivolous subtleties as their own inventions; since the same cavils were both observed and refuted by the ancients. Whoever wishes to see the whole doctrine of *Episcopius* completely overthrown, may consult the accurate and solid *Dissertation on the subjection of Christ*,* by *Andrew Essenius*,—a man whom I venerate as my Preceptor and Father in the Lord.

XXIV. It is not sufficient that our faith contemplate the Father as the eternal Father of Christ, unless we are also brought to him as OUR OWN FATHER through Christ. Christ himself leads us to him when he says, " I ascend unto my Father, and your Father;"[i] in which words he intimates that there is a resemblance, and, at the same time, a diversity, in the Father's paternal relation, as it respects himself and us. This was judiciously observed by the ancients. " He said not," says *Cyril* of *Jerusalem*,† " *to our Father*, lest the " creatures should have fellowship with the Only-be- " gotten; but *to my Father and your Father*—my " Father, in one respect, to wit, by nature—yours, in " another respect, to wit, by adoption."

XXV. In what way God is the Father of believers, we have shown at large elsewhere.‡ Yet, that nothing may be wanting to this Dissertation, we briefly notice, that God is called our Father, 1st, With respect to our supernatural *regeneration* by his Spirit, by which a new and heavenly life is begun within us, and we, in our measure and order, are even " made partakers of

* *Dissertatio de subjectione Christi*, cap. v.

† *Catechesis* vii. et xi.

‡ See the Author's *Economy of the Covenants*, book iii. chap. 10. and 11. T.

[i] John xx. 17.

the Divine nature."[j] Of this, the Evangelist John speaks in the following words: "Which were born, "not of blood, nor of the will of the flesh, nor of the "will of man, but of God."[k] 2dly, With respect to our *marriage* with the Lord Jesus; for when we become his Spouse, we pass into the Father's family, and the Father addresses us by the endearing name of "Daughter,"[l] while Jesus himself describes us, with the same breath, as "his Sister and his Spouse."[m] 3dly, With respect to *adoption*, by which we obtain the right and the privileges of sons, and the eternal inheritance is bequeathed to us by an immutable testament. We read, "Who hath predestinated us unto the adoption "of children;"[n] and "If children, then heirs."[o]

XXVI. The condition of the sons of God is truly excellent. If David accounted it so great a matter, to be called the son-in-law of such a king as Saul,[p] how highly should we esteem the honour of being called the sons of the living God? 1st, How unparalleled is that *dignity*, by which we trace our descent, not from an earthly prince or monarch, but from the King of heaven! 2dly, What can be more beautiful than that *Divine nature* which we obtain by a new generation![q] God himself glories in his sons as his peculiar treasure, and even calls them "the first fruits of his increase;"[r] who are to him for a praise, and a name, and an honour.[s] In this instance, his conduct almost resembles that of parents who glory before others in such of their

[j] 2 Pet. i. 4. [k] John i. 13.
[l] Ps. xlv. 10. [m] Song v. 1, 2.
[n] Ephes. i. 5. [o] Rom. viii. 17.
[p] 1 Sam. xviii. 23. [q] 2 Pet. i. 4.
[r] Jer. ii. 3. [s] Deut. xxvi. 19.

children as are remarkable for beauty. 3dly, What more desirable, also, than a *conjugal relation* to the First-begotten Son of God, who is " white and ruddy, the chiefest among ten thousands !"[t] Nothing can even be conceived, more delightful, more enriching, or more glorious. 4thly, Nothing, in fine, can be more excellent than that inheritance, which the sons of God obtain in right of their adoption, and which is assigned them by an irrevocable testament.

XXVII. It will not be unprofitable to prosecute this topic a little further; and, opening our Father's TESTAMENT, to inquire WHAT and HOW GREAT are the *Blessings* bequeathed, and under what STIPULATIONS, he has bequeathed them to us. By the TESTAMENT, we understand, *The last and immutable will of God, recorded in the sacred Scriptures, and confirmed by the death and blood of Jesus, by which he hath declared his chosen and believing people, heirs of the whole inheritance.*

XXVIII. The Testament is *the Will of God*, or that " counsel of his will,"[u] by which he has appointed both the inheritance and the heirs, and to which our Lord referred, when he said, " It is your Father's good pleasure to give you the kingdom."[v] I add, that it is *the last and irrevocable will* of the Father; for as this is is essential to a valid testament among men,[w] so it is not wanting to this testament. " Wherein God, wil-" ling more abundantly to shew unto the heirs of pro-" mise the immutability of his counsel, confirmed it by " an oath, that by two immutable things, in which it " was impossible for God to lie, we might have a strong

---

[t] Song v. 10.   [u] Ephes. i. 11.
[v] Luke xii. 32.   [w] Gal. iii. 15.

" consolation."ˣ   In this Will, he has assigned the inheritance as well of grace as of glory, of which we shall speak immediately.   He has also appointed the heirs, —not indefinitely, all that shall believe ; but these and the other persons particularly, whose " names are writ- " ten in heaven,"ʸ and " graven upon the palms of God's " hands."ᶻ   This his Will, he has expressed in both parts of the holy Scriptures, which are, therefore, called a Testament.ᵃ   In fine, that this Will might in no respect be defective, the whole is confirmed and sealed by the blood and death of the Lord Jesus.ᵇ

xxix. To understand this, we must observe, that God the Father, did, by testament, intrust his Son Jesus with this honour, that he should be the head of the elect, to excel them in glory, and to possess authority to impart to them, all his blessings.ᶜ   Jesus, again, by the power committed to him by the Father, bequeathes his benefits by testament, to the elect, that they may be joint-partakers of them with himself.   " I appoint " to you (by testament) a kingdom, as my Father hath " (by testament) appointed unto me."ᵈ   This making of the Testament, then, is originally the doing of the Father, but immediately of Christ the Mediator; who died, not to make void the inheritance by his death, for he is " alive for evermore,"ᵉ but to seal the promises, and to acquire for his people a right to the inheritance.⁴² Hence the blood which he shed, is called " the blood of the testament."ᶠ

ˣ Heb. vi. 17, 18.   ʸ Luke x. 20.

ᶻ Is. xlix. 16.   ᵃ 2 Cor. iii. 14.

ᵇ Heb. ix. 16, 17.   ᶜ Ps. ii. 8.

ᵈ Κἀγὼ διατίθεμαι ὑμῖν, καθὼς διέθετό μοί ὁ πατὴρ μѣ, βασιλείαν. Luke xxii. 29.

ᵉ Rev. i. 18.   ᶠ Zech. ix. 11.   Mat. xxvi. 28.

⁴² See NOTE XLII.

xxx. The BLESSINGS bequeathed in the Testament, are inestimable. We reduce them at present to three principal heads. The *first* is THE POSSESSION OF THE WHOLE WORLD; for it was promised to Abraham and his seed, that they " should be heirs of the world."[g] On these words, we may hear the commentary of *Ludovicus de Dieu:* " As sin, by separating us " from God and subjecting us to his curse, rendered us " exiles and outcasts, so that we had no spiritual right " or dominion, corresponding to the character of the " sons of God, over even the meanest of the creatures; " so, when God becomes our God and we become his " blessed people, we are restored, as sons, to the right " and dominion of the whole paternal inheritance: " And, since there is nothing besides God and the " world, we are made heirs of the world, both the " earthly and the heavenly, the present and the future. " Hence it is said, *All things are yours;*[h] and, amongst " these all things, are mentioned,[i] *the world,* and what- " ever is in it, *things present and things to come.*"

xxxi. This possession of the world, we may observe, consists in the following things. 1st, Every son of God possesses as much of the good things of this world as the wisdom of our heavenly Father judges sufficient for the support of the animal life, without exposing the spiritual to detriment; and so possesses, that, in the enjoyment of it, he may taste the love of his Father, who confers it upon him as a pledge of better blessings, and of his Elder Brother, who himself became poor, that his people might be rich.[j] This love of God the Father and of Christ, added to the smallest crumb of

----

[g] Rom. iv. 13.   [h] 1 Cor. iii. 21.
[i] Verse 22.   [j] 2 Cor. viii. 9.

bread or drop of cold water, renders them, beyond measure, preferable to all the most exquisite luxuries of the
rich of this world. " A little that a righteous man
hath, is better than the riches of many wicked."[k] 2dly,
All the creatures must serve the children of God as
steps by which they may ascend to the Creator. In all
of them, as in a bright mirror, they contemplate his
adorable perfections,[l] and thus find cause of exultation
and delight.[m] They perceive in them, in particular,
the love of God towards themselves. When they behold the sun, the moon, and the stars, they rejoice that
their Father hath lighted up so many luminaries for
them, of which they may avail themselves in performing works which become them as the sons of God. Nor
do they survey this display of his goodness with less
admiration, than if every individual had his own sun,
or his own moon, shining upon him.[n] They do not exceed the bounds of propriety, when they even entertain
the thought, that, for their sake, the world still remains
in its present state, and that for this the wicked are indebted to them ; for " the holy seed is the substance"
(the support) of the world.[o] 3dly, All the creatures,
and the whole administration of God towards them,
" work together for their good."[p] This holds so extensively, that angels in heaven and devils in hell, are
both obliged to bear a part in the service. As to angels
in heaven, " Are they not all ministering spirits, sent
" forth to minister for them, who shall be heirs of sal-
" vation ?"[q] As to the infernal spirit, the great teacher
of arrogance, was he not, when aiming at a very differ-

[k] Ps. xxxvii. 16.   [l] Ps. civ. 24.
[m] Ps. xcii. 4, 5.   [n] Ps. viii. 3, 4.
[o] Is. vi. 13.   [p] Rom. viii. 28.
[q] Πνεύματα λειτουργικα. Heb. i. 14. Ps. xxxiv. 7. xci. 11.

ent object, compelled, in spite of himself—by his buf-
fetings to teach Paul humility?[r] 4thly, If this world,
which, by reason of sin, is subjected to vanity, cannot
suffice them, God will from its ashes, after its destruction, form another, and make " a new heaven and a new
earth, wherein dwelleth righteousness."[s] Each of these
ideas may be included in the general promise of the inheritance of the world.[43]

XXXII. The *second* blessing of this testament, is A
SPIRITUAL KINGDOM. " I appoint unto you," says
Christ, " a kingdom."[t] To this kingdom, even such
of the children of God as are, in other respects, in the
humblest condition, the poor, and servants, and hand-
maids, are called. " Hath not God chosen the poor of
" this world" to become " rich in faith, and heirs of
" the kingdom, which he hath promised to them that
" love him."[u] To this belong, 1. The excellency of the
sons of God, by which they surpass all other men.[v]
2. Victory over sin and the unruly lusts of the flesh, to
which even kings and dreaded tyrants are enslaved.[w]
3. The treading of the devil under their feet.[x] 4. Triumph over a whole conquered world, in spite of whose
rage they shall be eternally saved.[y] 5. Inestimable
riches of spiritual gifts;[z] even in the midst of poverty.[a]
6. A holy peace of mind, and joy in the Holy Ghost.[b]
All these privileges are begun here in grace, and consummated hereafter in glory.

[r] 2 Cor. xii. 7.   [s] 2 Pet. iii. 13.
[t] Luke xxii. 29.   [u] James ii. 5.
[v] Prov. xii. 26.   [w] Rom. vi. 14, 18.
[x] Rom. xvi. 20.   [y] 1 John v. 4.
[z] Ps. xlv. 12.   [a] Rev. ii. 9.
[b] Rom. xiv. 17.
[43] See NOTE XLIII.

xxxiii. The *third* benefit is GOD himself. Hence says the Apostle, - - - " heirs of God."c Here, the inheritance is mutual. Believers are God's portion, and God is their portion, as these are made reciprocal by the Prophet : " The portion of Jacob is not like them ; " for he is the Former of all things ; and Israel is the " rod (the tribe) of his inheritance."d In this possession of God, his children find, 1st, Protection against every evil. " I will say of the Lord, He is my refuge, and my fortress." Why? He is " MY GOD, in him will I trust."e 2dly, The communication of every good.f For, 1. All that infinitude of perfections which is in God himself, will appear glorious and admirable in the sons of God, and will impart itself to them, that they may enjoy it for their consummate felicity. And what can the soul desire, beyond this infinite Portion ?g 2. What will not God give those, to whom he gives himself ?h

xxxiv. In this testament, if it is considered in its whole extent, with all its promises, there are no STIPULATIONS properly so called ; for it consists of absolute and unmixed promises, suspended upon no condition to be performed by our own strength. Yet the divine wisdom and care have so adjusted all things in it, that a certain and a wise connexion is established amongst them, and the improvement of the blessings promised first in order, paves the way for the possession of further benefits. We have elsewhere treated of this at large.[44]

---

c Rom. viii. 17.   d Jer. x. 16.

e Ps. xci. 2.   See Ps. xxvii. 1, 2.   Is. xliii. 2, 3.

f Ps. xxxvi. 8.   g Ps. lxxiii. 25.

h 1 Cor. iii. 22, 23.

[44] See NOTE XLIV.

xxxv. In the same books, therefore, in which the Testament is contained, God has enjoined every one that would take comfort from the promised inheritance, 1st, To love, search, meditate upon, and lay up in his heart, as no contemptible part of his inheritance, those writings which exhibit the Testament.[i] He must esteem them more than his necessary food.[j] 2dly, To value highly, as it deserves, the promised inheritance. 1. To hunger and thirst after it, and to be satisfied with nothing short of it.[k] 2. To consider all other things, in comparison of it, loss and dung;[l] and to be prepared, cheerfully to sell all that he hath, in order to obtain the pearl of inestimable worth.[m] 3. To glorify God for his great goodness.[n] 4. To keep, with care and diligence, what he has already received.[o] 3dly, To walk as becomes his present happy state, and the hope of so glorious an inheritance.[p] 4thly, To be ready to impart to his brethren what he has received from his Father, both in things temporal and spiritual;[q] and to exert his endeavours that others may be brought to possess the same inheritance with himself.[r] The individual sustains no loss, but rather derives an accession of happiness, from the numbers of his fellow-heirs; for the abundance of love serves wonderfully to heighten the joy.

xxxvi. It remains to be observed, that if, in a matter of so great importance, we would not impose upon ourselves by flattering imaginations, it is necessary carefully to examine ourselves, by those distinguish-

---

[i] Deut. xxxiii. 4. vi. 6.

[j] Job xxiii. 12.

[k] Mat. v. 6.

[l] Phil. iii. 8.

[m] Mat. xiii. 46.

[n] Ps. xxxi. 19.

[o] Rev. ii. 25. iii. 11.

[p] 1 Thes. ii. 12. 1 John iii. 3.

[q] Rom. xii. 13.

[r] Acts xxvi. 29.

ing characters of the children of God which the Scriptures supply. The chief of these are the following. 1st, The impression and expression of the Divine image, with a holy conformity to our Father. What is more natural than for a son to resemble his Father? The natural Son of God is " the brightness of the Fa- " ther's glory;" and it is fit that we, in our order and measure, should be so too. As corrupt Adam " begat " a son in his own likeness, after his own image;"[s] so God forms his children in his own likeness, " in righte- " ousness and true holiness."[t] This resemblance to God is gradually promoted by familiar intercourse with him, until, having obtained " the adoption, to wit, the re- " demption of our body," of which the Apostle speaks,[u] we shall become perfectly like him.[v]

XXXVII. 2dly, A new life, which is worthy of God, and the effect of the Spirit of adoption, who is the Spirit of life.[w] The life of creatures never fails to correspond to their spirit. The natural man has not a nobler spirit, nor a more excellent principle of life than his soul (*anima*); and consequently he lives merely an *animal* life. But as the children of God are endowed with a " free Spirit,"[x] who is also the Spirit of Christ;[y] so they, in their measure, live such a life as Christ lived, exerting their utmost efforts to copy after his example and pattern. " Be ye followers of God," says the Apostle, " as dear children."[z]

XXXVIII. 3dly, A true and sincere love to God. Nature itself teaches this; for what genuine son doth not

---

[s] Gen. v. 3.
[u] Rom. viii. 23.
[w] Rom. viii. 2.
[y] Gal. iv. 6.

[t] Ephes. iv. 24.
[v] 1 John iii. 2.
[x] Ps. li. 12.
[z] Ephes. v. 1.

love his father? This is not only a written law, but
born with us. Now this love to God arises, partly,
from the consideration of his infinitely amiable perfections, which his children are admitted familiarly to
contemplate, " their eyes seeing the King in his beauty ;"[a] partly from the beams of Divine love continually
shed forth upon them, by which they cannot fail to be
inflamed.[b] Whenever they attentively reflect upon this
love, they consider the whole capacity of their soul as
too limited to render adequate returns of love.

XXXIX. 4thly, Filial reverence and obedience.[c] This
arises from that love of which we have just spoken.
This love forbids a man to do any thing displeasing to
God, and inspires him with so ardent a zeal for his
glory, that he cannot, without anguish, see his honour
infringed by others.[d] It disposes him also to discharge,
with promptitude and alacrity, all the duties of religion.[e] Further, it does not suffer a man to be at ease,
if perhaps, by an inconsiderate action, he has offended
God, and forfeited those gracious smiles of his face
with which he was formerly cheered; it constrains him
at last to prostrate himself, with the profoundest reverence, at the feet of his heavenly Father, with sorrow
and tears to implore the pardon of his offences, and
to promise greater circumspection in his future conduct.[f] [45]

XL. 5thly, Undissembled brotherly love, which he
bears for all those in whom he perceives the Divine
image, and a participation of the same grace with himself. Whilst other evidences are often imperceptible,

[a] Is. xxxiii. 17. Ps. lxiii. 2.　　　[b] 1 John iv. 19.
[c] Mal. i. 6. 1 Pet. i. 17.　　　[d] Ps. xlii. 3, 10.
[e] John xiv. 21.　　　[f] Luke vii. 38.
[45] See NOTE XLV.

this brotherly love furnishes the doubting soul with a comfortable mark of its state.[g] It is impossible for the love of the brethren, to be separated from the love of God. Whoever loves the original, will also love the copy. Whoever loves God, will love him who belongs to God, in whom he discerns the excellencies of God, and whom he believes to be beloved of God.[h] Happy the man whose spirit bears witness with the Spirit of God, that these distinguishing characters of God's children, are found in himself.

[g] 1 John iii. 14.   [h] 1 John iv. 20.

DISSERTATION VIII.

ON THE CREATION.

I. THE work ascribed in the Creed to the Father is that of CREATION; on which we now proceed, concisely, to discourse. Let us begin with explaining the word. What the Latins call *Creare*, the Hebrews express by the term ברא (*bara ;*) which signifies, to produce some new thing, solely, by one's will and command, or nobly to effect and accomplish something by a surprising energy. Thus Moses says, " If the Lord " make a new thing,"[a] that is, produce a strange thing by his powerful word, causing the earth to open her mouth: and, likewise, Jeremiah, " The Lord hath cre- " ated a new thing in the earth,"[b] that is, hath commanded a thing to exist, nothing equal, or similar, to which was ever beheld.

II. We are not, however, to imagine, that the word ברא does uniformly, or by its own proper power, denote the production of a creature out of nothing. It is applied to those works which are expressly recorded to have been formed, during the first six days, from pre-

[a] בריאה יברא Num. xvi. 30.
[b] ברא יהוה חדשה בארץ Jer. xxxi. 22.

existent matter.[c] Though men are the offspring of their parents, too, by natural generation, God is deno-minated the *Creator*[d] of every man; and this not mere-ly with regard to the soul, which, indeed, he creates out of nothing, but with regard to the whole person, which owes its existence to his good pleasure, and is " fear-" fully and wonderfully made."[e] In like manner, it is said in the Psalms, " The people who shall be created " shall praise the Lord;"[f] and in Ezekiel, " I will " judge thee in the place where thou wast created, in " the land of thy nativity."[g]

III. Besides, no one doubts, I suppose, that the new heavens and the new earth, for which, according to the promise of the Supreme Being, we look, are to be con-structed out of the rubbish and ashes of the world which now exists. Yet God says of them, " Behold, I create " new heavens, and a new earth."[h]

IV. There is even a passage, where things which exist already, are said to be created, when new vi-gour is infused into them : " Thou sendest forth thy " Spirit, they are created; and thou renewest the face " of the earth."[i] From these instances it appears, that the word ברא is sometimes used in relation to things, which are, by no means, made out of nothing, and yet are so far created, that, by the will and command of God, they pass, in a certain respect, from a state of non-existence to a state of existence.*

---

* מאין ליש, as *Kimchi* speaks.

[c] Gen. i. 21, 27.   [d] בורא Eccles. xii. 1.

[e] נוראות נפלא Ps. cxxxix. 14.

[f] עם נברא יהלל יה Ps. cii. 18.

[g] נבראת Ezek. xxi. 30.

[h] הנני בורא Is. lxv. 17.

[i] תשלח רוחך יבראון Ps. civ. 30.

v. Correspondent to the Hebrew ברא, is the Greek verb κτιζω; whence κτισις, *creation,*[j] is derived; that is, an act which gives existence to a creature. But this word is also of extensive application, and signifies the producing of things in any way; as appears from the definition of *Hesychius,*[*] and from the Apostle Peter's denominating a magistrate divinely appointed for regulating the affairs of men, " an ordinance (a crea-" ture) of man."[k]

vi. The *Seventy Interpreters,* also, have not scrupled to make use of this term in reference to the supreme Wisdom, and as our Divines are accustomed to explain it, in reference to the generation of the Word.[l] The Chaldee Paraphrast, likewise, on the same passage, employs the word ברא. Some, too, derive from this Hebrew verb the noun בר, *a son;* the Latin word *parere,* (to beget;) and the Dutch word *baren.*[†] But, as these words have now a different signification in the schools of theology, I deem it neither prudent nor safe, whilst the heretics discover so much perverseness, for any Divine to imitate that phrase, when discoursing of the Only-begotten Son of God, by calling him *Created,*[‡] in whatever sense the expression be used.

vii. It may be added, that the Latin verb *creare,* in like manner, does not signify, precisely, what we now usually intend by this term. It may even admit of a doubt whether the ancient Romans ever recognised this signification. With them *creare* is *gignere,* (*to be-*

---

[*] Κτίσαι est 'ιδρυσαι, 'οικησαι, αρξασθαι. Κτισμα, ποιημα, 'οικοδομημα.

[†] The Scottish word *bairn,* (a child,) may, with equal probability, be traced to the same Hebrew origin. T.

[‡] נברא, κτισθεις, *creatus.*

[j] 2 Pet. iii. 4. Mark x. 6.

[k] 'Ανθρωπινην κτίσιν. 1 Pet. ii. 13.   [l] Prov. viii. 22.

get ;) *to make* in any manner ;† or even *to appoint to any dignity,* in which sense Consuls, Generals, and Magistrates are said *creari, to be created.*

VIII. Although it appears, then, that as well in sacred as in common use, the signification of these words is very vague and indeterminate ; yet, because that mode of creation by which something is produced out of nothing is the most excellent and wonderful, it is usual in theological discourses, for an act of this sort to be strictly called *Creation,* and to be distinguished from *generation,* and other modes of producing.

IX. To pass, therefore, from an examination of the word to the illustration of the subject ; CREATION IS THAT ACT OF GOD, IN WHICH, BY THE ALL-POWERFUL COMMAND OF HIS WILL, HE MADE OUT OF NOTHING, AND PERFECTED, THE WHOLE UNIVERSE, IN THE SPACE OF SIX DAYS.

X. Before the Creation, nothing at all existed, excepting God :—No world such as this we now behold, which some have falsely supposed to have been co-eternal with God :—No shapeless matter, from which, by means of motion, other substances were formed by some imaginary Mind ; according to the expression of *Anaxagoras* in *Laertius,* " All things existed in one irre-" gular mass ; then Mind came, and reduced them to " order :"‡—In fine, no spirits distinct from God, as, in opposition to Scripture, the adversaries of the eternal Divinity of Christ contend—But absolutely nothing.

---

* As in *Virgil, Sulmone creatos,* begotten, or born, at *Sulmo :* and in *Horace, Fortes creantur fortibus ;* The brave are begotten by the brave.

† *Ennius* accordingly says, *Dicitur Vesta hanc urbem creavisse ;* Vesta is reported to have created, that is, founded, this city.

‡ Πάντα χρήματα 'ην 'ομɛ͂· ɛιτα νοῦς ɛλθων, αυτα διɛκόσμησɛ.

XI. Satisfied with himself, with his own infinite perfections, and with the most ample knowledge, love, and enjoyment of those perfections, God found in himself the most consummate happiness, and happiness becoming his character; for which reason the Apostle Paul calls him, " the Blessed."[m]   It pleased him, however, to display his attributes in certain works that are *without himself*,* the form and image of which he had most wisely delineated in his mind from eternity. And since he needed no assistance from any, as nothing exists or even can exist independently of him, he commanded all things that are, to rise out of nothing, by the mere act of his sovereign will. " He hath made the earth by his power; he hath established the world by his wisdom; and hath stretched out the heavens by his discretion.[n]

XII. While Reason, particularly as now vitiated by sin, and disposed to raise its clamorous voice against God, dictates these truths somewhat obscurely; Faith, relying on the Divine testimony, embraces them without hesitation. " Through faith, we understand that " the worlds were framed by the word of God, so that " things which are seen were not made of things which " do appear."[o]

XIII. By the expression τους 'αιωνας, the Apostle means the same thing that the Hebrew Doctors intend by עולמים, to wit, *ages*, or *worlds*. He uses the plural number, because they distinguished betwixt three worlds; the *lowest*, which is the residence of plants, animals, and men; the *middle*, which is the

* *Extra se.*

[m] Ὁ μακαριος. 1 Tim. vi. 15.   [n] Jer. x. 12.

[o] Πιστει νοῦμεν κατηρτίσθαι τὰς αἰῶνας ῥήματι Θεῦ, 'εἰς τὸ μὴ ἐκ φαινομένων τα βλεπόμενα γεγονέναι. Heb. xi. 3.

region of the stars; and the *highest*, which is the habitation of angels, and blessed spirits.[46]

xiv. In these worlds, there is a *framing*,* a skilful arrangement of the parts, and an adaptation of every thing to purposes suitable to itself, and to the whole system. Whatever attention human reason may give to these matters, it is excited by faith to mark them more carefully, and to perceive them more distinctly. But faith supplies us, also, with further light and instruction, whether you consider the beautiful order and arrangement observed in the work of creation, which we learn only from Moses; or attend to the symmetry that is still discernible in the world, in which our carnal reason, from its arrogance and pretended wisdom, would presume to detect a variety of blemishes, were it not restrained by faith.

xv. This order and symmetry, thus recognised by faith, leads us to God, by whose *word*, that is, by whose command, the worlds were made; and so made that " the things which are seen,"† that is, the things which exist,‡ were made, μὴ εκ φαινομενων, " not of things which do appear." This expression is employed, by an *anastrophe*,§ which was made use of principally by the Hellenists, instead of ἐκ μη φαινομενων, *of things which do not appear*. The meaning is, as *Chrysostome* judiciously remarks, " the things which exist were made of things not existing."‖

---

* Καταρτισμὸς.   † Τα βλεπὸμενα.

‡ The Hebrews, whom the Apostle imitates, call such things הנמצאות, τα ἑυρισκόμενα, *the things which are found*.

§ An *anastrophe* is " a figure, whereby words which should have " been precedent, are postponed." T.

‖ Τα ὄντα ἐξ 'ουκ ὄντων.

46 See Note XLVI.

XVI. The word φαινεσθαι signifies originally, *to be brought forth into light;* and thence, simply, *to exist:* as when we read, "It was never so seen," it never so *appeared,* "in Israel."[p] The multitude, who uttered these words, by no means intended that similar works had, in reality, been done in Israel, though they had not appeared; but simply, that nothing similar had ever happened. "Things that do appear,"* are things actually existing, which stand in no need of the Divine call to cause them to be, or to appear. "Things which do not appear,"† are nothing,—"things not existing,"‡ which indispensably require to be called into existence by the power of God, before they can appear. Rom. iv. 17.

XVII. *Schlichtingius,* an erroneous interpreter, perverting, as usual, the sense of the Apostle, affirms that *the things which do not appear,* are those elements of things which were in a state of confusion at the beginning of the world. He infers from these words of the Apostle, what, he contends, is apparent also from the history of the creation of the world as recorded by Moses; that God, when he made this world, or when he began the creation described at the beginning of Genesis, did not make it absolutely of nothing, but of that mass which was without form, and covered with darkness. He quotes, too, this expression used by the writer of the book of WISDOM,[q] ἐξ 'αμορφου ὑλης, "of matter without form;" which the Latin Translator renders *ex materia invisa,* "of unseen matter." He affirms, at the same time, that no mention is made in holy writ of the creation of this matter. *Volkelius* reasons at

* Φαινομενα. † Μη φαινόμενα.

‡ Τα μη 'όντα.

p Mat. ix. 33. q Ch. xi. 17.

great length in the same absurd style,* and adds this observation; that in the Greek Version of the Old Testament, which the New Testament writers generally follow, the earth is called *invisible*† in that passage, where, in the Hebrew, it is denominated *void*.

xviii. The design for which these remarks are brought forward, is to make us believe that something besides God existed before the creation of the world, and to weaken the force of that argument in support of the true Deity of Christ, which our Divines are accustomed to derive from his existing before the world;—which, according to the language of Scripture, denotes eternity.

xix. But the heretics miss their aim; for the Mosaic history expressly declares, that God made that earth which was " without form and void,"‡ and covered with thick darkness. The words run thus : " In the " beginning God created the heaven and the earth. " And the earth was without form and void." The obvious meaning is, that *the earth*§ which God created was then, when first made, a mass without form and void. It was not, therefore, created out of a shapeless mass. Whence then was it created ? What remains but—nothing ?

xx. If they urge, that the first verse contains a summary of the whole work, and that, in the subsequent verses, it is particularly shown whence all other things were created; we answer, that, even allowing the first part of this assertion to be true, it was far from the intention of Moses to intimate that what in the first verse he calls " the heaven and the earth," was formed of that matter which in the second verse he calls the earth

---

* *De Vera Relig.* lib. ii. cap. 4.

† ᾿Αόρατος. ‡ תהו ובהו׃

§ הארץ with the demonstrative particle ה.

" without form and void." But, after he had comprehended all things under the denomination of the heaven and the earth, saying nothing further with regard to the highest heaven, in which God has prepared his throne, he shows, in the following verses, what was the state of the earth when it first proceeded from the hand of God, and in what manner and order all other things were formed out of it. *Vatablus,* to whom *Volkelius* appeals in this cause, expresses himself in the following terms: " You may clearly understand it thus;
" In the beginning, when God created the heaven and
" the earth, the earth was then without form, &c. By
" the heaven he intends the celestial bodies, and by the
" earth, the terrestrial. He sets forth, at first, the
" whole universe, that its Author may be known,—
" that it may be understood, both that the world did not
" exist from eternity, and also that God created some-
" thing out of nothing." Do writers who express themselves in such terms as these, agree with the heretics ?

xxi. It is not necessary for us, besides, to admit that the first verse briefly comprehends all those works which are afterwards particularly detailed. The opinion of *David Kimchi,* in which a great number of Divines both ancient and modern acquiesce, appears to me to be highly probable. He considers the order of the creation as here propounded by Moses in this manner: That, first of all, God created the heaven, that is, the highest heaven with the angels; then the earth, the first appearance and condition of which are described in the second verse, and out of which other creatures were subsequently formed. And it is called " without form and void," in opposition to heaven, which was immediately carried to its full perfection, and replenished with inhabitants.

XXII. Moses, indeed, mentions that the earth was at first covered with water, and involved in thick darkness; and the Greek Interpreters, failing to express properly the sense of the Hebrew term, have called it "invisible."[*] It cannot, however, be proved from any resemblance betwixt the expressions, which are considerably dissimilar, that the Apostle alluded to this passage. " The things which do not appear,"[†] mentioned by Paul, and " the invisible earth,"[‡] mentioned by the Greek Interpreters, are, in reality, quite different from each other. When Paul speaks of " the things which do not appear," he refers to the *state of things prior to the creation.*[§] " The invisible earth," on the contrary, does not signify a mass existing before the creation, but the second part of the universe, which, as well as the heaven, was created on the first day. Those who wrest these expressions to any other meaning, offer manifest violence, not only to the Mosaic history, but also to the whole tenor of Scripture. We have now spoken of the former; let us proceed to the latter.

XXIII. If this pretended matter of which the world was made, existed previously, I ask, was it previously made of nothing by God, or was it really self-existent, and co-eternal with God? The one or the other of these is unavoidable; but both are contrary to holy writ.

XXIV. The matter in question, was not made before the creation of which Moses gives an account: for the Mosaic creation took place " in the beginning;"[||] and the beginning of something else prior to this universal beginning cannot be alleged, without contradicting the sacred historian. The Scripture, too, makes the pre-

---

[*] 'Αόρατος.   [†] Τα μη Φαινομενα.

[‡] Γῆ ἀόρατος.   [§] *Creationis terminus a quo.*

[||] בראשׁית:

eminence of the Supreme Being above all others, to consist in this, that he existed " before the mountains were " brought forth, ere ever the earth and the world were " formed;"[r] and God himself urges this as a proof of his Deity; " Yea, before the day was, I am he."[s]   In short, whatever existed *before the beginning, ere ever the earth was,* existed before all time—according to the phraseology of Scripture, was ETERNAL—was *before the works of God*—and could not have been made.

xxv. Besides, whoever denies that this matter was made, is not afraid to contradict the four-and-twenty Elders in heaven, who thus address themselves to God in their song of praise: THOU HAST CREATED ALL THINGS.[u] Nor does he scruple to contradict the Apostles John and Paul, who teach the same doctrine in John i. 3. Col. i. 16.—passages which, in defiance of truth, are applied by the heretics to the new creation of things by the Gospel. If these declarations of the Elders and Apostles are certain, as unquestionably they are, it is also certain, that this original matter of the world is either a mere figment, and indeed absolutely nothing, or that it was created by God.

xxvi. Further, if this matter both existed from eternity, and existed of itself, and thus was indebted to God for nothing it possessed, what right had God to it ? or what title had he, to fashion it according to his pleasure ? *Basil* says, " If it was, in reality, uncreated, it " must be esteemed worthy of the same honours with " God."* Our adversaries, on other occasions, contend that every right of God in relation to the creatures arises either from a favour conferred by him upon them,

---

* *Hexaem.* Hom. ii.

[r] Ps. xc. 2.   [s] Is. xliii. 13.
[t] Prov. viii. 22, 23.   [u] Rev. iv. 11.

or from an offence committed on their part against God. According to the hypothesis, the first has no place here; of the last, brute matter is totally incapable.

Add to this, that it can hardly be conceived how the Creator took possession of that which might be considered not only equal, but in some respects superior to God. It was at least a thing of which he stood in need, and which supplied him with materials and facilities for his operations, and thus was greater than God who needed it; while this supposed matter stood in no need of him, or at least received nothing from him. But every one is dependent on him, whose assistance he needs to make use of; and every one, by employing what pertains to another, is inferior to him of whose property he avails himself. As the eloquent *Vogel-sangius* has acutely observed,* matter must have conferred a truly signal favour upon God, in furnishing him with the means, by which he might, to this day, be known, and acknowledged as Omnipotent. See an excellent discussion of this controversy by *Dionysius*, in *Eusebius*;† and another, in the same historian, by *Origen*, who refutes at large that exposition which the Socinians have thought proper to adopt.

XXVII. Nor shall the heretics elude the force of this argument, by a counterfeit modesty, whilst they pretend that because sacred writ is silent with regard to the creation of this matter, they also determine nothing. Though they should not presume to determine this point, one of two suppositions is true; the matter in question was either created before the Mosaic beginning, or it was not. There is no room for a third hy-

* *Disput. Physica de Mundo,* sect. viii.

† *De Præp. Evan.* lib. vii. cap. penultimo: περι τȣ μη αγεννητον ειναι την ὑλην.

pothesis. But we have shown the falsehood of both these suppositions.

xxviii. The passage of Paul, which we are now considering, ought not to be compared with WISDOM xi. 17. but rather with 2 MACCAB. vii. 28, where the pious mother animating her son to suffer martyrdom, charges him to look upon the heaven and the earth, and all that is in them, and *to consider that God made them of things that were not.** This has been observed even by *Grotius,* for whom *Schlichtingius,* (according to the testimony of *Lubieniecius,* in his preface prefixed to his Posthumous Commentaries,) entertained the highest esteem, and of whom he was wont to say, " that " the Christian world had waited for the appearance of " such a man, for more than fifteen centuries from the " days of the Apostles."

xxix. *Volkelius* objects that, in this passage of the Maccabees, the author intends *a privative nothing,* or matter destitute of that form which was to be superinduced: because what is affirmed of all other things, is here asserted concerning man in particular, that he was made of nothing; whereas, while it is certain with regard to several other creatures, it is peculiarly manifest with respect to man, that he was formed of the earth. But this exception has no weight. For, when that pious woman, in conformity with the sentiments of the Catholic Church, says, that all things, and mankind among the rest, were created of nothing, she refers to the first and universal origin of things; which were brought, not from a *privative nothing,* but from *nothing* in a *negative* and absolute sense. Although, when you consider every thing in detail, some are im-

---

* Γνῶναι ὅτι ἐκ 'ἐξ 'ὄντων 'ἐποίησεν αὐτὰ 'ὁ Θεός.

mediately, and others mediately, from nothing; yet ultimately, all things are made of nothing.

xxx. We might dismiss the expression adduced from the book entitled the WISDOM OF SOLOMON xi. 17,* with a short answer, by saying, that that author is not authentic either with us, or in the estimation of our adversaries; and that if he had imbibed this error from the dregs of heathen philosophy, it would have been proper to refute him from writers of undoubted credit, not to obtrude him as a sound interpreter of Moses or Paul.

xxxi. Yet I can scarcely bring myself to believe, that he held that opinion which the heretics impute to him. When he says that the almighty hand of God created the world of matter without form, he seems to speak not of the very first commencement of all things, but of the creation of terrestrial things of that matter which in GEN. i. 2, Moses takes notice of as made by God: For, in the ordinary language of men, the earth, with the things which it contains, is commonly called the world, in contradistinction to heaven. That the earth was, in reality, formed out of that shapeless or confused matter, is evident. That God created this matter, too, this writer by no means denies. He affirms, on the contrary, that " all things" were made by his word; v and, in this very chapter, he intimates, that nothing could exist " which was not called by God."w This must be true, also, with regard to the " matter without " form," of whatever sort it is.

---

* The entire verse from which the expression is quoted, is as follows: " For thy almighty hand, that made the world of *matter* " *without form,* wanted not means to send among them a multitude " of bears, or fierce lions." T.

v Chap. ix. 1. w Τὸ μὴ κληθὲν ὑπὸ τῦ Θεῦ, ver. 25.

xxxii. But, according to the testimony of *Jerome*, it is affirmed by several ancient writers, that this pretended *Solomon* was *Philo* the Jew, who was called *Moses Atticissans;** and were this certain, we could nowhere collect the meaning of this verse, more decisively than from *Philo*. Now this writer, in his book *on the Making of the World*,† expresses sentiments widely different from, the hypotheses of the heretics.

xxxiii. Not far from the beginning of the treatise, he has the following words : " But the great Moses was " of opinion, that what is uncreated, differs extremely " from what is visible; for whatever is sensible, being " capable of generation and liable to changes, never " continues in the same state. To that which is in- " visible, therefore, and perceptible only by the mind, " he attributes eternity, as allied and congenial to it; " whilst he applies generation as a proper term for dis- " tinguishing the objects of sense."

xxxiv. On these words, let it be remarked, 1st, That, conformably to the doctrine of Moses, *Philo* ascribes eternity, solely, to an invisible nature, which is perceived by none of the senses, but only by the mind, that is, to God. He does not, therefore, ascribe it to any original matter;—which no man, possessing the use of his reason, ever affirmed to be perceptible to the mind only, and not to the senses. 2dly, That he asserts that none of those things which are subject to change or alteration can be uncreated. But shapeless matter is, unquestionably, a substance of this sort. 3dly, To obviate a cavil which some might draw from the word, it may be added, that in *Philo*, as also in Moses,[x] *generation*

---

* That is, Moses imitating the language of Athens.   T.

† *De Opificio mundi.*

[x] Gen. ii. 4.

signifies the same thing which we commonly express by the term *creation*.

xxxv. When, therefore, he said a little before; " that " in reference to things that exist, it is indispensibly " necessary, that there be both an active cause, and " something affected by the cause ;" he did not intend by " something affected by the cause," matter that existed before the creation, but matter which was formed by the creating God. This is clear from the words which follow; " There is no connexion between what is not " made, and him who did not make it."

xxxvi. The ancient nation of the Jews were evidently of the same mind. The great *Rabbi Eliezer*, accordingly, says; " Before the Almighty created the " world, he and his name existed alone." See *Manasseh Ben Israel on the Creation ;** who shows that this opinion was received and approved by all the wise men of ancient times. As to the conceits which other Doctors advance about the making of another world before the present one, or the creation of many things before the world, they are cabalistical, mystical, and allegorical. Such also are the expressions of *R. Eliezer*, when he tells us, that heaven was made of the brightness of God's garment, and the earth of the snow which is under the throne of his glory. *Maimonides* affirms, that these assertions are so strange and marvellous, that he does not recollect to have seen the like, in the writings of any of those who observe the Jewish law.†

xxxvii. It is necessary, mean while, to maintain the distinction suggested above. If we consider the first origin of things, all of them were created of nothing. Some, however, were made immediately of nothing, as.

* *De Creatione*, Probl. iii.
† *More*, Part ii. cap. 27.

the first works of the first day, and all spiritual substances: others, mediately, as the works of the subsequent days, which indeed were made of matter; but of
matter that in itself was ill adapted to the purpose,
that bore no resemblance to the things produced from
it, and from which no such creatures could have been
produced by any natural energy.

xxxviii. This production of things was effected by
the mere will and command of God, by his *all-powerful will*,* as *Clement* of *Alexandria* expressed it; or,
which is the same thing, by his word, or fiat. "God said,
" Let there be light, and there was light."y "He spake,
" and it was done; he commanded, and it stood fast."z
" Thou hast created all things, and FOR THY PLEA-
" SURE they are, and were created."a The creatures
existed merely because God willed them to exist, without further effort, without laborious exertion. "The
" creation of the world," says the same *Clement*, "is
" the effect of his counsel alone:" and *Philo* agrees
with him, saying, "It seems reasonable to think, that
" in the works which he performs, God exercises not
" only power and authority, but also wisdom and intel-
" ligence."

xxxix. It is still more remarkable, that *Maximus
Tyrius*, a rural philosopher, and a stranger to recondite
learning, should have taught the same truth in the following eloquent passage: "By the will of Jupiter,
" the earth, and whatever is nourished by the earth,
" was established; the sea, and whatever is produced
" by the sea; the air, and whatever is supported by the
" air; the heaven, and whatever moves in heaven. All

* Παντοκρατορικῷ βελήματι.

y Gen. i. 3.   z Ps. xxxiii. 9.   a Rev. iv. 11.

" these were created by the will of Jupiter."* A little
before, too, he had said that all these are the works of
him, " whose comprehensive and perfect mind is never
" divided, but with incredible rapidity, in the twinkling
" of an eye, accomplishes and perfects whatever it
" touches." Truly Christian and pious expressions,
had he said JEHOVAH instead of Jupiter.

XL. Since these statements are just, we utterly detest that bold tenet of the new Philosophy, by which it
is maintained, " That, although God had, from the be-
" ginning, given no other form to the world than that
" of a chaos ; yet if, after having established the laws
" of nature, he had assisted its operations by that con-
" currence which he usually affords, it may be concluded,
" without any prejudice to the miracle of the creation,
" that, by this ordinary concurrence alone, all things
" purely material would, in course of time, have attain-
" ed the same state of perfection in which we now see
" them." The consequence of such notions is, that the
masters of the new Philosophy imagine, that by means
of natural generation, according to the rules of motion,
all natural things *could* by degrees have been produced
out of chaos, established and adjusted, (one of them even
says, supposing the ordinary concurrence of God, *must*
have been produced,) in the same manner as they have
now been produced, established, and adjusted by a supernatural creation ; and, consequently, that there was
no necessity for that miraculous work which is called
creation.

XLI. These sentiments have a *dangerous tendency.*†
It ought not to pass without severe reprobation as an instance of arrogant temerity, that poor pitiful man should

* *Dissert.* xxv.

† Πονηρᾶ κομματος, i. e. literally, are *of a bad stamp.* T.

boast that he has discovered a way, by which, under the conduct of motion alone, all whose laws he, no doubt, has been able to ascertain, those wonderful works, which, as now created by the powerful word of God, command the astonishment of all the choirs of angels in common with the holy prophets, could, and even must have come forth from chaos of their own accord. God spoke, of old, to Job out of the whirlwind, saying, " Gird up now " thy loins like a man; for I will demand of thee, and " answer thou me. Where wast thou when I laid the " foundations of the earth? declare, if thou hast under- " standing. Who hath laid the measures thereof, if " thou knowest? or who hath stretched the line upon " it?"[b] &c. But these audacious men, according to their hypotheses, would find an answer to return to God; to wit, that, in all those works, there is nothing too wonderful, to have risen spontaneously out of chaos agreeably to their own rules of motion. Without doubt, however, they deserve the same reproof which God administered to Job, " Who is he that darkeneth counsel " by words without knowledge?"[c]

XLII. Whatever may be pretended to the contrary, assertions of this kind are derogatory to the miracle of the creation. The most admirable circumstance in creation is, that, at the mere command of the Deity, all things rose into existence either out of nothing, or out of matter which was altogether inadequate, and bore no proportion to what was to be formed from it. But this wonder is, in a great measure, if not entirely set aside, when it is affirmed that, supposing the ordinary concurrence of God, all things would have come forth out of chaos in the same manner, of their own accord, or as

[b] Job xxxviii. 3, 4, 5.   [c] Verse 2.

Gregory of *Nyssa* speaks, " by a spontaneous concourse,"* provided it had pleased God, who now accele-
rated the work, to have indulged motion and chaos with
a certain period of time. According to this account,
what is miraculous in creation, this only excepted, that
it surpasses the ordinary production of natural things
as to the degree of rapidity with which it is accomplished ? The issue to which these notions gradually
lead, is to cause the true doctrine of the creation of the
world to be at last discarded with ridicule and disgrace.
A certain raw disciple of this school, has not been
ashamed, to deride that doctrine, in a book in which
he makes this newfangled philosophy the interpreter of
Scripture.

XLIII. Since it is manifest, then, from what has been
said, that Creation is the production of things from nothing, and this by a mere command and volition, the
natural consequence is that we must consider it as, indisputably, a work of the Divine omnipotence. Hence
God ascribes it to himself alone, and disowns every other
cause, whether co-ordinate or instrumental. " Lift up
" your eyes on high, and behold who hath created these
" things, that bringeth out their host by number : he
" calleth them all by names by the greatness of his
" might, for that he is strong in power; not one fail-
" eth." " Hast thou not known, hast thou not heard,
" that the everlasting God, the LORD, the Creator of
" the ends of the earth, fainteth not, neither is weary ?"d
" I am the LORD that maketh all things; that stretch-
" eth forth the heavens alone; that spreadeth abroad
" the earth by myself."e Parallel to this is the following

* Ἀυτομάτω συντυχία.
d I s. xl. 26, 28. See also verses 12, 13, 14. Ch. xxxvii. 16. xlii. 5.
e Is. xliv. 24.

expression in Job;—" Who alone spreadeth out the
" heavens, and treadeth upon the waves of the sea."ᶠ

XLIV. Pressed by testimonies so very clear, *Socinus*
perfidiously objects, " that these passages do not prove
" that, in creating and forming the world, God made
" use of the services of none at all, but only of none
" that did not entirely depend upon himself, and that
" had not derived from him the power of doing some-
" thing towards the creation of the world."   This is
boldly to contradict the prophets and God himself; for
since they expressly declare, that God stretcheth forth
the heavens ALONE, they exclude every other cause of
every sort; and since it is added that God spreadeth
abroad the earth BY HIMSELF, we are taught that this
is an *immediate* act, in which no cause, not even one
that is instrumental, and that operates by power derived from another, has any place. The Rabbinical
writers say,—" immediately, and without any concaten-
" ation of causes."

XLV. By this work, too, the God of Israel discrimi-
nates himself from all the pretended gods of the Gentiles, and vindicates his own majesty in opposition to
them.   " All the gods of the nations," says the Psalmist, are " idols; but the LORD made the heavens :"ᵍ
and we read in Jeremiah, " Thus shall ye say unto
" them, The gods that have not made the heavens and
" the earth, shall perish from the earth, and from un-
" der these heavens."ʰ Nor is it impertinent to remark,
that, whilst Jeremiah composed all his other writings
in the Hebrew language, this verse alone is found in
the Chaldee dialect; because it was proper that the

ᶠ Job ix. 8.   ᵍ Ps. xcvi. 5.
ʰ Jer. x. 11.

faithful should be armed against the temptations of the Babylonians, and learn, in due time, what answer they should return to those idolaters, in their own tongue.

XLVI. The following words of *Sophocles* are not unlike this dictate of Divine revelation: " He who made " the heaven and the extensive earth, is one God— " truly one."* These lines of *Pythagoras,* or of *Orpheus,* quoted by *Justin,*† bear a still closer resemblance to the language of Scripture.

" Say'st thou, I am a God, I am Divine? " Create a world like this, and call it thine." ‡

XLVII. The Apostle also teaches, in Rom. i. 20. that ever since the creation of the world, the invisible things of God are clearly perceived, being understood by the things that are made, and, in particular, his eternal power and godhead. We have elsewhere vindicated this passage from the perverse interpretations of heretics.§ We only remark at present, that the reasoning of the Apostle would have no force, if any other Creator of the world besides the one eternal and omnipotent Deity either existed, or could exist.

XLVIII. Further, that the act of creating is so peculiar to God that no creature can be admitted to any

---

* Ἐῖς ταῖς ἀληθείαισιν, ἐῖς ἐστι Θεος, ὁς οὐρανὸν τέτευχε και γαῖαν μακρὰν.

† *Lib. de Monarchia.*

‡ Ἐι τῖς ἐρεῖ, Θεός εἰμι παρὲξ ἑνὸς, οὗτος ὀφειλει

Κόσμον ἴσον τοῦτῳ στήσας εἰπεῖν, ἐμὸς οὗτος.

A learned man has translated this distich into Latin thus:

Qui Deus affectat dici, producére mundum

Huic similem tentato, suum quem dicere possit.

§ The Author here refers to what he had formerly said, Dissert. iv. Sect. 16. *et seq.* T.

share in it, may be demonstrated in the following manner. Creation is the production of a thing by the mere command of him that creates. If, therefore, we imagine that God communicates this privilege to any creature, that at his (the creature's) command, a certain other thing may exist, that thing would either exist without any co-operation on the part of God for effecting its existence, either by willing or commanding it to be, and would be wholly indebted for its existence to the fiat of the commanding creature; or it would exist in consequence of God's willing and commanding its existence, in concert with the creature which is supposed to create. Now, each of these ideas is most dishonouring to God, and involves a manifest contradiction. If the former is asserted, it is alleged that God wills that a creature may exist which does not depend upon himself in its operations, and that, by the mere and absolute command of this creature, something may exist even without his consent; than which, nothing more absurd can be conceived. If the latter is preferred, it is not properly the creature which is supposed to create, that would in reality create; since his command is not sufficient to give existence to the thing: but God would create at the command of that creature, upon whose willing the existence of something, God is supposed to will and command the same thing. This, however, is not only contrary to the hypothesis, but also makes God dependent, in his operations, on the will of a creature. Since these imaginations are extremely derogatory to the dignity of the Supreme Being, we must, of necessity, conclude, that the act and the power of creating are incommunicable to any creature.

XLIX. It is impossible, besides, even to imagine any kind of instrument of creation strictly so called. The reason is, not merely that every instrument requires some matter and subject on which it may operate in a way adapted to its capacity, while creation strictly taken supposes the absence of all pre-existent matter; but, chiefly, because creation is effected by the mere command and will of him who creates; which excludes every other concurring cause, whatever be its nature and kind, agreeably to the expression which we lately quoted from Isaiah : " I spread abroad the earth *by myself*." [i]

L. From the preceding reasonings, it indisputably follows, that the same Godhead which belongs to the Father, belongs also to the Son and the Holy Spirit. Although, for reasons which we have elsewhere assigned, the creation is, in the Creed, attributed to the Father, the sacred writings ascribe it also to the Son and the Holy Ghost. Each of these persons, it is clear, is frequently styled God. But, if, while they are called God, they have not made the heavens and the earth, they must necessarily be numbered among those gods who " shall perish from the earth, and from under these " heavens ;" [j]—which it would be blasphemous to allege.

LI. No man of piety will deny, that the world which God has created, is a most extensive theatre erected for the display of the Divine perfections, and that mortal men are unable to ascertain its exact dimensions. " Who hath measured the waters in the hollow of his " hand, and meted out heaven with the span, and com- " prehended the dust of the earth in a measure, and " weighed the mountains in scales, and the hills in a " balance ?" [k] " If heaven above can be measured, and " the foundations of the earth searched out beneath, I

[i] Is. xliv. 24.   [j] Jer. x. 11.   [k] Is. xl. 12.

" will also cast off all the seed of Israel for all that they " have done, saith the LORD."[1]   Yet that the world is infinite, or, which is the same thing, that its extent is without bounds, no sober-minded person will affirm. God attributes to himself that power of measuring the waters and the heavens, which he denies to man; but the universe could not be measured even by God himself, unless its quantity had bounds and limits.

LII. The distinction betwixt *infinite* and *indefinite* might be admitted on this subject, provided it were ingenuously and properly explained.   The world might be allowed to be indefinite with regard to us, as we are incapable of precisely assigning the bounds and measures of the universe; though we know in general, that it hath bounds and limits, and therefore is not infinite.

LIII. But, after you have affirmed, " that our under- " standing is able to conceive no bounds in the world, " and that this is owing not to the weakness of the hu- " man mind, but to the positive idea of the world, in " which we can imagine no bounds; and that, since " this idea of the world has not arisen from our preju- " dices, and can be traced to no other quarter, it neces- " sarily follows, that God has impressed it upon our " minds, and consequently, that it is true, and gives a " just representation of the nature of the world:"—After you have even said, " We know that this world, or this " universe of corporeal substances, has no limits to its " extent:"—After you have deliberately hazarded all these assertions, to subjoin, in order to escape the odium of so extravagant an opinion, " that you would rather " call the world *indefinite* than *infinite*, that the term " *infinite* may be reserved for God only,"—this is to amuse the reader in a manner contrary to all the laws

[1] Jer. xxxi. 37.

of candour. If the idea of the world as having no imaginable limits be true, and be divinely impressed on our minds,—if we know that it has no bounds to its extent, why have we recourse to subterfuges? Why do we meanly resort to evasions? Why do we not give every thing its appropriate name? Why not speak as we think, and call that which has no bounds or limits, *infinite?* Why do we seek a dishonourable and cowardly retreat, in the word *indefinite?* Let us speak roundly and properly. " Nothing remains but sound, " and the graces of language." *

LIV. " That is infinite," says Aristotle, " to which, " whatever quantity is assigned it, you may always as- " sign something further." † Now surely, the authors of the new philosophy give us an account of the world, which, this definition of what is infinite, exactly suits; for they affirm that whatever limits of the world be supposed, they always stretch beyond them, and conceive a further extension. Since, then, they boldly assert the thing, why do they, childishly and in a manner unworthy of men, cavil about the term *infinite?*

LV. Let us examine the thing itself. And, lest our arguments should be treated with supercilious contempt, because they are ours, let these candid gentlemen be obliging enough to allow us to make use, for a little, in this contest, of weapons with which we are furnished by the celebrated *Cocceius,* a name neither odious nor inconsiderable in their esteem. This writer reasons in the following manner. ‡

LVI. " *Melissus* the *Samnian,* a disciple of *Parmenides,* whom *Aristotle* refutes, affirmed, ' that the

* Τα δ' άλλα κομπος, και λογων ευμορφίαι.
† *Natur. Auscul.* lib. iii. cap. 9.
‡ *In Gen.* i. sect. 16.

" world is infinite.'* This doctrine is contrary to Scrip-
" ture. The heaven and the earth are not infinite; for
" the earth has bounds, and the heaven, whether the
" aerial, the starry, or the third heaven, according to its
" position with respect to us, is not infinite, but finite.
" That to which infinitude is denied, is wholly finite.
" We indeed are unable to measure the universe, and
" it surpasses our conception. But God bounds, and
" ' meteth out heaven with the span.'m Extension be-
" longs to all these parts of the universe; but the ex-
" tension of things which are extended, has both a be-
" ginning and an end. If it has not, the same thing
" will at once have, and not have, a certain number of
" spaces and parts. It will not have them, because it
" is infinite; it will have them, because it has parts be-
" yond parts. The human mind does not admit a num-
" ber actually infinite; for there is no number, to which
" something may not be added," &c.

LVII. Let those who contend that the arguments
against the existence of a body actually infinite, are
mere sophisms, now reply to this reasoning. Or if it
seem too obscure, which to men of erudition it ought
not to appear, I should be happy to learn what they
have to oppose to this single demonstration, which is
plain and easy. Every body has a certain quantity.
Every thing that has quantity, has parts beyond parts.
That which is infinite, cannot have parts beyond parts;
and, therefore, it can neither have quantity, nor be a
body. That what is infinite cannot have parts beyond
parts, is proved thus. Each of the parts supposed, must
be either finite or infinite. If they are infinite, each
part is equal to the whole; which is contradictory. If

* Ἄπειρον εἶναι τὸ πᾶν.
m Is. xl. 12.

they are finite, they cannot make a whole, actually infinite; for finite parts, to whatever extent they may be
multiplied, still remain finite.   Besides, it is a maxim
of unquestionable certainty, that the whole is not greater than all its parts taken together. If, therefore, finite
parts, even when all of them are taken together, still
continue finite, the whole which results from them, is
also necessarily finite.[47]

LVIII. As the world is finite with regard to EXTENT,
it is also finite with regard to DURATION. The Scripture everywhere teaches, that its existence had a beginning.   It is said, " In the beginning God created the
" heaven and the earth ;"[n]—which intimates that the
beginning of time, by which the duration of all created
things is circumscribed, coincided with the creation of the
world.   We read, too, of " the beginning, ere ever the
" earth was, (*the beginnings of the earth,**) when there
" were no depths ;"[o] and our thoughts are elevated to
that eternity of God, which preceded " the foundation
" of the world."[p]

LIX. The most shameless sophistry is employed by
those followers of *Socinus* mentioned by *Episcopius*,†
who infer that the mountains and hills existed from
eternity, because Jacob calls them " the everlasting
" hills."[q] *Episcopius* justly opposes to them the following passage in the Psalms : " Before the moun-
" tains were brought forth, ere ever thou hadst formed
" the earth and the world, even from everlasting to
" everlasting thou art God."[r]   The Patriarch's " ever-

---

* קדמי ארץ   † *Conci.* vi. *in Joh.* xvii.

[n] Gen. i. 1.   [o] Prov. viii. 23, 24.

[p] Ephes. i. 4. John xvii. 5.   [q] Gen. xlix. 26.

[r] Ps. xc. 2.

[47] See NOTE XLVII.

" lasting hills," *hills of ages*,* are hills that existed from the beginning, and that are coeval with the world; for which reason they are called by Moses " ancient " mountains."ˢ

LX. But, supposing that the creation of the world took place in time, which has now been evinced from Scripture, it is asked, was it not at least possible for the world to have been created from eternity? To this question, *Athanasius* appears to me to have returned an acute answer in the following words.† " That al- " though it may have been possible for God to produce " works from eternity, yet it was impossible that the " works made by him could have existed from eternity, " if they really emerged from things that were not, and " did not exist before they were made. But how could " things which had no existence before they were made, " be co-existent with God, who always existed?"

LXI. This demonstration may be thus elucidated. That all the perfections of God belonged to him from eternity, admits of no doubt. From eternity, therefore, he possessed the power to produce all things, whenever he pleased, by the mere act of his will. Yet as to the things to be produced, it is absurd to allege that they could exist from eternity; for that which is from eternity, exists necessarily, existed always actually, and at no time was merely possible. But with regard to that which God voluntarily effected *without himself*,‡ so that, had he pleased, he might not have effected it —it implies a contradiction to say that it never was merely possible, and never only *to be* done, and consequently that it never was without an actual existence.

---

* גבעות עולם

† *Contra Arianos*, Orat. ii.   ‡ *Extra se.*

ˢ הרי קדם Deut. xxxiii. 15.

Since these positions are sufficiently evident, I wish it had not been said by a learned man, " that it is diffi- " cult to refute those who hold, that the eternity of the " world was possible." See the ingenious and solid reasonings of *Cocceius* on this topic.*

LXII. It is disputed among chronologers, how many years have now elapsed since the creation of the world; and the matter still remains undecided. We consider this contest as hopeless, and take no part in it at present. Let it suffice to know in general, that the world has not yet reached the age of six thousand years.[48]

LXIII. It is somewhat easier to decide the question respecting the season of the year, in which the world was made; for those who refer the beginning of the world to the autumnal equinox, appear to support their opinion by the strongest arguments. 1st, It is certain that the civil year of the Israelites began in autumn, the first month of which is called *Tisri*,† *the beginning*, an old Chaldean word from the root *Sarah*,‡ *to begin.* See Exod. xxiii. 16. xxxiv. 22, on the use of this civil year. Now, according to *Eusebius*,§ *Alexander Polyhistor* informs us, that Abraham, having received this account of the year from Enoch, delivered it to his descendants, and introduced it into Egypt. 2dly, The same idea is confirmed by the Sabbatical years which commenced at the autumnal equinox, according to the command of God.ᵗ For what could be more proper than that the

---

* *In Gen.* i. *Sect.* 39. *et seq.* Itemque *Disputat. Select.* xxvii. Sect. 29, &c.

† חשרי ‡ שרה

§ *De Præpar. Evang.* lib. ix. cap. 4.

ᵗ Levit. xxv. 9.

[48] See NOTE XLVIII.

beginning of those years should be the same with the beginning of the world, that there might not remain the space of six months, not pertaining to the Sabbatical years. 3dly, The maturity of every sort of fruit adapted to the use of man, serves also to show, that autumn was more probably the time of the creation, than any other season of the year.

LXIV. Further, though it would have been easy for God to create all things in full perfection, " in a single " moment, and by a single act and movement,"* he was pleased to employ six days in this work; as the Mosaic history, which ought by no means to be debased by rash and unnecessary allegories, expressly states. From this circumstance we learn, that we must not be superficial and hasty in our meditations on the works of God; that each of them ought, on the contrary, to be inquired into with attention and diligence; and that the whole period of our life should be devoted to this exercise, till, with an understanding perfect in vigour, we behold all things in a state of the highest perfection, in a most blessed Sabbath of rest.

LXV. A question has lately begun to be agitated with reference to the progress of the works of God on each of the days; to wit, whether each of the works of a day was perfected in a single moment, or in some period of time? This controversy, however, is not of very great moment; nor do the sentiments held on either side seem, hitherto, to be either supported or overthrown, by cogent arguments from Scripture.

LXVI. As to the importance of this question, I rank it amongst those doubtful points, which may be disputed among the reformed, without any prejudice to faith or

* Ἐν μιᾳ καιρῷ ῥοπῇ, μιατε ὁρμῇ και κινήσει.

charity; provided it be firmly and conscientiously held, that there is a vast difference between the first *creation* of things, which was accomplished by the command of God, (in a manner quite different from that order which was subsequently to be observed,) and *natural genera-tion*, which proceeds gradually from suitable matter, according to the rules of motion. As the denial of instantaneous creation is a step by which some proceed to maintain that most absurd hypothesis respecting all things spontaneously rising into existence by mere motion, the ordinary concurrence of God being supposed, —I utterly detest the denial of such creation. In the solution of the question itself, to which we will immediately proceed, an excessive refinement must be carefully avoided.

LXVII. Those who apprehend that the different days were occupied by the different works of these days respectively, make use of this argument chiefly;—that, otherwise, it would have been said that on each of the days God rested the whole day excepting merely the moment alleged, whereas the Scripture only makes mention of God's resting on the seventh day. But this reason is of no weight. If you understand by *resting*, ceasing from the production of a certain work till a new work be begun, God, no doubt, rested on each of the days. It is clear from the sacred narrative, that his works did not so rapidly succeed each other as to admit of no interval between them. When the work of each day was finished, God first approved of it, before he proceeded to other works; and mention is made of his uttering several distinct words, or commands, at the production of the different works. A remarkable interval, too, in which it may be truly affirmed that God rested, took place betwixt the creation of other animals

and of man, and also betwixt the creation of Adam and
Eve. But the rest of the seventh day is quite of a different kind; partly, as it consisted in God's ceasing
from the creation of new species of creatures; partly, as
he beheld with complacency the fabric of the universe
which he had now completed. Further, as to what is
added respecting the single moment assigned to the
work of creation on each of the days, it seems intended
to excite an odium against the contrary opinion. Since
several different works are ascribed to each of the days,
no person, I apprehend, understands, that all those
works were performed at once in a single moment of
the day. This notion is expressly inconsistent with the
account of the works of, at least, the first and the sixth
day.

LXVIII. Those who hold, on the contrary, that the
different works were done in different *moments* of time,
support their opinion, principally, by the following argument. The creation, say they, is said to have been
effected by the call and command of God; but God,
when he enjoins any thing to appear, cannot be resist-
ed, and at his command, all things must be present
without delay. Neither does this argument, however,
seem incontrovertible. Although, when God by his all-
powerful command orders any thing to be present, it
cannot refuse to come at his call; yet it is not necessary that it should appear, that very moment, in all
its perfection. It is possible for God, to command it to
come forward within some period of time. The Divine
command is the cause of the existence of things; but
the manner of their existing depends on the pleasure
of him who commands them into being. If he command them to appear in a moment, in a moment they
will assuredly appear. If he command them to go for-

ward to perfection in some space of time, a space of time will consequently be requisite for this purpose. From the mere command of God, then, respecting the existence of creatures, nothing can be inferred as to the particular manner of their rising into existence. Some things, which are done at his command, are unquestionably accomplished in a continued space of time. For instance, the coming of the animals to Adam in order to receive their names from him as their lord, undoubtedly took place at the command of God, yet not without succession. Nor let it be objected, that the inclination to come was infused into the animals in a moment; for their coming itself, and not merely the inclination, was the effect of the Divine command.

LXIX. My judgment, therefore, is, that this question cannot be decided without making a distinction. Some things were certainly produced out of nothing, as the highest heaven, and the chaos of the earth, angels, and the souls of men. These could not be otherwise created than in a moment. Since no medium can be imagined between existence and non-existence, the transition from nothing to something does not admit of delay or succession.

LXX. Other creatures were formed of pre-existing matter by means of motion. " I apprehend," said *Gregory* of *Nyssa*, " that all those things which ap-" pear in the creation, and which were brought into ex-" istence by the will of God, were produced by means " of motion and rest."* We, for our part, are not inclined, at present, to adopt such unrestrained expressions. Some works, however, were certainly accomplished by means of motion; as the drying of the earth, and the collecting of the waters into one place, which the

* *De hominis Opificio,* cap. i.

Psalmist celebrates in the following manner: " The " waters stood above the mountains. At thy rebuke " they fled; at the voice of thy thunder, they hasted " away. They go up by the mountains; they go down " by the valleys unto the place which thou hast found- " ed for them."[u] This was probably the case, too, with regard to the division of the stars; which, being separated from the original globe of light, and formed into distinct parts, could not, without motion, be fixed in so widely distant regions of the heavens. Now, that motion cannot be performed in what is called a mathematical moment, excluding all succession, is thus demonstrated. The body would, in this case, be in several places at once; it would be, at the same time, in the place from which it departs, the place to which it is going, and the intermediate place. Nay, it would be, and would not be somewhere, at the same time; for it is implied in the very idea of a body being moved, that it ceases to be in the place whence it removes, and is not yet arrived at the place whither it is going.

LXXI. We must hold, nevertheless, that this motion was altogether extraordinary, and extremely rapid. It is by no means to be reduced to the ordinary rules of motion which are now observed; it owed its beginning, its progress, and its whole modification, to a Divine, and a special command.

LXXII. We ought not to imagine, that the production of herbs and trees from the ground, of fishes and reptiles from the waters, and, in fine, of all the animals from the earth, was performed in so rigid and laborious succession, that, the larger parts and the minutest particles being gradually prepared and arranged, the works, at last, with difficulty, attained their perfection, in the

[u] Ps. civ. 6, 7, 8.

course of the day. But, at the command of God, the herbs, the trees loaded with their respective fruits, the fishes, the birds, and the other living creatures, suddenly came forth in full maturity;—each of them in a very short space of time, which, in comparison of the succession of months and years during which they now spring and grow up to perfection, may be regarded as a moment. " In a single instant of time," says *Eustathius*, " those things which existed not before, sprung out of " the earth, each distinguished by its own properties."* The glorious change of our bodies at the last day, exhibiting a kind of image of the first creation, will, in like manner, be effected " in a moment, in the twink-" ling of an eye."ᵛ

LXXIII. Since, on each of the days, God performed various and highly magnificent works, and some of them posterior to others, (though most of them were accomplished in an exceedingly short time,) yet in such a manner that it is impossible for us to assign the moments of the commencement and termination of the works of each day to their own hours respectively,— Divines justly say, according to Scripture, that *six days*, not *six moments*, were employed in the creation of the world. It must not be thought that, like a workman restricted to his task or to his time, God laboured in the work from morning to evening.

LXXIV. There is only ONE world, this very world, of the creation of which we are now treating, which was made by Christ, into which Christ came, and which comprehends within its circuit all things that were made.ʷ To imagine a plurality of worlds, existing either

* *Hexaem.* This sentiment occurs in nearly the same words in *Basil. Homil.* iv.
    ᵛ 1 Cor. xv. 52.   ʷ John i. 3, 10.

at the same time or in succession, is the raving of men who are not afraid of " intruding into those things " which they have not seen, vainly puffed up by their " own fleshly mind."[x]

LXXV. That God could have created more worlds, distinct and separate from this one, had it so pleased him,—it is reasonable for all to believe, who devoutly acknowledge the immeasurable and inexhaustible power of the Deity. As to the objection adduced by some, that this world is *the universe*,* besides which nothing can be created without a contradiction, it is a childish cavil. This world is now called the universe, because all things which are created, are, in reality, contained within its compass : were another world created, this would cease to be the universe.

LXXVI. Nor is another reason alleged of greater force, namely, that there would either be something intermediate, or nothing ; if there were nothing, they would not be really different worlds ; if something, even this would serve to conjoin them. That things betwixt which no body intervenes, are not different, is not true. It is sufficient to make them different, that they do not approach, and are not in contact with each other. Nor is it material whether another body be actually placed, or it be merely possible to place it, between them ; neither of the extreme bodies being removed from its own station.

LXXVII. But it excites our surprise, that they who contend that more worlds similar to this universe cannot be made even by the Divine omnipotence, admit without difficulty a plurality of particular worlds, or bodies resembling the earth that we inhabit, in which

* Τὸ πᾶν.
[x] Col. ii. 18.

either men or other living creatures reside. Although, too, according to the modesty which they affect, they allege that on this point nothing must be either rashly affirmed or denied; they cannot restrain themselves from severely censuring those who, merely labouring under prejudices, and in a manner infatuated by self-love, imagine that we men are the sole delight of God, and that our earth is the most pleasant spot of the whole world;—which they suppose cannot be done without despising the other works of God. " We know " not, indeed," they add, " whether there be men or " other creatures in the Moon; but if we intend to " form any opinion at all, it seems more conformable " to truth to affirm, than to deny, that it is inhabited " by men."

LXXVIII. I know not whether the very learned men derive these notions from the Commentaries of *Lucian*, or from the report of that man of strict honour and veracity, who, not long ago, flying on the wings of a goose, took an accurate survey of those upper regions, which have been hitherto unknown to other mortals that are sustained by the fruits of this earth. I cannot help recollecting on this occasion, what I long ago read on this subject in *Lucian*; and for the sake of my pupils, I will here repeat the substance of it in a few words. His story is as follows:* After he himself, with his companions, had been carried through the air by a mighty whirlwind during seven days and an equal number of nights, he arrived in his ship on the eighth day at a certain great country in the midst of the air,—an island, which, having the form of a globe, glittered with a profusion of light. They found it both inhabited and

* *Primus verarum historiarum Liber.*

cultivated. But that they might not wander hither and thither, ignorant alike of the men and the places, and not knowing under what part of heaven or into what region of the world they were thrown; it fortunately happened, that certain *Horse-vultures*,* that is, men who rode on vultures instead of horses, and who were some of the King's principal servants, conducted the extraordinary strangers to the palace. The King, having learned from their appearance and dress that they were Grecians, politely informs them that his name is *Endymion*, and also that the region into which they were conveyed, after having traversed so vast spaces of air, is called by the Greeks ΣΕΛΗΝΗ, (the Latins call it LUNA,) the MOON. He told them that he was engaged in an arduous and dreadful war with the King of the Sun, (for that part of the world is no less fully peopled than the Moon,) and added many other stories of the same kind, which it would be improper now to rehearse.

The learned men, however, may choose rather, perhaps, to acknowledge themselves indebted to *Kepler*, the celebrated astronomer, who relates,† that he saw through an optical tube, on the spotted face of the Moon, lofty mountains, great valleys, a vast number of deep ditches, also extensive forests, seas, and many other things closely resembling what is found in the earth which we inhabit. He alleges, too, that the Moon is inhabited, and that its inhabitants are short-lived, but of a stupendous size, fifteen times larger than the men of the earth, equal to whales; and that they build towns in situations exposed to the warm beams of the Sun. Lest doubts of the truth of this account

---

* Ἱππογύποι; in Latin, *Equivultures*.

† In *Selenographia* sua.

should remain, *Kepler* conjectures that he saw the workmen employed in their labours.

LXXIX. But candidly to speak out what I think; I am fully convinced that it is not without exposing our holy religion to disgrace, that men devoted to the study of Theology thus contend for such notions; and that meteorologies of this sort furnish the profane, and the enemies of the Reformed Church, with copious materials for mockery and ridicule. Allowing that it appears from the observations of *Hevelius*, that there are in the Moon high and low places, similar to our mountains and valleys, what probable reason, I ask, have we to induce us to conclude, that it contains men, states, and commonwealths? Can even the slightest evidences of their existence be found, either in nature, or in Scripture?

LXXX. Nay, there are not a few passages of Scripture, that are contrary to this lunatic imagination. Moses, by the distinct account which he gives of the counsel of God respecting the creation of man, sufficiently shows, that at that time no living creature similar to him existed in the universe. Why should God be introduced, saying, " Let us make man in our " image," &c. as if he were preparing for the chief of his works, if, perhaps only two days before, he had peopled the Moon, or the Sun, or even the other stars with men? For what purpose is it related, that, having discovered, so to speak, that it would not be good for man to remain alone, he thought at last of forming a companion for him? These transactions indeed are related in terms which allude to human infirmity;* but the expressions would be utterly void of propriety, and could

* Ἀνθρωποπαθῶς.

afford no meaning worthy of God, if several pairs of the human kind had already existed elsewhere.

LXXXI. Add to this, that Isaiah ascribes it in a special manner to the earth, that it was not " created in " vain," but " formed to be inhabited."[y] Paul, too, whilst he affirms that " God hath made of one blood " all the nations of men to dwell on all the face of the " earth,"[z] acknowledges no other race of men that has sprung up elsewhere, and that inhabits the face of the Moon.

LXXXII. Reason, too, gives its suffrage in our favour. If there were men in the Moon or in the other stars, they must either have retained their original integrity, like the good Angels; or fallen into sin, as we have done. But it seems probable that neither of these would have been passed over in total silence in holy writ; especially since so many proper opportunities of mentioning them occur. Whether our sin were to be aggravated, or the unbounded mercy of God towards us extolled, or the extent of that blessed society in which we shall rejoice in heaven, to be shown; it would have been worth while, at least briefly to notice so many myriads of saints from another globe. This argument has the greater weight, as frequent mention is made, on such occasions, of Angels; who are no less the inhabitants of another world than the men supposed, and whose affairs seem not to concern us so much as those of the other race, who are of the same species with ourselves.

LXXXIII. But, if the men inhabiting the Moon, or the Sun, or Mercury, are involved in the same misery of sin with us, it may be affirmed, either that they all remain eternally wretched, or that some of them are, in common with us, redeemed by Christ, or that another way of salvation is discovered to them. But no one of these suppositions is at all probable.

LXXXIV. Not the *first:* For it may be gathered from PSALM lxxxix. 48. that God would have created all those sons of men in vain, if none of them are to adore his perfections, and celebrate his praise. On this supposition, too, Paul would have had a singularly apt opportunity of inculcating the same thing, in that passage where he makes mention of Christ's not taking hold of angels, but of the seed of Abraham.[a] He would, beyond question, have highly commended the love of Christ towards us, if he had chosen to add, that not merely angels that sinned, but also whole worlds of men of the same nature with us, were passed by, that so amazing an act of kindness and grace, might be done to the men of this earth alone, which is perhaps the least of them all.

LXXXV. The *second* supposition is equally void of probability. For since Christ has not assumed a human nature of the same blood with those men, he is neither their Brother, nor their GOEL.* Since he has neither lived nor suffered, nor taught in their world; since in fine, he has appeared in it neither in a humble nor in a glorious form, nor is to appear in it at the consummation of all things;[b] it is not probable that the

---

* GOEL, which is translated *Redeemer,* is a striking designation given to Christ in Job xix. 25. Is. lix. 20. and various other passages. It denotes the near relation in which he stands to us as " the man Christ Jesus," and his consequent right to accomplish our redemption. It exhibits him as the antitype of the *Goel,* or near kinsman who by the Mosaic law was entitled to redeem an inheritance, and also was permitted to avenge the death of his relation, by killing the slayer if he found him out of the cities of refuge. See Diss. xiv. sect. **33—38.**   [a] Heb. ii. 16.   [b] Acts iii. 21.

salvation which he has obtained for us only by his appearing amongst us, is obtained for them without an advent of Christ to them. I might also mention the preaching of the Gospel, of which the Apostle testifies, that its *sound went into all the earth, and its words unto the ends of the world ;*[c] but he has not ventured to assert that it has reached the inhabitants of the Moon or of the other stars. Is it likely, too, that nothing would have been said respecting them, in those passages which describe that glorious judgment which is to be conducted with incredible solemnity at the last day? It will redound greatly to the honour of the Lord Jesus, without doubt, if he is to be the Judge not only of this world, but also of other worlds of mankind, as well as of angels.

LXXXVI. Nor is the *third* supposition admissible. For neither is there salvation in any other ;"[d] nor would it become a Most Holy God to admit sinful men to communion with himself, without a satisfaction to his justice. Such a satisfaction, besides, can be made by none but a person who is GOD-MAN; which it is unnecessary to consider more fully here, as we have elsewhere proved it at large.* Indeed new schemes of Divinity widely different from that which our churches maintain, must be framed for the benefit of the men inhabiting the Moon; as has been avowedly done of late, for the sake of his *Pre-adamites,*† by him who has been the first to discover their existence.

LXXXVII. Since these things are so, it is truly sur-

---

* The Author here alludes to a discussion in the *Economy of the Covenants,* Book ii. chap. 4.   T.

† Men whom the writer alluded to represented as having existed before Adam.   T.

  [c] Rom. x. 18.   [d] Acts iv. 12.

prising that men of intelligence and discretion could have allowed themselves, amidst so much light and learning, publicly to affirm in their writings, that they who think that the Moon is inhabited by men, hold a more probable opinion than those who choose rather to believe that it is uninhabited. I should have deemed the puerile rant of these writers quite unworthy of a serious confutation, were it not that it seemed proper to avert from our churches the reproach of so monstrous opinions.[49]

LXXXVIII. Our plan does not lead us to speak particularly of the different works of each of the days. Let us only take a brief view of the order which God observed in creating. First of all, he made the heaven, the throne of his majesty, with the angels, his attendants, and the witnesses and spectators of his other works; as may be inferred from some expressions in Job.[e] He then prepared these lower abodes for the accommodation of the animal life; that we might be taught always to give the first and highest place in our esteem to divine and heavenly objects.

LXXXIX. At one and the same time he began, and finished the heaven of his glory, and replenished it with glorious inhabitants. But to other things, he, in the first instance, gave rude beginnings, and perfected them by degrees; demonstrating his power and goodness, first, in the imperfection and weakness, and, then, in the perfecting of the creature. Of this sort was the producing of the world without light, that light might arise out of darkness: From which, too, we ascend, in delightful meditation, to the procedure of God in forming the new world of grace;[f] where also, commencing

[e] Chap. xxxviii. 6, 7. [f] 2 Cor. iv. 6.
[49] See NOTE XLIX.

with slight beginnings, he gradually perfects his design, till, in the blessed day of an eternal Sabbath, he calmly acquiesces, with entire approbation, in the consummated work.

xc. After all his other works, he made man; after man, nothing. This teaches us, that the rest of the creatures were made for man, the highest heaven itself, with its angels, not excepted; but that man was made for God only, to worship and obey him; since nothing was made posterior to man, to which as his superior he might do homage.

xci. Nor must this observation be omitted, that God rested in none of his works, how magnificent soever, till he had made man; but when man was created, immediately " he rested, and was refreshed."g *Macarius* elegantly says; " Man is a creature of high dignity. " Behold the heavens and the earth, the sun and the " moon, and consider how great they are. Yet it did " not seem good to the Lord to rest in these works, but " in man only. Man is, therefore, more exalted than " all the other creatures."* This instance of the Almighty's acquiescence in man, intimates that it gives greater delight to God that he has man to hallow and glorify his name, than that he made heaven and earth, and a vast number of creatures, which, though otherwise admirable, are incapable of knowing and enjoying him.

xcii. Thus we are gradually led to the IMPROVEMENT of this article; which consists chiefly in these three exercises. *First*, That we attentively meditate on the works of God. *Secondly*, That by them, as by a ladder, we ascend to God. *Thirdly*, That we descend

---

* *Homilia* xv.

g ‏ינפש‎ Exod. xxxi. 17.

to ourselves.   The Psalmist has comprised all these in a few words :[h] " When I consider thy heavens," (behold the soul attending to the works of God) " the " work of thy fingers ; the moon and the stars which " thou hast ordained ;" (behold the mind ascending to God) " What is man that thou art mindful of him," &c. Behold man descending to himself.

XCIII. Faith certainly requires, in the first place, that we contemplate and meditate on the works of God.[i] It is the characteristic of beasts, or of drunkards, who are worse than beasts, that " they regard not the work " of the Lord, neither consider the operation of his " hand."[j] Even heathen philosophers often professed that they could experience no sweeter pleasure in life, than the contemplation of the stupendous works of nature ; on which you may consult *Seneca's Preface* to his *Questions on the Works of Nature.**   Yet they were unable to discern in those works what faith causes us to perceive ; to wit, the excellencies of God, not merely as an omnipotent Creator, but also as our most gracious Father.   It is certain, too, that man was created for this very purpose, that he might be, as *Gregory Nazianzen* calls him, " the spectator of the visible, the " priest of the intelligent, creation." †

XCIV. Now we ought to perform this duty, 1st, With care and attention.   " Lift up your eyes on high, " and behold who hath created these things."[k]   We should hold a kind of conference with the creatures, and examine each of them respecting their admirable

---

* *Prefatio Quæstionum Naturalium.*

† Ἐπόπτης της ὁρατης κτισεως, μύστης της νοȣμενης.

[h] Ps. viii. 3, 4.   [i] Noȣμεν, Heb. xi. 3.

[j] Is. v. 12.   [k] Is. xl. 26.

properties. " Ask now the beasts, and they shall teach
" thee, - - - or speak to the earth, and it shall teach
" thee."[1] 2dly, With admiration. " Marvellous are
" thy works," says the Psalmist.[m] " O Lord, how mani-
" fold are thy works! in wisdom hast thou made them
" all: the earth is full of thy riches."[n] 3dly, With joy
and exultation. " Thou, Lord, hast made me glad
" through thy work; I will triumph in the works of
" thy hands."[o] This has been the exercise of angels even
from the beginning. " When the corner-stone of the
" earth was laid, the morning stars sang together, and
" all the sons of God shouted for joy."[p]

xcv. Further, we should ascend by the creatures, as
by an erect ladder, to God the Creator; who exhibits
himself in them, not only to be seen, but also to be *felt*,[q]
—whose glory the heavens declare,[r] and to whom the
brute animals of the earth, and the dumb fishes of the
sea, bear witness, that they proceeded from his hand.[s]

xcvi. Nor is a general acknowledgment of this sufficient. But those perfections of God which he has
brightly displayed in the work of creation, ought to be
particularly observed:—that infinite Power, at whose
command all things rose into existence:[t]—that unbounded Goodness, to which alone the creatures must
own themselves entirely indebted for whatever portion
of good is in them:[u]—that unsearchable Wisdom, which
has arranged every thing in so beautiful an order, that
it appears no less admirable in the least than in the

---

[1] Job xii. 7, 8.
[m] Ps. cxxxix. 14.
[n] Ps. civ. 24. See also xcii. 5, 6. Job xxvi. 14.
[o] Ps. xcii. 4.
[p] Job xxxviii. 6, 7.
[q] Acts xvii. 27.
[r] Ps. xix. 1.
[s] Job xii. 9.
[t] Jer. xxvii. 5.
[u] Ps. cxlv. 9.

greatest works : ᵛ—that amazing Philanthropy, in fine, which he has shown towards man, not only adorning his body by so exact a proportion of all its parts, which has beyond measure astonished Hippocrates and other anatomists ; but also suspending in his soul, as in the golden vault of the temple, an image of himself and a representation of his own holiness ; and at the same time, granting him dominion over the rest of the creatures.

xcvii. "God," as *Philo* eloquently observes, "by en-
" dowing man with reason, having admitted him to
" communion with himself, which is the best of his
" gifts, by no means withheld other blessings; but pre-
" pared for him, as the most nearly related and the most
" dearly beloved of his creatures, all that the world
" contains. Having determined that he should be des-
" titute of nothing conducive either to his living, or to
" his living happily, the Creator made provision for
" the one, by the rich abundance of comforts that were
" given him to enjoy; and for the other, by the con-
" templation of heavenly objects, with which when the
" mind is affected, it is inspired with an ardent desire
" of the knowledge of them."*

xcviii. We should endeavour also to rise in our me-
ditations, by *the way of eminence*, as it is called, from the greatness, the beauty, and the excellence of the creatures, to the consideration of the greatness and the beau-
ty of God. I cannot better illustrate this than in the words of the truly *Great Basil.* " Let us glorify the
" adorable Author of nature, who has formed all things
" with consummate wisdom and skill. From the beau-
" ty of the things that are seen, let us learn his trans-

* *De Opificio Mundi,* p. 12.
ᵛ Ps. cxlvii. 5.

" cendant beauty; and from the magnitude of these
" sensible and limited bodies, let us infer the infinite
" and immeasurable extent of his greatness and power,
" which no created understanding is able to compre-
" hend." * Hence it follows, that it is our duty to
esteem the Creator above the creatures; by no means
to acquiesce in the creatures themselves, whose goodness is finite and circumscribed, and which are, consequently, incapable of imparting full satisfaction to the
mind; and not even to rejoice in the creatures, except
in so far as we observe the excellencies of their Maker
manifested in them, that thus our delight may be
placed, not so much in the creatures, as in and through
them, in God the Creator.[w]

xcix. In fine, we ought continually to honour the
glorious Artificer of the universe with our praises and
thanksgivings. The sweet Psalmist of Israel, unable
to satisfy himself with so ample and so choice a collection of hymns for this purpose, solicits the assistance of
all creatures in the discharge of this duty.[x] The exhortation of *Epictetus*† to celebrate the praises of God
as the Creator, is truly admirable; and I should have
added it here, were it not that I recollect I have given
it elsewhere.‡

* *Homil.* i. *in Hexaem. circa fin.* Quoted from the original Greek,
and from the Latin Version of *John Argyropilus.*

† Vide *Arriani Dissert.* lib. i. cap. 16.

‡ The Author gives the passage from *Epictetus* to which he here
alludes, in the 17th section of his 8th *Dissertation on the Lord's
Prayer.* As the reader may wish to see a quotation so highly commended by Witsius, it is here subjoined in English.

" If we were truly wise, what else would be our business both in
" public and in private but to magnify, to praise, and render thanks
" to the Deity? Should we not sing this Hymn to God, whilst we

[w] Ps. lxxiii. 25.   [x] Ps. cxlviii.

c. But we should also descend to ourselves. 1st, That we may learn to fear and venerate the great Creator. " Fear ye not me, saith the Lord? Will ye not " tremble at my presence, who have placed the sand for " the bound of the sea?"[y] All creatures are in his hand, to employ them either for us, or against us, according to his sovereign pleasure; and it is in him alone, too, that we ourselves live, move, and have our being.[z]

ci. 2dly, That we may render the worship and service due to Him, whom every kind of animals both in the earth and in the sea obey. When we behold all creatures hearkening to his word according to the laws

" handle the spade and the plough, and whilst we partake of our " food? ' Great is that God, who has afforded us those implements, " with which we cultivate the ground. Great is that God, to whom " we are indebted for hands, and for the power of swallowing and " digesting our food; who causes us to grow imperceptibly, and to " breathe when asleep.' These instances of the Divine goodness " ought to be particularly celebrated; and we should praise him in " the noblest and most sacred songs, because he has given us facul- " ties by which we perceive them, and are capable of employing " them aright. What then? Since we are generally blind and stu- " pid, ought not some one to discharge this office, and to celebrate " the praises of God on behalf of all? *And what else can I do, who* " *am old and lame, but show forth his praise. Were I a nightin-* " *gale, I would act the part of a nightingale; were I a swan, I would* " *act the part of a swan. But since I am a rational creature, I ought* " *to praise God. This is my work; this I will perform; nor shall* " *I desert this honourable employment, while I am permitted to pursue* " *it. And I invite you to unite with me in the same song.*"

To this remarkable quotation, Witsius adds the following re- flexion. " O how well calculated is this devout discourse, this pious " counsel of a heathen, to make us ashamed of our backwardness " and indolence! Doth a pagan philosopher speak and act in this " manner; and how do we Christians conduct ourselves?" T.

[y] Jer. v. 22. Ps. xxxiii. 6—9.   [z] Acts xvii. 28.

of nature,[a] truly we ought to be ashamed and blush, if
we who are enriched and distinguished above the rest
by so many benefits, and who alone, in common with
angels, are privileged with reason, are found rebellious
against him, without whom we can do nothing ; and
against whom, in consequence, it is highly criminal for
us to form one hostile purpose or thought.   Hence
God frequently makes use of the irrational creatures, to
reprove and put to shame the rational.[b]

CII. 3dly, That whilst we sincerely discharge these
duties of piety, we may comfort ourselves, in various
ways, in God our Creator.   1. If that God, who is the
omnipotent Creator, be our God, he will certainly provide for us all that is necessary to our welfare.   " The
" earth is the Lord's, and the fulness thereof; the
" world, and they that dwell therein."[c]   Since " he
" giveth to the beast his food, and to the young ravens
" which cry,"[d] how much less will he suffer men who
so far excel other creatures, and who call upon him as
their Father, to lack what is necessary ?[e]

CIII. A memorable instance of this care of Providence occurred to me to-day, when reading the *Monody*
of *Gregory Nazianzen* upon *Basil the Great.**   He
relates, that when *Maximian's* violent persecution was
raging with its utmost fury, the ancestors of *Basil* es-
caped with a few servants to a certain cave in a mountain.   Continuing there upwards of seven years, and
dwelling in the open air, they lived on bread alone ;
nor did they, like the Israelites in the wilderness, utter
any complaint on that account.   God, who fed the Jews

* *Monodia Gregorii Nazianzeni in Basilium Magnum.*
[a] Ps. cxlviii. 8.   [b] Is. i. 2. 3.   Jer. viii. 7.
[c] Ps. xxiv. i.   [d] Ps. cxlvii. 9.
[e] Ps. xxxvi. 7.   Mat. vi. 26—34.

in the desert with manna and with quails, supplied them with provisions which they neither prepared nor expected—deer in good condition, which came of their own accord, no man pursuing them; and of which they killed what were immediately necessary, and dismissed the rest, reserving them as in a storehouse, ready to appear when required for future use. " The young lions " do lack, and suffer hunger; but they that seek the " Lord shall not want any good thing."[f]

CIV. 2. If the Almighty Creator be our God, nothing is so wonderful but he is able and willing to effect it on our behalf. Jeremiah, accordingly, reasons thus: " Ah! Lord God, behold thou hast made the heaven " and the earth by thy great power and stretched out " arm, and there is nothing too hard for thee;"[g] or, as our Dutch translators have well rendered the expression, " *there is nothing too wonderful for thee*,*—nothing which thou canst not easily perform in favour of thy people. He will govern all the creatures, too, in such a manner that none of them can hurt his people,[h] but all of them, on the contrary, shall serve to promote their salvation.[i]

CV. 3. To conclude, how great is this felicity of the saints, that it is given them to inherit not merely the creatures,[j] but also the Creator himself! " The For- " mer of all things is the portion of Jacob;"[k] and our " Maker is our Husband;"[l] in whom we are not only

---

* *Nulla res mirabilis tibi erit.*

[f] Ps. xxxiv. 11.

[g] לא נפלא ממך כל דבר Jer. xxii. 17.

[h] Is. xliii. 2.   Dan. iii. 17, 27, 28, 29. vi. 22, 23.

[i] Rom. viii. 28.

[j] Rom. iv. 13.   1 Cor. iii. 21, 22.

[k] Jer. x. 16.   [l] Is. liv. 5.

allowed to repose our confidence through the whole course of our lives,[m] but to whom, also, in our dying moments, we may " commit our souls as to a faithful " Creator."[n]

[m] Ps. xxxvii. 5,   [n] 1 Pet. iv. 19.

DISSERTATION IX.

ON THE NAME JESUS.

———

I. HAVING considered with some attention what we are to believe in relation to the FIRST PERSON of the Adorable Trinity, we now proceed to speak of the SECOND; to whom four titles are ascribed in the Creed, to wit, JESUS, CHRIST, the ONLY SON of God the Father, and OUR LORD. The two first of these titles are names of *office;* the third indicates his *nature;* the fourth points out his *dignity,* and the relation in which he stands to us.

II. Some have ingeniously remarked with respect to his official names, that the one of them is Hebrew, and the other Greek; because the Son of God is given to be a Saviour alike to Hebrews and Greeks, to Jews and Gentiles; " a light to lighten the Gentiles, and the " glory of his people Israel."[a] Others add, that the first name is Hebrew, and the surname Greek; because " salvation is of the Jews," and because to them it was first announced and exhibited. " To the Jew first," says the Apostle, " and also to the Greek."[b] I shall

[a] Luke ii. 32. [b] Rom. i. 16.

not anxiously inquire at present into the solidity of this observation.   The circumstance itself which gave occasion to it, at any rate, is certain, honourable to Jesus, and delightful to us.

III. Some authors, with *Moschopulus,* derive the name 'Ιησους, JESUS, from ιω, the future of which is ιασω ; whence comes 'Ιασους, and, by changing the letter α into η, 'Ιησους, that is to say, *a person who heals.* But those writers are undoubtedly mistaken, and by such a derivation they would incur the ridicule of all who are acquainted with the Hebrew language, were we not to admit the remark of *Grotius,* that by a certain play of fancy they have found a Greek term which corresponds with the Hebrew ישע as well in sound as in sense ; in which they follow the example of *Philo,* who delights in alluding to Greek words so as to depart as little as possible from the Hebrew notation. It is certain that the Hebrew term ישע and the Greek 'ιασις are very near akin, both in sound and in signification ; and to this it seems to be owing, that several Jews, who resided among Greeks, having been called by this Hebrew name, assumed the name *Jason* in Greek.

IV. But *Theophylact* says with great truth, " The " name JESUS is not Greek but Hebrew ;"* and it becomes us to maintain that etymology which is suggested by the expression of the angel to Joseph ; " Thou shalt " call his name JESUS, for he shall SAVE his people " from their sins."[c] This conducts us, as if by the hand, to the Hebrew word ישוע which occurs in various passages,[d] and when written fully is יהושע. The Greeks, who were singularly fond of a soft and easy pronuncia-

* *In Mat.* cap. i.
[c] Mat. i. 21.
[d] Ezra ii. 2. iii. 2.   2 Chron. xxxi. 15.

tion, transformed this name into Ἰησους, JESUS; which
is irrefragably proved by the consideration that, among
them, Joshua, the son of Nun, is called by the same
name, JESUS.[e]

v. The following expressions which *Rabbi Hakka-*
dos is reported to have used,* are worthy of notice.
" Because the Messiah shall save mankind, he will be
" called *Jeschua.*†   But the people of another nation,
" who shall embrace his religion, will call him JESUS ;
" and, therefore, you will find this name JESU pointed
" out in Gen. xlix. 10. יבא שילהולי. For the first letters
" of these Hebrew words, joined together, will form the
" name ישו JESU."

vi. It is clear, therefore, that *Damascenus* has justly
said, that " the name Jesus is by interpretation a Sa-
" viour."‡ *Cicero*§ observes, that no one Latin word is
sufficient to express the entire meaning of the Greek
term ; for the name *Servator* does not exhaust its whole
energy. *Grotius* is of opinion, that the term *Sospitator,*
which is more ancient, but employed more in sacred
than in common discourse, is of the same origin and
force with the Greek word. The term *Salvator,* however, though possibly not so good a Latin expression,
has been generally used in the Church ; and in this we
readily acquiesce.

vii. Let it be considered, then, as decided, that JE-
sus is from JEHOSHUA, and that JEHOSHUA denotes
(Salvator) A SAVIOUR. But it is inquired among the
learned, whether or not it signifies something more.
Eusebius makes the following remark :   " The name

---

* *In libro* GALE RAZAJA.   † ישוע:

‡ Τὸ Ἰησῦς ὄνομα Σωτηρ ἑρμηνεύεται.   *De Orthodoxa Fid.* lib. i.
cap. 12.

§ Act. iv. *In Verrem.*

[e] Heb. iv. 8.

" Jesus, translated into the Greek language, signifies
" the salvation of God."* A little after he adds:
" Joshua is the Salvation of JAO (or JEHOVAH,) that
" is, the Salvation of God."† He seems to have thought
that in this word, as also in *Jehonathan, Jehotzedec,*
and the like, *Jeho* is from Jehovah.

VIII. Nor is this opinion utterly without foundation.
Though the genius of the language can easily admit
the verbal noun יהושע (*Jehoshua*) to be formed from
הושיע (*Hoshea,*) it was not without some important
reason that Moses changed the name of his servant, who
was formerly called *Hoshea,*‡ not merely into *Jeshua,*§
as it is written in Nehemiah viii. 17. but into *Jehoshua,*‖
Numbers xiii. 16. that it might contain all the letters
of the name JEHOVAH.¶ There is a certain remarkable emphasis in such prophetical changing of names,
importing an accession of honour and dignity. The
word *Hoshea,* when taken as a noun, without doubt,
means *a Saviour.* If *Jehoshua* signifies merely the
same thing, and superadds nothing at all to the sense,
why did Moses make this alteration of the name?
Why did the Holy Spirit deem it worthy to be transmitted, in immortal records, to the latest posterity?
The truth is, that he who from the private counsel and
pious wishes of his Parents, was formerly called *Hoshea*
or *Saviour,* is now by Moses, from a prophetic impulse,
denominated *Jehoshua,* or the *Saviour of the Lord;*
because he was appointed and sent by the Lord, to be
the Author of a certain great salvation to his people, and to

---

* Σωτηριον Θεῦ εἰς την Ἑλλαδα φωνην τὸ τῦ Ἰησῦ μεταληφθεν ὄνομα
σημαίνει. *Demonstration. Evangel.* lib. iv. cap. ult.

† Ἰωσυε δε ἐστιν Ἰαω σωτηρια, τῦτ᾽ ἐστιν Θεῦ σωτηριον.

‡ הושיע   § ישוע   ‖ יהושע

¶ The Author's expression is *Tetragramma,* that is, the sacred
name consisting of four letters.

be in this a distinguished type of Him who was to bear the name *Jehoshua* in the whole extent of its import, so as to be at once the Saviour appointed by JEHOVAH, and JEHOVAH the Saviour.*

IX. We may here add the comment of *John Gerhard,* which is as follows:† " Joshua, a type of our Sa-
" viour, was first called *Hoshea* : but Moses, by prefix-
" ing the letter *Jod,* changed this name into *Jehoshua:*
" 1st, To give the more certain assurance to Joshua
" himself and to the people, of that deliverance, and of
" that victory over the Canaanites, to be obtained by
" his instrumentality, of which the searching out of the
" land was the commencement. *Hoshea,* it should be
" noted, is formed from the imperative mood, and sig-
" nifies SAVE ; but *Jehoshua,* from the future, and sig-
" nifies, HE SHALL SAVE. 2dly, To intimate that
" God would confer many blessings on the man, whom
" he had honoured by adding to his name the first letter
" of his own distinctive appellation. 3dly, Because Mo-
" ses, by the Spirit of prophecy, foresaw that Joshua would
" prove a type of Jesus Christ both in name and in fact;
" to wit, by introducing the people into the land of Ca-
" naan. As God added the letter ה *He* from his own
" peculiar name, to Abraham and Sarah, to signify
" that he himself was to descend from them in human
" nature ; so to the name Joshua he added the letter
" י" *Jod* (for in this manner I apprehend it should be
read,) " that thus *Jehoshua* might contain all the let-
" ters of his own name ; and that it might be intimated
" that Jesus, of whom Joshua was a type, would be JE-
" HOVAH, that is, the true God."[50]

* Vide *Gomarum in Mat.* i. 12.
† *In Locis Communibus,* Loc. iv. cap. 1.
[50] See NOTE L.

x. It was not by private authority, nor merely by the direction of his pious mother, that this name was assigned; but by the express command of God the Father, which an angel was commissioned to announce.[f] It was expedient that whatever was performed towards Christ, should be done according to the appointment of God; and it became his heavenly Father to claim to himself the right of giving a name to his Only-begotten Son. Who else, indeed, was capable of doing this? " What is his Son's name, if thou canst tell?"[g] It was of great importance to us, in fine, to be assured that human wisdom bore no part in imposing that name, the contemplation of which is the foundation of all our comfort.

xi. This name was actually put upon Christ, and solemnly declared, in and with his circumcision,[h]—a circumstance which was conformable to an ancient custom of the pious.[i] Nor is it without its mystical import; for from his very circumcision, and even in it, Christ began to do what was necessary to be done for our salvation. By this sign he recognised his subjection to the law;[j] showed that he was *eminently** the seed of Abraham; poured out in his infancy the first-fruits of that most precious blood by which our consciences are purged; and obliged himself to do and to suffer all that was requisite to secure to the heirs of promise the blessings of the covenant made with Abraham. In fine, by the cutting off of a small particle from his natural body, he prefigured the subsequent excision of himself out of the land of the living for the salvation

* Κατ' ἐξοχήν.

[f] Mat. i. 21. Luke i. 31.   [g] Prov. xxx. 4.
[h] Luke ii. 21.   [i] Luke i. 59.
[j] Gal. v. 3.

of his mystical body.[k] What could be more proper
than that the name of JESUS, or the SAVIOUR, should
be given the Son of God, in that sacred rite, in which
so many signs and pledges of his procuring our salvation by himself were exhibited.

XII. Without controversy, this name is exceedingly
illustrious. It designates a work, and includes a glory,
which are proper to God only, and cannot be shared
with any that is not God. When understood, therefore, in its full import, it far surpasses at once the dignity and the power of all creatures. Hence his own
proclamation, " I, even I am JEHOVAH; and besides
" me there is no Saviour."[l] As to others besides our
Lord, that have been called by this name, it was in
them either an empty and high-sounding title, imposed
by human wisdom and ambitiously assumed; or conferred by the gracious indulgence of God on those
whom he employed as the instruments of a compara-
tively inconsiderable, a corporeal and temporal salvation, and whom he intended to be, in this respect, types
of his Son. Its signification, consequently, when applied to those persons, was as much lower as the shadow is inferior to the body. In its full signification, it
belongs, as well exclusively as eminently, to the Son of
God.

XIII. Yet, without doubt, an erroneous opinion is entertained by those who imagine, that the name Jesus,
as it is either expressed in writing or pronounced by
the tongue, is of such superior dignity above all the
other names of God or Christ, that it ought to be venerated either by the bending of the knee, or by any
other token of homage. The Apostle, indeed, teaches

[k] Is. liii. 8. Ephes. v. 23.
[l] ואין מבלעדי מושיע Is. xliii. 11.

us, that " at the name of Jesus every knee should bow.["m](m)
But in this passage, " the name" does not signify the
term, but the Person himself, and the dignity conferred on him, expressed by this term ; as may be frequently seen in sacred writ, and particularly in Acts
iv. 12. Let this passage also be compared with that
in Isaiah xlv. 23. to which the Apostle manifestly alludes : " Unto me every knee shall bow."

xiv. It is not possible for him to whom counsel be-
longeth,[n] to bear a title without performing the work
and possessing the honour it implies. Whatever, therefore, may be designated by the word SAVIOUR, is found
in reality in our Lord Jesus ; the angel having added
this reason for the name given him,—" for he shall save
" his people from their sins."

xv. Further, he is said to *save* us, not because he
has explained the doctrine of the Gospel of salvation in
the clearest terms, and has confirmed it at once by the
example of a most holy life, by stupendous miracles, by
an almost incredible patience under sufferings, and by
the martyrdom of a most grievous and bitter death ;—
not because he has openly shown the way to immortality by his resurrection, and has obtained authority
from God to bestow upon us everlasting life. This is
the Semi-Mahometan blasphemy of *Socinus.* If the
salvation of Christ consist in nothing else, how slight,
at least, is his superiority to several other Prophets,
and in particular, to his Apostles !

xvi. Nor does he sustain the name of Saviour for this
reason, that he has restored us to a state in which God,
without any remaining obstacle from his avenging justice, and according to the inclinations of his mercy, is
both able and willing to communicate his blessings

[m] Phil. ii. 10.   [n] Prov. viii. 14.

anew, in that manner and upon those conditions which seem good to him; while, however, this procuring of salvation by Christ, so far as the nature of the thing is concerned, (though God knew that the event would certainly be otherwise) may remain entire and perfect in itself, although there were none to whom it should be applied, and who should experience its happy fruits. In this manner the Remonstrants, in their synodical writings,* debase this magnificent title of our Lord.

XVII. Were these allegations true, he would not have obtained for mankind the actual restoration of any to a state of favour and acceptance; he would not even have acquired for them any thing by which they can be saved: but would merely have removed the impediment arising from punitive justice, and thus obtained for God the power of acting graciously towards men. Nay, he would not even have obtained this for God, since, according to their sentiments, God possesses this power of himself, without the intervention of Christ, and previously to any work which he has done. For they hold the following language in their *Apology*;† " To affirm that the avenging justice of God is so es-" sential to his nature, that by virtue of it God is " obliged and necessitated to punish sin, is very absurd, " and very unworthy of God." *Corvinus* in like manner says, " God could have saved us without the satis-" faction of Christ, but he would not do it."‡ These expressions obviously tend to make void, by bold inventions, the whole doctrine of Christ's having procured our salvation.[51]

* *Synodal. Script.* p. 283, 285.
† *Apologia,* p. 46.
‡ *Censura Anato. Molin.* p. 436.
[51] See NOTE LI.

xviii. In fine, he is not called a Saviour on this account, that by his sufferings and death he has made satisfaction for what they call *mortal* sins, and delivered us from eternal punishment, leaving it to believers themselves to satisfy for *venial* sins, and to suffer temporary punishment, partly by deeds of penance in this life, and partly by the torments of purgatory in the life to come:—or even because he merited by his own most perfect holiness, that those works of holy obedience which we are bound to perform, if done from faith, should, though imperfect, merit salvation itself; and that those which we perform beyond what is due, should also merit a certain eminent degree of salvation and happiness. In this manner, the Doctors of the Popish class most unjustly divide the work of our salvation between Christ and men; vainly attempting to shelter sentiments palpably erroneous, by closely heaping absurdities upon absurdities.

xix. To these prodigious errors we oppose the Apostle Peter's sacred announcement of the truth in the following words: " Neither is there salvation in any other; " for there is none other name under heaven given " among men whereby we must be saved."[n] Now Christ saves us, as he PROCURES for us and APPLIES to us, a *real*, spiritual, and eternal SALVATION.

xx. To attain a distinct view of this subject, it is necessary for us to consider, first, the SALVATION of which Christ is the author; and then, the ACTS OF CHRIST with respect to this salvation.

xxi. SALVATION consists of two parts; *Freedom from all evil*, and the *participation of all good*.

xxii. SIN is the greatest of all evils, the spring and origin of every other misery, and sufficient of itself to

[n] Acts iv. 12.

render a man extremely wretched. No other evil is mentioned by the angel, when he explains the reason of the name JESUS. That sin is the sum and quintessence of all misery, is demonstrated in the following manner.—The chief happiness of man consists in likeness to God. This is not only affirmed by the Apostle John,[o] but it was even discovered by the light of nature to several of the Heathen philosophers. It is a principle so evidently true, that the Devil himself, in his reasoning with our first parents, took it for granted as of unquestionable certainty. Hence it follows, that he who is the most unlike to the blessed God, is in by far the most miserable state. Besides, the unspotted holiness of God is the glory of all the Divine perfections; and, accordingly, he is called " glorious in holiness."[p] Sin is an evil extremely contrary to that holiness. We must conclude, therefore, that sin, which places man in a condition the most unlike, nay, diametrically opposite, to the Divine blessedness, is the greatest misery of man.

XXIII. The malignity of sin will still more deeply penetrate the conscience, if we consider that the three following things are in it. 1st, An extreme *pollution*, which infects the whole soul,[q] and which is directly contrary to the glorious beauty of the Divine image. 2dly, A *power* of tyrannical domination, by which it deprives men of all that liberty and dignity which are worthy of the sons of God, and wreathes about their neck a galling and oppressive yoke,[r] setting no bounds or measure to their labour, but, with the daughter of the horseleech, incessantly crying, *Give, give.*[s] 3dly,

[o] 1 John iii. 2. [p] נאדר בקודש Exod. xv. 11.
[q] James i. 21. [r] 2 Pet. ii. 19.
[s] Prov. xxx. 15.

Guilt, which renders the sinner obnoxious to every kind of punishment in soul and body, to be undergone through eternity. The truth is, that unless satisfaction to Divine justice arise from some other quarter, all hope of recovery being utterly cut off, there remaineth nothing to the man that has offended even in a single instance, but " a certain fearful looking-for of judge-
" ment and fiery indignation, which shall devour the
" adversary."[t] Thus all other evils and miseries may be referred to sin, because the obligation to suffer them arises from sin.

XXIV. But when sin is put away, no evil can remain. Why should God punish an admirable work of his hands, in which he finds nothing contrary to his nature, or offensive to the eyes of his holiness? Hence the blessedness mentioned by David ; " Blessed is the man
" whose transgression is forgiven."[u]

XXV. It is not intended, nevertheless, that the absence of this evil, or that freedom from misery, includes the whole of happiness ; for a state of perfect happiness also comprises the possession of all that is good. But as darkness is dispelled by nothing but light, as nakedness is remedied by nothing but garments, as poverty is removed by nothing but riches ; so sin can be removed,—with respect to its *guilt,*—only by such a righteousness as is, at the same time, the ground of a title to life ;—with respect to its *dominion* and *pollution,* only by the sanctification of the Spirit ;—with respect to the *curse* which it brings, only by the communication of the Divine favour. It is because these blessings cannot be separated, that our salvation is represented as consisting in the removal of sin.

[t] Heb. x. 27.   See Rom. i. 32. ii. 9.   [u] Ps. xxxii. 1.

XXVI. The following benefits are essential to salvation. 1st, The participation of a righteousness by which we may obtain " justification of life."[v] 2dly, " True " holiness," in which the glories of the Divine image may shine forth ;[w] which is the ornament of the house of God,[x] and the beauty of every daughter of the king.[y] 3dly, Communion with God in grace, so that we may say, The LORD is the Portion of mine inheritance, and of my cup; thou maintainest my lot.[z] This communion with God includes, not only the privilege of approaching familiarly to him, to behold him, with open eyes, in the sanctuary of devout prayer and meditation;[a] but also that *boldness** by which we can pour forth all the sorrows of a distressed heart into his bosom, and confidently express our stammering requests, soliciting a richer supply of grace ;[b]—that descent of divine grace, by which he kindly visits the soul whom he loves, and that loves him in return,[c] and by which he *speaks to the heart* in the most affectionate terms ;[d]—and, in fine, that enjoyment of God which consists in this, that the soul sweetly acquiesces in him as its treasure,[e] is enriched by his riches, nourished by his abundance, protected by his power, guided by his wisdom, refreshed by his goodness, replenished by his sufficiency ; so that it knows nothing desirable except the full enjoyment of him, a felicity of which in this world it has only the first fruits. 4thly, Then follow, peace of consci-

---

* Παῤῥησία.

[v] Δικαίωμα εἰς δικαίωσιν ζωῆς.   Rom. v. 18.

[w] Ὁσιότης της ἀληθείας.   Ephes. iv. 24.

[x] Ps. xciii. 5.   [y] Ps. xlv. 13.

[z] Ps. xvi. 5.   [a] Ps. lxiii. 2.

[b] Heb. iv. 16.   [c] John xiv. 23.

[d] Hos. ii. 14. marg.   [e] Ps. lxxiii. 28.

ence, " the riches of the full assurance of understand-
" ing,"[f] and the strongest certainty with regard to the
possession of perfect felicity in due season; from whence
arises a " joy unspeakable and full of glory." " In
' whom," says Peter, " though now ye see him not,
" yet believing, ye rejoice."[g] 5thly, The perfect enjoyment of God in glory; first, in the soul after its departure from the prison of this animal body,[h] and then
in body and soul together, when the body shall have
become glorious and heavenly, after a blessed resurrection.[i]

xxvii. Such is the salvation, in reference to which
the Son of God is called Jesus. We now proceed to
speak of his Acts with regard to it; of which the two
following, in particular, require to be considered : first,
the Impetration,* secondly, the Application of
it. Of these, the former gives us a title to Salvation;
the latter, the actual possession and enjoyment of Salvation. Jesus accomplished the one in his state of humiliation; he is constantly engaged in performing the
other in his state of exaltation till the end of the world.

xxviii. Jesus procured our salvation in the following manner. 1st, By taking upon himself the guilt of
our sins, and suffering the punishment due to them in
body and soul, he, being God-man and consequently a
person of infinite dignity, gave the most ample satisfaction to the avenging justice of God, and obtained for
us deliverance from all penal evil. " Christ hath re-

---

* The Latin word *Impetratio* signifies *procuring*, or *obtaining*. It
is here used by the Author to denote what is commonly called the
purchasing of our salvation. It seems proper to retain his own expression, in an English form. T.

[f] Col. ii. 2.   [g] 1 Pet. i. 8.
[h] 2 Cor. v. 1.   Phil. i. 23.   [i] Ps. xvii. 15.   Phil. iii. 21.

" deemed us from the curse of the law, being made a
" curse for us."ʲ 2dly, Having fulfilled the whole obedience of the law in our room by the most perfect holiness as well of his nature as of his actions, he has procured for us a right to that consummate felicity, the
only condition of possessing which, in a manner consistent with the veracity, purity, and justice of God, is the
persevering practice of perfect holiness, agreeably to
these words of the law, " The man that doth these
" things, shall live by them."ᵏ It was necessary, that
this righteousness of the law should be fulfilled by
Christ :ˡ and thus there is in Christ a righteousness,
which " comes upon all men to justification of life;" " by
" the obedience of one many are made righteous ;" and
" grace reigns through righteousness unto eternal
" life."ᵐ 52

xxix. The effect of this impetration, therefore, is
not a *bare possibility* of the remission of sin, and of our
reconciliation with God, as the Remonstrants contend;
but the *actual remission* of sin, and *actual reconciliation.* In consequence of what Christ has done and suffered, God cannot, consistently with his own truth and
justice, and consistently with the covenant which he
made with his Son, abandon to condemnation, or exclude from partaking of salvation, any one of the elect.
He has even declared, on the contrary, that, since satisfaction has been already made by his Son and accepted by himself, there is nothing which he can require his elect either to suffer or to do, in order to acquire for themselves exemption from punishment or a
title to life ; but that this one thing only remains for

ʲ Gal. iii. 13.   ᵏ Rom. x. 5.
ˡ Rom. viii. 4.   ᵐ Rom. v. 18, 19, 21.
        ⁵² See NOTE LII.

them, that they rejoice, each in his own order and time, in that title to salvation which Christ has obtained for them, and in the possession of salvation by virtue of that title. This is what the Apostle teaches in these words : " God was in Christ, reconciling the world unto " himself, not imputing their trespasses unto them."n *

xxx. Further, Jesus powerfully APPLIES the salvation which he has obtained. He applies it to all those, and to those only, for whom he obtained it ; that is, those whose sins he took upon himself, and whose persons, he, as their Surety, represented. They for whom Christ died, may boldly say, Who shall lay our sins to our charge ? " It is God that justifieth. Who is he " that condemneth ?"o They whom Christ hath redeemed from the curse of the law, remain no longer under the curse ; but the blessing of Abraham comes upon them.p Those for whom Christ gave himself, he has redeemed from all iniquity, and purified unto himself a peculiar people, zealous of good works.q In short, the impetration and the application of redemption are of equal extent : the object of both is evidently one and the same.

xxxi. Salvation is applied to the elect, *initially*, in this life ;—*perfectly*, in the future life. Even in this life, the first-fruits of the Spirit,r who is the Spirit of glory,s are imparted to the sons of God. " He that " believeth on the Son," not only shall have hereafter, but already " hath everlasting life ;"t and is " saved by

* The Author more fully illustrates the effect of Christ's satisfaction, and replies to the objections of *Arminius* in his *Economy of the Covenants*, book ii. chap. 7. T.

n 2 Cor. v. 19.   o Rom. viii. 33, 34.
p Gal. iii. 13, 14.   q Tit. ii. 14.
r Rom. viii. 23.   s 1 Pet. iv. 14.
t John iii. 36.

" hope."[u] He has received from Christ, not merely what serves to comfort him amidst the adversities of the present world, but also what enables him to infer the inexpressible greatness of that felicity which is reserved for him in heaven.

XXXII. The application of salvation, as to *the present life*, is effected by the following acts. 1st, Christ effectually calls, invites, and allures his chosen and redeemed to the participation of the purchased salvation, outwardly by the word of the Gospel, and inwardly by the Spirit of grace.[v] 2dly, By the same word and Spirit, he regenerates them, by implanting in them the principle of a new life, that they may be a kind of firstfruits of his creatures.[w] 3dly, Having given them faith, he justifies them.[x] 4thly, He admits them, when justified, to a blessed intercourse of peace and friendship.[y] 5thly, By a gracious adoption, he grants them the privileges of sons ; he blesses them with the Spirit of adoption, and by an unalterable testament, gives them a title to the heavenly inheritance.[z] 6thly, He adorns them more and more, with the beautiful garments of holiness.[a] 7thly, He seals and comforts them by his Holy Spirit, who is the earnest of the future inheritance.[b] 8thly, He keeps them by his power through faith unto salvation, ready to be revealed at the last, the appointed time.[c] 9thly, He sometimes affords, in fine, to the objects of his love, particularly amidst the approaches of death, so clear a vision, and so rich a fore-

[u] Rom. viii. 24.
[v] Is. xlv. 22.
[w] James i. 18.
[x] Rom. viii. 30.
[y] Rom. v. i.   James ii. 23.
[z] Rom. viii. 15, 16, 17.
[a] 1 Thes. v. 23.
[b] Ephes. i. 13, 14.
[c] 1 Pet. i. 5.

taste of celestial things, that they appear to see them before their eyes, and are affected by them just as if they were present in the place where these things are.

XXXIII. The *future life* may be considered, either with regard to the soul in the separate state, prior to the day of judgment; or with regard to the whole man, after the consummation of all things.

XXXIV. He receives the soul, immediately after it has finished the labours of this animal life, to heavenly joys and heavenly mansions. Its place of abode, as well as its state and condition, is gloriously changed.[d]

XXXV. But when all that respects the completing of the Church in this earth shall have been accomplished, Jesus himself will appear in the clouds of heaven, in all the splendour of Divine magnificence, to judge the world; will raise the bodies of his people from the dust of death, adorn them with celestial qualities, unite them to their blessed spirits, never again to be separated from them by death, and conduct them to his Father's house; where all things concurring to exhibit the brightest manifestation of the glory of God, the whole assembly of the elect shall be satiated with those felicities, which " eye hath not seen, nor ear heard, and " which have not entered into the heart of man."[e]

Since Christ is so illustrious an Author of so great a salvation, who would deny that he has every possible title to bear the name JESUS?

XXXVI. It now remains that every one prove himself, whether he truly believes that the Son of God is JE-SUS, that is, an all-sufficient and the only Saviour. Such self-investigation is highly necessary. Because

---

[d] Luke xxii. 43.   Rev. xiv. 13.   Heb. xii. 23.

[e] 1 Cor. ii. 9.   John xiv. 3.   1 Thes. iv. 14—18.   1 Cor. xv. 22—58.

we have heard of Jesus from our earliest years, because we are accustomed to call the Son of God by this name, because the profession of the contrary would justly sound horrible in the ears of all as a renunciation of the whole of Christianity—on these accounts, every one rashly persuades himself, without ever having rightly examined the matter, that he believes in the Son of God as Jesus, and his own Saviour; while a great number give evidence by the whole tenor of their life that they do not believe.

xxxvii. The man who, in reality, believes that Christ is JESUS, or in other words, that all his salvation is laid up in him alone, may be thus distinguished. 1st, He will undervalue all other things in comparison of Christ; and how excellent or splendid soever they may seem, yet if they are laid in the balance with the Saviour, or opposed to him, he will count them but loss and dung.[f] As the sun in the firmament darkens all the stars, so the glory of Christ's sufficiency, perceived by the eye of faith, eclipses the lustre of all other objects. After it is once fixed and settled in his mind that Jesus alone is all, the believer says, " What will " other things be to me, if I am destitute of Jesus? " What will riches avail, or honours, or pleasures, or " all those other enjoyments that are invidiously styled " good things, whether of fortune, of the body, or of " the mind? Since I am thoroughly persuaded that " salvation is found in Jesus alone, salvation cannot be " in those things. They can neither confer salvation " by their presence, nor take it away by their absence. " Without Jesus, they are nothing; because Jesus is " all. If they are any thing at all, when possessed in

[f] Phil. iii. 7, 8.

" Jesus, they derive their value entirely from him;
" from whose love they then proceed, and who has in-
" fused into them any slight taste they may have of
" his sweetness. If, therefore, they ought to be re-
" garded with any degree of esteem, it is merely because
" they come from Jesus, and lead to Jesus."

xxxviii. 2dly, He will desire Jesus above every other
object. According to the definition of Aristotle, " A
" good thing is what all desire."* When a man believes, therefore, that not merely a good, but the Chief
good, is found in Jesus Christ, and in him alone, it is
impossible but he must ardently love Jesus, hunger and
thirst after him,g and seek him by earnest prayer and
at any cost that may be necessary ; prepared to sell all
other things, that he may obtain this pearl, this true
and invaluable pearl.h In private and in public, at
home and abroad, in hours of leisure and in hours of
business, in solitude and in company, he will often say
in his heart with unutterable sighs, " Lord Jesus, O
" that I were thine ! O that thou wert mine !"

xxxix. 3dly, He will not be able, too, to acquiesce
in any thing short of the possession of Jesus, or to rest
until he arrive at certainty, and complete security, with
regard to the possession of him. If a merchant knew
that his whole property and treasure were contained in
one ship, what anxious days and nights would he spend,
and how would he tremble at every appearance of the
dark clouds collecting, at every burst of the raging
storm, never at ease till he see the longed-for vessel arrive in the harbour ? So also, he who believes that all
his salvation is laid up in Jesus alone, will experience

* Ἀγαθόν ἐστιν ὃ πάντα ἐφίεται.
g Ps. xlii. 2.   h Mat. xiii. 45, 46.

constant solicitude, till Jesus say to his soul, " I am " thy salvation."[i] In a matter of so great moment, he will not venture to depend on slight and insufficient grounds, or on the flattering suggestions of a fatally deceiving heart. An " exceeding and eternal weight " of glory," is of too great importance to be suspended on a spider's web,—on the slender thread of a presumptuous imagination.

XL. 4thly, In fine, when he is certain of his communion with Jesus, 1. He will exult in him, and rejoice with an inexpressible joy, the nature and properties of which we have elsewhere described.* 2. With all care and diligence he will solicitously keep possession of his Jesus, lest any thing intervene to mar the delightful enjoyment of his Saviour, and of the salvation which is in him.[j] 3. His heart will be dissolved in love to Jesus; and carried away by a sacred transport, he will not suffer himself to be torn from his embraces.[k]

XLI. These and similar affections, exercised towards Jesus by the believing and loving soul, are described by *Bernard,* in an elegant Song, which well deserves to be committed to memory, and to be frequently sung to the LORD JESUS, in spirit and in truth.[53] I will, therefore, give it here, for the sake of those who have not a copy of *Bernard's* Works.

---

* The Author probably refers to what he had said on spiritual joy in *Dissert.* v. sect. 13. *et seq.*, and to his remarks on the same topic in his *Economy of the Covenants,* book iii. chap. 14. sect. 10. T.

[i] Ps. xxxv. 3.   [j] Song iii. 4.

[k] Song viii. 6, 7.

[53] See NOTE LIII.

*Most blessed Jesus, dearest Friend,
Hope of my longing, panting mind,
I seek thee with my tears and sighs,
To thee my soul lifts up her cries.

O Jesus, cordial to the heart,
Who light and life dost still impart,
A living Fountain, full and fresh,
Surpassing every joy and wish;

When on my heart thou'rt pleas'd to shine,
My soul is cheered with truth divine;
All I contemn but things above,
My bosom glows with heavenly love.

Jesus, my chief and lasting Good,
My Saviour, strength, and precious food,
Thy presence grant, thy glory show,
Thy boundless love, cause me to know.

He whom the love of Jesus warms,
Approved by Jesus, knows his charms.
Bless'd is the man he fills with grace:
'Tis all I crave, to see his face.

* O Jesu mi dulcissime,
Spes suspirantis animæ,
Te quærunt piæ lachrymæ,
Te clamor mentis intimæ.

Jesu, dulcedo cordium,
Fons vivus, lumen mentium,
Excedens omne gaudium,
Et omne desiderium.

Quando cor nostrum visitas,
Tunc lucet ei veritas,
Mundi vilescit vanitas,
Et intus fervet charitas.

Jesu, mi bone, sentiam
Amoris tui copiam,
Da mihi per præsentiam,
Tuam videre gloriam.

Quem tuus amor ebriat,
Novit quid Jesus sapiat.
Quam felix est quem satiat!
Non est ultra quod cupiat.

Jesus, thou Lord of Angels bright,
Great source of all their radiant light,
Thy name's to me supremely dear,
Delightful music to my ear;

The choicest honey to my taste,
Celestial nectar, rich repast.
Nor nature's stores, nor toys of art,
Afford such pleasure to the heart.

A thousand sighs for thee I heave,
To thee, my Jesus, still I cleave.
When wilt thou come, and give me joy;
A joy that fills, but cannot cloy?

Now what I sought, my eyes descry;
Behold! he comes on mountains high.
My arms embrace my Saviour kind,
His love inflames, dissolves my mind.

Happy the flame his love creates!
Happy the soul his grace dilates!
How sweet my love for God's dear Son!
It makes me feel a heaven begun.

Jesus, thou art my heart's delight;
Love rises to perfection's height,

> Jesu decus Angelicum,
> In aure dulce canticum,
> In ore mel mirificum,
> In corde nectar cœlicum.
>
> Desidero te millies
> Mi Jesu, quando venies?
> Me lætum quando facies?
> Me de te quando saties?
>
> Jam quod quæsivi video,
> Quod concupivi teneo.
> Amore Jesu langueo,
> Et corde totus ardeo.
>
> O beatum incendium,
> Et ardens desiderium!
> O dulce refrigerium,
> Amare Deum Filium!
>
> Tu mentis delectatio,
> Amoris consummatio.

In thee alone, my song, my boast,
Dear Saviour of a world that's lost.
  In thee the choirs of heav'n exult,
To thee my heart doth sing and shout.
Thy glory, love, and mercy sure,
My cares dispel, my thoughts allure.
  Thou art the Martyr's crown, the prize,
Which every Christian soldier eyes.
Thou art the fair, th' unfading flower;
The lily, fragrant every hour.
  The virgin heart, the soul that's pure,
In thee finds peace and joy secure.
My humble suit, Lord Jesus, hear,
For then I live, when thou art near.

> Tu mea gloriatio,
> Jesu mundi salvatio.
>   Tu verum cœli gaudium,
> Jesu cordis tripudium,
> Tollent omne fastidium,
> Mel, nectar, melos suavium.
>   Jesu corona Martyrum,
> Et flos perennis virginum:
> Tu casti cordis lilium,
> Tu decertantis præmium.
> Exaudi preces supplicum,
> Nil extra te quærentium.

DISSERTATION X.

ON THE NAME *CHRIST.*

I. CHRIST is the second name of Jesus our Saviour. This designation is in Hebrew, MESSIAH,* pronounced by the *Hellenistical* Jews, MESSIAS;[a] and in Latin, UNCTUS.† Although it has been attributed to other illustrious persons, both amongst the people of God,[b] and amongst the Gentiles,[c] yet as ascribed to our Saviour, it is " a more excellent name ;"[d] for he is " Mes- " siah the Prince," [e]—being so called, by way of emi- nence, as one who is " higher than the kings of the " earth,"[f] and who " in all things has the pre-emi- nence."[g]

II. Owing either to ignorance or to malice, the hea- then populace and several profane writers, by changing one letter, transformed this venerable name of our Lord into CHREST. Thus *Lucian* says, " If indeed

---

* משיח   † In English, The ANOINTED.   T.
[a] John i. 41.   [b] 1 Sam. xxiv. 6.   [c] Is. xlv. 1.
[d] Διαφορωτερον ονομα.   Heb. i. 4.
[e] משיח נגיד.   Dan. ix. 25.
[f] Ps. lxxxix. 27.   [g] Col. i. 18.

" *CHREST* were among the nations."* *Tertullian*
and *Lactantius* have imputed this manner of expressing our Lord's name to ignorance. " Since," says the
former, " it is erroneously pronounced *Chrestian* by you,
" (for you know not even the name,) it is composed of
" gentleness and benignity. Thus an innocent appel-
" lation is hated in the innocent persons that bear it,
" and the sect is now hated under the name of its
" Founder."† " It is necessary," says the latter, " to
" explain the reason of this name, on account of the ig-
" norance of those who, by changing one of the letters,
" commonly call him *Chrest*." ‡ This mistake arose,
possibly, from a confusion in the pronunciation of the
Greek vowels (η) *Eta* and (ι) *Iota;* for the Æolians,
as grammarians affirm, often interchanged these two
letters. In consequence of the same erroneous mode
of pronouncing the letter *Iota*, the ancients sometimes
wrote the name with a diphthong, saying *Chreist* § instead of *Christ*.‖ But malice appears also to have had
its influence in producing this false pronunciation.
The true name of our Lord was so often to be heard
from the lips of his followers, that, at any rate, it could
not have remained unknown to most of the heathen.
Though the word *Chrestus*, too, signifies gentleness
and benignity, as *Tertullian* finely retorted, and though
Christ was in reality gentle,[h] yet a reproach and an in-
dignity were couched under this appellation. Thus
Capitolinus relates of *Pertinax* that he was styled

---

* Ἐι τόχοιγε ΧΡΗΣΤΟΣ καὶ ἐν ἔθνεσιν. *In Philopatri.*

† *Apologet.* cap. iii.

‡ *De Vera Sapient.* lib. iv. cap. 7.

§ Χρειστος.

‖ Vid. *Huet. Dem. Evang.* Propos. iii. Parag. 20.

[h] Χρηστος. Mal. xi. 30.

Chrestologus, that is, *smooth-tongued,* because he spoke well and acted ill, was kind in words, not so in deeds.

III. To the same cause I would also refer the following expression of *Suetonius* in his Life of *Claudius:* " While the Jews, at the instigation of *Chrest,* were " continually creating disturbance, he banished them " from Rome." * Though Christ himself had never been at Rome, yet the doctrine of Christ disseminated there by his disciples, might be the cause, at least the occasion, of great dissensions amongst the Jews who resided in that city; some of them embracing it with distinguished alacrity and fortitude, others resisting it with frantic zeal and inveterate obstinacy.[54] From those contentions the edict of *Claudius* took its rise; for, as *Marcellus Donatus* has learnedly observed on this passage of *Tranquillus,*† historians make no mention of any celebrated man of the name *Chrestus,* excepting *Chrestus* the Sophist of *Byzantium,* who was a scholar of *Herodes Atticus* at Rome, during the reign of the Emperor *Adrian.* But this we notice in passing. Let us now return to Christ our Saviour.

IV. In order to understand aright the import of this name, three things must be distinctly illustrated. *First,* What is signified by the Anointing, from which Christ receives the name. *Secondly,* To how many, and to what offices he was anointed. *Thirdly,* In what way all believers are admitted to a participation of that Unction, as also of the name. For his " name is as " ointment poured forth," [i] which he not only retains for himself, but also graciously imparts to " his fellows."[j]

---

* Judæos, impulsore CHRESTO, assidue tumultuantes, Roma expulit. *Suet. in Claudio,* cap. xxv.

† This is another name of *Suetonius.* T.

[i] Song i. 3.   [j] Ps. xlv. 8.   [54] See NOTE LIV.

v. The Anointing of Christ denotes two things. 1st His DESIGNATION to the Mediatorial office: for " he " glorified not himself to be made an High Priest,"[k] but God " hath ordained" him.[l] 2dly, The COMMU- NICATION OF THE GIFTS OF THE HOLY SPIRIT, who was not given him " by measure."[m] Each of these has its distinct seasons, and its several periods or de- grees.

vi. The DESIGNATION includes, 1st, The foreknow- ledge, pre-ordination, or predestination of the Son of God to the office of Mediator, which took place from eternity.[n] If we were chosen in Christ before the foun- dation of the world,[o] to be saved by him, Christ must of necessity have been chosen together with us, to be our Saviour.[p] 2dly, The promise of Christ in the pro- phecies, and a delineation of him so accurate, that as soon as he came into the world he might be immediate- ly recognised in his true character by those who waited for the Consolation of Israel, and duly considered him. " For him hath God the Father sealed:"[q] that is, he has so distinguished him by certain characteristics, and has impressed such marks and " engravings" upon him,[r] that by these he might be " declared to be the " Son of God with power."[s] 3dly, The introduction of Christ to his mediatorial work, by his mission into the world.[t] 4thly, The Father's bearing testimony to his Son by a voice from heaven; of which we have three instances. 1. Immediately after his Baptism at Jor-

---

[k] Heb. v. 5.   [l] $\Omega\rho\iota\sigma\epsilon$. Acts xvii. 31.

[m] John iii. 34. Is. lxi. 1. Acts x. 38.

[n] 1 Pet. i. 20.   [o] Ephes. i. 4.

[p] Comp. Is. xlii. 1.   [q] John vi. 27.

[r] Zech. iii. 9.   [s] Rom. i. 4.

[t] John x. 36.

dan.[u] 2. On the holy mount.[v] 3. When he had an anticipation of his passion.[w]—All these are comprised in the general idea of the Unction. The eternal pre-ordination, at least, of which the rest are only the execution and declaration, is expressly denominated the anointing. " I was set up, *anointed*, from everlasting, from the beginning, ere ever the earth was."[x]

VII. To the *Second* part of the Anointing I refer, 1st, That fulness of the Spirit which was imparted to the human nature of Christ from its conception and birth, by the indwelling of the Divinity in the flesh which he assumed.[y] Astonishing indications of this shone forth when he was a boy twelve years old; and the more illustrious instances of it which he gave as he made progress in life, excited the admiration of every spectator.[z] 2dly, The copious communication of those gifts of the Spirit, by which he was to demonstrate, in the public discharge of his office, that he is the promised Messiah, and infinitely superior to others who preceded him, either as the Preachers, or as in any respect the Authors, of salvation. This was denoted by the emblem of the Spirit descending upon him in the likeness of a dove, when by the baptism of John, and the testimony of the Father, he was publicly installed into his office.[a] 3dly, That unparalleled height of glory and joy, to which he was advanced, as the reward of his labours, after his resurrection from the dead and ascension to heaven. This idea is suggested by the following words of the Psalmist: " Thou lovest righte-

---

[u] Mat. iii. 17. John i. 32—34.

[v] Mat. xvii. 5.   [w] John xii. 28.

[x] Ante seculum inuncta fui, &c. Prov. viii. 23.

[y] Col. i. 19. ii. 9.   [z] Luke ii. 47, 52.

[a] Mat. iii. 16, 17.

" ousness, and hatest wickedness," thou hast fully accomplished the whole work of the office with which
thou wast intrusted; " therefore," as a recompence for
thy merits, " God, thy God, hath anointed thee with
" the oil of gladness," has honoured thee with distinguished glory, and with glorious joy, " above thy fellows." b 55

VIII. The three-fold anointing of David, seems, in
some measure, to correspond with these three degrees
of our Lord's unction. 1st, At Bethlehem by Samuel,
while Saul was yet living and reigning; c after which
he lived privately for a time. 2dly, At Hebron, when
he was anointed King of Judah, after Saul's death; d
at which period he took actual possession of the kingdom, yet had many conflicts to sustain with the house
of Saul. 3dly, At Hebron again, when he was proclaimed King of all Israel, with the universal consent
of the people, the family of Saul being now divested of
all authority; d—in consequence of which unction, finding himself confirmed in the kingdom, he took the
strong hold of Zion. In like manner, our Lord was
anointed with the unction of the Spirit, even when he
was yet leading a private life. He was enriched, too,
with an ampler measure of this unction, when he entered on the actual execution of his mediatorial office,
which he could not discharge without most arduous
conflicts. But after it was demonstrated by his resurrection that he had conquered and triumphed over all
his enemies, the oil of joy was poured without measure
on his head, and " the rod, *the sceptre*, of his strength,
" was sent out of Zion." e To this, if I mistake not,

b Ps. xlv. 7.   c 1 Sam. xvi. 13.
d 2 Sam. v. 3.   e Ps. cx. 2.
55 See NOTE LV.

Peter expressly referred when he said; " Therefore, let
" all the house of Israel know assuredly, that God hath
" made that same Jesus whom ye have crucified, both
" Lord and Christ."[f]

IX. The offices with which our Lord was invested by
the unction he received, are three; in conformity to the
three-fold order of those, who, according to the Divine
appointment, were sometimes anointed of old. These
were, first, PROPHETS, as is commonly inferred from
the instance of Elisha. " Elisha the son of Shaphat of
" Abel-meholah, shalt thou anoint to be Prophet in
" thy room."[g] With respect to this *anointing* of Elisha,
however, to the prophetical office, as also of Hazael to
be King of Syria, and of Jehu to be King of Israel, it
is disputed amongst the learned, whether it is to be understood properly and literally; or figuratively and *improperly*,* for *designating, constituting,* and *declaring.*
Some, for the following reasons, prefer the latter. 1st,
Because we nowhere read that either Hazael or Elisha
was anointed by Elijah. Jehu, indeed, was anointed,
but not by Elijah, nor even by Elisha, but by one of
Elisha's disciples; and the ceremony, too, was done in
a very slight and cursory manner.[h] 2dly, Because Elijah, when executing the Divine commission regarding
Elisha, is not said to have anointed him, but to have
" cast his mantle" upon him.[i] 3dly, Because we find
nowhere else either a command relative to the anointing of prophets, or an example of such anointing.

Such is the reasoning of our Protestant brother *Pis-
cator,* after *Theodoret, Abulensis, Salianus,* and others
quoted by *Cornelius a Lapide.* But in opposition to

* Καταχρηστικως.

[f] Acts ii. 36. [g] 2 Kings xix. 16.
[h] 2 Kings ix. [i] 1 Kings xix. 19.

these arguments, it may be said, 1st, That we ought not to depart from the proper and usual signification of a word, without urgent necessity; which cannot be pleaded in this instance. 2dly, Although it is nowhere recorded that Elijah anointed those whom he was charged to anoint, it does not follow that this was not done; since it is not even recorded that he announced Hazael king of Syria, and Jehu king of Israel, which, however, is supposed. 3dly, It would be an exceedingly harsh *impropriety of speech*,* if the designation of a Prophet were called an anointing, and yet in the ordination of the Prophet no anointing properly so called, took place. Thus it would be absurd to say, that the Roman Consuls were anointed to the Consulship. 4thly, There is nothing to hinder us from believing, that Elisha was called and invited to the prophetical office by more than one ceremony. *Sanchez* observes not amiss, that " the anointing made Elisha a " prophet; the mantle made him a colleague to Eli-" jah." † A mantle, however, seems to have been usually worn by the Prophets. j As to the expression which immediately follows in *Sanchez*,—" and a Monk," ‡ it is ridiculous and absurd. 5thly, We would not rashly allege, in the mean time, that Prophets were constantly and universally anointed. This command respecting Elisha is sufficient for our purpose, whether we consider it as a departure from the ordinary usage, or suppose that anointing was not uncommon on similar occasions.

x. Further, the PRIESTS, also, were anointed, ac-

---

* Καταχρησις.

† Unctio Elisæum fecit Prophetam; pallium, Eliæ contubernalem.

‡ Et Monachum.

j Zech. xiii. 4.

cording to the Divine appointment : " Thou shalt
" anoint Aaron and his sons, and consecrate them, that
" they may minister unto me in the priest's office."[k]
The Jewish Doctors affirm, that this precept is to be
understood in this sense, that all such descendants of
the sons of Aaron as were common priests, were to be
considered as anointed *in them*, without the repetition
of the ceremony towards those individually, who succeeded the dead, in the priestly office. They add, however, that a new High-priest was always anointed at
his instalment, as, also, the priest whom they call *the
anointed for war*,* according to the law recorded in Deu-
teronomy xx. 2. But they will have this anointing
to extend only to the period of the first temple ; for it
could be done only with that sacred ointment, which
was prepared agreeably to the Divine direction,[1] and
the making of any composition similar to which, was
strictly prohibited. [m] The Talmudists, however, affirm,
that this ointment was made use of for the purpose of in-
stallation and consecration till the reign of Josiah, who
hid it under ground in the temple, in a secret place,
which King Solomon had long before prepared with the
greatest care, after having learned from the predictions
of prophets that the time would come when the As-
syrians should level the temple with the ground. See
Cunæus,† *Outram*,‡ *Selden*;§ and particularly *Simeon*,||
who produces a long comment by *Aberbenel* on the

---

* משוח מלחמה, Unctus belli causâ.
† *De Republ. Hebr.* lib. i. cap. xiv.
‡ *De Sacrific.* lib. i. cap. v. sect. 7.
§ *De Success. in Pontif.* lib. ii. cap. 9.
|| *De Muis varia sacra.*

[k] Exod. xxx. 30.   [1] Exod. xxx.   [m] Verse 33.

thirtieth Chapter of Exodus, where the manner of anointing the priests is expressly treated.

XI. KINGS, in fine, were consecrated by anointing; which has been copiously and ably illustrated by *William Schickhard.** Yet the Talmudists hold, that all the kings were not anointed, but only those who were either the first in their own family, or whose pretensions to the kingdom were disputed by rivals. Saul, David, and others, were anointed for the first of these reasons; others, in consequence of opposition from an adverse party. Thus Solomon was anointed on account of Adonijah's party, Joash on account of Athaliah's, and Jehu on account of Joram's; though Jehu appears also to have been the first of his family that was advanced to the royal dignity. The modern Doctors, meantime, say they, have learned from wise and venerable men, that the kings of Israel, who, after the separation from Judah, made Samaria the seat of government, were not anointed with the oil which was prepared by Moses conformably to the Divine appointment; and that Elijah, consequently, made use only of common balsam, when he anointed Jehu the son of Jehoshaphat.

XII. In conformity to this three-fold order of persons that were anointed of old, the office of Christ consists of three parts. In the sixty-first chapter of Isaiah, there is a passage relating to his *Prophetical* unction which Christ applies to himself, Luke iv. 17, 18, 19. His *Priestly* unction is referred to in Psalm cx. 4. compared with Heb. v. 4, 5, 6. and Dan. ix. 24, 26., where we read of the *anointing of the most Holy*, that is, Christ, whose unction was prefigured by the anointing of the sanctuary and the ark; of the *cutting off of*

* *De Jure Regio.*

the Messiah; and of the confirmation of the covenant by the Messiah's being cut off. His *Kingly* unction is clear from Psalm ii. 6.—With regard to the order of these offices, and the question as to which of them ought first to be considered, it is scarcely worth while to contend. They are all so intimately blended together in their exercise, that it is more necessary to distinguish them from each other in their nature, than in respect to the time of their execution.

XIII. Agreeably to custom, therefore, we begin with the PROPHETICAL office. That Christ was a Prophet, not merely equal but superior to Moses,—a Prophet who was to speak *the words of God*, words which God had reserved for himself to declare in the last days, and which it was not lawful for a mere man to utter,[n] is collected from Deut. xviii. 18. compared with several other passages of Scripture.[o] He is denominated " the " Apostle of our profession,"[p] that is, one whom we confess as a Teacher divinely commissioned, who teaches doctrines which are to be believed with the heart unto righteousness, and confessed with the mouth unto salvation, and to whom we are bound in all things to hearken; vowing submission to his authority, and saying Amen to him when we make a covenant with God.[q]

XIV. The office of prophets consists of the three following parts. 1st, To teach the way of salvation. 2dly, To prophesy, or to foretel future events, otherwise unknown. 3dly, Rightly to confirm their doctrine and their prophecies, by a certain exemplary holiness of life, and if circumstances render it necessary, by miracles, and by martyrdom.

[n] 2 Cor. xii. 4. comp. John iii. 34.
[o] Heb. iii. 5. Acts iii. 22, 23. Is. xlii. 1. Joel ii. 28. John vi. 14.
[p] Heb. iii. 1.   [q] Comp. 2 Cor. ix. 13.

xv. Each of these is performed by Christ in the most excellent manner. 1st, He revealed, and placed in the clearest light, the mysteries of the kingdom of heaven, and the secret counsel of God respecting our salvation.[r] 2dly, He accurately foretold in his prophecies the various events that are to befal the New Testament Church till the end of the world.[s] 3dly, He confirmed his whole ministry, 1. By an exhibition, and an example, of the most unspotted holiness of conduct, both in his life, and at his death.[t] 2. By stupendous miracles, none equal or similar to which were ever beheld.[u] 3. By the martyrdom of his death, to which the Apostle refers when he says,—" Christ Jesus, who " before Pontius Pilate witnessed a good confession."[v] In reference to this, too, Jesus Christ appears to be called, " the faithful witness, and the first-begotten of " the dead."[w] *Gregory Nazianzen* calls Christ " the " chief Martyr :" * and that Christ might not seem to be deprived of any part of his honour, the Christians of Lyons and Vienne of old, chose rather to be called *confessors* than martyrs.†

xvi. We must not here omit to notice the superiority of Christ to other Prophets in every part of his office. If you consider his doctrine, not only did he utter dark sayings of old,[x] and reveal mysteries which were kept secret since the world began,[y] and which he

---

* Πρῶτος μαρτυς.   *Orat.* xviii.

† *Euseb. Hist. Eccles.* lib. v. cap. xv.

[r] John xv. 15. xvii. 8.   [s] Mat. xxiv. xxv. Rev. i. 1.

[t] 1 Cor. xi. 1. 1 Thes. i. 6. 1 Pet. ii. 21.

[u] Luke vii. 14, 15, 16. Mat. xi. 3, 4, 5.

[v] Ἰησῦ Χριστῦ, τῦ μαρτυρήσαντος 'επι Ποντιῦ Πιλατῦ την ` καλην ` ὁμολο-γιαν. 1 Tim. vi. 13.

[w] Ὁ μαρτυς ὁ πιστος. Rev. i. 5.

[x] Ps. lxxviii. 2.   [y] Rom. xvi. 25.

had learned from no other, but had seen in the bosom of the Father;[z] but he also taught inwardly by the Spirit, and "opened the understanding of his disciples, "that they might understand the scriptures."[a] He did not utter prophecies from any foreign impulse or inspiration; but from the fulness of the godhead dwelling in him bodily, he knew of himself all future events; and he instructed other Prophets by his Spirit.[b] He performed miracles by his own might; others performed them in his name, and by his power.[c] The pains of eternal death were added to the martyrdom of a bloody decease;[d] whilst other martyrs, on the contrary, have, in the midst of their tortures, been generally indulged with no slight foretastes of celestial joys.

XVII. Further, Christ discharged the office of a Prophet not only during the time of his abode upon earth, but also from the beginning; frequently appearing in a visible form, as a prelude of his incarnation, to give instruction to his favourites.[e] He went also by the Spirit and preached to the inhabitants of the old world;[f] and hence he says, "I have not spoken in secret from "the beginning."[g] Even now, too, he continues to instruct the Church by the Spirit, by the Scriptures, and by the ordinary ministry of pastors and teachers.[h]

XVIII. We must know, that what has been said respecting the holiness of Christ's life, his miracles, and his death, while it pertains to his prophetical office, is, in a different view, to be referred to his other offices. Holiness was indeed necessary to Christ as a Prophet,

[z] John i. 18. iii. 32. viii. 38, 40.
[b] 1 Pet. i. 11.
[d] Mat. xxvi. 38. xxvii. 46.
[f] 1 Pet. iii. 19.
[h] 2 Cor. v. 20.

[a] Luke xxiv. 45.
[c] Acts iii. 6, 12, 16.
[e] Gen. xviii.
[g] Is. xlviii. 16.

for two reasons. 1st, That he might teach, not only by words, but also by deeds, proposing himself as a pattern.[i] 2dly, That he might confirm his whole doctrine, and in particular his declarations respecting himself as the Messiah, the Son of God, and the Saviour of the world; which, certainly, he could not be, unless he were pure from every blemish.[j] But the same holiness was equally requisite to his Priestly office, and that, also, on two accounts. 1st, That he might be a holy Priest, and a holy victim, well-pleasing to God.[k] 2dly, That by fulfilling, in the capacity of our Surety, the whole righteousness of the law, he might supply our want of righteousness, and acquire for us a title to eternal life.[l] In fine, it belongs also to Christ's Regal office, which cannot be administered at all without holiness and righteousness.[m]

XIX. The same observation applies to the miracles of Christ. As his miracles not only testify, in general, that he is the Messiah promised of old to the church, and now sent by the Father,[n] but also confirm the truth of the doctrine he taught, they respect his Prophetical office.[o] As they included the removal of temporal miseries and the communication of corporeal benefits, which served to shadow forth the healing of the soul distempered with sin,[p] they are to be referred to his Sacerdotal office. Finally, as by his powerful word he controlled the winds and the sea, diseases and death, and him that had the power of death, that is, the De-

---

[i] Mat. xi. 29.　　　　[j] John viii. 28, 29, 46.
[k] Heb. vii. 26.　　　　[l] Rom. v. 19.
[m] Ps. xlv. 7. lxxxix. 14. xcvi. 10.
[n] John v. 36. x. 25.　　　　[o] Luke xxiv. 19.
[p] Mat. viii. 17. comp. Is. liii. 4.

vil, they were manifestations of a Royal authority, which every thing that exists is obliged to obey.

xx. In fine, although the death of Christ, as it was a martyrdom, may be referred to his prophetical office, yet it belongs chiefly to his priesthood; for, as we will show immediately, it included the oblation of Christ, and the expiation of our sins.

xxi. Since it was not sufficient that salvation be announced to us, unless it were also purchased and procured, it was necessary that Christ should not only be a PROPHET, but likewise a PRIEST. Paul, accordingly, ascribes to him a priesthood incomparably more excellent than the priesthood of Aaron.[q]

xxii. The business of a Priest, is, in general, to be employed in " things pertaining to God," for the benefit of the people.[r] More particularly, it includes three things. 1st, To offer gifts and sacrifices for sins.[s] 2dly, To intercede for the people :[t]—a service which was especially incumbent on the High-priest on the solemn day of expiation, when he entered into the Holy of Holies, with incense and the blood of the consecrated goat.[u] 3dly, To bless the people.[v] If we may give credit to the Hebrew Doctors, the prayers which were offered by the High-priest on the day of expiation had something remarkable in them—which it seems proper not to omit in this place. Three distinct formularies of prayer, they tell us, were made use of by the High-priest, on that sacred anniversary. He first prayed for himself, then for his relations and the whole family of Aaron, and lastly for all the people. The first prayer

[q] Heb. vii. 20, 21, 22. viii. 6.		[r] Heb. v. 1.
[s] Heb. v. 1.					[t] Joel ii. 7.
[u] Lev. xvi. 12, 15.
[v] Numb. vi. 23. Deut. xxi. 5. 1 Chron. xxiii. 13.

was presented at the offering of the bullock for the sin-offering, in this form of words: " I beseech thee, O " Lord; we have sinned, we have offended, we have re-" belled in thy sight, I, and my family, and the sons of " Aaron, thy holy people; I beseech thee, O Lord, for-" give now the sins, the offences, the rebellions, where-" by we have sinned, offended, and rebelled in thy sight, " I, and my family, and the sons of Aaron, thy holy " people. As it is written in the law of Moses thy ser-" vant, where it is said, on this day shall an atonement " be made for you, to cleanse you from all your sins; " you shall be made clean before the Lord." To this prayer of the High-priest, the priests made the follow-ing response: " Blessed be his name, and the glory of " his kingdom for ever and ever." In the other form, which was used when he laid his hands upon the goat that was to be carried away into the wilderness, the High-priest prayed for all the people in similar terms. To this prayer, the people, with the priests, responded as above. The third prayer was made, when the High-priest entered within the vail to burn incense, and to fill the holy place with a thick cloud of the incense; at his return, moving gently backwards step by step, he thus commended the people to God: " May it please " thee, O Lord God, to grant, that if this year the " weather shall be warm, the heat may be tempered " with showers; that the sceptre may not depart from " the family of Judah; that thy people Israel may not " be destitute of food; and that the imprecations of the " wicked may be without effect." It will appear from the sequel, that these ancient forms are not noticed here without cause.

XXIII. There is none of these parts of the priestly office, which our Lord doth not exactly perform; for

he is " a merciful and faithful High-priest in things
" pertaining to God, to make reconciliation for the sins
" of the people."[w] 1st, " Through the eternal Spirit,
" he OFFERED himself without spot to God, that by
" his own blood, he might purge our conscience from
" dead works ;"[x] and " by one offering he has perfected
" for ever them that are sanctified."[y] 2dly, He PRAY-
ED for his disciples on earth ;[z] and he still prays for them
in heaven ;[a] " appearing in the presence of God for us,"
not with blood of others, but with his own blood, founding his intercession upon the dignity and efficacy of his
oblation.[b] 3dly, He imparts a more than sacerdotal
BLESSING to his people, not only when dying on the
cross,[c] or when about to ascend to heaven ;[d] but, in particular, when reigning on his celestial throne ;[e] yet
most abundantly, at the last judgment.[f]

XXIV. In the OBLATION, the *Priest* is Christ as
God-man, but chiefly according to the Divine nature,
and the power of an endless life.[g] The *Sacrifice* is also
Christ, principally according to the human nature ;[h] to
which, at the same time, the Divinity, personally united
to it, imparted dignity and worth ; as it is owing to
this, that not the blood of a mere man, but " the blood
" of God"[56] was shed.[i]—As to the *Altar*, some hold that
it is the Divinity of Christ, others, the cross.[57] To us
it appears that both views are consonant to truth, ac-

[w] Heb. ii. 17.   [x] Heb. ix. 14.
[y] Heb. x. 14.   [z] John xvii. 9.
[a] Rom. viii. 34.   [b] Heb. ix. 24, 25.
[c] Gal. iii. 13, 14.   [d] Luke xxiv. 51.
[e] Ephes. i. 3.   [f] Mat. xxv. 34.
[g] Heb. vii. 16.   [h] Heb. x. 10.
[i] Acts xx. 28.

[56] See NOTE LVI.   [57] See NOTE LVII.

cording to the twofold use of the altar of old. The altar was intended, first, to support the victim to be offered by fire unto God; secondly, to sanctify the victim, which it did not effect of itself, but by the sacred fire that descended from heaven, and was a type and figure of the Holy Spirit. In the former respect, the cross on which Christ was lifted up, may and even ought to be called the altar.[j] In the latter, it must be referred to Christ's own Divinity, and his eternal Spirit, through which he offered himself without spot unto the Father.[k] In this way we may reconcile the seemingly contradictory expressions of the Dutch Annotators, who assert sometimes that the cross, and sometimes that the Divinity of Christ, was the altar upon which this sacrifice was offered.*

xxv. The oblation itself consists in the sufferings and death of Christ, as appears incontrovertibly from the reasoning of the Apostle, Heb. ix. 25—28. The flames with which he was burned, were zeal for the glory of God, and unbounded love towards his brethren;[l] to which was added the baptism of the fire kindled by the wrath of God against our sins.[m]

In this oblation of Christ, however, as in other sacrifices, three articles may be distinctly observed. Those sacrifices were first offered alive at the door of the tabernacle of the congregation;[n] then killed for the honour of God, and laid upon the altar, to be consumed by fire, either in whole or in part; lastly, the blood of some of them was carried into the most sacred apart-

---

* Compare the Notes on Psalm cx. No. 19. with those on Heb. xiii. No. 15.

j 1 Pet. ii. 24.   John xii. 32, 33.   k Heb. ix. 14.
l Ps. lxix. 9.   m Luke xii. 50.
n Lev. i. 2, 3.

ment of the tabernacle. Christ, in like manner, offered himself, 1st, While yet living and vigorous, when of his own accord he went to the spot, from which he knew he was to be led to judgment, and thence to the cross as an atoning sacrifice;[o] and voluntarily presented himself to God, to suffer impending death. Accordingly, he says, "For their sakes I sanctify myself," *I offer myself a sacrifice to God.*[p] To *sanctify** has sometimes the same meaning as to *offer*;† nor can the word well admit any other signification in this place. *Chrysostome* very properly explains the expression, "I sanctify myself," in this manner, "I offer myself a sacrifice to thee."‡ 2dly, When suffering and dying, and shedding his blood in the manner just explained, and for that purpose led forth without the gates of Jerusalem; as the sacrifices by which he was most remarkably typified were burned without the camp, and without the city.[q] 3dly, When he carried his blood, or his soul now separate from the body, (for the blood is taken for the *life*, the *soul*) into the holy place not made with hands, and presented it to his Father;[r] for Christ is in heaven not merely as a High-priest, but also as a Lamb slain.[s] I see no reason why we should deny that this entrance of Christ into the heavenly sanctuary, to present his blood as a token that the sacrifice was slain, belongs to his oblation.

XXVI. The end and effect of the oblation, is the full

* קדש or ἁγιαζειν.

† Προσφερειν.

‡ Προσφερω σοὶ θυσίαν.

[o] Luke xviii. 31.

[p] Ὑπερ αὐτῶν ἐγω ἁγιαζω ἐμαυτὸν. John xvii. 19.

[q] Heb. xiii. 11, 12.

[r] Heb. ix. 12.

[s] Rev. v. 6.

expiation and blotting out of our sin,[t] so that it can neither be imputed to believers in order to punishment, (a privilege which they possessed also in ancient times by virtue of the suretiship engagements of Christ, and the oblation which was, in due time, to be accomplished,) nor henceforth can any demand of the hand-writing be made, or any confession of guilt by reiterated sacrifices, as if it were not yet expiated; which is the consequence of the oblation's having been actually accomplished.[u]

XXVII. The INTERCESSION of Christ is not a mere presenting of petitions for us, similar to that which believers owe one another. It is, on the contrary, a glorious representation of that will of Christ, by which we are sanctified; founded on the dignity of his person, the efficacy of his oblation, the merit of that righteousness which he fulfilled in our stead, and on that sacred covenant by which he has obtained for himself the right not only of praying for favours on our behalf, but also of *demanding the heathen for his inheritance*,[v]—demanding them as a due reward, and the purchase of his labour.[w] Hence, with a certain authority, which would be indecorous in all excepting the Son of God and the Surety of so excellent a covenant, he says, " Father, I " WILL[58] that they also whom thou hast given me, be " with me where I am."[x] So great, indeed, is the dignity, authority, and efficacy of this intercession, that it can no more be transferred to another, than even the expiation of our sins, upon which it depends, and with which it is inseparably connected.[y] It is a work of the

[t] Heb. i. 3.   1 John iii. 2.   [u] Col. ii. 14.   Heb. x. 2.
[v] Poscendi gentes, &c.   Ps. ii. 8.   [w] Is. xlix. 4.
[x] Θελω.   John xvii. 24.   [y] 1 John ii. 1, 2.
                    [58] See NOTE LVIII.

God-man,—a work in which there is a joint concurrence of the human will of Christ, representing the right he has obtained, and praying from sympathy for our infirmities,—and of his Divine will, securing audience and an answer to his requests.

xxviii. But we must here notice the correspondence of the prayers of Christ with those which, as we have seen, the Jewish High-priest preferred on the day of atonement. As a threefold prayer is ascribed to the High-priest, so also we find that Christ, when discharging the most arduous part of his sacerdotal office, prayed chiefly thrice. First, when he was now ready to offer himself.[z] Again, amidst his sufferings themselves, which taken together constitute his oblation, when, though his prayers were several times repeated, they are comprised in one formulary, in the twenty-second Psalm. In the last place, after his entrance into the most holy place not made with hands; where he obtains by his intercession, that, amidst the violence of persecution, the Church may be refreshed with the dew and the rain of spiritual consolations, and become " as a wa-" tered garden;"[a] that his spiritual kingdom may be perpetual, like the sun and moon which endure throughout all generations;[b] that the souls of the priests may be satiated with fatness, and his people satisfied with his goodness; in fine, that all the malevolent wishes and machinations of enemies may prove abortive.[c] In that prayer too, which is recorded in the seventeenth chapter of John, we find that Christ observes the following order. He prays, first, for *himself*;[d] then, for the *Apostles* who were in a peculiar sense his own,

[z] John xvii. [a] Jer. xxxi. 12.
[b] Ps. lxxii. 5. [c] Jer. xxxi. 14. Is. liv. 14—17.
[d] Verses 1—5.

and formed, so to speak, his *family ;*[e] and, lastly, for *all the people*, for all that shall believe on him through their word.[f]

xxix. The sacerdotal BLESSING of Christ, is, in like manner, of an entirely different sort from that by which, either the pious wish all peace and prosperity to each other, or pastors express similar wishes for the Church. This kind of blessing consists merely in words, and the sincerity of the soul that desires good things for others; and is a beseeching of God to show kindness to men. But Christ's benediction consists in nothing short of deeds, and the real communication of spiritual benefits, which he does not solicit from another, but takes from what is his own, to impart unto us. Hence it is said in Ezekiel : " He shall give his sons inheritance, out of " his own possession."[g]

xxx. In reference to this sort of benediction, the maxim of the Apostle is indisputably certain : " With- " out all contradiction, the less is blessed of the bet- " ter."[h] This aphorism, which is not of universal ap- plication, ought to be restricted to that species of bles- sing, in which the person who blesses represents Christ, and either the Church or one of its members receives the benediction. Such was the typical blessing with which the priests blessed the people according to the command of God ; for a blessing of that nature was neither given by the people to the priests, nor by the priests to the High-priest.

xxxi. Even under the Old Testament, Christ exhi- bited some preludes of his priestly work. 1st, He took upon himself, as a Surety, the sins of the elect, to be ex-

[e] Verses 6—19. [f] Verses 20—24.
[g] Ezek. xlvi. 18. compared with John xvi. 14, 15.
[h] Heb. vii. 7.

piated at the appointed time;[i] and in the sacrifices, which were types of his oblation, he was " slain from " the foundation of the world."[j] Hence believers of those times obtained justification and other saving benefits.[k] 2dly, By virtue of his suretiship, he also made intercession for believers.[l] 3dly, He was the sole Fountain of all those blessings which were liberally imparted to the Old Testament Church.[m]

XXXII. We now pass on to the REGAL dignity of Christ. Here a distinction must certainly be made between the Divine, natural, and essential kingdom of Christ, which as God he possesses in common with the Father and the Holy Spirit; and the Personal, economical, and mediatorial kingdom, which is committed to him alone, by the Father. These kingdoms, however, are to be so distinguished from each other, as to show, that they do not differ so much in substance, as in a certain respect and application. The former kingdom belongs to Christ as God; the latter belongs to him as God-man. The one comprehends all creatures, as they depend upon God as the Lord of the universe, both for their existence and their attributes; the other has a special respect to the Church. Yet the economical kingdom of Christ is of such dignity and eminence, that it could not pertain to one that is not God, and it supposes or includes his Divine kingdom.

XXXIII. The Mediatorial kingdom, of which we are here to treat, may be considered in a threefold view. 1st, As a kingdom of POWER over all, not excluding even angels, whether good or bad; but yet with a certain reference to the Church, since he makes use of

[i] Ps. cxix. 122.   [j] Rev. xiii. 8.
[k] Heb. xi. 7.   [l] Zeph. i. 12, 13.
[m] Prov. viii. 18, 21.

all creatures for the benefit of the Church.[n] 2dly, As a kingdom of GRACE, which is exercised in the Church militant; of which we are to contemplate both the *external form*, consisting in a visible society, collected by the ministry instituted by Christ, in which sense even those belong to the kingdom of Christ, who lie to the King and yield him a feigned subjection;[o]—and the *internal form*, which is the mystical and spiritual sub-ordination of believers under Christ as their Lord and Head, in righteousness, and peace, and joy in the Holy Ghost.[p] 3dly, As a kingdom of GLORY, which is exercised towards the Church triumphant in heaven,—imperfectly at present, with respect to the souls of the saints,[q]—perfectly hereafter, with respect to their entire persons.[r]

xxxiv. The office of a King consists chiefly of the three following parts. 1st, To prescribe just and sacred laws for the people that are subject to him. 2dly, To rule, govern, and judge the people according to those laws. 3dly, Valiantly to protect and defend his people against enemies of every description.

xxxv. Nor is the Anointed of the Lord wanting either to himself or to his people, in the discharge of this office. 1st, Because he is the King, he is, of course, the Lawgiver of his people.[s] He is not indeed our Lawgiver, by promulgating a new law that is purer than the law of Moses, and to which as more perfect the promise of eternal life is annexed. Even the Mosaic law, as we will shortly show, was published by Christ our King; it demands, too, a holiness corresponding to the Divine

---

[n] Mat. xxviii. 18. Ephes. i. 20, 21, 22. Philip. ii. 9, 10, 11.

[o] Mat. xiii. 47. viii. 12. [p] Rom. xiv. 17.

[q] Heb. xii. 23. [r] 1 Cor. xv. 53, 54.

[s] Luke vi. 46. John xiii. 34. xv. 17.

image, that is, a holiness absolutely perfect; and it is only by virtue of the same law, as satisfied by Christ, that we expect eternal life. But Christ is our Lawgiver by inculcating that same law as a rule of new obedience and of gratitude.[t][59] 2dly, He rules his people in righteousness, holiness, wisdom, and clemency, according to the laws which he has given;[u] and, conformably to the same laws, he will one day judge the whole world.[v] 3dly, He powerfully protects his people, and, in spite of the utmost efforts of " the gates of hell,"[60] causes them to triumph over all their enemies.[w]

xxxvi. Christ employs the ministry of his word and the operations of his Spirit in the administration of his kingdom; but in a different manner and form from that in which he makes use of them in the discharge of his prophetical office. In the latter, he *instructs* them by his word, as " the Teacher of righteousness;"[x] in the former, he *commands*, as " a Leader and Com-" mander to the people."[y] In the one, he enlightens our minds by his Spirit to understand the truth;[z] in the other, he bends our hearts, and causes all our faculties, both of soul and body, to yield a prompt obedience.[a]

xxxvii. It cannot indeed be denied, that the kingdom of Christ is much more illustrious under the New Testament, than under the Old. Accordingly, the New Testament state, in contradistinction to the an-

---

[t] Mat. xxii. 37, 38, 39. [u] Ps. xlv. 7.

[v] Acts xvii. 31.

[w] Mic. v. 5, 6. Mat. xvi. 18. John x. 28. 2 Thes. iii. 3. Rom. viii. 37.

[x] המורה לצדקה: Joel ii. 23. *marg.* [y] Is. lv. 4.

[z] Luke xxiv. 45. [a] Jer. xxxii. 39, 40.

[59] See NOTE LIX. [60] See NOTE LX.

cient condition of the Church, is often denominated in the Gospel, *the kingdom of heaven*. The prophets, too, when prophesying of the introduction of the new dispensation, represent Jehovah as then taking possession of the kingdom.[b] But yet the Son of God was King of Israel even under the old dispensation.[c] He showed himself King, 1st, When he delivered the fiery law amidst thunders and lightnings in the presence of a very large assembly of people.[d] 2dly, When he instituted the whole hierarchy of elders, priests, and high-priests, who were merely the servants and officers of the Son of God in ruling and governing the people according to the laws prescribed;—of whom therefore we may consider these words of Wisdom as eminently true, " By me kings reign, and princes decree justice."[e] 3dly, When he so often rescued his people from their calamities, and so powerfully defended them against all their enemies.[f] For this reason King David himself adores the Son of God as King: " Thou art my King, " O God; command deliverances for Jacob."[g]

XXXVIII. But how splendid soever these displays of his royalty may seem, they were only faint shadows of a better kingdom which the Lord reserved for the New Testament economy; of which the beginnings were seen while Christ was yet alive, but the chief glory was displayed after his resurrection from the dead. Notwithstanding his being clothed with the form of a servant, the rays of his royal majesty shone forth in the days of his flesh, 1st, *At his birth*, which the heavenly

---

[b] Ps. xxii. 28. xcvii. 1. xcix. 1.　　　[c] Judg. viii. 23.

[d] Acts vii. 38. comp. with v. 35. Ps. lxviii. 8, 9. comp. with Ephes. iv. 8; Heb. xii. 26.

[e] Prov. viii. 15.　　　[f] Is. lxiii. 9.

[g] Ps. xliv. 4.

hosts joyfully celebrated, announcing that a Saviour was born, " who is Christ the Lord ;"[h] and which was honoured by the *Magi*, who came from a distant country, offering such gifts as are due to a King, or to one who is more than a King.[i] 2dly, *In the course of his life*; during which he exhibited, particularly to his disciples, proofs of his dignity, which compelled them to say with Nathanael, " Thou art the Son of God, thou art " the King of Israel."[j] With such authority did he command even the winds, and the sea agitated by the fury of the tempest, that the astonished spectators exclaimed, " What manner of man is this, that even the " winds and the sea obey him !"[k] But he gave the most signal display of his royal dignity on that occasion, when, in order to fulfil the prophecy contained in the book of Zechariah, he went in procession to Jerusalem sitting on an ass, amidst the acclamations of a vast multitude of people that preceded and followed him, crying out, " Hosanna to the son of David ! Blessed is he that " cometh in the name of the Lord !"[l] 3dly, *Amidst his deepest debasement* and most dreadful sufferings, when he asserted his royal dignity,[m] and was recognised as a King, not merely by the penitent robber,[n] but also by Pilate ; though the latter had a different purpose in view.[o]

XXXIX. But after Christ's resurrection from the dead and ascension to heaven, every thing became more bright and glorious. Here again, four principal periods present themselves to notice. 1st, In the gathering of the

[h] Luke ii. 11, 13.
[i] Mat. ii. 1, 2.
[j] John i. 49.
[k] Mat. viii. 27.
[l] Mat. xxi. 8, 9.
[m] Mat. xxvi. 64. John xviii. 36, 37.
[n] Luke xxiii. 42.
[o] John xix. 19.

Church from among Jews and Gentiles by the preaching of the gospel of the kingdom ;[p] with which the destruction of the Jewish polity and hierarchy, in subserviency to the erection of the kingdom of liberty, was connected.   To this we refer, Mat. xvi. 28. xxvi. 64. *Coming in a cloud* is the symbol of coming with power to inflict on a country some surprising and inevitable judgment.[q] 2dly, In the subjugation of the kingdoms of the world by Constantine the Great.   A great voice was then heard in heaven, saying, " Now is come salva-
" tion, and strength, and the kingdom of our God, and
" the power of his Christ,"[r] &c.   3dly, In the destruction of the kingdom of Antichrist and the Beast, which was begun at the Reformation,[s] and will be completed at the appointed time.[t]   4thly, In the conversion of the Jewish nation, and in the glory of the whole Church, with which that conversion will be attended.[u]   All will issue in the glorious appearing of Christ to judge the world.[v]

XL. The Scriptures often affirm, that the kingdom of Christ and its glory will be eternal.[w] Nor can it possibly be otherwise.   If a kingdom come to an end, this must be owing to one or other of the following causes. Either the king himself dies, or enemies deprive him of the kingdom, or the subjects rebel and withdraw themselves from his government, or he himself abdicates the kingdom.   But none of these events takes place here.

---

[p] Ps. cx. 1, 2.   [q] Comp. Is. xix. 1.
[r] Rev. xii. 10.   [s] Rev. xiv. 7. *et seq.*
[t] Rev. xix. 1.   [u] Rom. xi. 15. Is. lix. 19. lx. 1.
[v] Mat. xxv. 31.

[w] Ps. xlv. 6. 1 Chron. xxii. 10. comp. with Luke i. 32, 33. Dan. ii. 44. vii. 14.

XLI. Not the *first*;—for having died once to obtain this glorious kingdom, Christ lives for ever to retain it in secure and everlasting possession.[x] Not the *second*; —for because he has already vanquished and triumphed over all his enemies by his death, they have learned, in spite of themselves, to submit their stubborn neck to the yoke;[y] and if any thing of this sort remain to be done, the Father has taken it entirely on himself, Christ in the mean while resting securely at his right hand.[z] Not the *third*;—for his subjects are " a righteous na-" tion which *maintains universal fidelity*."[a] He establishes his kingdom in their hearts and wills, and implants such a holy fear of himself in their minds, that they cannot depart from him.[b] Whoever revolt from him, give evidence that they never pertained to the number of his faithful subjects;[c] and notwithstanding their defection, he will compel them to confess his power and dominion, " ruling them with a rod of iron, " and breaking them to shivers, as the vessels of a pot-" ter."[d] In fine, not the *fourth*;—for he will do nothing derogatory to the decree of the Deity, or to the promise of the Father, or to the predictions of Scripture, or to the fruit of his own merits, or to his own proper dignity, acquired at so vast an expense, with which the glory of the elect is indissolubly connected.

XLII. It is not, however, to be dissembled, that there are several expressions in the writings of Paul, which seem to intimate that Christ is one day to divest himself of the kingdom; in particular, 1 Corinth. xv. 24—28. This is truly a difficult passage; and many

[x] Rom. vi. 9, 10. Rev. i. 18.
[y] John xvi. 33. Heb. ii. 14. Col. ii. 15.　　[z] Ps. cx. 1.
[a] Is. xxvi. 2.　　[b] Jer. xxxii. 40.
[c] 1 John ii. 19.　　[d] Rev. ii. 27.

have used their endeavours to explain it, and to reconcile it with what has just been said. Let us, too, make
a similar attempt. We will first show, what of the
eternal glory of Christ, as King, and of his kingdom, is
quite indisputable; which, consequently, Paul does by
no means here contradict; and then, in what sense the
Apostle, nevertheless, may say, that there shall be an
end, and that the kingdom shall be delivered to God
even the Father, and that the Son himself shall be subject unto Him who subjected all things to him, in order
that God himself immediately, rather than the Mediator, may be all in all.

XLIII. It is certain, 1st, That the Divine, essential,
and natural kingdom of Christ, is eternal.[e] 2dly, That
the humanity of Christ will always remain personally
united with the Divinity, and will on that account enjoy a glory very far surpassing the glory of all creatures.
Even the human nature partakes, in its own place, of
that " name above every name," which God has given
to the Mediator, as a reward of his foregoing abasement.[f] 3dly, That Christ will always be the Head,
that is, by far the most noble member of the Church,
and as such will be recognised, adored, and praised by
the Church.[g] 4thly, That the Mediatorial kingdom itself will be eternal as to its glorious effects, as well in
the Head, as in the members. Some of those effects
are,—in Christ, the effulgence of the Divine Majesty
shining most brightly in his Person as God-man, which
will never be diminished in any degree;—in the elect,
complete liberty; the subjugation of all their enemies;
the entire abolition of sin, as to its guilt, dominion, remains, and all its direful consequences; and unutterable

[e] Dan. iv. 34.   [f] Philip. ii. 9.   [g] Rom. viii. 29.

joy, arising from intimate communion with God. These will to eternity be acknowledged and celebrated as the blessings of Christ our King, and as flowing from the indwelling of his Spirit, who is always the Spirit of Christ.[h] In these respects, then, the kingdom of Christ is eternal; and Paul is here so far from opposing these sentiments, that, on the contrary, he teaches them at great length.

XLIV. It must be confessed, however, that after the day of the last judgment, the exercise of Christ's Kingly office, and the form of his mediatorial kingdom, will be widely different from what they now are. 1st, The economical government of this kingdom, as now exercised by an ecclesiastical ministry, and by civil authority as conducive to the protection of the Church, will then cease, " when he shall have put down all rule, " and all authority, and power."[i] 2dly, After the last judgment, Christ will render an account to God the Father, of his whole mediatorial office, as most perfectly accomplished, in what relates not only to the purchase, but also to the full application of salvation to the whole Church; presenting to him a truly glorious Church, not having spot or wrinkle, or any such thing. This will be an evidence that he has in no respect been wanting to the office committed to him; and to this may be referred the expression, " He shall deliver up " the kingdom," that is, the Church in her perfect state, " to God, even the Father." 3dly, That account having been rendered, the godhead itself without the intervention of a Mediator, (for which there seems no more occasion, sin with all its remainders and consequences being entirely removed) will hold communion

[h] Gal. iv. 6.　　　　　　[i] 1 Cor. xv. 24.

immediately with the redeemed, in almost the same manner in which it holds fellowship with angels; with this difference, however, that the redeemed will through eternity acknowledge themselves indebted to the merits of Christ for this immediate communication of the Deity. This is what is intended by the expression, "that God " may be all in all."j 4thly, Then also Christ, no longer discharging any part of the Mediatorial office, will, with regard to his human nature, be subject unto God, as one of the brethren, possessing manifold and most excellent glory, without any diminution of the glory which he now enjoys. In this view, he may be compared to the Son of a King, who, having received from his Father a commission and supreme authority to subdue a number of rebels, and to rescue citizens from a tyrannical usurpation, after accomplishing every thing with happy success according to the will of his Father, resigns a laborious authority which is no longer necessary, and lives in security, enjoying an honourable repose amidst the delights of the royal habitation. This seems to be intimated by these words, " And when all " things shall be subdued unto him, then shall the Son " also himself be subject unto him that put all things " under him."k 5thly, Thus far there " shall be an " end" of the mediatorial kingdom, the exercise of which supposes some imperfection in the Church; and this end will be so far from reflecting any dishonour on Christ as King, that, on the contrary, it will redound to his glory, agreeably to the following expression of Paul; " When that which is perfect is come, then that " which is in part shall be done away."l It is an end

j Verse 28.   k Verse 28.
l 1 Cor. xiii. 10.

of such a nature, as brings all things to a state of complete and endless perfection. *[61]

XLV. It is, doubtless, a signal instance of the power, wisdom, and goodness of God, that Christ, by these three offices, remedies all those defects, and delivers from all those evils, which render us miserable. He cures our ignorance and blindness, as a Prophet; expiates the guilt of our sins, as a Priest; perfects his strength in our weakness, as a King. As a Prophet, he shows the way of salvation; as a Priest, obtains a title to salvation; as a King, bestows salvation itself. As a Prophet, he furnishes our understanding with a spiritual knowledge of spiritual things; as a Priest, cleanses us from all pollution of the flesh and of the spirit; as a King, bends our wills into obedience to himself.

XLVI. Happy, then, the diligent disciples of so great a TEACHER!—who instructs them in most important, and most wonderful, saving truths, " which angels de- " sire to look into;"[m]—instructs with a perspicuity which " makes wise the simple,"[n] and with an almost incredible sweetness and *grace*,[o] which is not only extolled by the Church in words breathing pure affection,[p] but acknowledged, in their own way, even by carnal men, and enemies themselves.[q] Nor doth he merely exhibit those sublime mysteries externally to the ears and eyes; he also gives inwardly the Spirit of wisdom and revelation in the knowledge of himself,[r] and grants his disciples a new and heavenly understanding that they may

* Τέλος τελειότητος, τέλος οὐκ ᾽εχον.

[m] 1 Pet. i. 12.   [n] Ps. xix. 7.

[o] Ps. xlv. 2.   [p] Song v. 16.

[q] Luke iv. 22.   [r] Ephes. i. 17.

[61] See NOTE LXI.

discern divine and heavenly things in their native beauty, and know the truth " as the truth is in Jesus,"[s] and may even " have the mind of Christ."[t] What is the most delightful and most efficacious of all methods of instruction,—this incomparable Teacher presents his truths not only to be seen, but also to be *tasted* and experienced.[u] The genuine disciple of Christ not merely knows, and not merely believes, but sometimes tastes and feels what is implied in the remission of sin, in the privilege of adoption, in familiar intercourse with God, in the grace of the Spirit dwelling in the breast, in the love of God shed abroad in the heart, in the hidden manna, in the sweet embraces of Jesus, and finally, in the earnest and pledge of perfect felicity. This kind Teacher brings his followers into his school, as into a banqueting-house, and says, " Eat, O friends; drink, " yea, drink abundantly, O beloved;"[v] and being thus liberally entertained, not by a generous Father, but by the blessed Redeemer, they obtain far clearer eyes for contemplating celestial objects, than Jonathan had of old, after having tasted of the honey-comb.[w] With great truth, therefore, the Supreme Wisdom uttered this, as well as every other expression that proceeded from her lips: " Blessed is the man that heareth me, " watching daily at my gates, waiting at the posts of " my doors."[x]

XLVII. Happy, also, are contrite sinners in so great a HIGH-PRIEST!—who is both " merciful and " faithful in all things pertaining to God;"[y] and who " by one offering hath perfected for ever them that are

[s] Ephes. iv. 21.   [t] 1 Cor. ii. 16.

[u] Ps. xxxiv. 8.   [v] Song v. 1.

[w] 1 Sam. xiv. 27. [x] Prov. viii. 34, 35, 36.

[y] Heb. ii. 17.

" sanctified."[z]   The whole guilt of our sins being thus expiated, there remains no condemnation to us ;[a] and we have boldness to enter into the holiest by the blood of Jesus, by a new and living way which he has consecrated for us through the vail, that is to say, his flesh.[b] Besides, this unparalleled High-priest, " when he had " by himself purged our sins, sat down on the right hand " of the Majesty" of God " on high ;"[c] and there he makes continual intercession for us.   Our prayers truly are often so frigid and languid, that we can scarcely hear them ourselves, and much less can we presume to imagine they have entered into the ears of the Lord of Hosts, unless perhaps to solicit vengeance against us for not treating his Majesty with becoming reverence. How rich the consolation, then, that we have a High-priest so near to God, who is always interceding for us, and whose intercession is never disregarded by the Father ;[d] who, putting our prayers into his golden censer, offers them with his own incense upon the golden altar which is before the throne, that they may be a fragrant odour to the Lord ![e]   Whilst he does this for us, he cannot fail at the same time to enrich us with his most abundant and delightful benedictions, that so we may " come and sing in the height of Zion, and flow to- " gether to the goodness of the Lord, that our soul " may be like a watered garden."[f]

XLVIII. Happy, in fine, the faithful subjects of so great a KING !—all whose laws are at once wise, just, holy, and good, and rejoicing to the heart ;[g] whose

---

[z] Heb. x. 14.   [a] Rom. viii. 1.
[b] Heb. x. 19, 20.   [c] Heb. i. 3.
[d] John xi. 42.
[e] Rev. viii. 3.   See also Heb. iv. 14, 15, 16.
[f] Jer. xxxi. 12, 13, 14,   [g] Ps. xix. 8.

whole administration is full of righteousness, wisdom and equity; and whose protection is omnipotent, so that none can hurt any one of his people, none can destroy in all his holy mountain.[h]

XLIX. But whoever wish to be partakers of this inexpressible happiness which is found in Christ, must by faith receive him in all his offices, and in the whole extent of his character. He cannot possibly be divided into parts.[i] He is either wholly enjoyed, or wholly lost. If men have no inclination to acknowledge him as a Prophet, to whose instructions and discipline they must cordially submit, and as a King, whose will they must obey with alacrity and reverence, it is certain that their glorying in him as a Priest is vain and presumptuous. He expiates the sins of none as a Priest, but of those whom he also instructs as a Prophet, and governs with sovereign authority as a King. The same persons are at once his disciples, his clients, and his subjects.[62]

[h] Is. xi. 9.   [i] 1 Cor. i. 13.
[62] See NOTE LXII.

DISSERTATION XI.

ON THE NAME *CHRISTIANS*.

———

I. ALL believers are called CHRISTIANS, from CHRIST, their Master, Lord, Husband, and Head. They are partakers of his anointing, and consequently of his name.

II. Of the origin of this denomination, which occurs but thrice in the sacred volume,[a] we have an account in Acts xi. 26. - - - " And it came to pass that a whole " year they assembled themselves with the Church, and " taught much people. AND THE DISCIPLES WERE " CALLED CHRISTIANS FIRST IN ANTIOCH." Here the exchange of the ancient and more simple name for the new and more significant one, and also the time when, and the place where, this alteration was introduced, are distinctly stated.[63]

III. The faithful were originally denominated either *disciples* absolutely, or *the disciples of the Lord*.[b] Christ had given it in charge to his Apostles to make disciples of men of all nations, by the preaching of the

---

[a] Acts xxvi. 28.   1 Pet. iv. 16.   [b] Acts ix. 1.
      [63] See NOTE LXIII.

word;[c] and the whole ministry of the Gospel was subservient to this object, that those who were once disciples of men that were teachers of wisdom falsely so called, whether Jewish or Pagan,—disciples of Satan that most artful seducer,—and disciples of licentious appetites and passions, which instil nothing good into the ear or mind, might become disciples of God and Christ, lovers and students of true, heavenly, and divine wisdom. The name of disciples is peculiarly suited to them who sedulously cultivate this wisdom; for it denotes both diligence and modesty; and it served to remind believers, that they ought carefully to search the oracles of God, and to hang submissively on the lips of one Teacher; and also, that, whatever proficiency they may have made, they should always remember that they occupy the place of learners.

IV. But, as the followers of philosophers usually receive their designation from the founders of the sects to which they respectively belong, so it seemed proper to the Holy Spirit, that the disciples of Christ should henceforth be termed *Christians*, from Christ himself. There is none more worthy than this greatest of Prophets, " of whom the whole family in heaven and earth " is named;"[d] and it was truly honourable for Platonists, Aristotelians, and the pupils of Gamaliel the Hebrew, renouncing their former studies and sects, to give their name to Christ, and to receive a name from Christ in return. " Who teacheth like him?"[e] " What " know I," says *Tertullian*,[*] " but under any discipline, " a name may pass from the Master to his followers? " Are not philosophers styled Platonists, Epicureans,

---

[*] *Apologet.* cap. iii.
[c] Μαθητεύσατε παντα τὰ ἔθνη. Mat. xxviii. 19.
[d] Ephes. iii. 15.　　　　[e] Job xxxvi. 22.

" and Pythagoreans, from their respective leaders? Do
" not the Stoics and Academicians receive their deno-
" mination even from the places to which they com-
" monly resorted, and where they held their assem-
" blies ?* Do not physicians derive a name from *Era-*
" *sistratus*, grammarians from *Aristarchus*, and even
" epicures from *Apicius* ?"

v. Divine Providence, which is so conspicuous in
every thing, appears particularly admirable and adorable, in the *time* and the *place* of the giving of this
name to the faithful. The name of Christians was not
given them, till, in Cornelius and his family, the first-
fruits of the Gentiles were dedicated to God, and it became evident to the Church that " God had also to the
" Gentiles granted repentance unto life ;"f—till a great
number of Grecians,64 to whom men of Cyprus and
Cyrene preached the Lord Jesus, believed and turned
to the Lord ;g—till, in fine, Paul and Barnabas had
for a whole year taught a great multitude, consisting
principally of Gentiles. The Jews might, perhaps,
have somewhat indulged in superciliousness, had this
honourable name of Christians been granted first to
themselves, and at a time when the word of life was
confined within the narrow limits of their nation. It
was, therefore, given in the first instance to Gentiles,
or at least to a Church composed partly of Jews but
chiefly of Gentiles, and that in a Gentile city; that

---

* The Stoics, it is well known, derived their name from the
Stoa, portico, or covered walk, where *Zeno*, the Father of that
sect, instructed his pupils; and the Academicians received their designation from the *Academia*, the place in the suburbs of Athens
where *Plato* met with his disciples. T.

f Acts xi. 18.   g Verses 20, 21.

64 See Note LXIV.

thus it might be clear to all, " that God is no respecter
" of persons, but in every nation he that feareth him
" and worketh righteousness, is accepted with him ;"[h]
and that, " in Christ Jesus, neither circumcision avail-
" eth any thing, nor uncircumcision, but a new crea-
" ture."[i]

VI. Several circumstances relative to Antioch, are
worthy of notice. 1st, That it was a Gentile city,—
lest Jerusalem should boast of the illustrious name of
Christians as having been first given to her own citizens. 2dly, That it was the metropolis of Syria, and
the principal residence of the tyrannical *Antiochus,*
who, by the dreadful havoc which he made of the ancient Church, approved himself the Antichrist of that
period, and the forerunner and type of the great Antichrist of latter days. Thus Christ Jesus erected his
trophies in the same city, where the throne of Satan
and of his noted Enemy had been established; and
caused the name of his kingdom and people to go forth
to the whole earth, and to the remotest parts of the
globe, from that very place, whence the most horrible
persecution of his people and profanation of his sanctuary had taken their rise. 3dly, That it was, at that
time, the greatest and most powerful city in all Asia,
as Alexandria in Africa, and Rome in Europe;—not
merely that the splendour of the city might impart a
certain lustre to the giving of this name of *Christians,*
but, chiefly, that it might be diffused through the world
with the greater ease and rapidity.

VII. It was inconsiderate, however, in the Church of
Antioch to conclude from this circumstance, that they
were entitled to a preference above other Churches.

---

[h] Acts x. 34, 35.   [i] Gal. vi. 15.

This presumptuous notion was long ago reproved by *Chrysostome*, who addresses himself to the inhabitants of that city in the following words :* " But, if any dis-
" pute about honour and precedency arise, you, from an
" extravagant ambition, contend that you are entitled
" to preside over the whole world; overvaluing your-
" selves for the distinction, that this your city first gave
" the name of Christians to the faithful." Ambition of this kind amongst the churches, is, in reality, very pernicious. They are all equal in Christ, " having ob-
" tained like precious faith ;"ʲ they are sisters in the same family ; nor are they at liberty to glory against one another, or to exalt themselves, on account of the external magnificence of their cities, the greatness of their numbers, the antiquity of their origin, or for any peculiar privilege. In other respects, the Church of Jerusalem, doubtless, was immensely superior to the rest of the churches; for she not only had the whole company of Apostles, but the Lord himself for her immediate Teacher and Founder, and the greater part of the stupendous transactions recorded in the Gospel, took place in her presence.

VIII. In vain also does *Baronius* adduce it as an argument in vindication of Peter's pre-eminence, that the highly auspicious name of Christians originated in the Church of Antioch, which he pretends was the seat of Peter, and was erected and founded by that Apostle. It is without authority from Scripture, and even in opposition to its statements, that all these assertions respecting Peter are made. It is not true, that he erected or founded the Church of Antioch. The first that

* *Homil.* vii. *in Mat.*
ʲ Ἰσότιμον λαχȣσαι πιστιν. 2 Pet. i. 1.

preached the Gospel there, were the disciples of Jerusalem who were scattered abroad by the persecution which arose after the martyrdom of Stephen. These were succeeded by certain Cyprians and Cyrenians. Barnabas, by common consent, was afterwards commissioned from Jerusalem for that purpose; and, in fine, he was joined by Paul, whom he brought from Tarsus to Antioch, to assist him in the work.[k] Of Peter we read not a word. These facts are so manifestly certain, that they have extorted from *Baronius* himself the confession, how reluctant soever, that the Gospel was not first preached at Antioch by Peter.[*] Now what is it to found and erect a church, but by means of the preaching of the Gospel, to lay the one only Foundation, namely Jesus Christ, and to build believers upon him, " for an habitation of God through the Spirit."[l] But these services are by no means conducive to pontifical greatness. The Father of the *Annals* had quite a different matter in view. " It is to be understood," says he, " that the Church of Antioch is said to be found-
" ed by Peter in this respect, that the chief dignity
" was conferred on it by Peter, that thus it might be
" called, and be in reality, the greatest of the Oriental
" Churches. It is to be affirmed, also, that Peter first
" erected or established the patriarchal seat of Antioch;
" for effecting which, Peter was under no necessity of
" taking a journey to Antioch; since, wherever he
" might be, he was able to do this, by his pre-eminent
" authority." But, pray, Baronius, why should this be affirmed, understood, and believed? What passage of Scripture attests it? Where does the Holy Spirit, when making mention of the founding or building up

---

[*] *Annal.* tom. i. p. 272. *juxta edition. Antverp. An.* 1612.
[k] Acts xi. 19, 25.   [l] 1 Cor. iii. 10, 11. Ephes. ii. 20, 21, 22.

of a church, intend the establishment of a patriarchal seat? Where does Luke, or any other authentic and credible historian of the Acts of the Apostles, if you know of any such, show by satisfactory proofs that Peter was the Patriarch of Antioch? These assertions do not accord with the simplicity of the Apostolic Church. They are quite foreign to the diction of the Holy Spirit. They are at variance, too, with the sacred history. For when a contention respecting ceremonies arose at Antioch, recourse is not had to Peter, to terminate the controversy by interposing his patriarchal authority, which, no doubt, ought to have been done; but the matter is referred to the whole college of Apostles, whose decision is sent to Antioch by chosen men, no mention being made of a patriarch.[m] Dismissing, therefore, this fictitious eminence of the Church of Antioch derived from its having been the seat of Peter, let it suffice us to know, that God made choice of that Church to give the name of Christians to believers.

IX. This name was no less despicable and odious in the esteem of the heathen, than it was grateful, precious, and glorious, in the eyes of the faithful. To the heathen, Christians appeared men of no consideration. If the apparel of a Christian did not accord with the pomp and fashion of the world, he was everywhere insulted in the streets by the cry, *There goes an impostor and a knave!*[*] The name alone was deemed a sufficient crime. " With such wilful blindness," says *Tertullian*,[†] " was it generally hated, that men, when " bearing a favourable testimony to a Christian, com-

* The expression in the Latin is, *Impostor et Græcus est.* A *Grecian* was then a term of reproach for an arrant knave. T.

† *Apol.* cap. iii.

[m] Acts xv.

" bined with it a reprobation of the name. ' *Caius Sejus*,'
" says one, ' is a good man, but he is a Christian.' ' I
" wonder,' says another, ' that *Lucius*, who is a man of
" intelligence, suddenly turned Christian.'" *Justin* says
in like manner, " You sustain the name as evidence
" against us :"* and again, " We are hated merely for
" Christ's name's sake."† This, as *Eusebius* shows at
large,‡ was exactly conformable to our Lord's prediction.[n]
Neither incest, nor parricide, nor sorcery, was judged worthy of severer punishment than the mere name of Christianity ; by which, as *Tacitus* alleges,§ they were con-
victed of no particular crime, but of hatred against the
human race. It was not thought sufficient to employ
the usual instruments of torture and death, iron-hooks,
plates of burning iron, stakes, engines resembling a
horse, crosses, melted metals, wild beasts, examples of
burning alive. New forms of punishment were indus-
triously contrived to expiate the crime of this name.
It seemed too humane, that Christians should be bound
with a girdle of branches, and burnt at a stake formed
of a plank or pole split into two parts ; and that so frequently, that they were thence branded with the designations of *the Branch-people*,‖ and *the people igno-
miniously bound.*¶ [65] A severity unknown to the ancients required, that when the light of day failed, they
should be burnt for the purpose of giving light by night,
being covered all around with torches, paper, and wax,
and with a coat bedawbed and interwoven with com-
bustible substances ; while a stake was thrust through

* *Apol.* p. 156. † *Apol.* p. 144.
‡ *Demonstr. Evan.* lib. iii. cap. 5. p. 77. *Edit. Steph. An.* 1545.
§ *Annal.* 15. ‖ *Sarmentitii.* ¶ *Semaxii.*
[n] Mat. xxiv. 9.
[65] See NOTE LXV.

the middle of their bodies, and made to come forth at the mouth. The mode and circumstances of this punishment, worthy of *Nero* its inventor, are exactly depicted by *Calvisius.** Besides, who can enumerate all the different kinds of torture and of death, of scourges, pulleys, gibbets, wheels, pressures, gridirons, burning pots, racks, and goblets, which *Baronius* describes;† and of the engines of torment mentioned by *Eusebius.*‡ To justify all this outrageous barbarity, crime enough was implied in the innocent name of Christian, without further evidence or trial; of which *Justin, Athenagoras, Clement* of *Alexandria, Tertullian, Jerome, Augustine,* and others, no less justly than freely complained.

x. Notwithstanding the extreme detestation in which the name of Christians was held, the faithful exulted in it so much, that, rather than renounce it, they were willing to undergo a thousand deaths. In reply to questions put to them, or even of their own accord, they not merely acknowledged, but boasted, that they were Christians; and that at a time when such a profession might seem unseasonable and hazardous. When charged with Christianity, they rejoiced; to be accused of it, was their wish; to be punished, their felicity. When branded with it, they gloried; when arraigned, they made no defence; when condemned, they gave thanks. While tormented with hooks, or suspended on crosses, or encompassed with flames, or beheaded with swords, or exposed to wild beasts, they discovered a resolute mind and a cheerful countenance, and gloried that they were Christians. *St Lucian,* according to

* *Ad annum* lxiv.   † *Martyrolog. Roman.*
‡ *Lib.* v. *cap.* 1. *Lib.* viii. *cap.* 7. et 9. et 11. *Lib.* vi. *cap.* 39. alibique passim.

Chrysostome's account, when asked, " What is thy na-
" tive country? answered, I am a Christian.—What is
" thy occupation?—I am a Christian.—Who were
" thine ancestors?—In reply to every question, still he
" said, I am a Christian."

XI. Nor, indeed, is it surprising, that the followers
of Jesus put so high a value on this name of Christian;
for it comprehends almost every relation in which they
stand to Christ, the communication of his mystical
unction, and the participation of his offices; and it binds
its professors to a contempt of the world, and to more
than human undertakings. Each of these things must
now be considered with some attention.

XII. We have seen above, that nothing is more usual
than for scholars to receive their denomination from
their Teacher. We have also shown elsewhere,* that,
in Eastern countries, the names or distinguishing marks
of Masters, were imprinted with red hot iron upon the
foreheads of their servants. This practice is more than
once alluded to in the book of Revelation. The Angel
said, " Hurt not the earth, neither the sea, nor the
" trees, till we have sealed the servants of our God in
" their foreheads."[o] The Lord Jesus himself says of
his people in like manner, " I will write upon him the
" name of my God, and the name of the city of my
" God, which is new Jerusalem, which cometh down
" out of heaven from my God; and I will write upon
" him my new name:"[p] That is, I will show by my
conduct, and by conferring a most ample reward,
that I recognise him as a faithful servant of my Father,
as a citizen of the spiritual Church, and as my property,

---

* See the Author's *Economy of the Covenants,* Book iii. chap. 12.
sect. 8. T.

[o] Rev. vii. 3. See also chap. xiii. 16.   [p] Rev. iii. 12.

and *peculiar treasure.** Further, for a Wife to be named from her Husband, is not only sanctioned by modern custom, but authorised also by a most ancient and primitive appointment: " She shall be called Wo-" man, because she was taken out of Man."q Such, in fine, is the union between the head and the members, that they are justly included under one name.

The single name of Christians, therefore, happily expresses the dignity and felicity of believers, as standing in all those relations to Christ. It characterises them as the disciples of Christ, their Teacher ;r the servants of Christ, their Lord ;s the bride of Christ, their Bridegroom ;t and the spouse of Christ, their Husband.u In fine, they are members of that mystical body, of which Christ is the Head ;v for which reason, the society of believers is called not merely *Christian,* but also *Christ,* the members being reckoned with the head: " For as the body is one, and hath many members, and " all the members of that one body, being many, are " one body; *so also is Christ.*"w

XIII. Besides, since the name Christian is derived from Christ, and Christ, the Anointed, from *anointing,* and since this name can, in no respect, be empty and void of meaning; it must necessarily signify, that believers are partakers of the same anointing with Christ. And truly *his name is as ointment poured forth ;*x— poured forth, not upon himself merely, without measure, and most abundantly; but so as to flow down to all the members of his spiritual body, to the remotest

---

* סגולה, περιποίησις.

q Gen. ii. 23.
s John xiii. 13.
u Ephes. v. 25. Rev. xix. 7.
w 1 Cor. xii. 12.

r Mat. xxiii. 8.
t John iii. 29.
v Ephes. i. 22.
x Song i. 3.

extremities of the hands and feet, to the fingers and toes, and so to speak, even to the nails;—just as the precious ointment poured upon Aaron's head, ran down upon the beard, and descended to the skirts of his garments.[y] This is what John affirms, when he says, " Ye " have an unction from the Holy One ;"[z] and again, " The anointing which ye have received of him, abid- " eth in you."[a] Now this unction consists in a partici- pation of the same Spirit; and hence says Paul, " Now " he which stablisheth us with you in Christ, and hath " anointed us, is God; who hath also sealed us, and " given the earnest of the Spirit in our hearts."[b]

XIV. We may here observe that believers can attain no privilege, more *profitable*, or more *joyful*, or more *glorious*, than this participation of the unction of Christ.

XV. In ancient times, wrestlers, and others that con- tended in gymnastic games, endeavoured to make their nerves supple, and their limbs active, by frequent anointing. Anciently, wounds were usually cured by wine and oil; and perhaps more successfully than they are now healed, by the tedious applications of a laborious surgery.[c] In the primitive Church, in fine, many sick persons were healed, when anointed with oil.[d] *Tertullian* affirms,* that, among others, *Severus,* the father of *Antoninus,* was recovered in this way from an illness under which he laboured, by *Proculus,* a Christian. If we may give credit to *Jerome,*† even dead persons were, in some instances, thus restored to life.

* * *

* *Ad Scapulam,* cap. iv.   On this passage see the observations *de la Cerda.*

† *In vita Hilarionis.*

[y] Ps. cxxxiii. 2.   [z] 1 John ii. 20.
[a] Verse 27.   [b] 2 Cor. i. 21, 22.
[c] Luke x. 34.   [d] Mark vi. 13. James v. 14, 15.

So likewise, by the participation of the mystical oil, or the Spirit of Christ, we who are dead are quickened,[e] for he is " the Spirit of life ;"[f]—we who are diseased are healed ;[g] and the wounds which our sins have inflicted on our consciences, are cured.[h] We are girded also with strength, and our feet are made like hinds feet ;[i] so that we are enabled to lift up the hands which hang down, and the feeble knees, and to make straight paths " for our feet."[j] Anointing with the Spirit, and anointing with power, are united in Christ the head ; and also, in his believing members.[k] And how can it be otherwise ? The Spirit with whom we are anointed, is " the Power of the Highest,"[l] and " Power from on " high."[m]

XVI. *Joy,* and the gladness of a soul exulting in the grace of God, spring also from this unction. Oil, by its natural virtue, " makes the face to shine;"[n] and amongst the ancients, anointing with ointment was an indication of mirth.[o] Hence Jesus directs his disciples to conceal the severity of a fast, by anointing their head with oil.[p] But nothing possesses so great an exhilarating virtue as the shedding abroad of the love of God in the heart by the Holy Ghost; who, on this account, is called " the oil of gladness."[q] The Psalmist cordially congratulates himself on this felicity, saying, " Thou " anointest my head with oil."[r] Hence, too, arises so

[e] John vi. 63.	[f] Rom. viii. 2.
[g] Ps. ciii. 3, 4.	[h] Ps. li. 10—14.
[i] Ps. xviii. 33, 34.	[j] Heb. xii. 12, 13.
[k] Acts x. 38. Gal. iii. 5.	[l] Luke i. 35.
[m] Luke xxiv. 49.	[n] Ps. civ. 15.
[o] Eccles. ix. 8.	[p] Mat. vi. 17.
[q] Ps. xlv. 7.	[r] Ps. xxiii. 5.

exuberant a joy, that even the valley of the shadow of death can neither strike terror into the mind, nor deprive it of serenity. This is the true reason why Christians have undergone, sustained, and overcome, the most cruel tortures of every sort, not merely with constancy, but with incredible alacrity, leaping and singing for joy. They were refreshed to a degree which can neither be expressed nor conceived, by the delightful odour and powerful fragrance of this anointing, from which they derived that abhorred name, which was the cause of their tortures. To this the Spouse refers, when she sings thus ; " Because of the savour of thy " good ointments,—therefore do the virgins love thee."[s]

XVII. In fine, distinguished *honour* and glory arises to believers from the fragrance of this unction, which diffuses itself on every side.[t] It was anciently no inconsiderable part of the magnificence of Kings that wherever they went, they spread around them an extensive and delightful perfume.[u] *Antiochus Epiphanes* discovered great profuseness in this respect ; for when one of the people accosted him in these words, " Happy art " thou, O king, who sendest forth so sweet a perfume," he replied ; " As to this, truly I shall always gratify, " and give you full satisfaction ;" and instantly caused a vessel containing about two gallons, full of the most precious ointment, to be poured upon his head ; from which so vehement a fragrance arose, that it immediately attracted, and brought together to the spot, a great multitude, from the forum itself, and from the remotest parts of the city.* But Christ, by the commu-

---

* This is related from *Polybii,* lib. xxvi. by *Athenæus,* lib. x. *pag. mihi* 438. Compare also *Athen.* lib. v. p. 194.

[s] Song i. 3.   [t] Compare John xii. 3.

[u] Ps. xlv. 8.

nication of his anointing, performs far greater wonders on believers. He causes them to diffuse the fragrance of their odour through the whole world, and, by the sweetness of their conversation and the undissembled probity of their lives, to allure not only to the admiration, but also to the love, the reception, and the profession of Christianity, a countless multitude of men, called forth far and wide from their habitations. Nay, the odour of those garments which they receive from the ivory palaces of Christ, is not merely to men, but even to God himself, " as the smell of a field which the " LORD hath blessed."[v]

XVIII. An interesting story, after having pervaded the whole of the East, has lately reached the ears of Europeans. It is reported that in the month of October, in the year 1655, certain *Maronite* shepherds, whilst they were feeding their flock on the mountains of Nebo and Abarim, frequently observed, that several goats wandered abroad, and kept at a considerable distance from the flock for two or three days, and that, when they returned, their hair had a singularly pleasant smell. The shepherds thought proper to inquire into a circumstance so surprising. Committing themselves, therefore, to the direction of the goats, they came to precipices of an immense depth, within which they found a small but most delightful valley, the descent to which was very difficult, through rocks that to appearance had been torn up from it by an earthquake. There they discovered an exceedingly sweet-smelling cave, and, in the middle of it, a sepulchre of fresh-looking stone, having several characters inscribed upon it. The astonished shepherds, having retraced their steps, spread

[v] Gen. xxvii. 27.

wide around them a sweet odour proceeding from their
bodies and their otherwise sordid clothes; and, being
struck with the singularity of the matter, related to
the Patriarch of the *Maronites* [66] on mount Lebanon
all that they had seen and found.   The extraordinary
sweetness of the odour seemed to confirm their account.
Two priests were, therefore, sent to the spot, who found
the monument, on which were inscribed, in Hebrew
letters, these words, MOSES THE SERVANT OF THE
LORD; and who, with a delusive joy, persuaded themselves that they had found the sepulchre of Moses the
Prophet, which God had so carefully concealed.*   This
story indeed has more the appearance of fables than of
truth.   But the sweet odour which was rashly believed
to proceed from the sepulchre of Moses, is, in reality,
exhaled from the sepulchre of Christ. All his sheep are
attracted by it; and they find it so abundant, that, when
returning from the sepulchre of Christ, that is, when
enriched with the merits of his death, they are a sweet
savour of Christ, both to men and to God.[w]

XIX. Further, as Christ was, by his unction, installed into his three offices, the prophetical, the sacerdotal,
and the regal; so those who derive the name of Christians from him, are in their measure, prophets, priests,
and kings.   I say, in their measure; for these offices
in Christians, are, doubtless, of a kind and order widely different from the offices of Christ.   Since his whole
Mediatorial function consists in these offices, they can
no more be shared with others than his mediation itself.
But these designations, as conferred upon us, bear an
analogy to the offices of Christ, which though neces-

* See *Hornii Histor. Eccles.* p. 262.
[w] 2 Cor. ii. 15.
[66] See NOTE LXVI.

sarily slight, is sufficiently close to exalt us to high honour and happiness. That believers are made *Prophets*
we infer from Joel ii. 28, 29. " And it shall come to
" pass afterwards, that I will pour out my Spirit upon
" all flesh, and your sons and your daughters shall pro-
" phesy," &c. To this promise Peter refers, when he
says, " For the promise is unto you, and to your chil-
" dren, and to all that are afar off, even as many as the
" Lord our God shall call."x That they are also *Priests*
and *Kings,* appears from 1 Pet. ii. 9. " But ye are
" - - - a royal priesthood ;" and from Rev. i. 6.—" And
" hath made us kings and priests unto God and his
" Father."

xx. The Prophetical character of believers, as distinguished from the public and authoritative office of
teachers, is either *extraordinary*, being peculiar to some
in the primitive Church ; or *ordinary*, extending to all
Christians in all ages.

xxi. The *extraordinary* prophesying was, that believers in private stations, appointed to no ecclesiastical
office, and even young virgins, were endowed with so
great a fulness of the Spirit, that, on a sudden, they
discoursed on divine subjects to the astonishment of
the hearers, spoke languages with which they had formerly no acquaintance, and were enabled to foretel future events. Of this we have many testimonies and
examples in Scripture.y It pleased God in this manner
to confirm the truth of Christianity. But when the Gospel was sufficiently established for convincing the Gentiles and for rendering the Jews inexcusable, and was
also clearly and fully exhibited in the sacred books, these

x Acts ii. 39.

y Acts x. 44—46. xix. 6. xxi. 9. 1 Cor. xii. 9, 10. xiv. 26. and
in other passages.

unusual operations of the Spirit gradually ceased as
well among teachers, as among common believers. At
what precise time they were withdrawn, I presume not
to determine. The ancients pronounce high encomiums
on the prophecies of *Melito*, of *Methodius*, and of *Gregory* of *Neocesarea*, who is called *Thaumaturgus*.
That those prophecies were either fraudulently con-
trived by holy men, or of a still blacker origin, not to
say diabolical, it is difficult to suppose, and hard to affirm. I cannot, however, approve of the extravagances
of *Basil*,* and *Gregory* of *Nyssa*,† who ascribe to
Gregory of *Neocesarea* the same Spirit as to the Prophets and Apostles, and even make him almost equal
to Moses. It is manifest, at least, that the Spirit of
prophecy has now ceased. As to the prophecies of the
Reformation that was to take place in the Church by
the instrumentality of Luther and other men of God,
a vast number of which *Micrælius*‡ and *John Gerhard*§
have collected;—those prophecies were partly pious
wishes, and partly probable conjectures; for amidst an
extreme degeneracy of manners, men are wont to prog-
nosticate better times; they in part contain an application of the sacred book of the Apocalypse to those
times, and in part are entitled to no credit. And with
regard to the prophecies which *Comenius* has, with great
zeal, obtruded lately on the Church, their futility
has been demonstrated in a learned dissertation by
Arnold, our venerable colleague. Whatever the Spirit of God, whom we must not presume to limit, may
be pleased to reveal to this or the other individual re-

* *Libro de Spiritu Sancto,* cap. xxix.
† *In vita Gregorii Thaumaturgi.*
‡ *Histor. Eccles.* lib. iii. sect. 2.
§ *Loco de Ecclesia,* paragr. 292.

specting some particular future events, the inspired volume is to us a sufficient rule. " To the law and to " the testimony." See the learned Dissertation of *Voet on Prophecy and Prophets.** Some remarkable particulars of the prophecies of *Usher* are related by *Richard Parr*, in his Life of that distinguished Prelate, published at London, in the year 1686. To these may be added similar instances in certain Scottish Ministers, narrated by *Fleming*, a pious and learned man, in an English Treatise, entitled, *The Fulfilling of the Scriptures.*† [67]

XXII. Let us now inquire into that which is *ordinary*, common to all Christians, and extended to all ages. As the office of the ancient Prophets included two things, namely, that they themselves were taught by an immediate illumination from God, and that when thus taught, they instructed others; so these two things are observable in the prophetical character common to believers.

XXIII. All Christians are *taught of God*,‡ and, as *Tertullian* expresses it,§ " watered, *inundated*, with " the Divine Spirit."[z] " They have an unction from " the Holy One, and they know all things; and need " not that any man teach them, as the same anointing " teacheth them of all things."[a] " The God of our " Lord Jesus Christ, the Father of glory, gives them " the Spirit of wisdom and revelation in the knowledge " of him, the eyes of their understanding being en-

---

* *De Prophetia et Prophetis,* tom. ii.

† *Pag.* 353. *et seq. et* 392.　　　　‡ Θεοδίδακτοι.

§ Spiritu Divino inundati.

[z] Is. liv. 13. John vi. 45.　　　　[a] 1 John ii. 20, 27.

[67] See NOTE LXVII.

" lightened."[b] Though the external ministry of men is employed, this is ineffectual, unless it be accompanied with the internal and immediate revelation of the Spirit;[c] which is granted, in various degrees, to individual Christians, according to the measure of divine grace ; but allotted to all of them in sufficient proportion ; for " no man can say that Jesus is the Lord, but " by the Holy Ghost."[d]

xxiv. To this revelation of the doctrines of the Gospel with which all believers are favoured, is sometimes added a more special and familiar manifestation of the Lord Jesus to the soul ; when, taking it, so to speak, by the hand, " he brings it into his chambers ;"[e] and, having drawn aside the curtain and opened the sanctuary of heaven, he exhibits the glories which are within the vail, the felicities of heaven, and the joys of immortality ; that the understanding may contemplate, and the mind by anticipation enjoy, these exalted delights. This is a privilege he has promised to them that love him : " He that loveth me shall be loved of my Father, " and I will love him, and will manifest myself unto " him."[f]

xxv. In some instances, the Spirit of God even pourtrays on the imagination of believers, as well when awake as when asleep, very bright images of heavenly things ; which they appear not only to perceive with the mind, but also to behold immediately with their eyes, in a manner nearly resembling that in which the prophets anciently saw the objects represented to them in their visions.   That this frequently happens to the afflicted and the dying, is evident from the memoirs of

[b] Ephes. i. 17, 18.   [c] Acts xvi. 14.
[d] 1 Cor. xii. 3.   [e] Song i. 4.
[f] John xiv. 21.

the life and death of the godly, and is well known to those who are frequently employed in visiting the sick. We have examples of it in *Olympia Fulvia Morata,* a learned and celebrated female in her time, concerning whom see the famous *Voet;**—in *Caspar Olevian,* of whom the particulars are detailed by *Melchior Adam;* —in *John Holland,* of whom see *Bolton and Hoornbeeck;*†—in *Wenceslaus Budowick,* and *Caspar Kaplin,* two Bohemian noblemen, of whom *Lætus* gives an account in his History;‡—and in others without number. The visions of several Martyrs in Africa, recorded in an Epistle written from prison by the Confessors, are related by *Baronius.*§ It cannot admit of a doubt, that, in reference to such internal and immediate revelations, Christians may be accounted Prophets.

XXVI. It pertains also to the prophetical character of Christians, that they teach the truths which they have learned from God. They are enabled to " show " forth the praises of Him who hath called them out of " darkness into his marvellous light."g This they do, with their *mouth,* by their *life,* and by their *death.*

XXVII. They do it with their *mouth,* 1st, By a confession of the name of Christ.h 2dly, By pious and holy conferences and communications respecting the common salvation, with their domestics, their acquaintances, and

---

* *Disput. Select.* Tom. ii. p. 691.

† *De Desertione Spirituali,* cap. iii.

‡ *Histor. pag. mihi,* 528.

§ *Tom.* ii. *ad Annum.* cclxii. *Num.* 8. et. seq. *iterumque Num.* 26, 27, 28. *rursus* 44—46.

g 1 Pet. ii. 9.

h 2 Cor. iv. 13. Rom. x. 10. Mat. x. 32. Compare *Dissert.* iii. sect. 39.

others, as opportunities occur.[i]   3dly, By singing sacred hymns,[j] which is spoken of as a species of prophesying.[k] *Jerome* bears a signal testimony to the Christians of his own age and place, when, in a letter which he wrote to *Marcella,* inviting her to the country of Bethlehem, he says : " To whatever side you turn, the " ploughman sings hallelujahs, whilst holding the " plough ; the laborious reaper entertains himself with " hymns ; and the vine-dresser, whilst he dresses the " vines with the pruning-hook, sings one of the Psalms " of David.   In this province these are the songs ; " these, as it is commonly expressed, the songs of love." Justly, also, do we turn to the honour of our own ancestors what was affirmed by *Strada,* a reviling Jesuit, in order to expose them to reproach and disgrace. " That translation," says he, " of hymns," namely the translation of *Marotus* and *Beza,* " though abandoned " and condemned by the Catholics, was zealously and " pertinaciously retained by the Heretics ; and the " custom of singing Psalms in the French language, " according to the fashion of the *Genevese,* in compa- " nies, in places of public resort, and in shops, became " thenceforth, a peculiar characteristic of the Heretics."* Thus the Papists distinguish Heretics by the same peculiarity by which the ancients distinguished Christians.

XXVIII. But Christians teach also by their *life,* that is, by the exemplary holiness of their conduct ; by which,—the perverseness of a world lying in wickedness is reproved—the beauty of true virtue displayed even before the eyes of men unwilling to behold it—

---

* *Decad.* i. lib. iii.

[i] Ephes. iv. 29. vi. 4.   Philip. ii. 16.

[j] Ephes. v. 19.   Col. iii. 16.

[k] 1 Sam. x. 10. xix. 23, 24.   1 Chron. xxv. 1, 2, 3.

and the wonderful fruits of that Divine Spirit by whom Christians are actuated, appear, to the conviction of others and the glory of God.[1] *Tertullian* finely says ; " Though, owing either to the want of eloquence or to " the suggestions of modesty, (for philosophy is content " with the silent life,) no voice or sound be heard, the " practice utters an audible sound—at my very pre- " sence, vice is covered with confusion."*

xxix. In fine, Christians complete their prophesying by their *death;* such of them, in particular, as God calls to martyrdom. The truth of the Christian Religion has been asserted with incredible freedom, propriety, copiousness, and resolution, before princes, kings, emperors, and ingenious sophists, by men and women, old men and youths, and even by boys and girls. For the sake of this Religion, they have submitted, with unheard-of magnanimity, to the most terrible deaths, confessing and commending Christ, under the scourge and the sword, on wheels and pullies, in the midst of flames, and in burning goblets—and that even sometimes, when, to render the miracle the more illustrious, their tongues were cut out. All Christians are not called to martyrdom ; yet all ought to be prepared to suffer it, when called. It is one thing for a person who has the resolution to suffer martyrdom, to escape it ; and another thing, to be void of resolution for martyrdom. The former happens to many Christians ; the latter is becoming in no Christian. These words of our Lord are obligatory upon all : " Be thou faithful unto

---

* Etsi eloquium quiescat, aut infantia subductum aut verecundia retentum (nam et elingui philosophia vita contenta est) ipse habitus sonat—De occursu meo vitia suffundo. *De Pallio,* cap. vi.

[1] Mat. v. 16. Philip. ii. 15. 1 Pet. ii. 12. iii. 1.

" death, and I will give thee a crown of life;"[m] and
again, " If any man come to me, and hate not his fa-
" ther and mother - - - and his own life also, he cannot
" be my disciple."[n]

xxx. To the prophetical dignity of Christians is
added the *Priesthood:* " But ye shall be named the
" Priests of the Lord."[o]   Their priesthood, however,
does not consist in sacrificing irrational animals to God,
as was done by the Old Testament priests; for, Christ
having obtained the remission of our sins, " there is no
" more offering for sin."[p]   Nor doth it consist in daily
offering to the Father an unbloody sacrifice, and even
Christ himself, under the appearance of bread and wine,
for expiating the sins as well of the dead as of the living; as the Popish priests impiously contend.   For
" now once, in the end of the world, hath Christ ap-
" peared to put away sin, by the sacrifice of himself;"[q]
and by that " one offering he hath perfected for ever
" them that are sanctified."[r]   But the priesthood of
Christians is entirely spiritual—" to offer up spiritual
" sacrifices, acceptable to God by Jesus Christ."[s]

xxxi. Their priesthood consists in this, that they
are near to God, and have liberty of familiar access
to him.   *Cohen,** the Hebrew word for *priest*, properly signifies a servant who is peculiarly near the
King, and admitted to his most secret counsels.   Thus
Ira the Jairite is termed David's *Cohen,* " a chief
" ruler about David;"[t] which *Kimchi* explains thus;
" His servant and counsellor, to whom he showed more

* כהן

m Rev. ii. 10.   n Luke xiv. 26.
o Is. lxi. 6.   p Heb. x. 18.
q Heb. ix. 26.   r Heb. x. 14.
s 1 Pet. ii. 5.   t 2 Sam. xx. 26.

" attention than to the rest."*   The sons of David,
too, are called *Cohanim*, " Chief rulers,"[u] that is, as it
is elsewhere explained, " Chief about the King."[v]   In
like manner we read, that " Jehu slew all that remain-
" ed of the house of Ahab in Jezreel, and all his great
" men, and his kinsfolks and *Cohanaiu*," that is, his
intimate friends.[w]   Now God is the King of heaven,
and the Lord of all lords.   He, too, has his *Cohanim*,
or Priests, who have the privilege of " coming near to
" him,"[x] and are persons " that come nigh him," or his
intimate friends.[y]   All Christians have this dignity;
they are the friends and favourites of the King of heaven, and have " boldness to enter into the holiest by
" the blood of Jesus, by a new and living way which
" he hath consecrated."[z]

XXXII. It is also a part, and indeed the principal
part, of the priesthood of Christians, devoutly to offer
up to God all kinds of spiritual sacrifices.   By the
mortification of their " members which are upon the
" earth,"[a] they slay the old man for his honour.   They
dedicate to Him the *gift* † of alms;[b] the incense of
prayer;[c] the *sacrifice* ‡ of praise, that is, the fruit of
their lips, giving thanks to his name;[d] and, in fine, the
thank-offering of their souls and bodies,[e]—prepared, if
circumstances render this necessary, even " to be offered
" *as a drink-offering* upon the sacrifice and service of the

---

עבדו ובעל עצתו *   מנחת †   תודה ‡

[u] 2 Sam. viii. 18.

[v] הראשונים ליד המלך   1 Chron. xviii. 17.

[w] ומידעיו וכהניו   2 Kings x. 11.

[x] Exod. xix. 22.   [y] קרוביו   Levit. x. 3.

[z] Heb. x. 19, 20.   [a] Col. iii. 5.

[b] Heb. xiii. 16.   [c] Rev. viii. 3, 4.

[d] Heb. xiii. 15.   [e] Rom. xii. 1.

" faith" of their brethren. [f] The character of the Christian, as a priest, is not inelegantly described by *Tertullian* in the following words: " As his servant, I wait " upon him alone; I am slain for the sake of his reli-" gion; I offer him a fair and an excellent sacrifice, " which himself hath required,—Prayer proceeding " from a chaste body, from an upright mind, from the " Holy Spirit:—Not one pound of grains of frankin-" cense, nor gum-drops distilled from an Arabian tree, " nor two drops of myrrh, nor the blood of a worthless " bull desirous of death; nor, in addition to all other " polluted offerings, a defiled conscience." These words of *Tertullian* are quoted twice by *Eusebius.*[*]

XXXIII. Further, since it belongs to Priests to be occupied " in things pertaining to God,"[g] and in " all " the work of the place most holy,"[h] and consequently to " stand by night in the house of the Lord;"[i] let Christians remember that it pertains to their priesthood, to be " always abounding in the work of the " Lord,"[j]—frequenting his sanctuary to bear a part in divine worship,[k]—and consecrating the chambers of their own houses, and the innermost recesses of the soul, as an august temple to God, where acts of devotion may be continually performed.

XXXIV. It was the will of God, that, in ancient Israel, the priestly mitre and the royal diadem should not be worn by the same person; whilst he so parted these dignities, that the one was allotted to the tribe of Levi, the other to that of Judah. In the spiritual Is-

* *Demonst. Evang.* lib. i. p. 21. *iterumque* p. 27. *ad finem* lib. i.

[f] Philip ii. 17. 2 Tim. iv. 6.

[g] Heb. v. 1.   [h] 1 Chron. vi. 49.

[i] Ps. cxxxiv. 1.   [j] 1 Cor. xv. 58.

[k] Heb. x. 25.

rael, however, both are united; for, to the same priest-hood of which we have just been speaking, it is said, " Thou shalt also be a crown of glory in the hand of " the Lord, and a royal diadem in the hand of thy " God."[1]

xxxv. These spiritual *Kings* are animated by a re-markably generous mind, a " free spirit,"[m] " an excel-" lent spirit;"[n] for which they are compared not only to " a company of horses in Pharaoh's chariots,"[o] but even to Jehovah's " goodly horse in the battle."[p] This generous spirit disposes them to fix their eyes and their mind upon invisible, celestial, and eternal enjoyments, and to regard those objects which the rest of mankind admire, as toys, as of no value, nay, as " loss and dung;"[q] and to account even the pleasures and the pomp of a royal court contemptible in comparison of " the reproach " of Christ."[r] A certain holy *ambition,** also, stimu-lates them to strive to excel other men,[s]—to surpass them in the riches of sacred wisdom, in the beauty of spiritual grace, in the lustre of Christian virtues, and, in short, in all that is really excellent, as far as kings surpass their subjects in earthly dignity and magnifi-cence. Whilst they who distinguish themselves by such conduct, are the admiration not only of men, but of an-gels in heaven, and even of God and Christ;[t] they con-scientiously guard against all ostentation and pride: for as *Basil* of *Seleucia* finely says, in a discourse on these words of our Lord, " Except ye be converted and

---

* Φιλοτιμια. 2. Cor. v. 9.

[1] Is. lxii. 3.   [m] רוח נדיבה Ps. li. 12.

[n] רוח יתירא Dan. v. 12. vi. 3.

[o] Song i. 9.   [p] Zech. x. 3.

[q] Philip. iii. 7, 8.   [r] Heb. xi. 26.

[s] Prov. xii. 26.   [t] Song vii. 1.

" become as little children, ye shall not enter into the
" kingdom of heaven :"—*The degree of humility is the
measure of improvement.** That princely spirit which
animates believers, produces in them, also, such a high
esteem for their dignity, that they would choose rather
to suffer a thousand deaths, than to do any thing disgraceful to their exalted character; of which we have
very striking instances in Nehemiah,[u]—in Daniel's
companions,[v]—and in countless myriads of martyrs, as
well in the times of the Maccabees, as in subsequent
periods.

XXXVI. But what would a King be, without a kingdom and *power*? Of this, therefore, all Christians are
possessed, and that to a great extent, whether, as to
their worldly circumstances, they be rich or poor, free-
men or slaves. They have power, 1st, Over the whole
world; whose long established but corrupt customs, by
which as by a strong fetter, though in reality a slender
straw, even the noblest of worldly men are, like despicable fools, enslaved and bound,—they magnanimously
despise, reject, and trample under foot; not suffering
themselves " to be brought under the power of any."[w]
" Whatsoever is born of God, overcometh the world."[x]
2dly, Over *sin* and the lusts of the flesh, of which even
kings and dreaded tyrants are the miserable and truly
abject slaves.[y] Although this legion of most audacious
enemies sometimes makes an assault upon Christians
with such impetuosity that they seem almost overthrown, yet even when lying on the ground, they re-
sume their courage, and renew the contest on their

* Γίνεται μετρον αυξήσεως της ταπεινοφροσύνης ή δύναμις.
[u] Chap. vi. 11.   [v] Dan. iii. 16—18.
[w] 1 Cor. vi. 12.   [x] 1 John v. 4.
[y] Rom. vi. 14.

knees; and though, to appearance, nearly vanquished in the battle, they prove " more than conquerors" in the war.[z] 3dly, Over *Satan* himself, whom the God of peace bruises under their feet.[a] A convincing evidence of this was given in primitive times, when, at the command of Christians, devils, with reluctance and rage, departed from the bodies of those whom they had possessed,—according to our Lord's promise ; " These " signs shall follow them that believe; in my name " shall they cast out devils, &c."[b] *Grotius*, in his notes on this passage, has proved, by express testimonies from *Justin, Irenæus, Tertullian*, and *Origen*, that in the age when these Fathers flourished, Christians in various countries, exercised this power, to the astonishment of the heathen. *Eusebius* also says; " Still he con-" tinues, as we know by experience, to display the en-" ergy of divine power, expelling foul and malignant " demons from the souls and bodies of men, through " the silent invocation of his name."[*]

XXXVII. Thus, with Christ their head, they rule in the midst of their enemies.[c] A blessed kingdom of righteousness and peace, is, meanwhile, erected in their souls; where the Spirit of Christ holds the sceptre, love is law, and all their faculties of soul and body voluntarily submit themselves to the Spirit; which produces incredible tranquillity and gladness of heart. This is that kingdom of Christians, which Paul describes in the following words : " The kingdom of God is—righte-" ousness, and peace and joy in the Holy Ghost."[d]

---

[*] *Adversus Hieroclem.*

[z] Rom. viii. 37.   [a] Rom. xvi. 20. Rev. xii. 10, 11.

[b] Mark xvi. 17.   [c] Ps. cx. 2.

[d] Rom. xiv. 17.

XXXVIII. To this power are added royal *wealth*, and royal *majesty*. Their wealth is not secular, but heavenly and spiritual. " God hath chosen the poor of this world, " rich in faith and heirs of the kingdom."[e] The riches of the Christian are, the word of God laid up in the sacred treasury of the mind[f]—the wisdom derived from that word[g]—store of divine grace, the least drop of which is more precious than all the gold of the whole world—and, in fine, the abundance of heavenly bliss that awaits them, of which they enjoy the first-fruits in the present state.[h] Solacing themselves in these treasures, they are truly and spiritually rich ; they equal kings in wealth. Such, then, is the royal opulence they possess.

XXXIX. Their wealth is accompanied with a *majesty* and dignity which render them venerable and sacred, as well with God as with men. God suffers none to injure them with impunity : " Yea, he reproved kings " for their sakes, saying, Touch not mine anointed, " and do my prophets no harm."[i] The following words of God in Isaiah are truly magnificent : " Since thou " wast precious in my sight, thou hast been honoura- " ble, and I have loved thee : therefore will I give men " for thee, and people *at thy request*."[j] He makes them equally venerable to their friends and their ene- mies. As to their friends, we have the following tes- timony, than which nothing of the kind more glorious, could be said : " And kings shall be thy nursing-fa- " thers, and their queens thy nursing-mothers : they

---

[e] James ii. 5.
[f] Ps. cxix. 72.   Job. xxiii. 12.
[g] Job xxviii. 15.   Prov. iii. 14, 15.
[h] Ps. xxxi. 19.   [i] Ps. cv. 14, 15.
[j] Is. xliii. 4.

" shall bow down to thee with their face towards the
" earth, and lick up the dust of thy feet; and thou
" shalt know that I am the LORD: for they shall not
" be ashamed that wait for me."[k] Of their enemies it
is in like manner said : " The sons also of them that
" afflicted thee, shall come bending unto thee, and all
" they that despise thee shall bow themselves down at
" the soles of thy feet," &c.[l]

XL. From the copious illustrations which have now
been given, it clearly appears, that the name of CHRIS-
TIANS, if taken, as it ought to be, in the whole extent
of its meaning, is highly magnificent. As it is a source
of unparalleled consolation to all those whom, not the
excessive civility of men, but the mouth of God himself
has expressly called by this new name;[m] so let all who
glory in this illustrious name, know that they are bound
to perform the noblest actions, and to cultivate a holiness remarkably exact and almost similar to the holiness of God; lest their profession, not corresponding
with their life, involve them in a condemnation equally
certain and dreadful. O how justly does *Chrysostome*
say ! " The greater the honour to which God has ad-
" vanced us, the higher in proportion are the attain-
" ments in virtue to which we are obliged to aspire."*
Equally elegant are these expressions of *Ambrose* :
" Let us discover what profession we make, rather by
" our conduct than by our name ; that our name may
" accord with our conduct, and our conduct correspond
" with our name : LEST OUR NAME BE VAIN, AND
" OUR GUILT ENORMOUS." We conclude with the

* *In Johan.* xiv.
[k] Is. xlix. 23.
[l] Is. lx. 14.   See also Rev. iii. 9.
[m] Is. lxii. 2.

excellent words of *Augustine:* " Let us not satisfy
" ourselves merely with the appellation of Christians ;
" but let us reflect that we are to be judged in reference
" to this,—whether we presumptuously arrogate a name
" to which we have no title."*

* *De vita Christiana.* See *Gregory* of *Nyssa, De perfecta hominis
Christiani forma.*

DISSERTATION XII.

ON JESUS CHRIST,

THE ONLY-BEGOTTEN SON OF GOD.

————

1. IT becomes every one who earnestly desires the eternal salvation of his own soul, to exert his best endeavours to attain " all riches of the full assurance of " understanding, to the acknowledgment of the mystery " of God, and of the Father, and of Christ; in which* " are hid all the treasures of wisdom and knowledge."[a] These words intimate, that there is a GOD, by whom the world exists, of whom, and to whom we all are;[b] and who can prove to his rational creatures, and even to sinful man, what he is to himself, the Fountain of consummate blessedness."[c] In the Godhead, we must know, there is a FATHER, who is able to restore life to that which was lost, to renew his own image in the sinner, to admit a person who had been alienated from him to the embraces of his fatherly love, and, in fine, to make him an heir of heavenly and eternal blessings.[d] The Father, too, hath a SON, of the same na-

* See NOTE XXXII.

[a] Col. ii. 2, 3.   [b] 1 Cor. viii. 6.   Rom. xi. 36.
[c] 1 Tim. vi. 15.   [d] Luke xii. 32.

ture and of equal dignity with himself, whom, according to the counsel of peace which takes place between God and the Man whose name is the BRANCH,[e] he could send into the world, clothed with human flesh, and made under the law;—so that, the law having received full satisfaction from him to all its demands, he can exercise his goodness and mercy towards the sinner, in consistency with righteousness, holiness, and wisdom.[f] To this work the Son was appointed from eternity;[g] and being endowed with the richest gifts of the Spirit,[h] he is called CHRIST, that is, the Anointed. This is a " mystery," which no man could know, unless it were revealed by God;[i] and which, even when thus revealed, no mortal can fully comprehend.[j] In this mystery, is "wisdom and knowledge;" for without knowing it, we neither understand the manner of the Divine operations, nor can we conceive any thing that is worthy of God, in the plan of our salvation. Wisdom is an invaluable " treasure:"[k] but it is " hid" and laid up in this mystery; for when this is not revealed or not known, we cannot fail to remain ignorant of the wisdom of God; and whoever meditates with due attention on this incomprehensible topic, will continually discover new treasures which he had not formerly perceived. To consider this mystery for a little, therefore, and in the exercise of faith to contemplate Christ as the ONLY-BEGOTTEN SON of the Father, and OUR LORD, will be a pious, a becoming, and a profitable employment. Nothing, certainly, can be more repugnant to the mind of Paul, and to the genius of the

[e] Zech. vi. 12, 13.   [f] Gal. iv. 4, 5.
[g] Prov. viii. 23.   [h] Is. lxi. 1.
[i] Mat. xi. 27.   [j] Prov. xxx. 4.
[k] Job xxviii. 15—19.

Christian Religion, than this blasphemy uttered by *Ostorodus:* " In order to know the will of God to-" wards us so far as is requisite to salvation, it is not " at all necessary to know the nature of Christ, but " merely his office."*

II. We confess in the Creed, that Jesus Christ is, *First,* The Son of God. *Secondly,* Begotten of God. *Thirdly,* His Only-begotten.

III. That he is the Son of God, Christ himself protested in an assembly of those who are termed,[1] but in a far lower sense, " Children of the Most High;"[m]— the Father proclaimed by a voice from heaven;[n]—and the Holy Spirit proved by descending upon him.[o] The sacred Scriptures, too, represent it as the sum of our confession and faith relative to Christ, to believe and profess that Jesus is the Son of God.[p]

IV. This name, when attributed to Christ, is *more excellent*[q] than any that is given to Angels; though they also are denominated " Sons of God."[r] By the expression *more excellent,* the Apostle indicates a difference not merely in *degree,* but also in *kind;* that this name may be completely and directly distinguished, and as applied to Christ, have a signification totally different. For a difference in degrees is not sufficient to constitute a *difference*† in name. The King of Assyria, for example, or of Persia, was, by many steps of dignity, superior to any King of Cappadocia, or Pontus, or Lacedemon; yet the name of King is not *more*

---

* *Instit.* cap. vi.   † Διαφορα.

[1] Ps. lxxxii. 6.   [m] Mat. xxvi. 64.

[n] Mat. xvii. 5.   [o] Mat. iii. 16.

[p] John xx. 31. 1 John iv. 15. Mat. xvi. 16. John vi. 69. Acts viii. 37. ix. 20.

[q] Διαφορωτερον, Heb. i. 4.   [r] Job i. 6. xxxviii. 7.

excellent when ascribed to the Persian or the Assyrian monarch, than when it is applied to the ruler of Cappadocia, Pontus, or Laconia.   Nor is it unworthy of notice that the Apostle affirms, that Christ hath *obtained by inheritance** this name.   The expression intimates, that, like an inheritance, it is Christ's indisputable and unalienable property; nay more, that he possesses it not as a mere voluntary gift, nor as the recompence of his labour or the consequence of his merit, but as an inheritance to which he has an original right, arising from the intimate relation between the Father and him.⁶⁸   In virtue of that relation he is evidently entitled to this name; nor could he, by any power or means, be precluded from obtaining it, or divested of his right to be acknowledged by God the Father and by men, as what he really is, the Son of God.   We indeed are heirs of God, because we are sons;ˢ and because we have received Christ, and are, in the manner competent to us, born of God, " power is given to us " to become the sons of God;"ᵗ or owing to the divine condescension and liberality, we may dare to consider ourselves as such.ᵗ   But nowhere are we said to have *inherited* the name of the sons of God.

v. It serves to establish the same point, that the Apostle speaks of Christ as, ὁρισθεντα υἱον Θεου ἐν δυναμει, " declared to be the Son of God with power."ᵘ Ὁρίζειν is to *define*, to determine, to fix a thing within its bounds and limits, so that one may perceive what it is in itself, and how it differs from other things; or to designate any thing precisely and particularly, to the

* Κεκληρονομηκεναί.

ˢ Rom. viii. 17.   ᵗ John i. 12.
ᵘ Rom. i. 4.
          ⁶⁸ See NOTE LXVIII.

exclusion of every thing else.* Christ is elsewhere
said to be, ὡρισμενος, " ordained," *determined*, particularly designated, " of God to be the Judge of quick
" and dead."ᵛ So here he is " declared, *determined*, to
be the Son of God," that is, placed within such bounds,
so separated by those bounds from other persons, and
so particularly declared to the exclusion of others, that
it is equally unlawful and impossible not to consider
him as the Son of God. It is added,—" with power."
This may either be connected with the word " declared,"
and thus it is affirmed that Christ is " declared, *deter-*
" *mined*, with power," that is, demonstrated by the
strongest evidence to be, in a peculiar sense, the Son of
God; or it may be joined with the expression, " the
" Son of God," and then the meaning is, that Christ is
the Son of God with power. Whether you choose the
one or the other, the result is almost the same. According to the former construction, Christ is " declared,"
determined, in all the emphasis of the term, conformably to its strongest and most proper signification. According to the latter, he is " the Son of God with
" power," that is, the power which is absolutely so called, and is peculiar to God, (who is therefore denominated by the Hebrews *the Power*,†) and in reference to
which Christ is called " the mighty God."ʷ Of these
two modes of construing the sentence, however, the
latter appears the more simple and the more nervous.

---

* *Hesychius* explains ὁριζει by ῾ιστησει, ὁρον διδωσι, κρινει, θεματιζει,
διαιρει, ἀφοριζει; he fixes, limits, determines, establishes in a certain
position, distinguishes, separates.

† הגבורה, ἡ δυναμις.

ᵛ Acts x. 42. See also Ch. xvii. 31.

ʷ אל גבור Is. ix. 5.

vi. Further, Christ as the Son of God, is BEGOT-
TEN of God; for the Father thus addressed him,
" Thou art my Son; this day have I BEGOTTEN
" thee :"ˣ that is, I have caused thee to go forth from
myself.   The word ילד is commonly applied to mothers, because they bring forth children immediately
from themselves.   " Ask ye now and see, whether a
" man doth travail with child."ʸ   Fathers are usually
said הוליד, to *beget,* to make another bring forth, to
be the cause of fruitfulness to another.   Here God applies to himself that which is proper to mothers, because the going forth of the Son is immediately from
himself.   Nor does this passage relate to the formation
of the human nature in the womb of Mary, in reference
to which, the term הוליד might seem more pertinent,
because the power of the Deity was the cause of fruitfulness to the Virgin ;—but to the generation of Christ
*as a Divine person.**   This observation which I owe
to a very accurate Interpreter, is particularly useful for
repelling the impious cavils of the Socinians.   You
may compare it with the remarks formerly made in the
eleventh Section of the *seventh Dissertation.*

vii. But since mortals find themselves at a loss to
explain particularly the generation of even the minutest
creature in the world, who among them is able to conceive in his mind, or to declare by his tongue or pen,
in what the generation of the Son of God consists ?
This one thing, however, we may safely affirm, because
we learn it from the word of God himself, that the generation in question is such a communication of life
that the Son hath " life in himself."ᶻ   It is such a

* Κατα Θεολογίαν.

ˣ Ps. ii. 7.   ʸ אם יולד זכר, Jer. xxx. 6.
ᶻ John v. 26.

communication of the Divine, living, and life-giving essence, that the Son hath this essence, not as adventitious, recent, or dependant upon another,—but " in " himself," as the Father hath it " in himself;" whilst in the Son it is the foundation of that power of which he as Mediator is possessed, to impart life to dead sinners,—a spiritual and holy life in this world, as well as a blessed and everlasting life in the world to come. See the *Dissertation* just referred to, *Section tenth.*

VIII. This generation of the Son of God is from eternity. For thus the Supreme Wisdom speaks of itself, " The LORD possessed," or *got* " me, in the " beginning," or *the beginning*, " of his way, before his " works of old."[a] Wisdom here ascribes to itself a generation, in consequence of which God hath it as a Son; for the term קנה is applied to one that brings forth, as in these words, " I have gotten a man;"[b] and also to one that begets, as in the following expression, " Is not he thy Father that hath *got* thee ?"[c] She calls that generation, " the beginning of the ways of God," because it is a kind of *procession*, or *going-forth*,[d] and there was no procession in the Deity prior to this,— none either possible or conceivable. Or we may so construe the expression, that Wisdom herself may be called " the beginning of the ways of God," because God does nothing but in and by the Son, who, on that account, is denominated " the beginning of the creation of God."[e]—This possessing by generation, this

---

[a] קנני ראשית דרכו   Prov. viii. 22.

[b] איש קניתי   Gen. iv. 1.

[c] הוא אביך קניך   Deut. xxxii. 6.

[d] מוצא   Mic. v. 1.

[e] ʽΗ ἀρχη της κτισεως τῦ Θεῦ.   Rev. iii. 14.

" beginning of the ways of God," precedes *his works ;**
that is, not merely external works, but every kind of
preparations and decrees.[f] Wisdom proceeded from
the Father before the going forth of the Divine decrees,
not with respect to time, for the decrees were also eternal, but in the order of nature ; for no decree was formed without the Son. *Of old* † denotes eternity ; for
that which was in some respect prior to the eternal decrees of God, cannot but be eternal. It is added,
" When there were no depths, I was brought forth."[g]
But the deep was from the beginning.[h] And to place
it beyond a doubt that this discourse relates to the Personal Wisdom, or the Son of God, it follows, " Then I
" was by him as one brought up with him."[i] The
word in the original properly signifies a *nursling,* ‡ a
son carried in the bosom ; as may be gathered from this
expression in the book of Numbers : " Carry them in
" thy bosom, as a nursing-father beareth the *sucking-*
" *child.*"[j] Now the same representation is given of
Christ in the Gospel of John, when he is called " the
" only-begotten Son who is in the bosom of the Fa-
" ther,"[k] that is, most intimately related to the Father,
both by nature, and by mutual love.[69]

IX. We must not here omit the following remarkable announcement in the prophecies of Micah : " Out
" of thee," O Bethlehem, " shall he come forth unto
" me that is to be Ruler in Israel ; whose goings forth

---

* מפעליו   † מאז

‡ 'Εγκόλπιος.

[f] See Mic. ii. 1. Ps. lvii. 3.

[g] חוללתי verse 24. Comp. Ps. li. 5. Is. li. 2.

[h] Gen. i. 2.   [i] Verse 30. אמון.

[j] האומן Num. xi. 12. [k] John i. 18.

[69] See NOTE LXIX.

" have been from of old, even from everlasting."[1]   A certain learned man has made an observation which deserves to be repeated here.   He shows from this passage that there is a threefold *going forth* of Christ.   One is *external* and visible, namely, his going forth out of Bethlehem at his birth, when he assumed our nature. The word יצא " come forth" is frequently used in reference to birth,[m] and even to the birth of Christ himself; as when we read; " their Governor *shall proceed*," that is, shall be born, " from the midst of them."[n]   Of this going forth it is said that it was to be unto God. He shall come forth *unto me ;** that is, by my power, through my goodness and faithfulness, for the promotion of my glory.   Another going forth is *internal* and *everlasting*, to wit, that generation of the Messiah, by which he is in reality, and is called the Son of God; and which secures to him this dignity, that in all the emphasis of the term, he is the Ruler of that free people, whose blessed liberty consists in their being subject to God only.[o]   This generation according to the Spirit, is here opposed to the other, which is according to the flesh ; in exactly the same way as in Rom. i. 3, 4. and chap. ix. 5.   It took place מקדם " from of old."   This word, when applied to duration, sometimes denotes indefinitely time long since past; and sometimes eternity, as in the following passages : " The eternal God, " *the God of eternity*, is thy refuge :"[p] " He that abid- " eth of old, *he that inhabiteth eternity :*"[q] " Art thou

---

לי *

[1] ומוצאתיו מקדם מימי עולם   Mic. v. 2.

[m] Gen. xvii. 6. 2 Kings xx. 18.

[n] יצא   Jerem. xxx. 21. Compare Is. xi. 1.

[o] Is. xxxiii. 22.   [p] אלהי קדם   Deut. xxxiii. 27.

[q] יושב קדם   Ps. lv. 19.

" not from everlasting, O LORD."ʳ　From this last
passage it appears not only that קדם signifies *eternity*,
but also מקדם, *from eternity*.　Yet since those " go-
" ings forth," which are distinguished from the going
forth out of Bethlehem, are mentioned in the plural
number, it is right to conceive of a *third*, which took
place from the days of old, besides that which is from
eternity, namely, the going forth of the Messiah in the
word of the most ancient promise.　The expression
" going forth," or proceeding, is applied to speech, as
when it is said, " Man doth not live by bread only, but
" by every word that proceedeth out of the mouth of
" the Lord."ˢ　And together with the word of promise
and of grace, the Messiah himself goes forth in the
word, and comes to the relief of the disconsolate sinner.
Hence says the Psalmist, " Ride prosperously *upon*
" *the word of truth*."ᵗ　This going forth in the promise
took place *from the days of old*,* from the most ancient
times, from the beginning of the world, from the period
when the days of time began to run, in paradise itself.
The expression designates the remotest period of anti-
quity.ᵘ　It ought by all means to be compared with
these words of the Apostle : " In hope of eternal life,
" which God that cannot lie promised *before the world*

---

* מימי עולם

ʳ הלא אתה מקדם יהוה　Hab. i. 12.

ˢ מצא פי יהוה　Deut. viii. 3. Add Ps. lxxxix. 34. and Dan. ix.
25. מז מוצא דבר, " from the going forth of the commandment."
See also verse 23. and Est. i. 19. Luke. ii. 1. ἐξῆλθε δόγμα, " there
" went out a decree."

ᵗ Ps. xlv. 4.

ᵘ See Mic. vii. 14. Mal. iii. 4. Is. li. 9. lxiii. 9, 11. Deut.
xxxii. 7.

" *began.*" ᵛ ⁷⁰   Nor do I know an instance, in which it denotes an absolute eternity, without beginning.

x. In reference to this generation Christ is called God's OWN *proper* SON ;ʷ not his Son metaphorically, nor by adoption, nor in the same sense in which others are his sons, but his natural Son, (just as Simon is called Andrew's *own, proper, brother ;*ˣ) and on that account " equal" to the Father.ʸ   It was not improperly, or in opposition to the mind of the Lord Jesus, that the Jews inferred from his expressions, that he made himself equal with God.   For in that case he would have accused them of calumny, he would have protested that injustice had been done him ; and if he be nothing more than a mere man, he would have vindicated himself most effectually from the charge of a blasphemy so horrid, so extremely injurious to God, and so unworthy of his own characteristic humility.   He sought not his own glory, but his glory that sent him.ᶻ   And, therefore, because the Father can be honoured only in the Son,ᵃ he taught expressly—his whole discourse was adapted to this purpose—all his reasonings were directed to this object, to make it perfectly manifest, that he is so the *proper Son* of his *proper Father*, that he possesses the same essence, power, and dignity with him. Nor does John relate what the hearers either properly or improperly concluded from Christ's discourse, but what Christ himself both said and did.   As he truly

---

ᵛ Πρὸ χρόνων αἰωνίων.   Tit. i. 2.

ʷ Τῷ ἰδίῳ υἱῷ.   Rom. viii. 33.

ˣ Τον ἀδελφον τον ἴδιον.   John i. 42.

ʸ John v. 18.   ᶻ John viii. 50. vii. 18.

ᵃ John v. 23.

⁷⁰ See NOTE LXX.

said that " God was his proper Father," so he truly
" made himself equal with God."

XI. For the same reason we are taught that " the
" name of God is in him."[b] " The name of God" signifies those attributes of God, those perfections and excellencies, by which he makes himself manifest to men
in his works, especially in the work of our salvation;—
those attributes which God ascribed to himself when
he proclaimed his name before Moses;[c] and in reference
to which, Christ, having not only promulged them by
his doctrine, but also shown them forth by his work,
protests that he has "manifested the name of God unto
" men."[d] This name, indeed, involves Deity itself in
its import; nor can it be communicated to one who is
not God, any more than the glory of Deity, from which
it is hardly, if at all to be distinguished.[e]

XII. Near akin to this expression is the title of " the
" angel of God's face."[f] This designation is given him,
not merely because he always contemplates the face of
God, which indeed he doth in a manner far superior to
other angels, insomuch that it is said, " No man know-
" eth the Father save the Son;"[g] but also because the
face of God, as reconciled and gracious, is nowhere exhibited to the view of sinful men but in Christ.[h] Now
what else is the face of God in this sense than the glory
of God as it is displayed in glorifying the elect; or, to
use Paul's expression, " the light of the knowledge of
" the glory of God in the face of Jesus Christ?"[i] Since
the face of God is so exhibited in Christ, that " he that

b Exod. xxiii. 21.　　　　c Exod. xxxiv. 5, 6, 7.
d John xvii. 6.　　　　　 e Is. xlii. 8.
f Is. lxiii. 9.　　　　　　 g Mat. xi. 27.
h John i. 18.　　　　　　 i 2 Cor. iv. 6.

" hath seen Christ, hath," of course, " seen the Fa-
" ther,"ʲ it necessarily follows that Christ is possessed
of the same glory and godhead which belong to the Father.

XIII. Nay, he is also denominated THE FACE OF
GOD. " When God said, Shall MY FACE go before
" thee to give thee rest?[71] Moses said unto him, If
" THY FACE go not with me, carry us not up hence."ᵏ
God had formerly promised that the Angel " in whom
" his name is," to wit, his Son, the Messiah, should go
before them in the wilderness, to bring them to the
place which he had prepared; but offended by their
horrible idolatry in making and worshipping the golden
calf, he proposed to send one of the ordinary angels to
expel the nations from the promised land, and threatened that himself would not go with them. Yielding, however, to the importunate supplications of Moses, who solicited the accomplishment of the former
promise, he inquires if he cannot rest unless his OWN
FACE go with him, that is, the same Angel of whom
he had formerly spoken. The same thing, if I am not
mistaken, is intended in Malachi,ˡ when it is said,
" Behold, I will send my messenger," that is, John the
Baptist, " and he shall prepare the way לפני FOR MY
" FACE;" that is Christ, for it follows: " and the LORD
" whom ye seek, shall suddenly come to his temple."
It deserves also to be considered whether we may not
refer to Christ that expression of David: " As for me,
" I will behold thy face in righteousness, I shall be sa-
" tisfied, when I awake, with THY LIKENESS."ᵐ What

ʲ John xiv. 9.   ᵏ Exod. xxxiii. 14, 15.

ˡ Chap. iii. 1.   ᵐ תמונתך Ps. xvii. 15.

[71] See NOTE LXXI.

should hinder us from comparing these words with 1 John iii. 2.; for Christ is both the face and the image of God.[n] Nor is it unnatural to understand in the same sense this phrase, " the similitude of the Lord;"[o] for it seems to be numbered amongst the peculiar honours by which Moses was distinguished from the rest of the prophets, that the Son of God addressed himself immediately both to his eyes and his ears, while to other prophets he generally disclosed his secrets by the intervention of angels.

xiv. It is, at all events, a very memorable eulogy with which Paul adorns our Lord, when he calls him " the brightness of the Father's glory, and the express " image of his person."[p] These titles may be given to Christ in reference to his office; but they belong to him primarily and more eminently, in relation to his person. As the Son of God, he is " light of light," and the most illustrious effulgence of the Father's glory. " We beheld his glory," says John, " the glory as of " the only-begotten of the Father."[q] In the Apocryphal writings, Wisdom is denominated " the bright- " ness of the everlasting light."[r] " He sent forth " the Son," says *Anastasius*, " as beams, as an efful- " gence upon the earth."[*] The expression intimates both that the glory of the Son is equally bright with that of the Father, and that the Son's going forth from the Father is natural. *Oecumenius*, accordingly, makes this remark: " By the term *brightness*[†] he shows that " the going forth of the Son from the Father is natu-

* Ὑιὸν δὲ ὡς τὰς ᾿ακτινας ἀπέστειλε, τὸ ἀπαυγασμα ἐπὶ γης.

† Ἀπαυγασμα.

[n] Col. i. 15.   [o] תמונת יהוה Numb. xii. 8.

[p] Ἀπαύγασμα της δόξης, καὶ χαρακτηρ της ὑποστασεως αὐτȣ. Heb. i. 3.

[q] John i. 14.   [r] Ἀπαυγασμα φωτὸς ἀϊδιȣ. Wisdom vii. 26.

" ral, and not by grace or adoption ; for brightness pro-
" ceeds naturally from any luminous body, as the sun
" or a fire."

xv. He is also " the express image of the person,"
the *hypostasis,* of the Father. In expounding the word
hypostasis, we sometimes indulge, I doubt not, in excessive refinement. Being treated certainly in too
scholastic a manner, it was understood in a variety of
different senses, and occasioned numerous disputes and
contentions in the Church. See on this subject, among
the ancients, *Socrates,** *Theodoret,* † and *Rufinus* ; ‡
amongst the moderns, *Forbes.* § We, for our part,
prefer nothing to simplicity. The words themselves
appear to require that *hypostasis,* and *character,*‖ " the
" express image," be understood as corresponding exactly to each other. The same form which in the seal
may be called *hypostasis,* is, in the wax, termed *character :* and here, as *Gomar* has judiciously remarked,
there is an elegant figure. As the *character* agrees in
form with the archetype, or model, so Christ agrees in
essence with the Father ;—but in a more excellent manner, since he is one with him in essence, not in species
but in number. Hence he is described as " being in
" the form of God."ˢ Again, as the *character* differs
from the archetype in its mode of subsisting, the archetype having communicated the form, but the *character*
having received it by the impression ; so the Father
hath Deity from himself, which he communicated to
the Son by eternal generation, while the Son received

---

* *Histor. Eccles.* lib. iii. cap. 7.   † Lib. ii. cap. 8.
‡ *Histor.* lib. i. cap. 29.
§ *Instruct. Histor. Theol.* lib. i. cap. 11. sect. 8.
‖ Χαρακτήρ.

ˢ Philip. ii. 6.

it from the Father. The Son is, therefore, not the Father, but is spoken of as distinct from the Father.[t] In fine, the *character*, though it is not the model, yet fully expresses it; and, in like manner, the Son exhibits the Father in himself, and reveals him to us. *Theophylact*, after *Gregory* of *Nyssa*, says very finely: " Neither doth the *character* excel the *hypostasis*, " because in so far as it might excel, it would have no " *hypostasis* or model; nor is the *hypostasis* greater " than the *character*, for then it would have something " not expressed in the *character*."

XVI. The acute *Bisterfeld*,* when vindicating this passage against *Crellius*, premises, that the Apostle, in his Epistle to the Hebrews, makes use of such descriptions and such terms as have their foundation in the Old Testament; adding this as a universal maxim, " that, with the exception of terms merely historical, " all the phrases and words employed in the New Tes- " tament to express any mystery of faith, are taken " from the Old." To this last sentiment, I dare not give an unqualified assent; but of what he says in reference to this place in particular, I cordially approve. Let us see then what there is in the Old Testament corresponding to this expression of Paul. *Bisterfeld* does not give me full satisfaction here. He thinks that " the brightness"[†] corresponds to the Hebrew word rendered " apparently." [‡] But that word signifies rather *sight, appearance.* [§] The phrase " apparently " and not in dark speeches,"[u] may be considered as in some degree parallel to the following expression of Paul:

---

* Lib. i. Sect. 2. Cap. 30.

† Το ἀπαυγασμα.

‡ מראה Num. xii. 8.

§ Ἐιδος.

[t] John v. 17.

[u] מראה ולא בחידות Num. xii. 8.

" We walk by faith, not by sight."[v] " Faith" may
correspond to " dark speeches," and " sight" to " apparently."   To me it seems more probable that there is a
reference to that " brightness"* of the divine glory which
was above the ark, and which, as well as the ark itself,
was a shadow, whose truth and body is in Christ :[w]—
or to that which shone forth in the face of Moses, or in
the Cherubim which appeared to Ezekiel, to which the
word " bright"[x] is applied, an expression very similar
to that which Paul employs:—or (what I would prefer
to all the rest, if it seem improper to include the whole)
to that splendour of the Divine Majesty, which sometimes shone upon the Prophets when they beheld God
in a human form.   Thus, not to mention others, Ezekiel speaks of " the appearance of the brightness - - -
" the appearance of the likeness of the glory of the
" Lord."[y]   With this compare the following expression
of Isaiah, namely,—" the abundance, *brightness*, of her
" glory."[z]   When Paul, therefore, describes the Messiah in nearly the same magnificent terms, what does
he intend to teach, but that he is the same person, who,
to give a prelude of his future incarnation, presented
himself to the view of the prophets under so august an
appearance of Divinity ?   *Bisterfeld* comes nearer the
truth when he observes that *character*† is a term parallel to *Temuna ;*‡ for each of these words signifies a certain figure, engraven and impressed according to a certain measure and proportion.   But when he adds, " *Te-*
" *muna* is derived from *Mijn,*§ that is, *number*, and

* 'Απαυγασμα.   † Χαρακτηρ.
‡ תמונה   § מין

[v] Δια πιστεως περιπατουμεν, ε δια ειδες. 2 Cor. v. 7.
[w] Col. ii. 17.   [x] נוגה Ezek. i. 13.
[y] מראה הנוגה מארה דמות כבוד יהוה Ezek. i. 28.
[z] זיו כבודה Is. lxvi. 11.

" thus signifies a most accurate impression," his observation, I apprehend, is incorrect; for *Mijn* does not
signify the number, but the species or kind of things.
Temuna is a likeness of that sort which bears the very
species and form of an object, by which it is discriminated from all other objects;—just as the *character* exhibits the whole figure that is in the archetype.

XVII. Possibly, however, it may seem better to compare the Apostle's expression with that passage in Hag-
gai, where it is said to Zerubbabel, that is, according
to some interpreters, to Christ, who was the son of Zerubbabel and prefigured by him: " I will make thee as
" a signet,"[a] or a seal-ring. In a signet there is a *cha-*
racter. The sense then might be this: ' I will imprint
' on thee an exact likeness of myself; I will demon-
' strate that thou art a Son the same with me in sub-
' stance and equal in glory, and I will make it manifest
' by every evidence that thou art, in reality, such a Son.'
Add to this the following words in Zechariah; " I will
" engrave the gravings thereof;"[b] that is, ' I will cause
' to appear in him, all those marks and excellencies,
' which are the characteristics of the Messiah and my
' Son.' But whatever be the meaning of these passages, we conclude, that the Son of God, for this precise reason that he is begotten of God, is in all respects
like and equal to God the Father who begat him, and
is the true God and one with him.

XVIII. It is impossible that more than one should be
the Son of God in this sublime sense; and the Scripture, accordingly, represents him as the ONLY-BEGOT-
TEN Son of the Father.[c] Believers indeed are " be-

---

[a] חותם Hag. ii. 23.   [b] Zech. iii. 9.
[c] John i. 14, 18. iii. 16, 18. 1 John iv. 9.

" gotten of God ;"d and this generation of believers is
the communication of exactly the same essence, or " di-
" vine nature,"e which is communicated to Christ.*
Yet that communication of the same divine nature, and
consequently that generation from God, which is the
privilege of believers, is entirely of a different order and
kind from that which is attributed to Christ. The former is improper, metaphorical, gratuitous, importing
some resemblance to God, such as is competent to man ;
but by no means equality, least of all, identity. The
latter, on the contrary, is such as may appertain to a
Divine person,—proper, natural, eternal, implying *equality, oneness, identity*† with God the Father. This is
clearly taught by John, who, after having affirmed that
believers are " born" or " begotten of God," in order to
preclude all doubt that the sonship of Christ is widely
different from the sonship of believers, testifies more
than once, with the same breath, and almost in the
same sentence, that Christ is the " Only-begotten Son
" of God."f Were it not for this, the inspired writer
would certainly have avoided so harsh an *appearance
of contradiction ;*‡ and after having taken notice of
many sons that are begotten of God, would have deemed it better to say, that Christ is the most distinguished
Son, and more excellent than the rest, than to call him
the " Only-begotten."

XIX. Truly impious in a high degree is the cavilling
of *Socinus* on this topic. With a view to overthrow

---

* On the Divine nature's being *communicated* to Christ, an expression which repeatedly occurs in this Dissertation, the reader will
find some remarks in NOTE XXXIX. T.

† Ἰσότης, ἑνότης, ταυτότης.   ‡ Ἐναντιοφανεια.

d John i. 13. James i. 18. 1 John iii. 9. v. 1.

e 2 Pet. i. 4.   f John i. 13, 14. 1 John iv. 7, 9.

the true and eternal sonship of the Son of God, he not only substitutes in the room of an incomprehensible generation, which is the fundamental and only cause of that sonship, those things which are merely manifestations and posterior evidences of it; but also denies, that Christ is called the Only-begotten Son of God because he alone was begotten of God. This is expressly to contradict the Holy Ghost, and indeed himself also; for if others besides Christ are begotten of God by the same kind of generation, Christ is certainly not the Only-begotten.

xx. But what reason does he assign for this designation? For having rejected the true cause of the Scripture's calling Christ the " only-begotten Son" of God, he must needs contrive others foreign to the purpose. He compares Christ with Isaac, whom Moses calls the *only Son* of Abraham,[g] and Paul *his only-begotten Son;*[h] while it is evident that at the very time when he is so termed, Abraham had another son, namely, Ishmael, as really begotten by him as Isaac. He pretends that there are chiefly two reasons for that designation. The *first* is the peculiar love which his Father bore for him; just as Solomon says that he was an " only" Son " in the sight of his mother,"[i] although he was not the only son born to David of the same mother.[j] The *second* is, that he alone was to succeed to the whole inheritance. *Socinus* vainly alleges that Christ is in like manner termed the only-begotten Son of the Father, because he is peculiarly dear to the Father, and is appointed the sole Heir of all things.[k]

xxi. It is readily admitted, that the comparison

g יחיד Gen. xxii. 2, 12.
h Μονογενῆ. Heb. xi. 17.
i Prov. iv. 3.
j 1 Chron. iii. 5.
k Heb. i. 2.

which he institutes between Christ and Isaac would be
legitimate, had he remembered that in Isaac there was
only a faint shadow of those things, which in Christ
are found in the highest perfection; and had he not,
from the similarity of several terms which, with some
note of imperfection, are applied to Isaac, taken occasion to obscure the glory of Christ, to whom " a more
" excellent name" belongs. As to the rest, the heretic
both deceives and is deceived.   Isaac is styled an *only*
Son to Abraham, because he alone was born by virtue
of the promise, and because it was solely on his account
that his Father's name was changed and enlarged. He
is called his *only-begotten*, because he alone was born
of Sarah, his lawful wife.   These circumstances gave
rise to the designations *only* and *only-begotten*, and
were the reasons of his tender love for him, and of his
appointing him heir of all that he had.   Abraham's
peculiar affection for Isaac, and his making him heir
of all his possessions, were not, on the contrary, the
reasons of these designations.   The love shown him,
and the inheritance he received, gave evidence that
Isaac was the only-begotten, but did not make him so.
And the same thing must be affirmed with regard to
Christ.   Because Christ is the only-begotten Son of
God, God loves him with a tender and peculiar love,
and he has declared him Heir of all things.

   XXII. The objection from Prov. iv. 3. where the expression is, " the only one in the sight of my mother,"*
has no weight.   For, 1st, The Hebrew word rendered
only† does not, in its native signification, exhaust the
whole meaning of the Greek term which corresponds to

*only-begotten.** *Only* is one expression, and *only-be-gotten* is another. If *only* mean dearly beloved when the subject so requires, it does not, for that reason, signify *only-begotten.* David, too, called Solomon *my only Son,*[1] chosen of God, dear to me, more excellent than the rest; he did not call him *only-begotten.* 2dly, Who will assert that what is here mentioned may not be understood as having at least commenced when Solomon was in reality his mother's only-begotten Son, though several brothers were afterwards added to the number? For it clearly appears, that he was Bathsheba's first born after the child that was conceived in adultery.[m] 3dly, What should hinder us from explaining these words as spoken figuratively by Solomon,—as if an only-begotten Son, not Solomon himself precisely, were represented as expressing himself in this manner?†

XXIII. It is by no means sufficient, however, for the purposes of faith, thus to consider Christ as the ONLY-BEGOTTEN SON OF GOD, unless we contemplate also his relation to us, and our relation to him. And here what first presents itself to view is that unbounded love of God the Father, which prompted him to exalt us who are by nature " the children of wrath,"[n] and the offspring " of our father the Devil,"[o] to so high a dig-

---

* Μονογενης.

† The Author's expression, corresponding to the general word *figuratively* in this sentence, is *per* προσωποποιίαν, that is, *by a prosopopœia,* or personification. This figure of speech is commonly defined " that by which things are made persons," or " that by which we " attribute life and action to inanimate objects." But it includes also one person's speaking and acting in the name of another; and in this view the term *prosopopœia* is here employed by our Author. T.

[1] בני אחד 1 Chron. xxix. 1.   [m] 2 Sam. xii. 24.
[n] Ephes. ii. 3.   [o] John viii. 44.

nity as to become, not indeed equal, yet in our measure similar to his only-begotten Son,—"to be con-"formed to his image, that he might be the first-born "among many brethren."[p]

XXIV. But again, it is an evidence of still greater love, that, in order to our obtaining this dignity, he spared not his only-begotten Son, but gave him to us, and delivered him up for us.[q] Abraham was regarded, and not unjustly, as having done a great thing, when he withheld not from God his son, his only son Isaac, whom he most tenderly loved. But Isaac was nothing more than a man and a sinner; he was due to God, and was given to God; given in purpose rather than in fact; it was not possible for him to die more gloriously than as a consecrated victim which God desired, and which exhibited in his death a type of the Messiah, who was to be offered in sacrifice in due time; nor after all did he die. What is the son of Abraham, besides, compared with the Only-begotten Son of God, who was given to us insignificant men, to be actually sacrificed and slain for our salvation, to be burned and consumed both in soul and body, by the fire of Divine justice, kindled against our sins!

XXV. How amazing also is the kindness of the Lord Jesus Christ towards us, who, notwithstanding his greatness, and our extreme insignificance, "is not "ashamed to call us brethren!"[r] Truly infinite is the distance with regard to dignity between Christ and us, —Christ, the only-begotten Son of God, and us, who, considered in the most favourable light, are as persons "born out of due time."[s] To Saul it appeared highly

[p] Rom. viii. 29. [q] John iii. 16. Rom. viii. 32.
[r] Heb. ii. 11. [s] 1 Cor. xv. 8.

indecorous in Jonathan, the son of a king, to entertain
a brotherly affection for David the son of Jesse.[t] But
how much lower doth the Son of God condescend to
stoop, in calling us his brethren, and in allowing us to
use the same familiarity towards him! And see what
an astonishing wonder of love is here! In order to di-
minish, in some degree, the inequality of condition, the
Son of God, " who being in the form of God, thought
" it not robbery to be equal with God, made himself
" of no reputation, took upon him the form of a ser-
" vant,"[u] and, what is by far the lowest step of his de-
basing assimilation to us, appeared " in the likeness of
" sinful flesh ;"[v]—and hath exalted us at the same time
to the greatest height of dignity of which we are capable, by giving us the glory which the Father gave
him,[w] and by making us " partakers of the divine na-
" ture."[x] These indeed are demonstrations of an almost incredible love.

xxvi. But the generosity of our Brother doth not
stop even here ; for he admits his chosen to the name
and the privileges, not only of the sonship but also of
the primogeniture.[y] This is truly wonderful, and far
surpasses human reason ; for it seems impossible, in the
nature of things, that there should be more than one
First-born among many brethren. The Son of God
has neither sold his birth-right, after the example of
the profane Esau ; nor, like Reuben, forfeited the primogeniture by any instance of misconduct. That dignity, in fine, which he obtains by the right of his Sonship, is no less unalienable, and no less incommunica-

[t] 1 Sam. xx. 30.   [u] Philip. ii. 6, 7.
[v] Rom. viii. 3.   [w] John xvii. 22.
[x] 2 Pet. i. 4.
[y] Exod. iv. 22.   Heb. xii. 23.   James i. 18.

ble, than his eternal Divinity. Whence then do we receive the name of the primogeniture, and, since the name cannot be nugatory, its privileges also? Truly our holy religion is full of mysteries, that are not to be measured by reason, but embraced by faith. Christ has not *resigned* his own birth-right, but bringing us by his Spirit into a state of the most intimate union with himself, he has made us partakers of himself, and of all his benefits, and consequently of his primogeniture. He has not, profanely *sold* his own, but has generously *purchased* ours for us, and acquired it by the spotless purity of his meritorious obedience. And as he doth not cease to be the *only-begotten* Son of God, though we are said to be *begotten* of God; so neither is it prejudicial to his primogeniture, that we are recognised as the first-born of the same Father; for our primogeniture is quite of a different kind and order from his. We obtain this advantage from it, in the mean time, that we are lords of all our brethren, who are born of the same blood, but not of the same Spirit with us; and that, receiving more than a double portion above them, we are heirs of all our Father's goods,[z] and joint-heirs with Christ.[a]

xxvii. It becomes us, however, to attend particularly to our conduct, and to take heed that we do nothing unworthy our relation to so illustrious a Brother. 1st, Since we are now bound by the vow which was made of old by the Spouse, and since Christ has become our " Bro- " ther, sucking the breasts of our mother;"[b] it remains that, having found him, we " kiss" him with a kiss of inviolable love. If Joseph in this manner embraced his brethren, and Benjamin more than the rest;[c] how

[z] Gal. iv. 1.   1 Cor. iii. 21.   [a] Rom. viii. 17.
[b] Song viii. 1.   [c] Gen. xlv. 14, 15.

much greater cause have we to embrace Christ Jesus our Brother; who comes to us not to take away corn, but to bring us food sufficient to nourish an immortal life! 2dly, As he is not only our Brother, but our First-born Brother,[d] and " the First-born of every creature, in all things having the pre-eminence;"[e] we ought also to render him all possible homage, treating him with at least no less respect than Jacob treated his ruthless brother Esau.[f] 3dly, It should be delightful to us to enjoy his familiar fellowship; for it is good and pleasant for brethren to dwell together in unity.[g] And in proportion as he is more excellent than any Jonathan, so much the more bitter should be that lamentation which the want of his valued intercourse calls forth.[h] 4thly, Let us take him in all things for our " exam-" ple,"[i] that by bearing as close a resemblance to him as possible, we may be assured of our sonship. 5thly, For his sake let us also love all who are his,—all in whom even a faint resemblance, and consequently some relation to him, may be discerned; as David resolved to show kindness to all that were of the family of Saul, for the sake of his brother Jonathan.[j] 6thly, Let us never allow ourselves to be ashamed of Christ, of his Gospel, or of his cross;[k] but in distressing as well as in comfortable circumstances, in adversity no less than in prosperity, let us, with alacrity and joy, confess him as our Brother, lest he be ashamed of us in the glorious day of his second coming, when his people will enter on the full possession of the heavenly inheritance.

[d] Rom. viii. 29.　　　　　　　　[e] Col. i. 15, 18.
[f] Gen. xxxii. 4. xxxiii. 3.　　　　[g] Ps. cxxxiii. 1.
[h] Comp. 1 Sam. xx. 41.　　　　　[i] 1 Pet. ii. 21.
[j] 2 Sam. ix. 1.
[k] Mark viii. 38.　Rom. i. 16.　Gal. vi. 14.

DISSERTATION XIII.

ON JESUS CHRIST,

OUR LORD.

---

1. IT is no inconsiderable part of civility and politeness to address every one by his proper titles; and in
showing each other this mark of respect, the primitive
Christians, as appears from numerous examples of sacred monuments, were by no means deficient. But in
proportion as the only-begotten Son of God excels all
mankind in glory, with so much the deeper veneration
and heart-felt regard doth it become us to do him homage. We ought carefully to guard against every
appearance of neglecting any expression of respect to
which he is entitled; for it is the will of the Deity,
" that all men should honour the Son, even as they
" honour the Father."[a] That celestial urbanity, however, which is not merely the language of the lips but
the effusion of the heart, is taught and learned only in
the school of the Spirit. " No man can say that Jesus
" Christ is LORD, but by the Holy Ghost;"[b] that is,
—so as rightly to know, acknowledge and celebrate the

---

[a] John v. 23. [b] 1 Cor. xii. 3.

lordship of Jesus, with its grounds and consequences, and to have the whole soul suitably affected towards him as Lord. Let us now attempt, therefore, in dependence on the Spirit of Christ, accurately to show what it is to call him LORD, in spirit and in truth.

II. Christ is, in reality, "the LORD;"[c] "the Lord from " heaven."[d] He requires us to honour him with this compellation; " Ye call me Master and Lord; and ye " say well, for so I am."[e] Faith addresses him at once with the heart and the mouth, saying, " My Lord, and " my God;"[f] and indeed every tongue is bound to confess, " that Jesus Christ is Lord, to the glory of " God the Father."[g]

III. It is the subject of dispute among the learned, whether the Son of God, to whom the title Κυρίος, (*Kurios*,) is usually ascribed, be also called Δεσπότης, (*Despotes*;) and what difference there may be betwixt these two words. Some would have us to believe, that Δεσπότης is never used in holy writ but with reference to the Father, and that He is called Δεσπότης in allusion to servants that are obliged to obey; but that Christ is termed Κυρίος, because he has an inheritance as his peculiar property. This distinction of the words is, in their apprehension, deducible from the fourth verse of the Epistle of Jude, where God is called Δεσπότης, *Master*, because he has power over all; and Christ Κυρίος 'ημων, *our Lord*, because he has authority over us, as his property, and a possession which he has purchased for himself. The latter term, they allege, must certainly add something to the former, as otherwise there is a vain repetition of a word entirely synonimous.

---

[c] האדון. Mal. iii. 1.   [d] 1 Cor. xiv. 47.
[e] John xiii. 13.   [f] John xx. 28.
[g] Philip. ii. 11.

Ammonius seems to countenance this distinction; for at the word Κυρίος, in his book *concerning similar and different expressions,** he says : " Κυρίος and Δεσπότης " differ. A husband is called Κυρίος in relation to his " wife, and a father is so called in relation to his chil- " dren; but one is denominated Δεσπότης in reference " to those that are bought with his money." He ex- presses himself almost in the same manner at the word Δεσπότης. And I own that, influenced by the authority of eminent men, I formerly acquiesced in these state- ments.

IV. But having examined the matter more carefully, and observed the way in which the terms are employ- ed, I saw reason to conclude that this distinction is not well founded. Κυρίος is the most general word, and signifies *a person having authority and power* † over any thing, in whatever manner it is acquired ; Δεσπότης is used in reference not only to servants, but likewise to all sorts of persons that are subject to one's autho- rity and government. Δεσποτης παντων 'ανθρωπων, " the " *Despotes* of all men," occurs in *Æschines.*‡ *Demos- thenes,* in like manner, says ; Δεσποτης, 'ηγεμων, κυριος παντων,§ " the *Despotes,* the ruler, the lord of all;" where these terms, it is to be noticed, are used as syno- nymous. In *Plutarch* we have the expression, δεσποτην σοῦ καὶ ἀδελφὸν, ‖ " thy *Despotes* and brother." Nay, any one is called the *Despotes* of his *peculiar property.*¶ Thus *Lucian* has τ8 δακτυλιοῦ δεσποτης, " the owner of " the ring ;" and *Theophylact* uses the phrase, δεσποτης

* *De similibus et diversis dictionibus.*
† Τον κύρος ἔχοντα.   ‡ *Contr. Ctesiph.*
§ *Pro Cor.*   ‖ *In Artarx.*
¶ Περιποιήσεως.

χρημάτων,* " the proprietor of the goods." The Greek Interpreters of the Old Testament, also render the Hebrew word אדון, *Adon,* by Κυριος and Δεσποτης indiscriminately ; though indeed by the former term more frequently than the latter. There is no example, besides, to prove that in the style of the New Testament these words are distinguished from each other in the manner alleged; for we will show immediately that the passage produced from the Epistle of Jude, is explained better as relating to Christ. Nor does the accumulation of equivalent words, make an unbecoming tautology; it rather expresses the sense the more emphatically, and is often made use of for this purpose, both by sacred and profane writers. We have just seen an instance of this in *Demosthenes;* and with that example you may compare the following ; " the Blessed and the only Poten-" tate, the King of kings, and Lord of lords."[h]   If any distinction at all is admissible, what consideration should induce us to choose that which the learned men are pleased to prefer? " If there is any difference," says *Erasmus,*† " Δεσπότης is a term denoting private right; " Κυριος is a name of honour and authority ; for mothers " are required 'οικοδεσποτειν, *to guide the house;* not " κυριευειν, *to rule with sovereign authority.*"

v. Nor is there any reason why we should hesitate to call Christ *Despotes,* or to affirm that he is so called in Scripture. Since, as God, he has all things in common with the Father, he is unquestionably *Despotes* in the same sense with the Father. In that passage, too, in the second Epistle of Peter, [i] where this word occurs, it is far more natural to explain it as relating to Christ

---

* *Epist.* xix. *Vid.* Stephani Thesaurum.
† *In Scholiis.*
[h] 1 Tim. vi. 15.   [i] Ch. ii. 1.

than to the Father; for the expression *bought* leads us
to this interpretation, and false prophets have more generally directed their attacks immediately against Christ
than against the Father. Nor is it necessary to insert
a point between the words in Jude, in order that God
the Father alone may be called *Despotes,* and Jesus
Christ Κυριος ἡμων, " our Lord." That this is not allowed by the article, which, being common to all the
epithets, shows that the subject is one and the same,—
Beza contends against *Erasmus,* and *Bisterfeld* maintains in opposition to the objections of *Crellius.** Add
to this, that in several manuscripts the words are these;
" the only Lord and our Lord Jesus Christ" †—the
word " God" being omitted. The Complutensian
edition obviates all doubt, giving the words thus : " the
" only God and Lord, our Lord Jesus."‡ The Syriac,
the Ethiopic, and both the Arabic versions, take the
expression in the same sense. May we not also refer
to Christ the cry of the slain martyrs ? " How long, O
" *Lord* holy and true, &c." ʲ It is certain that Ecclesiastical writers often give this name to Christ.§ *Isi-*
dorus of *Pelusium* says, " Our Lord and *Master*
" Christ."‖ " Herod," says *Photius,* " missed the
" *Lord,* but murdered a great number of infants."¶
And, according to the testimony of *Eusebius,*** the descendants of our Lord's family, were denominated
Δεσποσυνοι, persons related to the *Despotes.* Let us

---

* Lib. i. sect. i. cap. 7.

† Τον μονον δεσποτην και κυριον ἡμων Ἰησῦν Χριστον.

‡ Και τον μονον θεον και δεσποτην τον κυριον ἡμων Ἰησουν.

§ Vid. *Libros responsionum ad Orthodoxos.*

‖ Τὸν Κυριον ἡμῶν και δεσπότην Χριστόν.

¶ Ἡρωδης μεν δεσποτῦ διήμαρτε, φονευς δε πολλῶν νηπίων γινεται.

** Lib. i. cap. 7.

ʲ Ἑως ποτε ὁ δεσπότης, &c. Rev. vi. 10.

then desist from building important propositions upon a distinction by no means solid. Neither the authority of Christ, nor the credit of our religion, depend upon the niceties of words.[72]

VI. Further, this title of honour is, in all reason, due to Christ; for he is JEHOVAH, and possesses in himself the whole excellence of Deity, which is the root and foundation of Divine dominion. He is expressly called Jehovah in Isaiah;[k] " The voice of him that " crieth in the wilderness, Prepare ye the way of JE- " HOVAH," that is, Christ; for this is the language of John his harbinger. And again, " Surely shall one " say, In JEHOVAH have I righteousness and strength; " even to him shall men come."[l] That these expressions relate to Christ, is not only evident from the scope of the passage itself, but also confirmed by the authority of Paul, who applies to Christ the verse immediately preceding.[m] Now Christ being JEHOVAH, he is for this very reason LORD,—having the same authority and power with the Father over all things that are without himself, and that are indebted to him for whatever they possess. " All things were made by him, " and without him was not any thing made that was " made;"[n] and upon that account he has dominion over all. The Apostle says emphatically, " There is one " Lord Jesus Christ, by whom are all things, and we by " him."[o] In this respect Christ has a lordship purely *Divine*, in reference to which all creatures, and in particular all rational creatures, angels as well as men, are his servants, being dependant upon him, and bound to take his law for the rule and standard of their actions.

[k] Chap. xl. 3.   [l] Chap. xlv. 24.
[m] Rom. xiv. 11.   [n] John i. 3.
[o] 1 Cor. viii. 6.
[72] See NOTE LXXII.

The winds and the sea obey him; and whilst the good angels willingly and cheerfully recognise his authority, it is acknowledged, although with reluctance, even by the bad.[p]

VII. But besides that lordship which he possesses over all *as God*, on account of the unbounded excellence of his nature; he has another lordship *as Mediator*, which is given him by the Father, and exercised in a special manner over the elect, who are his property and inheritance, and as Peter says, " a peculiar " people."[q]

VIII. Christ's authority over the elect as his peculiar property is consummated by three different steps. 1st, The original foundation of it is in the eternal decree of the Father, by which they were given to him, that he might acquire and redeem them for himself. Accordingly he renders thanks to the Father, saying, " Thine they were," as all creatures are thine; " and " thou gavest them me,"[r] by a special decree thou didst exempt them from the common condition of others, thou didst commit them to me to be redeemed and called by me in due time. In the same sense he denominates the elect of the Gentiles, when neither actually redeemed nor called, *my sheep;*[s] because by the Father's appointment he was already their Lord.

IX. 2dly, This authority, however, was more fully acquired by actual purchase, when he delivered up himself in our stead, that we, being bought with a price, might be no longer our own.[t] As when the price is paid, the right to the thing purchased is transferred to the purchaser; so from the time when Christ gave his

[p] Mat. viii. 27, 31.   [q] Λαὸς εἰς περιποίησιν. 1 Pet. ii. 9.

[r] John xvii. 6.   [s] John x. 16.

[t] 1 Cor. vi. 19, 20. vii. 23.   1 Pet. i. 18, 19.   Rev. v. 9.

own blood for them as the real price of their redemption, he was constituted the sovereign Lord of all the elect. The Father then said to him, " Ask of me," according to thy right (in conformity to the covenant, of which we read, Isaiah liii. 10.) " and I shall give " thee the heathen for thine inheritance, and the ut-" termost parts of the earth for thy possession."[u]

x. 3dly, By virtue of this right he now watches over the elect as his property, sustains them in life, affords them the means of salvation, preserves them from the sin against the Holy Ghost, and does many things towards them, by which, as by a sort of preparatory measures, he begins to claim for himself his own. But at last he comes to take actual possession of them, when, by his Spirit, he effectually calls, regenerates, and blesses them with faith. Although, in point of right, they were long before the property of Christ, yet, in point of fact, they continue under the power of the devil, sin, and their own corruptions, until being freed from every other dominion by the powerful operations of the Spirit of Christ, they are completely vindicated and appropriated to him alone. Then they renounce Satan, sin, and themselves, and acknowledge Christ their Redeemer as their lawful and only Lord. In this manner he " delivers them from this present evil " world,"[v] " brings them" to himself,[w] and purifies them unto himself a peculiar people.[x]

xi. This lordship of Christ was recognised by ancient believers before his incarnation, for David in spirit calls him his Lord ;[y]—and also by those who conversed with him on earth, whilst his majesty was yet concealed. It

[u] Ps. ii. 8.
[w] John x. 16.
[y] Ps. cx. 1.   Mat. xxii. 44.

[v] Gal. i. 4.
[x] Tit. ii. 14.

was, however, graced and aggrandised by splendid accessions, when he was advanced to the right hand of God the Father, and solemnly proclaimed King and Lord of his Church. Of this Peter speaks in the following words; " Therefore let all the house of Israel " know assuredly, that God hath made that same Jesus " whom ye have crucified, both LORD and Christ."[z]

XII. But he also powerfully asserted his dominion, and gave a striking demonstration of it in the sight of the whole world, when he punished the refractory nation of the Jews with a dreadful overthrow, destroyed their polity, burned their temple, and abolished the whole assemblage of those carnal ceremonies by which the glory of his spiritual kingdom was not a little obscured.[a] He asserted it too, when, after the numerous and bloody contests in which his Church was involved, he enabled her to triumph over the barbarous tyrants both of the East and West, established her liberty under Constantine the Great, and either made the rulers of the earth affectionate nursing-fathers to the Church, or compelled them to render him a pretended subjection. In fine, he exhibited a remarkable proof of his sovereign dominion, when, in the days of our fathers, he greatly reduced the tyrannical power of Antichrist, who usurps his throne, and caused the everlasting Gospel, in which he is preached as the only Lord of the Church, to be published through the whole world.

XIII. There are also displays of his authority which are yet to take place. He will demonstrate that he is Lord, when he shall convert the Israelites to himself, overturn the profane throne of Antichrist, and destroy the destroyers of the earth,—and when the dominion and

[z] Acts ii. 36. See also Ephes. i. 20—23. Philip. ii. 9, 10, 11.
[a] Comp. Luke xix. 27.

the greatness of the kingdom under the whole heaven shall, in consequence, be given to him and to the people of the saints of the Most High,—when all the kingdoms of the world shall become the kingdoms of our Lord and of his Christ, and the Church shall, under his pacific reign, be enriched with the most abundant gifts of the Spirit. In what surprisingly magnificent language the Scriptures both of the Old and New Testament, describe those happy times, we shall elsewhere have a more convenient opportunity of showing at large. That blessed period will at length be succeeded by the last act of the lordship of Christ, when, having judged men and devils, and having trampled all his enemies under his feet, he shall bring the whole assembly of his people home to himself in heaven,—being glorified in his saints, and admired in all them that believe. Such then is the dominion of Christ; nor is it merely such, but far surpasses all that it is possible for us to express or conceive.

XIV. To give evidence that we rightly acknowledge and truly believe the lordship of Christ, it behoves us to be affected towards him in a manner worthy of those who remember that they are his, and not their own. They who call Christ Lord, not only with the mouth and from custom, but from the secret teaching and influence of the Spirit, behold in him, in reality, such Divine excellence, such a height of Divine perfection, so rich an abundance of grace, in short, such a venerable majesty resulting from the glories of his character, and diffusing its lustre on every side, that whatever once seemed bright and magnificent in the world, and whatever seems illustrious and splendid in the choirs of the Seraphim and Cherubim, appears, in comparison with Him, as smoke, or the shadow of a shadow. Such did the Spouse represent him to herself, when she described him as " white and ruddy, the chiefest among " ten thousands," surpassing all those eulogies in which she so copiously and so affectionately celebrates his excellence.[b] Such did Peter, with his companions, behold him on the holy mount.[c] Such did John see him more than once ;[d] and in preceding times, Isaiah,[e] and Ezekiel,[f] and Daniel.[g] Such do all his servants believe him to be, though they may have never seen him but with the eye of faith, as he is represented in the spiritual glass of the Gospel, or as, without any visible splendour, he shines on their hearts by the beams of his majesty. No one, doubtless, rightly venerates the sovereign authority of Christ, who does not deliberately consider him as infinitely more excellent than all creatures, and does not regard him as a person of so transcendant worth that it becomes all orders of angels in heaven, and all the princes, kings, and emperors on earth, to unite with himself in worshipping, praising, and adoring him with the profoundest reverence, casting their crowns at his feet,—and who is not, in fine, so transported with admiration for his unparalleled glory, that to be wholly devoted to it, is his earnest desire and his unspeakable delight. " He is thy Lord," says the Psalmist, " and worship thou him."[h]

xv. Further, it is necessary for every one who acknowledges Christ as his Lord, to renounce Satan, the world, sin, and even himself, that he may belong to none but Christ. It is absolutely impossible to serve

---

[b] Song v. 10—16.
[d] Rev. i. 13—16. xix. 11—16.
[f] Ezek. i. 26.
[h] Ps. xlv. 11.

[c] 2 Pet. i. 16, 17.
[e] Is. vi.
[g] Dan. vii. 13, 14.

at the same time two masters that are so contrary to one another, and the one of whom, at least, justly demands the submission of the whole man.[i] Whoever belongs to Christ, doth not belong to Satan; he is rescued from his tyranny.[j] " In time past," but only in time past, he " walked according to the prince of the " power of the air, the spirit that now worketh in the " children of disobedience."[k] He doth not belong to the world; he is " delivered from this present evil " world,"[l] and he has learned that " the friendship of " the world is enmity with God."[m] He doth not belong to sin; he is dead to sin, through the death of Christ.[n] Formerly indeed he was its servant; but being now made free from sin, he has become the servant of righteousness.[o] He doth not belong to himself, that he should desire to be the master of his own actions, or the disposer of his own lot, his own foolish concupiscence giving him law. But his affections being reduced to order, the desires of the flesh being subdued, and the remains of his own will gradually vanishing away,— Christ alone begins to live and to reign within him.[p] It is certainly the characteristic of all the servants of Christ, that they hate, dread, and detest the cruel dominion of those lords, or rather tyrants, whom they formerly served, and whatever they know to be conducive to their interest.

XVI. The dominion of those tyrants was solemnly renounced by believers in ancient times, when they gave their name to Christ in baptism. It was a truly pathetic address which, according to the custom then ob-

[i] Mat. vi. 24. [j] Heb. ii. 14, 15.
[k] Ephes. ii. 2. [l] Gal. i. 4.
[m] James iv. 4. [n] 1 Pet. ii. 24.
[o] Rom. vi. 18. [p] Gal. ii. 20.

served, the Patriarch, on the sixth day of Easter-week, delivered from his chair to those that were about to be baptized. We shall here exhibit a part of that address, adapted to our present purpose.* " You intend this " day to show the hand-writing of your faith to Christ. " Your conscience will be the pen, ink, and paper; " your tongue, the form. Attend then to the manner " in which you subscribe this profession. Beware of " committing a mistake, lest, peradventure, you should " be deceived. Men that are about to die make a tes- " tament, and appoint another to inherit their posses- " sions. To-morrow night you, too, are going to die " to sin; and now your renunciation is a testament; " you make the devil the heir of your sins, and you " leave them to him as an inheritance. If any of you " then retains in his mind any thing which belongs to " the devil, let him renounce it as one that is about to " die, who is no longer master of his own possessions. " Let none amongst you, therefore, retain in his heart " any thing that pertains to the devil. Cast in the " devil's face all the remainders of filthiness and wick- " edness, and be joined with Christ. See that none of " you be negligent, or high-minded; stand with trem- " bling. The whole transaction in which you are now " engaged is awful and tremendous. All the powers " of heaven are present in this place; all the angels and " archangels, though invisible, are recording your words; " the Cherubim and Seraphim are bending from hea- " ven in order to receive your engagements and pro- " mises, and represent them to the Lord. Take heed, " therefore, how you resist the devil, and adhere to the " Creator of the universe." A little after, he thus ad-

* Ex *Barberino MS. Sancti Marci.*

dresses them: " What I say, say you also in like man-
" ner: I renounce Satan, and all his works, and all his
" service, and all his angels, and all his pomp."   He
says these words thrice, and they all respond.   Then
he interrogates them, saying; " Have you renounced
" Satan?" to which they reply, " We have renounced
" him."   Immediately he rejoins, " Stand with trem-
" bling.   What I say, do you also say: And I am
" joined with Christ," &c.   He says these words also
thrice, while they all respond.   He next asks them this
question thrice: " Are you joined with Christ?"   And
when they have replied, " We are joined," he makes a
short prayer, and then subjoins the following admoni-
tion: " Behold you have renounced the devil, and are
" joined with Christ.   The records are completed, and
" Christ confirms them in heaven.   Be faithful to your
" engagements.   Preserve these records for yourselves,
" for they are to be publicly produced in the day of
" judgment," &c.*

How pious, solemn, and devout this ancient observance! Would to God that we never forgot the day
in which we were devoted to the service of Christ,
whilst his name was invoked over us!   Would that
we never forgot that sacred obligation which is sealed
by baptism!   It is useful, however, by some affecting
form of speech, to press these things again and again
upon the minds of those who have been initiated into
Christ, and have called him Lord.   And for that purpose we now make use of this form in conversing with
our young people.

xvii. Further, it behoves the man who makes an
honest profession of Christ as his Lord, to submit to

---

* Vide *Fehlavii notas ad Christophorum Angelum*, p, 482, &c.

his will with the greatest alacrity. Without contradiction, and without murmuring, he must acquiesce alike
in his *commanding* and *disposing* will; that he may
cheerfully *perform* the duties required, and patiently
suffer the evils inflicted. It is reasonable that the will
of the servant be in all things conformed to the will of
his Lord, and, so to speak, absorbed in it, so that from
the heart he may say, " Not my will, but thine be done."
Even the heathen, that knew not Christ Jesus, the
Lord that bought us, saw from the dim light of nature,
that this is a debt which they owe to God. *Epictetus*
divinely says; " Will thou nothing but what God
" wills." *

XVIII. Let us speak first of his COMMANDING will.
As many as call Christ Lord, and do not at the same
time obey his precepts because they are his, make, without doubt, a false and hypocritical profession. " Why
" call ye me, Lord, Lord, and do not the things which
" I say?"q If the authority of a centurion over his soldiers and his servant is such, that they go and come at
his pleasure, and promptly obey his orders,r how much
greater the authority over his people, which belongs to
Jesus, our supreme Commander and Lord! " The life
" of every man," said *Epictetus*,† " is a military ser-
" vice,—both long and diversified. Thou must act the
" part of a soldier, and perform without reserve what-
" ever thy Commander may require, even anticipating,
" if possible, his will." But *Epictetus* was ignorant of
Christ, the Commander in the Christian warfare. Thou
knowest him, and therefore it becomes thee to say with
Paul; " Lord, what wilt thou have me to do?"s—

* Μηδειν αλλο θελε, 'η α 'ο θεος θελει. Apud *Arrian.* lib. ii. cap. 17.
† Apud *Arrianum,* lib. iii. cap. 24.
q Luke vi. 46.   r Mat. viii. 9.   s Acts ix. 6.

waiting only the intimation of his will, and obeying with alacrity and promptitude all and each of his commands, how ungrateful soever they may appear to the flesh, and how different soever from the dictates of disordered reason—although he should command thee to go even to inevitable death. If the heroes of David, on hearing the king express his ardent wish that one would give him water to drink from the well of Bethlehem which was before the gate, broke through the host of the Philistines, drew water out of that well, and brought it to David,[t] what service that we know to be well pleasing to our Lord, should appear to us arduous! A *Socrates* could say to God; " Whatever " place or rank thou mayest assign me, I would die a " thousand deaths rather than abandon it."[*] And shall not we say with Paul; " None of these things " move me, neither count I my life dear to myself, so " that I might finish my course with joy, and the mi- " nistry which I have received of the Lord Jesus?"[u]

XIX. Nor is it enough to do those things which Christ hath commanded us, unless we do them, also, because he hath commanded them. The formal nature of obedience consists in this, that we recognise and submit to the authority of Christ. In all Christ's precepts, indeed, there is the highest equity, pleasantness, and utility, which we are bound to consider and admire, and which ought to make those precepts themselves amiable in our esteem. But his sovereign lordship over us will only appear, when the mere will of Him who commands, stands in the place of every reason; even though, as often happens, owing to the blindness of our minds, we should discern nothing in the command, either

* *Arrian.* lib. iii. cap. 24.
[t] 2 Sam. xxiii. 15, 16.   [u] Acts xx. 24.

equitable, or pleasant, or useful. Hence such expressions as the following are frequently annexed to the precepts of Scripture : " I am the LORD ;"ᵛ " Have not
" I commanded thee ?"ʷ " In order to obviate our dif-
" ficulties," says *Tertullian,* with his usual energy, " we
" inculcate this one thing, that what God commands
" is good, and the best that can be done. I esteem it
" daring presumption to question the excellence of a
" Divine command ; for we ought to obey it, not mere-
" ly because it is good, but because it is the command
" of God. The majesty of the Divine authority should
" operate as the chief inducement to obedience. The
" authority of Him who commands deserves considera-
" tion, prior to the advantage of him that serves." *
This reasoning of *Tertullian* is strongly confirmed by
Chrysostome in the following words; " When God
" commands, it is not our part to inquire curiously into
" the nature of the things prescribed, but merely to
" obey." And again, " God hath commanded ; make
" no farther inquiry." † In the passage whence these
words are quoted, you will find a copious illustration of
this topic ; and the whole deserves a perusal.

xx. It is incumbent on every one who duly acknowledges the lordship of Christ, to submit himself also in
the same spirit to his DISPOSING will. If he is Lord,
and if we are his property, who can hinder him from
doing what he will with his own ?ˣ " Nay but, O man,
" who art thou that repliest against God ? Shall the
" thing formed say to him that formed it, Why hast
" thou made me thus ? Hath not the potter power

---

* *De Pœnit.* cap. iv.
† *Orat.* ii. *adversus Judæos.*
ᵛ Lev. xviii. 2, 4, 5, 6, &c.   ʷ Josh. i. 9.
ˣ Mat. xx. 15.

" over the clay?"ʸ We have noble examples of this submission in Aaron,ᶻ in Eli,ᵃ in David,ᵇ in Hezekiah.ᶜ It becomes all to discover the same temper. To contend with the providence of God, is equally vain and criminal. It is *vain*, for he leads the willing, and drags the refractory. " I know that thou canst do every " thing, *and that no thought can be withholden from* " *thee*,"ᵈ—none of thy thoughts can be frustrated; or, *no thought is too hard for thee*,—there is no thought which thou canst not overcome, or which does not strive with thee in vain. It is *criminal*; for reason says, that it becomes thee to yield to the Lord, and not the Lord to thee; and that it is better thou shouldst be involved in total ruin than that even the least part of his most holy will should fail to be accomplished. Our Lord is at once *righteous*,ᵉ " excellent in judgment, and in " plenty of justice, so that he will not afflict;"ᶠ—and *wise*, knowing infinitely better than we ourselves what is conducive to our interest;—and *good*, attending more carefully than we to the preservation, the honour, and the improvement of his property, and overruling all events for the benefit of his people, not excepting those which are apparently the most destructive. The man who is not firmly persuaded, that it will be better for him that things proceed according to the will of the Lord Jesus, than according to his own inclination, throws a most unjust aspersion upon the government of Christ.

XXI. It is truly base and disgraceful, if faith does

ʸ Rom. ix. 20, 21.   ᶻ Lev. x. 3.

ᵃ 1 Sam. iii. 18.   ᵇ 2 Sam. xv. 25, 26.

ᶜ Is. xxxix. 8.

ᵈ ולא יבצר ממך מזמה Job xlii. 2.

ᵉ Rom. ix. 14.   ᶠ Job xxxvii. 23.

not teach us that submission towards Christ, which nature taught the heathen towards God. Even these saw
that " it is the part of a good man to yield himself to
" fate, * and " without murmuring to follow God, by
" whose appointment all things take place."† They
knew that nothing is more reasonable than to refer our
will to the will of God, or rather to give it up without
reserve to be absorbed by that supreme will. Hence
says *Epictetus,* in language surpassing that of a philosopher : " I have surrendered my inclination to God.
" Is it his will that I should be sick of a fever ? it is
" my will also. Is it his will that I should direct my
" attention to any thing ? it is my will too. Is it his
" will that I should earnestly desire any thing ? it is
" likewise my will. Is it his will that I should obtain
" the possession of any thing ? I also am so inclined.
" Is it not his will that I should obtain it ? Neither is
" it mine."‡ *Seneca* says to the same effect : " Let
" man be pleased with whatever has pleased God."§
They taught that the man who contends with the Divine will, wearies himself in vain ; which is the scope
of the following elegant distich :‖

> Whate'er the course fate thee assign,
> Submit with pleasure, ne'er repine :
> Although you fret, and vex your soul,
> Unyielding fate you can't control.

---

* *Seneca de Provid.* cap. v.
† *Epist.* cvii.
‡ Apud *Arrian.* lib. iii. cap. 26.
§ *Epist.* lxxiv.
‖ *Palladæ in Anthol.* lib. i. cap. 13.

    Ἐι τὸ φερον σε φερει, φερε και φερου, ἐι δ' ἀγανακτῆς,

    Και σαυτον λυπεῖς, και το φερον σε φερει.

They regarded it as an established maxim, that what God wills is better for us than our own choice. " I al-" ways acquiesce," says *Epictetus*, " in that which comes " to pass; for I deem that which God wills, better than " what I will. To him I adhere, as his servant and " follower; my wishes and desires are in unison with " his appointments; whatever he wills, I will."* Nay, they went so far as to argue, that all things should be received from God not only with patience, but also with joy and thanksgiving; nor did they merely argue thus. The same *Epictetus*, (from whom I am at present often quoting, having lately read his writings, and being un-able to withhold from my hearers these very beautiful quotations,)—*Epictetus*, I say, has the following ex-pressions : " To a good man nothing is evil, either liv-" ing or dying. What then shall I think, when God " doth not afford me the means of subsistence ? What " else, but that as a good Commander he sounds a re-" treat for me ? I submit, I follow, commending my " Leader, and praising his works. I came when it " seemed good to him, and now I retire when he pleases; " and while I lived, this was my employment, to praise " God, whether alone or with others, whether with one " or with many."† And again ; " Rendering thanks " to God for all things, blaming nothing whatever that " is done by him."‡ From all this they inferred, that nothing is more worthy of a virtuous man, or more con-ducive to his happiness, than to follow God whitherso-ever he calls him,—charging men to keep always in

---

* Apud *Arrian*. lib. iv. cap. 7.
† Lib. iii. cap. 26.
‡ Lib. iv. cap. 7.

remembrance the lines of *Cleanthes,* which may be thus translated :*

Father of all ! great Ruler of the sky !
Thy power I own, thy wisdom still descry.
Whate'er the paths through which thou'rt pleas'd to lead,
With joy I follow, and obey with speed.
Were I to fret, and act a wayward part,
Follow I must, though with an aching heart.
Fate leads the willing, drags th' unwilling soul ;
Tranquil, the good ; the bad, compell'd to howl.

These are choice and invaluable sentiments, which it becomes us to wrest from Heathen moralists as unlawful possessors, to transcribe into our own philosophy, and in our practice itself to transfer to Christ ; if whilst we call him Lord, we are anxious to guard against falsehood and hypocrisy.[73]

XXII. Besides, who can doubt that it is a source of the greatest consolation to the pious, that, delivered from the cruel dominion of the most dreadful tyrants, they no longer belong to the devil, or to sin, or to themselves, but to Christ Jesus, the Lord. It is truly *honourable* to serve a Lord so wise, so just, so mighty, so blessed, and so glorious in every respect.[g] It is truly *pleasant* also to be subject to him, whose " sceptre is " a sceptre of righteousness :"[h]—whose " statutes are

---

* Quod *Seneca* ita transtulit, *Epist.* cvii.

        Duc me Parens, celsique Dominator poli,
        Quocunque placuit ; nulla parendi mora est.
        Assum impiger : fac nolle, comitabor gemens.
        Ducunt volentem fata, nolentem trahunt.
        Malusque patiar, quod pati licuit bono.

  [g] Comp. 1 Kings x. 8.   [h] Ps. xlv. 6.

    [73] See NOTE LXXIII.

" right, rejoicing the heart, and more to be desired
" than gold, yea, than much fine gold; sweeter also
" than honey, and the honeycomb :"[i]—who has rescued
us not only from the yoke of sin and Satan, to which all
mankind were subject, but also from the yoke of the
ancient ceremonies which lay grievous on the necks of
the fathers; and has put upon us his own yoke, which
is light and easy, consisting merely in the delightful
offices of charity and love :—who, in a word, requires
nothing from his disciples of which he has not previously exhibited an example in his own conduct :[j]—
whose goodness and clemency surpass the kindness of
all mortals, as far as the heaven is higher than the
earth :[k]—who regards his disciples not as " servants, but
" friends,"[l] and, as we have lately seen, even honours
them as " brethren." It is truly *advantageous*, in fine,
to have Him for our Lord, who is most wise, to provide for the interests of his people,—most powerful, to
protect them alike against the violence and the fraud
of their enemies,—most opulent also, and most liberal,
to enrich them with abundance of good things, temporal as well as spiritual and heavenly, and at last to make
them possessors and partakers of all that glory which
belongs to himself. It were easy to illustrate these
ideas at length, and they furnish ample matter for pious meditations. But we hasten to consider the economy
of our Saviour's incarnation.

[i] Ps. xix. 8, 10.   [j] John xiii. 15.
[k] Ps. ciii. 11.   Micah vii. 18.   [l] John xv. 14, 15.

NOTES

CRITICAL AND EXPLANATORY.

NOTES

CRITICAL AND EXPLANATORY.

Note I. Page 1.

A TREATISE on what is usually styled the Apostles' Creed, ought, no doubt, to contain a correct copy of that ancient summary. For the accommodation of some readers of these Volumes, it seems proper to insert it here, in parallel columns, in Greek, Latin, and English.

ΣΥΜΒΟΛΟΝ ΤΩΝ ΑΠΟΣΤΟΛΩΝ.

ΠΙΣΤΕΥΩ εἰς Θεὸν Πατέρα παντοκρατορα, ποιητήν ουρανῦ καὶ γῆς· καὶ εἰς Ἰησουν Χριστὸν τον υἱὸν αὐτῦ τον μονογενῆ, Κυριον ἡμων, συλληφθέντα ἐκ πνευματος ἁγιῦ, γεννηθεντα ἐκ Μαριας της παρθενου· παθοντα ἐπι Ποντιῦ Πιλατῦ, σταυρωθιντα, θανοντα, και ταφεντα· κατελθοντα εἰς ᾅδῦ τῇ τριτῃ ἡμερα ἀνασταντα ἐκ νεκρῶν· ἀνελθοντα εἰς ἐρανους, καθεξομενον ἐκ δεξιῶν τῦ πατρος παντοκρατορος· ὁθεν μελλει ἐρχεσθαι κρῖναι ζῶντας και νεκρους.

Πιστευω εἰς Πνευμα ἁγιον· πιστευω τήν ἁγιαν ἐκκλησιαν καθολικην, ἁγιων κοινωνιαν, ἀφεσιν ἁμαρτιῶν, σαρκος ἀναστασιν, ζωὴν αἰωνιον. Ἀμην.

SYMBOLUM APOSTOLICUM.

CREDO in Deum Patrem omnipotentem, Creatorem cœli et terræ. Et in Jesum Christum, Filium ejus unigenitum, Dominum nostrum: qui conceptus est de Spiritu Sancto, natus ex Maria Virgine, passus sub Pontio Pilato, crucifixus, mortuus, et sepultus; descendit ad inferna; tertio die resurrexit a mortuis; ascendit ad cœlos; sedet ad dextram Dei Patris omnipotentis; inde venturus est judicatum vivos et mortuos.

Credo in Spiritum Sanctum. Credo sanctam Ecclesiam Catholicam; Sanctorum communionem; remissionem peccatorum; carnis resurrectionem; et vitam æternam.

AMEN.

THE APOSTLES' CREED.

I BELIEVE in God the Father Almighty, maker of heaven and earth; and in Jesus Christ his only Son, our Lord, who was conceived by the Holy Ghost, born of the Virgin Mary, suffered under Pontius Pilate, was crucified, dead, & buried; he descended into hell; the third day he arose again from the dead; he ascended into heaven, and sitteth at the right hand of God the Father Almighty: from thence he shall come to judge the quick and the dead.

I believe in the Holy Ghost, the holy Catholic Church, the communion of saints, the forgiveness of sins, the resurrection of the body, and the life everlasting. AMEN.

Note II. Page 5.

No reader has cause to be surprised at the venerable Author's expression respecting the uncertainty of the *Titles* of the Sacred books, and of the short notices, commonly called *Subscriptions*, subjoined to the Epistles of Paul. It is generally admitted in reference to both, that they are not authentic. With regard to the former, it may suffice to quote the words of the late Dr George Campbell in his Note on the Title of the Gospel by Matthew : " The title," says that celebrated critic, " neither of this, nor of the other histories of our Lord, is to be ascribed to the penmen. But it is manifest," he adds, " that the title was prefixed in the earliest times by those who knew the persons by whom, and the occasions on which, these writings were composed."

As to the *Subscriptions* of the Epistles, many Critics and Interpreters have proved, that the inaccuracies they often contain supply satisfactory evidence that they are a mere human addition, and generally the work of a later age.—Archdeacon Paley, for example, in the 15th Chapter of his ingenious book entitled *Horæ Paulinæ*, has particularly shown that " six of these are false or improbable, i. e. absolutely inconsistent with the contents of the Epistles, or difficult to be reconciled with them." The Epistles referred to are the 1st to the Corinthians, the Epistle to the Galatians, the 1st and 2d to the Thessalonians, the 1st to Timothy, and the Epistle to Titus. —On this topic Dr Doddridge has the following strong expressions in a Note, in his *Family Expositor*, on 1 Cor. xvi. 8. *But I will tarry at Ephesus until Pentecost :* " I look upon this as a very plain intimation that he was now at Ephesus ; and consequently that the inscription added at the end of this Epistle, which tells us it was written *from Philippi*, is very far from being authentic ; and I hope it will be remembered that no credit is to be given to any of these additions, which have been presumptuously made, and I think very imprudently retained."

Note III. Page 7.

Various names were anciently given to the Creed, as the *Canon* or rule of faith, μαθημα the *lesson*, γραμμα and γραφη the *writing*. But its most usual designation is the *Symbolum* or Symbol.

Our Author does not deny, that this word may signify a *Collection ;* and this sense is favoured by its etymology. He agrees, however, with the best Grammarians and Critics, in representing its

most frequent import to be a *sign*, and a sort of military *oath*.*——
The learned *Saurin* gives his opinion of the meaning of this term in
a passage of his instructive Catechism, which may be thus translated.

" Quest. What is the meaning of the word Symbol? Ans. It
has two senses, both of which are adapted to the Creed of which we
now speak. Q. Which is the first sense? A. The word *Symbol*
may signify a Collection, *une Collection,* or *un Recueil,* of certain
truths. Q. How can that sense agree to the Apostolic Creed?
A. It is a Collection, or *Recueil,* of the principal truths which the
Apostles taught. Q. What is the second sense that may be given
to the word *Symbol?* A. This appellation was anciently applied to
certain marks or signs, *marques,* which people gave to one another
when they made an agreement, and which served to distinguish the
parties in that agreement from those who had no concern in it.
Q. How can this meaning suit the Apostles' Creed? A. Because the
profession of faith in the truths contained in this Creed, is the mark
by which Christians testify their submission to the doctrine which
the Apostles taught, and by which they distinguish themselves from
those who reject it."†

Sir Peter King, after mentioning several other senses which have
been put upon the term, expresses his own sentiments thus: " In
my opinion, the signification of the word is more naturally to be
fetched from the *sacra* or religious services of the heathen, - - -
where those who were initiated in their mysteries, and admitted to
the knowledge of their peculiar services, which were hidden and concealed from the greatest part of the idolatrous multitude, had certain signs or marks, called *Symbola,* delivered unto them, by which
they mutually knew each other, and upon the declaring of them
were without scruple admitted in any temple to the secret worship
and rites of that God, whose symbols they had received. These
symbols were of two sorts, either *mute* or *vocal,*" &c.‡   But this derivation of the word seems quite inadmissible. There is no evidence
or authority to prove that Christians adopted the term in imitation
of that practice which prevailed amongst idolaters; and it is in itself
highly improbable that they derived the designation of this Sum-

---

* *Schrevelius,* accordingly, in his *Lexicon,* renders the word Συμβολον, *signum,*
tessera militaris, symbolum, pactum ; and *Hedericus* makes it *indicium, tessera,*
auspicium, collatio, conventum, pactum. Scapula, too, gives a similar explication
of the term.
  † Abregé de la Theologie et de la Morale Chretienne en forme de Catechisme,
par Jaques Saurin, p. 99, 100.
  ‡ Critical History of the Apostles' Creed, ch. i. p. 11.—3d edit.

mary from the impure and detestable mysteries of the heathen gods. On these grounds, Sir Peter King's opinion is rejected by *Bingham;* who deems it most likely that the word *Symbol* was chosen, because the Creed " was, like the *Tessera Militaris* among the Roman soldiers, a sort of mark or badge, by which true Christians might be distinguished from infidels or heretics."[*]

Note IV. Page 10.

Our Author justly affirms, not only that Luke takes no notice of the Apostles' Creed in the *Acts,* but also that the Apostles make no mention of it in their Epistles. It seems proper, however, to remark, that several expressions occur in the Epistles, which, not without probability, have been supposed to refer to some ancient summaries of the Christian doctrine. Archbishop *Secker,* in his Lectures on the Creed, after stating that the necessary doctrines " have from the earliest times been collected together, and that the profession of them hath been particularly required of all persons baptized," adds,— " These Collections or Summaries are in Scripture called *the form of sound words,* 2 Tim. i. 13 ; *the words of faith,* 1 Tim. iv. 6 ; *the principles of the doctrine of Christ,* Heb. vi. 1."[†] *Whitby,* too, considers the following expressions as referring to such summaries— " the mystery of faith," and " the mystery of godliness," 1 Tim. iii. 9, 15, 16 ; " the faith once delivered to the saints for which they are to contend," Jude 3 ; " the παρακαταθηκη or *depositum* of Christian doctrine which Paul commands Timothy to keep," 1 Tim. vi. 20 ; and " the good thing committed to him which he is to keep by the Holy Ghost," 2 Tim. i. 14.[‡]

The following Extract from a Sermon on 2 Tim. i. 13. will form an appropriate conclusion to this Note. " The word translated *form* signifies a *pattern,* an *exemplar,* an *outline,* and may be supposed to comprehend all the doctrines of the Apostle with which Timothy had been made acquainted by word and by writing. Many, however, think that something more particular is meant ; or that ' the form of sound words' mentioned in this place was a formulary or summary of doctrine which Paul had put into his hands, that he might follow it as his guide in preaching the Gospel. If this be the proper sense of the term, it corresponds with the *Articles,* and the *Confessions of Faith,* which are still used by the Churches as standards to which the public and private instructions of their Ministers

---

[*] Bingham's Antiq. of the Christian Church, book x. ch. iii. sect. 1.
[†] Secker's Works, vol. iv. pp. 264, 265.
[‡] See Whitby's Note on 2 Tim. ii. 2.

ought to be conformed. Some have even imagined that this form of sound words is still in existence; and they refer us to that compendious Creed which bears the name of the Apostles. For this opinion however," adds the Preacher with great propriety, " there is no foundation except an improbable, and even ridiculous tradition concerning the composition of it by the Twelve."*

Note V. Page 14.

The Church of Scotland, in common with other Protestant Churches, has not omitted to avow her esteem for the Creed as a Summary of doctrine conformable to Scripture; and, although the public recitation of it in Christian assemblies forms no part of her worship, she has not neglected to inculcate a becoming attention to it on all her members. In the Sum of the first Book of Discipline, No. xiii. entitled " The Table," we read—" Who cannot say the Lord's Prayer and the *Articles of the Faith,* and declare the sum of the Law, should not be admitted." The Creed, too, is subjoined to the Shorter Catechism for the instruction of youth; and we are informed in a Note, that it is annexed there, " Not as though it were composed by the Apostles, or ought to be esteemed canonical Scripture, as the ten Commandments and the Lord's Prayer, (much less a prayer, as ignorant people have been apt to make both it and the Decalogue,) but because it is a brief sum of the Christian faith, agreeable to the word of God, and anciently received in the Churches of Christ."

Although some Protestant Divines may have formerly spoken of the Creed as " almost authentic," no enlightened Protestant of the present day, it is presumed, would choose to honour it with that epithet. Secker, after commending it in terms abundantly strong, thus qualifies his eulogy : " But neither this, nor any other Creed, hath authority of its own equal to Scripture; but derives its principal authority from being founded on Scripture." †

That imperfection which characterises every human performance, may, without question, be discovered in the Creed. Its warmest admirers need not blush to concede, that, with regard to fulness of doctrine, as well as accuracy of expression, it is susceptible of improvement. To many it has justly appeared surprising, in particular, that while it states the facts of our Lord's suffering, crucifixion, and death, it doth not more explicitly exhibit the grand doctrine of his submitting to sufferings and death, in order to expiate the guilt

---

* Dr Dick's Sermon on Confessions of Faith, pp. 4, 5.
† Secker's Works, vol. iv. p. 265.

of his people, and bring in everlasting righteousness. That all the necessary articles of our Religion are not *expressly* contained in the Creed, is clearly shown by Witsius himself in the 18th Section of the 2d Dissertation. But, notwithstanding its defects, the Creed is a venerable Summary; and it is to be regretted, that some of the friends of truth have allowed themselves to criticise it with unjustifiable severity. We particularly allude to the rough treatment it has met with from an admirable defender of the Saviour's divinity.*

Note VI. Page 17.

That some doctrines of Scripture are of such importance that the knowledge and faith of them are necessary to salvation, is a position extremely offensive to many professed Christians. What more fashionable than the vague assertion, that, provided a man's practice be good, his faith is of no consequence. How repugnant this sentiment is at once to sound philosophy and revealed religion, it were easy to demonstrate. If correct knowledge is of little value, and if it be of small moment to distinguish betwixt truth and error, why is man at all endowed with the powers of understanding? Why, in that case, did the Son of God appear on the earth in the capacity of a great Prophet and Teacher? or, why does he send the Holy Spirit to guide his disciples into all truth?—Has not God an equal title to the homage of the understanding, and the obedience of the heart? Is it not expressly said, too, in sacred writ, " That the soul be without knowledge, it is not good,"† and, " He that believeth shall be saved?"‡ The state of the understanding, it is obvious, never fails to affect, in a great degree, the state of the will and affections. The faith of the Gospel is the appointed mean of the purification of the heart; and it is clear from observation and experience, that, whilst the darkness of ignorance and the mists of error administer powerful support to the reign of superstition, ungodliness, and vice,—just and noble sentiments sincerely entertained in the understanding and judgment, exert the most salutary influence on the dispositions and the conduct.—But to discuss this important topic at large, would not consist with the limits of these Notes. It is illustrated, in some measure, by our Author's observations on the distinguishing marks of fundamental articles.—Whoever wishes to see the preciousness of Divine truth amply unfolded and irrefragably proved, would do well to peruse the writings of the late Rev. An-

* Mr Thomas Bradbury's Sermons on the Mystery of Godliness, vol. 1. Ser. 16. p. 232.
† Prov. xix. 2.   ‡ Mark xvi. 16.

drew Fuller, particularly his " Calvinistic and Socinian Systems examined and compared as to their moral tendency." Some excellent remarks on this subject occur also in Dr Witherspoon's works; as in his " Essay on Justification," and in his Sermons on " the ab-
" solute necessity of salvation through Christ," and " the trial of religious truth by its moral influence."

Note VII. Page 20.

It may be proper to state, that *Remonstrants* was a name early given to the followers of *Arminius*. " They received," says Mosheim,* " the denomination of *Remonstrants* from an humble petition entitled their *Remonstrances,* which they addressed, in the year 1610, to the States of Holland. And as the patrons of Calvinism presented an Address in opposition to this, which they called their *Counter-remonstrances,* so did they, in consequence thereof, receive the name of *Counter-remonstrants.*"

The Arminian system, it is well known, is just a modification of the errors of *Pelagius.* At an early period of its history, it was considered as extending merely to the five following points : 1. The cause and object of predestination ; 2. The object and efficacy of the death of Christ ; 3. The power of man's free-will in his fallen state ; 4. The efficacy of converting grace ; 5. The perseverance of the faithful, and the possibility of their total apostacy. A considerable number, however, of the admirers of this specious and unscriptural scheme, departed much farther from the truth than Arminius himself, and embraced erroneous views on a variety of other articles. The orthodox Divines in Holland were alarmed, in particular, at their apparent indifference to all the most vital peculiarities of the Gospel, and at the friendship which, in many instances, they cultivated with the professed followers of *Socinus.* " Those who are well informed and impartial," says the learned Historian just quoted, " must candidly acknowledge that the Arminians were far from being sufficiently cautious in avoiding connexions with persons of loose principles, and that by frequenting the company of those whose sentiments were entirely different from the received doctrines of the Reformed Church, they furnished their enemies with a pretext for suspecting their own principles, and representing their theological system in the worst colours.—See also some short historical notices of the Arminian controversy in that truly valuable work, *Theol. Pet. Van Mastricht,* lib. viii. cap. 3. sect. xliii. p. 1152, *et seq.*

* Eccles. Hist. Cent. xvii. Sect. ii. Part 2. ch. 3.

Note VIII. Page 25.

The 15th and 16th verses of the 1st Epistle to Timothy have been the subject of much controversy and critical discussion, both as to the genuine reading of the text and the meaning of the terms. The construction adopted in the authorised English Version, it may be remarked, does not appear quite so unnatural, or so injurious to the interests of truth, as some writers apprehend. Admitting that the Church is spoken of as " the pillar and ground of truth," it is evident that this must be understood in a qualified sense; and the expression, as has been shown by Calvin and Whitby on the passage, affords no countenance to the absurd claims of infallibility advanced by the Romanists. Besides, taking the punctuation as it stands, the essential importance of the articles respecting our Saviour, stated in the 16th verse, is still asserted in a manner which ought to make Socinians ashamed. If the Apostle brings forward those articles as constituting " the mystery—the *great* mystery of godliness," every candid reader must allow that he represents them as fundamental doctrines. The energy, however, of Paul's declaration concerning the paramount importance of these doctrines is, without doubt, considerably increased by the construction proposed by *Cameron*, and approved by the other celebrated Critics mentioned by our author. Nor, although great caution in the interpretation of Scripture is highly commendable, does there seem sufficient ground for the scrupulosity which Witsius discovers on this occasion. According to *Michaelis* and other eminent Critics, the *points* of the New Testament are not to be received as genuine. While they admit the possibility of the Apostles having employed the full point, or left a blank where the sense of the period ended, they affirm that the most ancient manuscripts do not satisfactorily show where the Apostles made these stops, and that, in construing passages, it is best to follow the direction of common sense and sound rules of interpretation. Cameron's construction of this passage has, accordingly, been adopted without scruple, and defended with ability, by many of the most respectable modern Divines; as Dr Doddridge in his *Expositor ;* the Rev. Thomas Bradbury in his Sermons on the Mystery of godliness ; * and the late venerable Dr Erskine in his Discourses on the same subject.† Doddridge's translation of the verses is as follows : " But if I delay, that thou mayest know how it becomes thee to converse in the house of God. The pillar and ground

---

* Vol. i. Sermons 1. and 2.
† Vol. i. Discourse 10.

of truth, and confessedly great, is the mystery of godliness : God was manifest in flesh," &c.

It is not the writer's intention here to institute an inquiry with regard to the disputed word Θεος, *God,* in the 16th verse. On this subject the inquisitive reader may consult the Appendix to Dr Erskine's first Discourse on 1 Tim. iii. 16,[*] where he abridges the criticisms of Mosheim on the passage ; *Griesbach's* Notes on this verse ; Dr Lawrence's Remarks on Griesbach's Classification of Manuscripts ; Dr Wardlaw's Note C, subjoined to his excellent Discourses on the principal points of the Socinian Controversy ; and the very candid as well as considerably minute discussion of the question in the Christian Observer.[†] It has been well proved by *Cyril,* as well as by several modern writers, that even were the word Θεος given up, the doctrine of Christ's divinity is clearly taught in the passage. But the inquirer who is at once unbiassed by prejudice, and disposed, in examining a point of this sort, to allow to internal evidence its due share of weight, will probably find it difficult to avoid the conclusion strenuously urged by Mosheim and Lawrence, that Θεος, and not ὁς or ὁ is the genuine reading.

Note IX. Page 30.

Our author justly inculcates a sacred reverence for the whole body of revealed truth. It ought not to be forgotten, that all the doctrines which the Scriptures teach, and all the facts which they relate, as well as all the precepts they deliver, are supported by the same authority. If no man is permitted to violate the least of God's commandments, it is equally certain that no man is at liberty to disregard any fact recorded, or to treat with indifference and contempt any doctrine taught in the Holy Scriptures. Were the principle once admitted, that a man may without crime bring the truths of God to the bar of his own reason, and that he is at perfect liberty to credit or discredit, to esteem or despise them, as they shall appear to him to be true or false, important or unimportant,—it would be easy, by means of this single principle, to discard all that is momentous and interesting in the sacred volume. Nothing is of small consequence, as the eloquent *Saurin* somewhere remarks, in a religion of love ; for love naturally prompts us to please its object even in the minutest affairs. There are such mutual connexions and dependencies, too, betwixt the various contents of Divine revelation, that an article apparently trivial may be of considerable importance to the

* Vol. i. pp. 369—372. † Vol. for 1809, pp. 269—277.

strength, beauty, and symmetry of the whole edifice. Thus, the free and unconditional exhibition of the Saviour to men as sinners is deemed by some that have no small pretensions to orthodoxy, a questionable or a very unimportant point; and yet it may be safely affirmed, that scriptural views of this article are intimately connected with right apprehensions of the grand doctrine of justification by the grace of God. To give another instance—a fastidious reader may be apt to presume that Paul descends to frivolous matters, and trifles in a manner hardly befitting the dignity of an Apostle, when he requests Timothy to bring with him the cloak which he had left at Troas, or when he intermingles a weighty exhortation relating to the discipline of the Church with this condescending suggestion, " Drink no longer water, but use a little wine for thy stomach's sake and thine often infirmities :" Yet, not to mention other useful purposes which such passages are calculated to serve, it has been ably demonstrated by *Paley*, that these references to minute circumstances and occasional interruptions of the sense, so exactly according with the natural ease and freedom of epistolary writing, afford a powerful argument for the authenticity of the Epistles of Paul, and consequently for the Divine authority of all the doctrines and precepts they contain.

From these remarks, however, let none conclude, that all the facts and truths of Scripture are of equal importance with regard to their *matter ;* and let none suppose that such was the opinion of Witsius. Who would choose to affirm that the birth of John the Baptist is a fact of equal moment with the birth of our Lord, or that the doctrine of infant-baptism is no less important than that of the atonement ? If, in the code prescribed for the regulation of our conduct, there are duties which may justly be denominated " the weightier matters of the law," it seems to follow, by parity of reason, that the system of truth revealed for the direction of our faith, contains some doctrines " weightier" than others; that is, more strikingly illustrative of the Divine perfections, and more immediately and powerfully conducive to the glory of God, in the comfort, holiness, and final happiness of man. Nor have we cause to complain that we are furnished with no means of ascertaining the relative importance of truth, or, as to this point, are left entirely " to the guidance of our own fallible and fanciful ideas, or the diversity of human sentiment ever variable and fleeting." The same unerring oracles which show us what is truth, discover, to a certain extent at least, what is the most important truth. See Isaiah xxviii. 16. 1 Cor. xv. 1—4. 1 Tim. iii. 15, 16. The Scriptures do not enable us, indeed, to distinguish precisely, in every instance, betwixt essential and non-essential doctrines. It is impossible, as our Author shows, to form an exact list of fundamental points; nor was such a list necessary. But the whole of his reasoning, in his second Dissertation, proceeds on the supposition that, while some doctrines are fundamental, there are others which, though Divinely attested and unquestionably useful and salutary in their own place and proportion, are *not* fundamental. And to deny or overlook this distinction, is, in reality, more injurious to the cause of truth and the interest of genuine religion than some are aware. Unhappy consequences, no doubt, have arisen from the abuse of this distinction. But the denial, and even the neglect of it, has also been productive of very considerable mischief. To represent all the doctrines of Scripture as of equal magnitude and necessity, serves to give an unnatural and distorted view of Divine truth, exceedingly derogatory to its beauty and credit;—to create a pharisaical attachment to subordinate articles unfavourable to the right improvement of the most essential, and injurious to the interests of personal piety;—to proscribe mutual forbearance from the list of Christian duties, and to contract, beyond measure, the terms of Christian communion;—to give rise, in fine, either to a blind and implicit uniformity, or to endless strife and divisions.

NOTE X. Page 33.

Few readers will need to be informed, that the term *Consubstantial* was employed to designate the true divinity of Christ as a Person of the same substance or essence with the Father. At the Council of Nice in Bithynia assembled by Constantine, A. D. 325, the doctrine of Arius was condemned, and Christ declared ὁμοὖσιος τῶ πατρὶ, " consubstantial with the Father."*

Whoever is inclined to question the expediency of Creeds and Confessions, might peruse, with advantage, *Walker* of *Dundonald's Vindication* of the discipline and constitutions of the Church of Scotland, Dr Erskine's *Sketches of Church History*, vol. i. pp. 1—15. and Dr Dick's Sermon on this topic from 2 Tim. i. 13.—There is considerable force in the observations of Witsius himself respecting the propriety of including in a Confession of faith some articles not absolutely fundamental, and of employing, for the illustration and defence of the truth, well-chosen terms not contained in Scripture.

---

* See the *Nicene* Creed, and Mosheim's Ecclesiastical History, vol. i. p. 414. *et seq.*

Nor can it be denied, that those who have zealously contended for making Confessions extremely short and general, and for entirely excluding from such formularies all expressions, however consonant to sacred writ, that are not literally the very language of Scripture, have often discovered a predilection for the most radical and pernicious errors. Our candid and venerable Author, however, must not be understood as accusing of damnable heresies every individual, or every Church, that questions the propriety of having a very long Confession, or of loading a Creed with a great multitude of human expressions. Much less is he to be considered as imputing heresy to those who refuse to esteem it almost as criminal and presumptuous to alter or improve a Confession of human compilation, as to attempt an alteration or improvement of the sacred volume itself. Our first Reformers, though well aware of the expediency and utility of subordinate standards, manifested a deference for the supreme rule of faith and practice, highly deserving the respect and imitation of their professed admirers. It may suffice to quote the following passage from the Preface to the Old Scottish Confession, authorised by Parliament in the year 1560.

————" PROTESTING that if any man will note in this our Confession any article or sentence repugning to God's holy word, that it would please him, of his gentleness and for Christian charity's sake, admonish us of the same in writing. And we - - - do promise unto him satisfaction from the mouth of God (that is, from his Holy Scriptures) or else reformation of that which he shall prove to be amiss."*

NOTE XI. Page 37.

Our Author, when entering on his illustration of Saving Faith, very properly reminds us that the Understanding and the Will are not separate and independent principles, but faculties appertaining to one and the same soul, and closely interwoven in their various operations. In his treatise *on the Covenants*,† he refers to *Scotus* on this topic, and also quotes a passage from *Scaliger* to the same effect. If the sentiments of men of science are of any importance on this subject, we might avail ourselves of the authority of one of the most profound Philosophers of the eighteenth century, who, after adverting to the common division of the powers of the human mind into the powers of the *understanding* and those of the *will*, proceeds to

---

* The *Collection of Confessions*, printed at Glasgow 1761; pp. 25, 26.
† Book iii. ch. 7. sect. 5.

remark that we are not to conceive of this division, " as if in those operations which are ascribed to the understanding, there were no exertion of will or activity, or as if the understanding were not employed in the operations ascribed to the will." Having illustrated this position, he concludes with the following words: " It is therefore to be remembered, that in most, *if not all,* operations of the mind, both faculties concur; and we range the operations under that faculty which hath the largest share in it."*

On all spiritual subjects, however, the plain dictates of sacred writ are far more satisfactory than the most respectable human authority, or the most ingenious discussions of any philosopher. And whoever examines the language of Scripture with attention and candour, will be apt, one should think, to acquiesce in the remark which Dr Owen makes in his Catechism, with regard to the seat of Faith—" It is in the understanding, in respect of its being and subsistence; in the will and heart, in respect of its effectual workings." The proper object of faith, without doubt, is truth. To believe, is, primarily, an act of the understanding. Yet the doctrines of the cross are of so spiritual and humbling a nature, and so contrary to the corrupt bias of the human will and affections, that they are never sincerely believed till the whole soul is regenerated by the Spirit of God; and it is equally certain that whenever the faith of these glorious and interesting doctrines is produced in the human understanding, it cannot fail to have corresponding effects on the dispositions and movements of the heart. The Scriptures every where represent the faith of God's elect as a vital and holy principle. It works by love, purifies the heart, overcomes the world, and renders those who believe in God careful to maintain good works. How widely different such a faith must be from that which terminates in mere speculation, and is " a simple act of the understanding, having no moral virtue or holiness attached to it," it is unnecessary to say. See Dr Erskine's Dissertation on the nature of Saving Faith, and Fuller's Letters on *Sandemanianism.*

It may be alleged, with some appearance of reason, that our Author, in this Dissertation on Faith, would have treated the subject to greater advantage, had he more scrupulously distinguished between faith strictly so called, and its various attendant graces and holy fruits. Owing to the self-righteous disposition of the human heart, the inconsiderate reader may deduce erroneous conclusions from his extensive and somewhat desultory mode of explaining the

---

* Dr Reid's *Essays on the Intellectual Powers of Man,* Essay i. ch. 7. p. 67.

matter, and be led to place that confidence in the operations and fruits of faith which ought to rest solely on its glorious object. But let not the Author be mistaken, or blamed to excess. With laudable solicitude, be it remarked, he warns his readers, in the 6th and 19th sections, against misapprehensions injurious to the freedom of grace in the justification of believers. It was his decided conviction, that men are justified by faith, not as a work or duty, not as a principle of holy obedience, or as the surrender of the soul to Christ as Lord and King, but merely as an instrument by which the meritorious righteousness of Christ is received and applied. His sentiments on this topic are clearly stated and defended in his Treatise on the Covenants,* and in his *Irenicum.*†

Note XII. Page 41.

Amongst the points which it is necessary for a man to know in order to his becoming a believer, the Author very naturally mentions, in the first place, the doctrine of our corrupt, ruined, and helpless state. This is a doctrine which, however repugnant to the self-exalting imaginations of the human heart, and how much soever it has been impugned and derided, is clearly taught in the sacred records, obviously implied in the whole system of revealed truth, strongly supported by fact and experience, and powerfully confirmed by the dictates of every enlightened conscience. The natural tendency, too, of this humbling tenet, is highly salutary. The man who truly knows and believes it, is prepared to glorify God by a cordial approbation of the scheme of mercy, to acquiesce in Christ as " all his salvation and all his desire," and successfully to cultivate humility, meekness, patience, contentment, self-denial, and every other Christian grace. Ignorance, and inconsideration with regard to this doctrine, as well as direct and avowed opposition to it, are extremely pernicious.

The formularies of the Protestant Churches in general, and the writings of the most eminent Reformed Divines,‡ discover the high importance attached to the doctrine of man's lost and helpless state among all that are sound in the faith. It is truly gratifying also to see this necessary article expressly stated and ably defended in a Summary of Christian Divinity written by *Platon*, late Metropoli-

---

* Book iii. Chap. 8. Sect. 47—56.

† See Mr Bell's Translation of that work, chap. x. p. 108, *et seq.*

‡ See Calvin's Institutions, Dickinson's " Discourse on Original Sin," Edwards on " the Christian Doctrine of Original Sin," Halyburton's Great Concern, Boston's Four-fold State, Richard Taylor's Discourses on the Fall and Misery of Man and on the Covenant of Grace, Haweis' Fifteen Sermons, &c.

tan of Moscow; which is highly esteemed in Russia, and commonly made use of in the seminaries of education in that extensive empire. " Out of this state of utter ruin," says this distinguished member of the Greek Church, " *the human race could have no hope of saving themselves.* The dead can never raise themselves to life, nor can he who has fallen into a deep pit ever get out of it without the help of another. But, according to Paul, man is dead in sins, Ephes. ii. 5 ; and the comparison used by Christ, Mat. xii. 11, represents him as fallen into the pit of misery. Therefore it was altogether impossible for him to deliver himself out of this state of utter ruin." After demonstrating the insufficiency of repentance and amendment, and pointing out our absolute dependance on Divine mercy, he adds,

" Let no man, however, suppose that because God is infinitely merciful, or rather mercy itself, he can, without regarding men's imperfections and their falling into sin, out of his mere goodness pardon men, and render them fit to be partakers of his blessedness and glory. Such reasoning is base and sinful; it makes the mercy of God blind; it presupposes a God not possessed of eternal and inviolable rectitude. It obliges him to regard the righteous and the wicked alike—a supposition which it is dreadful to apply to the living God.

" Does any one ask, By what way then can man be saved? By that way, I answer, which infinite wisdom has devised, and in which the mercy of our God is united with a full satisfaction to his justice in the work of our salvation."*

Note XIII. Page 42.

No considerate reader will rashly ascribe to rank enthusiasm the strong expressions of our Author relating to the internal evidence of " the glorious Gospel." Why should it be deemed incredible that a revelation from heaven is distinguished by certain intrinsic characters of its Divine original, which, how imperceptible or how revolting soever to the natural man, are clearly discernible to the enlightened mind, and, by a sweet yet irresistible energy, command its assent? —Dr Owen's Treatise on the Reason of Faith, Fuller's Gospel its own Witness, and a recent little work by Thomas Erskine, Esq. entitled, " Remarks on the Internal Evidence of the truth of Revealed Religion," well deserve the attention of those who wish to examine particularly this important subject. A few excellent observations on

* *Platon's Summary*, &c. translated from the *Slavonian* by R. Pinkerton, p. 127. See also pp. 74—78.

it occur also in the 4th section of Dr Erskine's Dissertation on Faith. Nor ought we to omit the judicious *Halyburton's* Essay concerning the Reason of Faith, subjoined to his Treatise on the Necessity of Revealed Religion—of which the late *Mr Newton* says; " I set a high value on this book of Mr Halyburton's, so that unless I could replace it with another, I know not if I would part with it for its weight in gold."*

NOTE XIV. Page 43.

The expression in Luke i. 1, rendered by Beza *quarum plena fides nobis facta est,* and in our authorised English Version " things which are most surely believed among us," is one of those about the precise meaning of which interpreters are not agreed. Whitby's paraphrase on the words is thus expressed—" things which are most surely believed *(or have assuredly been performed)* among us *(by the Lord Jesus)":* and in his Note on the verse he adds ;—" When St Luke saith they were πεπληροφορημενων εν ημιν, he does not mean only that they were done, but that they were performed with such circumstances as gave them ' the full assurance of faith' (Heb. x. 22.) as to the truth of the doctrines taught and the works done by Christ and his Apostles." Dr Doddridge renders the expression " those facts which have been confirmed among us with the fullest evidence ;" and says in a Note, that he thinks the expression is " rather to be understood as referring to the fulness of that *evidence* with which the facts were *attended,* than to the *confidence* with which they were *believed.* Dr Hammond, agreeably to the Vulgate, renders the expression more simply, the things " that have been performed among us ;" and Dr Campbell to the same effect, " the things which have been accomplished among us." This version is defended with great ability by the last mentioned writer, and, in the opinion of *Parkhurst,* not without success. But admitting that Hammond and Campbell give the most correct translation of the expression in Luke i. 1, it is allowed on all hands that πληροφορεω signifies not only to perform, to accomplish, but also to *convince,* to *persuade,* to *embolden ;* and that the proper meaning of the noun πληροφορια is *full conviction* or *assurance.*—If the reader wish to see any farther illustration of the other two Greek terms explained by our Author, namely *hypostasis,* and *elenchus,* he may consult Dr Owen's critical remarks on them in his Commentary on Heb. xi. 1.

* *Cardiphonia,* Vol. i. p. 140. 4th edit.

NOTE XV. Page 47.

In confirmation of the lively interest which the Christian takes in the truths of the Gospel, as they exhibit an astonishing display of the glorious perfections of God, our Author very properly quotes Rom. iv. 20. But he seems not altogether so happy in referring to John xii. 43, where it is said of the Pharisees who did not confess Christ lest they should be put out of the synagogue, that " they loved the praise of men more than the praise of God." By *the praise of men* we are evidently to understand the praise which men confer; and by *the praise of God*, the praise and honour which God is pleased to bestow upon men—not the praise or glory which is due to God. Such is the interpretation which the antithesis and connexion obviously require, and which is generally adopted by interpreters. Whitby's comment on the words is, accordingly, as follows; " They valued their reputation with men more than that honour which cometh from God only. John v. 44."

NOTE XVI. Page 49.

Christ and all his benefits are here spoken of as freely offered to *the sick and weary soul.* In the 24th section of this Dissertation, too, it is said—" Christ offers himself as a complete Saviour to all that are labouring and heavy laden, hungering and thirsting, to all that receive him and are disposed to surrender themselves to him:" and in Diss. xix. sect. 37, our Author, perhaps inadvertently, represents the extensive call to sinners in Isaiah lv. 3, as addressed to *the elect.*

Now, the sick and weary soul, and such as are labouring under a sense of guilt and danger, and longing for deliverance, are, without doubt, included among those to whom the free offers of Christ and his salvation are made. Nay, that some of our Lord's invitations and calls are addressed, in particular, to awakened sinners, may be readily allowed.

But let it be remembered, that it is not as *elect* or *non-elect,* but as *guilty and perishing,* that men are invited to receive Christ and his blessings; and that the invitation is by no means restricted to those who are awakened and convinced. That the Gospel contains a free and full exhibition of Christ and his benefits to sinners of every class and of every character, is an important truth, clearly founded in the sacred oracles, intimately connected with the glory of the grace of God and with the honour of Christ as the Lord our Righteousness, and eminently conducive at once to true spiritual comfort and to the

interest of holiness in the heart and conduct.   But to establish this
doctrine at large, to obviate the various objections which have been
urged against it, and to illustrate its salutary tendency, would far
exceed the limits of these Notes.   May the writer be permitted to
recommend the careful investigation of this point to those young inquirers who may cast their eyes on this work, and to request them to
peruse, with impartiality and candour, the arguments adduced in its
favour in the Books mentioned at the foot of the page.*   From these
and other writings that might be referred to, it is sufficiently evident,
they will observe, that the doctrine of a free and universal exhibition
of Christ and his righteousness and blessings to men as sinners, is
by no means a distinctive badge of any one denomination of Christians, but a tenet conscientiously maintained in common by enlightened and faithful men of various persuasions—men who are anxious
to guard, with equal scrupulosity, against *Arminian* and *Antinomian*
errors.   Some apology may be made for the incorrect expressions of
Witsius and other excellent writers of his age in reference to this
article; but since the subject has, in later periods, undergone so
much discussion, and been placed by respectable authors in so clear
a light, it may justly be expected that young theologians will give
it an adequate share of their attention, and be prepared to declare
the whole counsel of the grace of God.

Note XVII. Page 49.

That *appropriation*, or personal application, is included in the nature of faith, is the general sentiment of evangelical Divines; and
with whatever zeal it has been attacked, not only by the followers
of *Arminius,* but by the professed disciples of a purer creed, it must
be neither renounced, nor thrown into the shade.   The friends of
this tenet may have sometimes made use of incautious language, and
of undignified allusions.   Some of them, it is admitted, have occasionally employed weak and inconclusive arguments.   Much stress, for
instance, has been laid by several writers on the expressions *believing
in* and *believing on,*—which, to any one that attends to the remarks
of *Witsius* in another part of this work,† will appear a feeble resource.

* See the Marrow of Modern Divinity with Boston's Notes; the Act of the
Associate Presbytery concerning the doctrine of grace; Brown's System of Divinity, pp. 385—388, 1st ed.; Brown (of Whitburn's) Gospel Truth accurately stated
and defended; Beart's Vindication of the eternal Law and everlasting Gospel,
part ii. sect. 2; Booth's Glad tidings to perishing sinners; a truly valuable Sermon
on the nature of the Gospel and its universal spread, by the late Rev. John Russel of Stirling; and Letters designed to illustrate the nature and tendency of the
Gospel, by the Rev. David Russel of Dundee, Let. 3d and 14th.
† Dissert. iv. sect. 3.

That personal application, nevertheless, is really involved in the faith of the Gospel, is a principle capable of the most satisfactory proof. Considered even as an act of the enlightened understanding, true faith must include application. The Gospel is a testimony of universal concern. It presupposes the ruined condition of all mankind by nature, and exhibits a gracious provision adapted to the circumstances of every individual. " Unto you, O men, I call," says Wisdom, " and my voice is to the sons of man." * No one therefore, in reality, believes the Gospel, unless he believes it with application of the truth to himself. No man knows and is persuaded that the whole world of mankind are naturally in a perishing state, and that Jesus Christ is an all-sufficient Redeemer, able and willing to save sinners of every description, without being convinced of his own lost condition, and without looking to Christ for the salvation of his own soul.

A more particular statement of the sentiments of Witsius on this topic may be seen in the 9th Chapter of his *Irenical Animadversions.* The Translator of that little work, too, has a judicious Note on that Chapter ; at the conclusion of which he refers to the *Answers by the twelve Brethren to the Commission's Queries,* p. 66. Several other publications, which illustrate less or more the doctrine of appropriation, are specified at the bottom of this page. †

Martin Luther and the other leaders in the Reformation, with their immediate successors, it is well known, were in general warmly attached to this doctrine. The same sentiments have also been held by many eminent Divines in subsequent periods. In Mr Bell's Treatise on Faith, p. 320. *et seq.* the reader will find a pretty large specimen of the expressions which Protestant Ministers and Churches have employed on this topic.—It is a pleasing circumstance which is related of the celebrated *Lavater,* that from his childhood he experienced great delight in cultivating intercourse with the God of Heaven as *his own* God. ‡—Amongst the more recent testimonies in

---

* Prov. viii. 4.

† The Rev. Eben. Erskine on the Assurance of Faith, Sermons, Vol. i. pp. 286—380. Dr Witherspoon's " Leading Truths of the Gospel," Ser. 4, " On the Nature of Faith." Mr Andrew Swanston's Sermons, Vol. i. pp. 111—158, Brown's Gospel Truth, pp. 225—272, 297—302. Rev. Arch. Hall's " Treatise on Faith." Bell's " Treatise on the nature and effects of Saving Faith," contained in the same volume with his " View of the Covenants," pp. 299—419. The Review of Mr Arch. M'Lean's Treatise on the Commission of Christ to his Apostles in the Missionary Magazine, Vol. iii. p. 123: And the First and Third Conversations between John a Baptist and Ebenezer a Seceder, on the faith of the Gospel, occasioned by Mr M'Lean's Treatise.

‡ " To *use* God," says he, " as my *own* God, was one of the earliest and most deeply impressed ideas in my mind." See an interesting Memoir of Lavater by *Dr C. F. Steinkopff,* one of the Secretaries of the British and Foreign Bible Society, in the Evangelical Magazine, Vol. xiii. p. 4. See also, pp. 6, 50, 53, 54.

favour of the appropriating nature of faith, we might refer to a Note by the judicious writer of the Memoirs of the late *Dr Alex. Stewart*, pp. 71—73, and to some passages in *Sargent's* Memoir of the *Rev. Henry Martyn*. No man of piety can peruse the following quotation from the Diary of the excellent Martyn, without perceiving most sensibly that the appropriating exercises of faith are accompanied with inexpressible consolation, and signally calculated to support and animate the Christian in the path of duty, amidst the greatest difficulties and trials in which he can be involved. Having left England on the 14th of September 1805, he soon after expressed himself thus; *

" After a long and blessed season in prayer, I felt the Spirit of adoption drawing me near to God, and giving me the full assurance of his love. My fervent prayer was, that I might be more deeply and habitually convinced of his unchanging everlasting love, and that my whole soul might be altogether in Christ. I scarcely knew how to express the desires of my heart. I wanted to be all in Christ, and to have Christ for my ' all in all'—to be encircled in his everlasting arms, and to be swallowed up altogether in his fulness. I wish for no created good, or for men to know my experience ; but to be one with thee and live for thee, O God, my Saviour and Lord. O may it be my constant care to live free from the spirit of bondage, at all times having access to the Father. This, I feel, should be the state of the Christian : perfect reconciliation with God, and a perfect *appropriation* of Him in all his endearing attributes, according to all that he has promised: it is this that shall bear me safe through the storm."

Note XVIII. Page 53.

For the satisfaction of some readers, it may be proper to state that the *Talmudists,* whom the Author repeatedly mentions in these Dissertations, are the writers of the Jewish *Talmud,* a most voluminous work, comprizing the oral law, which, according to the absurd notion of the Jews, was received from God by Moses on Mount Horeb, and handed down by tradition, and the commentaries of their learned men upon it. The ground-work of the Talmud is the MISHNA, that is, *Traditions,* which were compiled about the middle of the second Century by *R. Judah Hakkados,* Rector of the school at Tiberias in Galilee ; and which contain six books, each consisting of several tracts, which in all make up the number of sixty-three. To this are added the GEMARA, that is, the *complement,* being ancient

* Pp. 121, 122. 4th edit.

commentaries on the *Mishna*, and so styled because by them the *Mishna* is fully explained, and the whole traditionary doctrine of their law and religion completed.

This description is applicable both to the *Jerusalem Talmud*, which was written by the Jews of Judea, and completed about the beginning of the fourth Century; and to the *Babylonish Talmud*, which was compiled by the Jews of Babylon, and finished about the commencement of the sixth Century. The former has been repeatedly published in one large volume *folio ;* but the latter, which is chiefly and almost exclusively followed by the modern Jews, extends to twelve Folio Volumes. *Maimonides* has composed an abridgment of the Talmud, entitled *Yad Hachazakah*, which is of much greater value than the original work.*

NOTE XIX. Page 66.

The words in the last part of Zech. ix. 17, in the text of our authorised English Version, are these ; " Corn shall make the young men cheerful, and new wine the maids." But " new wine, which makes the maids eloquent," is a literal rendering of the expression as quoted by our Author from the Latin Translation by *Junius* and *Tremellius*. This rendering agrees also with one of the marginal readings in the English Version. The Hebrew term ינובב signifies literally *to cause to grow, or increase,* but metaphorically, *to render eloquent.* See *Buxtorf* and *Parkhurst* on the word נב.

NOTE XX. Page 67.

Although our Author takes notice of the ancient practice of presenting children to the *Bishop,* let it not be inferred that he considered *Diocesan Episcopacy* as of Divine origin. That a distinction between Bishops and Presbyters was early introduced into the Christian Church, and that many of its ministers, particularly after Constantine gave Christianity a splendid establishment, began to distinguish themselves more by the love of power and pre-eminence, than by a disposition to learn of their meek and lowly Master, are facts which it were vain to dispute. But, according to the Scriptures, the word ἐπίσκοπος, *bishop,* or rather *overseer,* and πρεσβύτερος, *presbyter* or elder, uniformly denote the same office. Observe Acts xx. 17, 28. Tit. i. 5—7. 1 Pet. v. 1, 2; and see Dr Campbell's Lectures on Ecclesiastical History, Lect. iv. Campbell remarks, that

---

* See *Prideaux's Connection*, Part i. Book 5. Vol. ii. pp. 465—472, 9th edit. and the *Christian Instructor*, Vol. ix. p. 41.

" all the Commentators of any note, except *Dr Hammond*, agree that by *bishops* in Philip. i. 1, is meant the ordinary pastors or presbyters." It is worthy of notice, too, that, according to *Michaelis*, in the ancient Syriac Version, συν ἐπισκοποις, Philip. i. 1, is rendered by an expression which signifies *with the elders*, and ἐπισκοπη, 1 Tim. iii. 1, *the office of an elder.*

While fidelity seemed to the writer to require the caution now given with regard to Episcopacy, he will add that he intends no uncandid reflexion against them who are conscientiously attached to that mode of Church government; nor is he insensible to the value of those services to the common cause of Christianity, which have been rendered by an Usher, a Beveridge, a Lowth, a Paley, a Hervey, a Newton, a Wilberforce, a Martyn, and many other members of Episcopal Churches.

Note XXI. Page 68.

What account is given by the learned *Durel* of the custom of the English Church referred to, the translator does not know. Durel appears, however, to have been too zealous a defender of the peculiarities of his own Church. " In the controversy against the Puritans, he had recourse to irritating and contemptuous expressions."[*] The very title of the work to which our Author refers is—" A Vindication of the Church of England against the unjust and impious accusations of Schismatics."—Of the ceremony of Confirmation, as practised in the Church of England, it is not intended to speak particularly. It seems proper to remind the reader, however, that to English Dissenters, and to many other Protestants, that ceremony appears too much akin to the Romish sacrament of Confirmation, which Calvin[†] clearly proves to be superstitious and absurd; and that, in their apprehension, no reasoning can be more inconclusive than that by which its supporters have attempted to establish its Divine authority from those passages in " the Acts" where we read of the Apostles confirming the souls of the disciples, or laying hands on their converts, and imparting the gifts of the Holy Ghost. " We shall not enter into any controversy," says Dr Doddridge on Acts viii. 15,[‡] " as to the foundation this has been supposed to lay for the rite of *Confirmation* as now practised in some Christian and Protestant Churches. It may be sufficient to observe, that here were *extraordinary gifts* evidently conferred by *extraordinary officers.*"

[*] Aikin's General Biography, Art. DUREL.
[†] *Institut.* lib. iv. cap. 19.
[‡] Family Expositor on Acts viii. 15. note *b.*

Yet let it not be imagined, that they who cannot approve of the rite of *Confirmation*, as practised even by several Protestant Churches, are averse to the use of scriptural and proper means for instructing and impressing the minds of the young, and for confirming them in the way of truth and duty. All pious ministers of Presbyterian Churches are accustomed to converse seriously with young people about the nature and design of their Baptism, as opportunities occur, and particularly when they apply for admission to the Lord's Table; and some of them are in the habit of requiring, what in the judgment of our Author is highly desirable, a public profession of their faith in the presence of the congregation. See " The Young Communicants' Catechism, with a Proposal for a public renewing of the baptismal Covenant," by the late Rev. John Willison of Dundee; and also " A Catechism for the instruction and direction of Young Communicants, to which is added a Compendious View of the baptismal profession and engagement," by Dr Colquhoun of Leith.

The reader will find an able and keen discussion of the subject of this Note in a Review which appeared some time ago in the Christian Instructor,* of a Sermon on Confirmation, preached by Archdeacon *Loving* at St John's Cathedral in Calcutta, on the 28th May 1815.

Note XXII. Page 70.

By the *Hellenists* we understand those Jews who spoke the Greek language, and made use of the Greek Translation of the Old Testament Scriptures, commonly called the Septuagint. The word ἱλληνισται occurs, indisputably, at least twice, in the New Testament, viz. Acts vi. 1, and ch. ix. 29, in both of which places it is rendered by our translators *Grecians*. There is, however, an obvious difference betwixt ἱλληνες, the word uniformly employed to signify *Greeks* or *Grecians*, and 'ἱλληνισται, *Hellenists* or *Grecizers*. The former denotes persons of Greek, or more largely of Gentile, extraction; the latter, those who wrote or spoke Greek. *Beza,* *Wolfius,* and some others, have contended that by the Hellenists is meant " such persons as had been converted from Heathenism to Judaism." But this opinion is inconsistent with the Syriac Version, which renders the expression, " Jews that understood Greek ;" and contrary to the testimony of Chrysostome, who affirms that it means " those that speak Greek," in opposition to the βαθεις Ἑβραῖοι, the *profound* or *deep* Hebrews. See the Notes of Hammond and Doddridge

* Vol. xv. p. 121, *et seq.*

on Acts vi. 1. The interpretation of *Hellenists* now given, is ably defended also by *Jennings*,* and by Dr Campbell.†—Compare NOTE LXIV.

The Hellenists, while they spoke the Greek language, very naturally made use of the Hebrew idiom which prevails in the Septuagint. It were vain, too, to dissemble, that the inspired penmen of the New Testament itself very generally employ modes of expression borrowed from the Hebrew, and thus deviate from the classic purity of the Greek tongue. But what reasonable and impartial man could allow himself for a moment to entertain the idea, that this circumstance, which so well accords with the situation and acquirements of these " holy men of God," serves, in any degree, to weaken the authority, impair the dignity, or detract from the value, of their inestimable writings?

NOTE XXIII. Page 72.

The first argument employed by our Author to prove the existence of the Deity, is that which is taken from the abstract idea, implanted in the mind, of an infinitely perfect Being. The honour of inventing this argument, which has been falsely ascribed to *Des Cartes*, seems to belong to *Anselm*, a native of Italy, and Archbishop of Canterbury in the twelfth century.‡ The argument, it must be allowed, is abstruse, if not unsatisfactory; and it might have been omitted without impropriety. But from the subsequent reasonings of *Witsius*, it is evident he must not be considered as placing his chief dependance upon this proof of the grand article in question, or as subjecting himself to the rebuke administered to a certain class of writers by the celebrated *Locke*, in the following passage of his Essay on the Human Understanding.§

" *How far*," says that profound writer, " the idea of *a most perfect Being* which a man may frame in his mind doth, or doth not prove *the existence of a God*, I will not here examine. For in the different make of men's tempers and application of their thoughts, some arguments prevail more on one and some on another, for the confirmation of the same truth. But yet, I think, this I may say, that it is an ill way of establishing this truth and silencing Atheists, to lay the whole stress of so important a point as this upon that sole foundation, and take some men's having that *idea* of God in their

---

* Jewish Antiquities, Book i. chap. 3. pp. 59—61. Edinburgh edit. 1808.
† Preliminary Dissertations, pp. 5—10. 1st edit.
‡ See Aikin's General Biography, Art. ANSELM.
§ Book iv. chap. 10. § 7.

minds - - - as the only proof of a Deity; and out of an over-fond-
ness for that darling invention, cashier, or at least endeavour to invalidate all other arguments, and forbid us to hearken to those proofs,
as being weak or fallacious, which our own existence and the sensible
parts of the universe offer so clearly and cogently to our thoughts,
that I deem it impossible for a considering man to withstand them.
For I judge it as certain and clear a truth as can any where be delivered, that *the invisible things of God are clearly seen from the creation of the world, being understood by the things that are made, even
his eternal power and godhead.*"

The argument for the existence of God taken from those numberless displays of his unbounded might, wisdom, and benignity, which
the creation exhibits, is incomparably more clear and convincing than
the argument *a priori*, even when stated in the most perspicuous and
unexceptionable manner. Some authors, accordingly, who put a
great value on the latter, are compelled to admit the superior utility,
if not the superior weight, of the former. " Because we can have
no true appropriate and distinguishing *idea*," says *Howe*,* " or conception of *Deity*, which doth not include a necessity of existence in
it, we might have gone that *shorter way* immediately to have concluded the existence of God from his idea itself. And I see not but,
treading those wary steps which the incomparable Dr Cudworth, in
his ' Intellectual System,' has done, that argument admits, in spite
of cavil, of being managed with demonstrative evidence. Yet since
some most pertinaciously insist that it is at the bottom but a mere
sophism; therefore, without detracting any thing from the force of
it as it stands in that excellent work and the writings of some other
noted authors, I have chosen to go *this other way*, as plainer and less
liable to exception, though further about; and begun lower to evince,
from the certain present existence of things not existing necessarily,
or of themselves, their manifest dependance on what doth exist necessarily or of itself."

" The argument *a posteriori*," says even *Dr Clarke*,† " is, indeed,
by far the most generally useful argument, most easy to be understood, and in some degree suited to all capacities; and therefore it
ought always to be insisted upon: But for as much as atheistical
writers have sometimes opposed the being and attributes of God by
such metaphysical reasonings as can no otherwise be obviated than
by arguing *a priori*; therefore this manner of arguing also is useful

---

* Living Temple, Part i. chap. 2. Vol. i. p. 38.
† See *Encyc. Britan.* Art. CLARKE (DR SAMUEL.)

and necessary in its proper place." To this may be added the answer he returned to *Mr Whiston* on this subject, as narrated by the latter in his " Historical Memoirs." " When Clarke brought me his book, I was in my garden against St Peter's College in Cambridge, where I then lived. Now I perceived that in these Sermons he had dealt a great deal in abstract and metaphysical reasoning. I therefore asked him, how he ventured into such subtleties, which I never durst meddle with; and showing him a nettle, or some contemptible weed in my garden, I told him the weed contained better arguments for the being and attributes of God than all his metaphysics. Clarke confessed it to be so, but alleged for himself, that since such philosophers as *Hobbes* and *Spinoza* had made use of those kinds of subtleties *against,* he thought proper to show that the like way of reasoning might be made better use of, *on the side of* religion : which reason or excuse I allowed to be not inconsiderable."[*]

Note XXIV. Page 74.

In quoting Psalm xxvii. 8, here and elsewhere,[†] our Author, it is proper to observe, adopts a mode of rendering the verse, which is approved by respectable interpreters, and corresponds with the old English Version of the Psalms, where it is thus expressed; " Mine heart hath talked *of thee,* Seek ye my face : thy face, Lord, will I seek." " The verse," says the judicious *Pool,*[‡] " may be thus translated : ' Concerning thee (as the particle *Lamed* is often used, or *for* or *instead of thee,* as it is unquestionably used Gen. xi. 3. Exod. xiii. 16. Prov. xxi. 18.) my heart said, Seek ye my face ; thy face, Lord, will I seek.' "

Note XXV. Page 78.

The intelligent reader will not need to be reminded, that whilst he is referred to those admirable illustrations which the Sacred Volume supplies of that argument for the existence of God which arises from the works of his hand, our Author is decidedly of opinion, that this argument, even independently of Scripture, is calculated to convince and satisfy every upright and candid mind. On this subject much has been excellently written. Dr Clarke [§] recommends the following books on " the wisdom of God in the final causes of things," viz. Galen *De usu partium,* Cicero *De Natura Deorum,* Mr Boyle on *Final Causes,* and Mr Ray on *the Wisdom of God in the Creation.*

---

[*] See *Encyc. Britan.* Art. CLARKE (DR SAMUEL.)
[†] See Dissert. v. Sect. 6.   [‡] Annotations, *in loco.*
[§] Discourse concerning the Being and Attributes of God, p. 112.

Amongst the later publications on this topic, Dr Derham's " Physico-Theology," and his " Astro-Theology," Sturm's " Reflexions on the Works of God," and Archdeacon Paley's " Natural Theology," have been particularly honoured with the stamp of public approbation. It may be added, that there is an able and popular discussion of the argument in question, in President Dickinson's Sermon on Rom. i. 20, and that it is concisely but clearly and forcibly stated by Archbishop Secker in his sixth Lecture on the Creed.*

Note XXVI. Page 85.

Dr Clarke's " Demonstration of the Being and Attributes of God," † contains a passage on the evidences of the Divine wisdom afforded by the phenomena of the heavenly bodies, particularly worthy of attention. He begins with remarking, that " the older the world grows, and the deeper men inquire into things, and the more accurate the observations they make, and the more and greater the discoveries they find out, the stronger this argument continually grows." Having made this general and important remark, he proceeds, in a great variety of instances, to contrast the stupendous discoveries of modern times with the ancient state of astronomical science, and to show what a vast accession of weight and evidence this argument has received since the days of Cicero. The passage is too long to be quoted here ; but without question, it is by far the most striking and entertaining in that work.

Whilst the instructive and beautiful sayings of ancient philosophers are presented to view, their lamentable errors and defects ought not to pass unnoticed. It seems proper here to call the attention of the reader to that ignorance or indifference with regard to the *unity* of God, which *Cicero* and *Zaleucus* discover in the same sentences, in which they most seriously and decidedly disclaim the principles of atheism. The former says, " Who is so stupid and infatuated as not to perceive, after having looked up to the heavens, that there are *Gods ?*" The latter, in like manner, required the Locrians, first of all, to believe that there are *Gods*. This is but a slight specimen of the language in general use among the wisest of the heathen. Many other examples are produced by the learned *Dr Leland*, who treats the subject at great length, and adduces it as one evidence of the insufficiency of the light of nature with respect to the know-

* Works, &c. Vol. iv. pp. 266—272.
† Prop. xi. p. 177. *et seq.*

ledge and worship of the one true God, that " the greatest and best of the ancient pagan philosophers generally express themselves in the polytheistic strain, and instead of leading the people to the one true God, they speak of a plurality of Gods, even in their most serious discourses." *

Note XXVII. Page 197.

The venerable Author here speaks of the Christian's favourable " conclusion" respecting his interest in God, as " the *foundation* of all comfort." The expression, it may be admitted, is not very happily chosen ; for, in strict propriety of speech, our Lord Jesus Christ alone is the Foundation of all comfort.† Yet it was obviously the intention of Witsius, merely to impress the mind of his readers with the importance of the conclusion he speaks of as a mean of possessing that spiritual consolation which is truly desirable.

It seems proper further to observe, that our Author's remarks concerning the temerity and arrogance of those who make presumptuous pretensions to an interest in the Divine favour, must not be understood in a sense prejudicial to the gracious calls and invitations of the Gospel. Something has been said, in a preceding *Note*,‡ respecting the free and unconditional access of sinners to the Saviour. But if sinners are, in reality, warranted by the Gospel, in their native character *as sinners,* to believe and rely on Christ as their all-sufficient Redeemer from sin and wrath, it appears equally certain that they are fully authorised, " by him to believe in God who raised him up from the dead and gave him glory,"§ and humbly to trust in the Father, now reconciled in his beloved Son, as their own God and Portion. It is said of the converted Jailor, that he " rejoiced, believing *in God* with all his house."|| This expression, indeed, may be applied immediately to Christ, whom Paul and Silas had just exhibited as the object of faith,¶ and who is most certainly " the true God and eternal life." ** But perhaps it is more natural to refer it to the Father, whom the believing Jailor now contemplated with joy as a reconciled God in Christ. To all to whom Divine revelation extends, Jehovah is pleased to address himself in these gracious terms ; " I am the Lord thy God ; - - - Thou shalt have no other gods before me." If, therefore, encouraged by his kind declaration, and stimulated by his express command, we " acknowledge God to

---

* The Advantage and Necessity of the Christian Revelation, &c. Part i. ch. 14.
† 1 Cor. iii. 11.   ‡ Note XVI.   § 1 Pet. i. 21.
|| Acts xvi. 34.   ¶ Verse 31.   ** 1 John v. 20.

be the only true God and our God," we are far from involving ourselves in the guilt of presumption, temerity, or arrogance. It is to
those who spurn at the tender mercies and trample on the high authority of the living God, and even to those who, on various pretexts, *defer* till a future opportunity believing in the Saviour and
coming to God by him, that presumption, temerity, and arrogance
may justly be ascribed. *

There is a confidence, however, it is readily conceded, which is
hypocritical, presumptuous, and vain ; and true faith is known by its
fruits. Our Author, therefore, very properly inculcates self-examination, and specifies some scriptural marks, by which the Christian,
under the guidance of the Holy Spirit, may obtain satisfaction with
respect to his spiritual state. Self-investigation is an exercise which,
no doubt, is often conducted in a manner highly improper and injurious. Thousands, in particular, have examined themselves under
the influence of a self-righteous temper, and instead of glorying only
in the cross of Christ, have manifested an inclination to depend on
the evidences of vital religion which they can discover in their own
hearts and conduct, as the cause of acceptance and the ground of
peace. Yet to eraze self-examination from the catalogue of Christian duties, and to represent it as altogether hurtful, or as an unnecessary and unprofitable employment, is equally contrary to Scripture and reason. Were the improprieties and faults incident to fallen
mankind, and even to saints on earth, in the manner of performing
a duty, or the unwarrantable views they may less or more cherish
while discharging it, to be held as a sufficient reason for despising
or neglecting the duty itself, where is the duty—where the obligation to God or man, which might not on this ground be undervalued
and omitted ?—The neglect of serious, frequent, and impartial inquiry into their own state and character is ruinous to the souls of
men. See Psalm iv. 4. 1 Cor. xi. 28. 2 Cor. xiii. 5. Gal. vi.
3—5. On this topic the reader will find some excellent observations in *Bearts'* " Eternal Law and Everlasting Gospel."†

Note XXVIII. Page 108.

We often read in the Scriptures of God's *hiding his face* from his
people, as well as *causing his face to shine* upon them. These expressions, which are obviously metaphorical, are considered by some
as uniformly referring to the external dispensations of his Provi-

* See the Rev. Eben. Erskine's Sermon on Exod. xx. 2, 3. Vol. ii. p. 294,
1st edit.
† Part Second, Chap. v.

dence, prosperous and afflictive; and it were absurd to deny, that in various passages, as in Deut. xxxi. 16—18, and Psalm xliv. 3, they do refer to such events. But there are other portions of sacred writ, in which, without violent perversion, they must be interpreted as relating, at least in part, to spiritual concerns. When the Psalmist, for instance, prefers the following petition, " There be many that say, Who will show us any good ? Lord, lift thou up the light of thy countenance upon us,"* who can justly consider him as intending any display of goodness short of those manifestations of the Divine favour to the soul, and those cheering influences of the Spirit, which are peculiar to " the godly man," and which create a joy of heart inexpressibly superior, in its nature and tendency, to the delight arising from the richest abundance .of " corn and wine." It is no less evident, that in those verses in the 27th, 88th, and 143d Psalms, where the Psalmist deprecates or complains of the hiding of God's face, the expression chiefly refers to the suspension of the joy of God's salvation. " I know, my brethren," says Dr Witherspoon,† " that the distress of serious souls, when mourning after an absent or an angry God, crying to him in secret, and following hard after him in his ordinances, is by many treated with the highest degree of contempt. But surely, if peace of mind from a well-founded hope of the Divine favour is the greatest of all present blessings; and if this, from the variableness of our own conduct, is sometimes more, sometimes less strong, and sometimes wholly suspended; when this last is the case, it must occasion inexpressible concern, and there can be no greater evidence of irreligion and impiety than to call it in question."

It has been the subject of dispute, whether God's hiding his face from his people is always the fruit of their own sin, or whether it is, in some instances, to be regarded as a mere act of wisdom and sovereignty. The truth, however, seems to lie in the middle betwixt two opposite extremes. The Almighty, without doubt, does nothing contrary to righteousness and equity. When the saints find themselves utterly destitute of spiritual comfort and joy, they may conclude with certainty, that unless their distress be occasioned by some constitutional disorder, it is owing, if not to any gross provocation or allowed departure from the living God, at least to culpable ignorance of evangelical truth, or else to the staggerings of unbelief, or the latent operation of remaining depravity. The footsteps of Di-

* Psalm iv. 6.
† See his Works, Vol. iv. Ser. 3. pp. 42, 43.

vine sovereignty must, at the same time, be recognised, in the varied measures of consolation allotted to different saints, who are equally solicitous to keep a conscience void of offence; and to affirm that God, in no instance, suspends for a time the consoling influences of his Spirit, except where some *special provocation* has been given him, would be to hazard an assertion which cannot well be supported by facts. On this subject, unguarded expressions have doubtless been sometimes employed by practical writers. Yet, in all probability, it will be difficult to confute the following sentiments expressed by the celebrated Witherspoon in the sermon just referred to. " Sin separates between God and his people, and causes him to hide his face from them. Nay, sometimes though there be no *particular or provoking crime* as the cause of his controversy with them, he may withdraw from them the light of his countenance, to exercise their vigilance, or try their patience."

Witsius, when adverting to the sorrow which the hiding of God's face produces in the Christian, alludes to that passage where our Lord says, " Can the children of the bride-chamber mourn as long as the bridegroom is with them ?"* It may be stated, in passing, that Dr Campbell, in his Translation of the Gospels, instead of " children of the bride-chamber," employs the word *bridemen;* and observes in a Note that the Greek phrase, υιοι τȣ νυμφῶνος, denotes no more than the English word *bridemen,* namely, the young men who at a marriage are attendants on the bride and bridegroom; whereas the phrase in English *the children of the bride-chamber* suggests a very different idea.

Note XXIX. Page 114.

Part of the Author's language relative to *spiritual joy* will be apt to be regarded by some as grossly fanatical. His expressions on this subject, however, are not only characteristical of his fervent piety, but justified by the doctrine and phraseology of Scripture. In the sacred volume, the " joy of faith" is repeatedly contrasted with the pleasure resulting from corporeal indulgence. " Eat, O friends," says the Saviour, " drink, yea drink abundantly, O beloved."† " Be not drunk with wine," says Paul, " wherein is excess; but be filled with the Spirit."‡ Whoever reads the Author's Dissertations with attention, will do him the justice to acknowledge, that he is far from inculcating or approving a religious joy which is founded rather in the reveries of a heated imagination than in scriptural apprehensions

---

* Mat. ix. 15. † Song v. 1. ‡ Ephes. v. 18.

of the truth, or which evaporates in mere emotion, and has no salutary influence on the temper and practice.

A hypocrite, indeed, may counterfeit the joy of the Christian; and the Christian himself, when his vigilance is relaxed, may make a perverse use of the delight he has experienced in the ways of God, and derive from it fuel for the remaining pride of his heart. But it is an important duty to " rejoice evermore;" and if humility and watchfulness keep pace with our joy, this grace can never be exercised to excess. The Divine wisdom and goodness, mean time, should be recognised and adored in proportioning the consolations of the Christian to the conflicts awaiting him, or the trials in which he is involved. The joy of the Lord is the strength of his people; and from the whole tenor of ecclesiastical history it clearly appears, that the joy which is " unspeakable and full of glory" operates with the most powerful energy, and shines with the brightest lustre, when they are called to suffer great tribulations, and to encounter death in the most appalling forms.

Note XXX. Page 124.

" The sanctification of a sinner is the consequence of the grace and merits of Christ." In this, and in some other passages, as in the 11th section of this Dissertation, our Author, when referring to our Lord's meritorious obedience and satisfactory sufferings, doth not scruple to make use of the expression *the merits of Christ*.* The same expression is employed also by many other evangelical writers. But, although it may not deserve to be entirely erazed from the vocabulary of orthodox Divines, and for the sake of variety may sometimes be employed, it is by no means so precise and unequivocal as some other phrases they are accustomed to use on that interesting topic. The remarks of *Mr Hervey* on this expression, however scrupulous and antiquated they may appear, are worthy of attention. In a controversial performance, written with considerable ability and spirit,† after having quoted the following question proposed by *Mr Wesley*, " Is justification more or less than God's pardoning and accepting a sinner through the merits of Christ?" he expresses his willingness to acquiesce in this definition, " if somewhat explained and a little improved." - - - " *The merits of Christ*," he adds, " will certainly comport with Popish or with Socinian notions. It abounds in writers of the former sort, and it is to be found in the latter. Therefore, to be more explicit: By *pardoning*, I mean God's acquit-

* *Meritum*, and sometimes *merita Christi.*
† *Aspasio Vindicated*, pp. 47—49.

ting a sinner from guilt of every kind and of every degree. By *ac-cepting*, I mean still more, God's receiving him into full favour, considering and treating him as righteous, yea, perfectly and gloriously righteous. By *the merits of Christ*, I would always be disposed to signify his active and passive obedience, all that he wrought and all that he suffered for the salvation of mankind." " *The merits of Christ*," he subjoins in a Note, " is an ambiguous phrase, and what I can by no means admire. But as it occurs in Mr Wesley's Letter, and in many valuable writers, I have, led by their example, occasionally used it in the following debate, understanding it and still using it in the sense explained above." After a few sentences in the text, Mr Hervey has this additional note. " To gratify Mr Wesley, I have admitted his phrase *the merits of Christ*, though as it is a phrase of dubious import, and what almost any sect or heresy will subscribe, I should much sooner choose to abide by *Aspasio's* language. And why should we not all speak with the Scriptures? Why should we not use the expressions of the Apostle? He says, ' justified by the blood of Christ;' he says, ' made righteous by the obedience of Christ.' When therefore we say, sinners are pardoned and accepted through the blood and through the obedience of Christ, we have a warrant for our doctrine which is indisputable, and a precedent for our language which is unexceptionable."

Note XXXI. Page 127.

The good sense of the Author appears in the conciseness and simplicity with which he has treated the doctrine of the Trinity. Nor is it the design of the Translator, either to bring forward those " subtle refinements of the schools," which are justly stigmatised by Witsius as bold and presumptuous; or, what indeed, if executed with propriety, might prove a more rational and profitable service, —to illustrate and vindicate particularly those passages of Scripture which establish this momentous article of the Christian faith. It seems right, however, to suggest a few hints on a topic so sacredly important, though keenly controverted.

Amongst the numerous publications that have appeared in defence of this doctrine, few perhaps are more satisfactory, or at least more useful, than the small Treatise by the *Rev. William Jones*, entitled " the Catholic doctrine of the Trinity proved by above an hundred short and clear arguments, expressed in the terms of the Holy Scripture." This little work is warmly recommended by the Rev. John Newton in one of his letters; and the sentiments with which he accompanies the recommendation are so instructive, and so worthy of the Author as a friend and pattern of evangelical and vital religion, that it would be almost a crime to omit the opportunity of quoting the whole passage.

" It gave me great comfort," says that excellent man to a pious correspondent, " to find that what I wrote concerning the Divine character of Jesus as God manifest in the flesh, met with your approbation. This doctrine is, in my view, the great Foundation-stone upon which all true religion is built. But, alas! in the present day, it is the stumbling-stone and rock of offence, upon which too many, fondly presuming upon their own wisdom, fall and are broken. I am so far from wondering that any should doubt of it, that I am firmly persuaded none can truly believe it, however plainly set forth in Scripture, unless it be revealed to them from heaven; or in the Apostle's words, that ' no one can call Jesus Christ Lord, but by the Holy Ghost.' I believe there are many who think they believe it, because they have taken it for granted, and never attentively considered the difficulties with which it is attended in the eye of fallen reason. Judging by natural light, it seems impossible to believe that the title of ' the true God and eternal life' should properly belong to that despised man who hung dead upon the cross, exposed to the insults of his cruel enemies. I know nothing that can obviate the objections the reasoning mind is ready to form against it, but a real conviction of the sinfulness of sin, and the state of a sinner as exposed to the curse of the holy law, and destitute of every plea and hope in himself. Then the necessity of a Redeemer, and the necessity of this Redeemer's being Almighty, is seen and felt, with an evidence which bears down all opposition; for neither the efficacy of his atonement and intercession, nor his sufficiency to guide, save, protect, and feed those who trust in him, can be conceived of without it. When the eyes of the understanding are opened, the soul made acquainted with and attentive to its own state and wants, he that runs may read this truth, not in a few detached texts of a dubious import, and liable to be twisted and tortured by the arts of criticism, but as interwoven in the very frame and texture of the Bible, and written, as with a sun-beam, throughout the principal parts both of the Old and New Testament. If Christ be the Shepherd and Husband of his people under the Gospel, and if his coming into the world did not abridge those who feared God of the privileges they were entitled to before his appearance, it follows by undeniable consequence that he is ' God over all blessed for ever.' For David tells us, that his Shepherd was Jehovah; and the Husband of the Old Testament Church was the Maker and God of the whole earth, the Holy One of Israel, whose name is the Lord of Hosts. Psalm xxiii. 1. Isaiah liv. 8. with xlvii. 4. I agree with you that, among the many attempts which have been made to prove and illustrate the scripture-doctrine that the Father, the Word, and the Holy Spirit are one God, there have been many injudicious, unwarrantable things advanced, which have perplexed instead of instructing, and of which the enemies of the truth have known how to make their advantage. However, there have been tracts upon these sublime subjects, which have been written with judgment and an unction, and I believe attended with a blessing. I seem to prefer *Mr Jones's* book on the Trinity to any I have seen, because he does little more than state some of the scripture-evidence for it, and draws his inferences plainly and briefly; though even he has admitted a few texts, which may perhaps be thought not quite full to the point; and he has certainly omitted several of the most express and strongest testimonies. The best and happiest proof of all, that this doctrine is true in itself and true to us, is the experience of its effects. They who know his name will put their trust in him; they who are rightly impressed with his astonishing condescension and love, in emptying himself and submitting to the death of the cross for our sakes, will find themselves under a sweet constraint to love him again, and will feel a little of that emotion of heart which the Apostle expresses in that lively passage, Gal. vi. 14."*

Whilst the New Testament unquestionably supplies more ample testimonies to the doctrine of the Trinity than the Old, the latter furnishes evidence more abundant and decisive than some are willing to admit. The passages in Genesis, the Psalms, and the Prophets, referred to by Witsius, and many other texts that might be produced from these ancient books, are sufficient, at least when taken in connexion and allowed to shed light on each other, to show that there are in reality more than one Person in the godhead, and even that the Persons are Three in number. In several places of the Old Testament, as in Isaiah ix. 6. xl. 3, 4, 9. Jerem. xxiii. 6. Zech. xiii. 7. and Mal. iii. 1, the true divinity of the Messiah is expressly and copiously declared. This indeed is a principle pervading the whole system, or, to use Mr Newton's expression, " interwoven in the very frame and texture," of ancient predictions and promises. And if the divinity of the Son of God, the promised Redeemer, was

---

* *Cardiphonia,* Vol. ii. p. 10. *et seq.* See a similar passage on the same subject in Letter 2d to the Rev. Mr S——— Vol. i. pp. 138, 139.

so clearly and fully taught in the days of old, who can suppose that the sublime doctrine of Three in one was entirely unknown to the Old Testament Church ?   On this subject, Bishop Horsley's Sermon from Mal. iii. 1.; Dr Dick's Sermon from Isaiah ix. 6, in which he shows that the ancient Church expected a Divine person in the character of Messiah, and that none but a Divine person could have realized the hopes of the Church ; and Dr Wardlaw's Discourse* on the Unity of God and the Trinity of Persons in the Godhead, are highly worthy of attention. The reader may also consult, with much advantage, *Dr Dwight's* Sermon entitled, " Testimonies to the Doctrine of the Trinity from the ancient Christians, Jews, and Heathens."† When quoting the sentiments of ancient Jews, Dwight states, that *Philo,* who flourished in the first century, calls the *Logos* " the eternal Logos, or God ;" and says, " he is necessarily eternal, and the image of the invisible God."   He shows, too, that similar expressions were employed by the Chaldee Paraphrasts, and other Jewish commentators. They hold, it appears, that " there are three degrees in the mystery of *Aleim* or *Elohim ;*" and these degrees they denominate " persons."   They affirm of them,—" they are all one, and cannot be separated."   *R. Judah Hakkados,* who lived in the second century, uses the expression " God the Father, God the Son, God the Holy Spirit,—three in unity, one in trinity."

Of the four passages in the New Testament Scriptures, cited by Witsius to show that the three Divine persons are the Father, the Son, and the Holy Spirit, two are at once clear and indisputable, namely, Mat. xxviii. 19. and 2 Cor. xiii. 14.   The other two are Rom. i. 4. 1 John v. 7.

With regard to Rom. i. 4, it unquestionably makes mention of Christ as *the Son of God,* and thus alludes also to the first person in the godhead under the character of *the Father.*   But if the worthy Author intended to intimate, that the expression " according to the Spirit of holiness" refers to the third person, usually called the Holy Spirit, the accuracy of his interpretation may certainly be questioned.   Calvin, Doddridge, and several other respectable interpreters indeed, have adopted the same view of this phrase.   Many judicious writers, however, are of opinion, that it refers, not to the Holy Spirit, but to Christ's own divinity ; which is contrasted with *the flesh,* or human nature, mentioned in the preceding verse.   Such were the sentiments of, at least, Tertullian and Ambrose among the ancients.   The same interpretation is embraced by a large propor-

* Discourses on the Socinian Controversy, Disc. i.
† System of Theology, Ser. lxxi.

tion of modern critics and divines, including Pareus, Erasmus, Cameron, Hammond, and the continuators of Pool. Beza reasons powerfully and successfully in its defence. Dr Macknight translates the verse thus—" But was declared the Son of God with power; with respect to his holy spiritual nature, by his resurrection from the dead." Dr Guyse, in fine, has the following Note on this verse: " If *the Spirit of holiness* is here considered as *expressive of the sense* in which Christ was *the Son of God*, it evidently signifies his own *Divine nature*, in opposition to what he was *according to the flesh;* and so the *antithesis* is very beautiful between (*κατα πνευμα*) *according to the Spirit* here, and (*κατα σαρκα*) *according to the flesh*, ver. 3. But if we consider it as *the principle* of the power by which Christ was raised from the dead, for demonstrating him to be the Son of God, it may signify either his own divine nature, or the Holy Spirit, the third Person in the adorable Trinity. And yet, unless his own divine power concurred in raising him from the dead, his resurrection, abstractly considered in itself, no more proved him to be *the Son of God*, than the resurrection of believers by the power of God, and by *his Spirit, who dwells in them*, (Rom. viii. 11.) proves any of them to be so."

With respect to the other distinguished text referred to, to wit, 1 John v. 7, its authenticity has been warmly disputed. Dr Mill, Bengel, Pool in his *Synopsis Criticorum*, Dr Hammond, Sloss, Whitby, Brown, and many more, zealously contend that it is genuine; whilst Michaelis, Griesbach, and others, no less strenuously urge that it is spurious.* The doctrine of the Trinity, it is of importance to remark, by no means hangs on this, or any other single verse of Scripture; and although its spuriousness were established by irrefragable proofs, the believer in the Sacred Three has no just cause of alarm.

The laws of candour, too, it should be noted, strictly forbid us to consider one's doubting or even denying the genuineness of this controverted text, an unequivocal evidence of heresy. *Luther* would never admit it into his German translation of the Scriptures; and *Calvin*, in his Commentary on the passage, while he expresses an inclination to retain it, yet, on account of its being omitted in many Greek Manuscripts, intimates a doubt of its authenticity in these words, " *Vix quicquam asserere audeo*," i. e. " I can hardly venture to make a positive assertion on the subject." The orthodoxy, never-

---

* According to these writers, all that is genuine in verses 7th and 8th is thus expressed in English,—" For there are three that bear record, the Spirit, and the water, and the blood; and these three agree in one."

theless, both of Luther and Calvin, with regard to the true divinity of Christ and the Holy Spirit, is completely indubitable. The learned *Griesbach* himself, though, in consequence of his *Diatribe* on 1 John v. 7, 8, and several other critical discussions of a similar nature, some have rashly regarded him as a patron of Socinian errors, most solemnly professes his persuasion of the Saviour's divinity, in a passage which has been thus translated,—" I publicly declare, and appeal to God for my sincerity, that I never doubted of the truth of the doctrine of the divinity of Christ. There are, indeed, arguments and passages of Scripture in its support so numerous and so satisfactory, that I am at a loss to conceive how any person who admits the authority of Scripture, and adopts a fair method of interpretation, can call it in question. That single passage, John i. 1—3, is itself so plain, and so free from every just exception, that the boldest efforts of interpreters and critics will be found incapable of wresting it from the hands of the defenders of the truth." *

From the manner in which Witsius refers to 1 John v. 7. it appears that he was one of those who consider this verse as forming a part of the inspired record; and his Translator, though he does not pretend to be very thoroughly acquainted with the numerous writings on the question, will take the liberty to say, that he has not yet seen sufficient reason to embrace the contrary opinion. It gives him pleasure also to find, that, although it has now become very fashionable to abandon the defence of this text, its spuriousness is by no means universally admitted by the learned. *Bishop Horsley* supports its authority with his usual decision. *Milner* seems to have viewed it in the same light, and adduces an historical argument on its behalf, of considerable weight. " It deserves to be noticed," says he, " that in their exposition of the Apostles' Creed, the Waldensian Reformers give us the well known text in 1 John v. 7. as a proof of the doctrine of the Trinity. They were, it seems, perfectly satisfied of its authenticity, and most probably, at that time, had never heard of any suggestions to the contrary."† *Dr Macknight* also, whilst he declines " passing any judgment on a matter which hath been so much contested," makes the following remarks in its favour. " 1st,

---

* This faithful translation of Griesbach's words is copied from a Review of *Dr Jack's* useful " Lectures in vindication of some of the most important doctrines of the Christian Religion," which appeared in the *Christian Repository*, Vol. ii. pp. 159, 160, where the original Latin is also quoted from the Preface to Griesbach's 2d vol. of the Greek Testament, which he published in 1775. It is to be regretted, that in the Preface dated 1806, prefixed to the 2d vol. of the work, as printed at London 1818, this interesting declaration respecting the divinity of Christ is omitted.

† Milner's History of the Church of Christ, vol. iii. p. 467. 3d edit.

That this verse, properly interpreted, instead of disturbing the sense of the verses with which it is joined, rather renders it more connected and complete. 2dly, That in verse 9th *the witness of God* is supposed to have been before appealed to ; *If we receive the witness of men, the witness of God is greater.* And yet, if verse 7th is excluded, *the witness of God* is nowhere mentioned by the Apostle."*

On the whole, amidst the difficulties arising from an acknowledged deficiency in the proofs from ancient copies, versions, and quotations, and amidst the jarring accounts which learned critics, in some instances, have given of the reading in the same Manuscript, the *internal* evidence for the genuineness of the text is considerably powerful. Notwithstanding the attempts which have been made to account for the insertion of the 7th verse by a mystical interpretation of the 8th having been inserted in the margin, and at last introduced into the text, still greater probability appears to attach to the conjecture, that, owing to the similarity of the beginning of the 7th and 8th verses, or to some other cause, a transcriber might incautiously slip over the seventh. Were we to entertain the harsh and improbable supposition, that, on one side or other, unhallowed liberties have been wilfully taken with the apostolic record, it admits of no doubt, as it is expressed by Dr Guyse, that " the *Trinitarians* had less occasion to interpolate this verse, than the *Anti-trinitarians* had to take it out of the sacred Canon."

The objections urged against the doctrine of the Trinity, though repeated very frequently by its enemies with an air of triumph, have often received satisfactory answers. Nothing can be more unjust, as well as uncandid, than the reiterated attempts which are made to convict Trinitarians of holding a contradictory doctrine. Did they affirm, indeed, that the Father, Son, and Spirit are three *in the same sense* in which they are one, and one *in the same sense* in which they are three, they might be justly accused of self-contradiction. But this is by no means their doctrine. They assert that the Divine Persons are three in a certain respect, and one in another respect ; whilst they frankly acknowledge their incapacity fully to comprehend or explain the manner in which these Three subsist in the same uncreated and undivided essence. On the testimony of God, who no doubt possesses a perfect and infallible knowledge of himself, and who cannot possibly lie or deceive, they believe a sublime and, to fallen mankind, a deeply interesting fact relative to the Divine be-

* Macknight's Literal Translation of the Apostolic Epistles, with a Commentary and Notes, *in loc.*

ing, while the *modus* of the fact confessedly surpasses the comprehension of mortals. And why, it may be boldly asked,—why should *such believing* be deemed preposterous, or irrational? " We may be unquestionably sure of many things as to their *existence*," says *Bishop Wilkins*, " and yet we may not be able to explain the nature of them. No man in his wits can make any doubt whether there be such things as motion, and sensation, and continuity of bodies : and yet these things are commonly esteemed inexplicable. So that our not being able to see to the bottom of things, and to give a distinct account of the *nature* and *manner* of them, can be no sufficient cause to doubt of their being."*—Reason has its mysteries as well as Revelation. That the Almighty existed from eternity, is unquestionably a doctrine of Natural Religion. " The invisible things of Him from the creation of the world, are clearly seen, being understood by the things which are made, even his *eternal* power and godhead." Yet every one capable of reflecting on the subject, must be sensible, that it is no less impossible for us to form an adequate conception of the doctrine of God's existing from eternity, than of his subsisting in three distinct persons. No man, therefore, who admits the one doctrine notwithstanding its mysteriousness, and rejects the other because it exceeds his comprehension, can be successfully vindicated from the charge of gross inconsistency. But instead of prosecuting this subject farther, suffice it to refer the reader to Wardlaw's Discourse on the Unity of God mentioned above, and to an enlightened and able " Review of the Socinian and Unitarian Controversy" in the *Christian Instructor*.†

Note XXXII. Page 130.

" All the treasures of wisdom and knowledge," says the Author, " are hid in the mystery of God, and the Father, and of Christ." In the authorised English Version of the Bible, we read, Col. ii. 3. " In whom (i. e. in Christ) are hid all the treasures of wisdom and knowledge." The original expression, however, ἐν ᾧ, rendered " in *whom*," is equally capable, as is obvious to every one at all acquainted with the Greek language, of being translated " in *which ;*" and might, therefore, be referred to *the mystery* mentioned in the 2d verse. Our Translators have done well in referring it to " Christ ;" but Witsius is not singular in applying it to " the mystery." Dr Hammond decidedly refers it to the mystery " of the Gospel, or

---

* Principles and Duties of Natural Religion, Book i. ch. 3. sect. 3.
† Vol. 12th, pp. 28, 176, 323, 386, *et seq.*

Christianity ;" " that is," he adds, " of the course which hath more obscurely been taken by God the Father under the Old Testament, and more clearly now by God in Christ under the New, to bring sinners to salvation. Verse 3. In which course is wrapt up all the depth of wisdom imaginable." Dr Whitby's opinion is, that it refers to the person of Christ, and in support of this interpretation he quotes Philip. iii. 8. compared with verses 11, 12. and also Col. ii. 8, 9. Yet he allows, " that there seemeth to be no great difference between referring this to his person, and referring it to his doctrine." Calvin, too, in his Commentary on the passage, while in common with the most of writers, he prefers applying it to the person of our Lord, admits that there is little difference betwixt the two applications. Compare Dissert. xii. Sect. i.

Note XXXIII. Page 133.

To entertain the reader with minute and acrimonious discussions relative to those minor points with regard to which a diversity of sentiment and practice prevails among serious and intelligent Christians, is by no means the design of these Notes. A decided persuasion in one's own mind, regarding such matters, is not at all inconsistent with candour towards them who embrace a different view of the subject; or with admitting that the arguments employed in defence of the contrary tenet, though not conclusive, do possess such a degree of weight or of speciousness, that, in this imperfect state, it is not wonderful men of integrity should acquiesce in them as fully satisfactory. When Christians shall have learned to avoid irritating expressions, and to manifest towards each other the true spirit of forbearance and charity, and, at the same time, calmly and impartially to investigate the truth, determined, with the docility of children, to acquiesce in the will of Christ,—a much greater unity of sentiment will assuredly be attained.

" It must be confessed on all sides," says Mr Bradbury, " that good people have been intemperate with one another, and argued with a warmth that has done little service to the cause ; first, about the *subject* of baptism, whether it may be administered to infants or no ; and secondly, about the *manner* of performing it, whether by sprinkling or plunging. I dare say there are many of both opinions, who bewail the excesses that have come into the controversy, and could wish that the disputants were *Christians* as well as *orthodox ;* that in maintaining the truth they would not grieve the good Spirit of God, but that all bitterness and wrath, partiality, noise, clamour, and *evil-speaking, be put away, with all malice ;* that " the argument may be as gentle as the cause it maintains."*

The reign of bitterness and wrath, it may be hoped, is rapidly hastening to an end. Every man ought, meanwhile, in the spirit of Christianity, to embrace proper opportunities of stating those sentiments which appear to him to be consonant to Scripture. On this principle, and in order to prevent misapprehensions of our Author's meaning, it seems right to observe, that although, when discoursing on the doctrine of the Trinity, he quotes with approbation a passage from *Ambrose,* in which that venerable writer speaks of Christians having been *immersed* at their baptism, we ought not to conclude that immersion or plunging is essential to the ordinance, or that Witsius looked upon it in this light. His views on this topic appear to have coincided with those which the compilers of the *Westminster Confession of Faith* have very cautiously and judiciously expressed in the following terms—" Dipping of the person into the water is not necessary ; but baptism is rightly administered by pouring or sprinkling water upon the person ;"†—and agreeably to which, also, the definitions of Baptism in the Larger and in the Shorter Catechism, represent this Christian rite under the general notion of " a *washing* with water." Without entering further into this contested point, or adverting to the numerous publications in which it is discussed, it may suffice to cite a passage from our Author's work *on the Covenants,* where he states his views of the subject at large.‡

Having proposed the question, " Whether baptism is rightly administered only by immersion, or whether it may be done also by pouring water from a vessel, or by sprinkling ?"—he admits, in reply, that both John the Baptist and our Lord's disciples *usually* baptized by immersion, and that the native signification of the Greek terms βαπτειν and βαπτιζειν is *mergere, tingere,* to plunge, to dip.

Yet, after having made these and some other concessions, in which the advocates for sprinkling are far from being universally inclined to acquiesce, he thus proceeds. " It must not, however, be supposed, that immersion is so necessary to baptism, that it cannot be rightly performed by *pouring* or *sprinkling*. The following arguments in favour of pouring and sprinkling, are of considerable force. 1. If we find that the Apostles did baptize by immersion, it doth not follow that they uniformly observed this method. It is more probable that the three thousand who were baptized in one day (Acts ii. 41.) had

* The Duty and Doctrine of Baptism, in thirteen Sermons, p. 4.
† Chap. xxviii. sect. 3.
‡ Book iv. ch. 16. sect. 13, 14.

water poured or sprinkled upon them, than that they were immersed.
It is not likely, that the Apostles, being completely occupied in
preaching the Gospel, could have found leisure to accomplish a work
which must have required so much time and labour, as immersing
so many thousands. Nor is it probable that Cornelius, and Lydia,
and the Jailor, who were baptized in private houses together with
those of their household, had baptisteries at hand, in which they
could be entirely immersed. *Vossius* * has produced instances of
sprinkling from antiquity, which *Josua Arndius* † has related in
the same order, without acknowledging his obligations to Vossius.
2. Although βαπτιζειν properly signifies *mergere*, to immerse, it is
used more generally to denote any kind of washing, as Luke xi. 38.
Dominicus a Soto ‡ has well observed, ' That in baptism there is
something *essential*, as *washing*, agreeably to the expression Ephes.
v. 26. where the Apostle calls baptism *a washing with water;* and
something *accidental*, namely, whether the washing be done in this
way or that.' 3. The thing signified by baptism is expressed by
pouring and sprinkling, both in the Old and New Testament. On
pouring, or affusion, see Isaiah xliv. 3.; on sprinkling, see Isaiah lii.
15. Ezek. xxxvi. 25. Heb. xii. 24. 1 Pet. i. 2. In these places of
Scripture, there is an allusion, I admit, to the Levitical sprinkling;
yet from this it is evident, that the application of the blood and Spirit
of Christ, which believers under the New Testament experience, was
properly represented by the rite of sprinkling. This is expressly suggested by the Apostle, Heb. ix. 13, 14. ' For if the blood of bulls
and of goats, and the ashes of an heifer *sprinkling* the unclean, sanc-
tifieth to the purifying of the flesh, how much more shall the blood
of Christ - - - purge your conscience from dead works?' 4. Add to
this, that the whole genius of the New Testament dispensation, being distinguished by liberality and gentleness, seems to preclude the
necessity of stripping and immersing feeble infants when baptized,
particularly in northern climates."—After some further remarks, the
Author observes, that, from what he had said, it follows, " that those
Greeks, who in the council of *Florence* pronounced the Latin Christians *unbaptized*, because they had not been immersed in water,
acted an exceedingly rigorous, and, at the same time, an unreasonable part."

Ambrose, in the quotation from him to which this Note refers, alludes, the reader will observe, to a *three-fold* immersion, which seems

---

* *Disput.* i. *De Baptism.* Th. 9.   † *Lexic. Antiq. Eccles.* p. 66.
‡ *Distinct.* iii. *Quæst. un.* Art. 7.

to have been customary in his age.   It is proper, therefore, to add, that our Author adverts to this practice in the same chapter of the *Economy of the Covenants*,* from which we have just quoted these remarks in favour of sprinkling.   It is of small moment, in his opinion, whether immersion or sprinkling be done *once* or *thrice.* Amongst the early Christians, he concedes, from the idea that a three-fold immersion or sprinkling implied a marked confession of the adorable Trinity, and also of our Saviour's rising from the dead on the third day, the rite was generally performed three times. About the beginning of the seventh century, however, the Arians in Spain, having begun to pervert this practice, for the support of their own errors in dividing the godhead, it was determined, as our Author states, at the fourth Council of *Toledo,* that both forms are irreprehensible in the Church of God, and the application of water *once* only was pronounced the more eligible mode.

NOTE XXXIV. Page 138, line 15.

Although the Author affirms, that " the economy of the Three Persons manifested itself no less" † in the first creation, than in the new creation, or work of redemption, his meaning must have been, that the discovery of the Three Persons in the former was equally *certain* as in the latter, not that it was equally *ample* and *bright.* If the wisdom, power, goodness, and other attributes of the Deity as one God possessing infinite perfection, are more illustriously displayed in the new creation than in the old, and if angels, in consequence, sing " Glory to God in the highest," it is at the same time evident, that redemption exhibits the clearest and most impressive manifestation of Jehovah as Three in one.   The distinct characters sustained by the Father, Son, and Spirit, and the distinct parts which they respectively fulfil in the plan of our recovery, most assuredly place this glorious mystery in a new point of light, inexpressibly more conspicuous and interesting than that in which it appeared at the original creation of man.

The whole passage in this Dissertation, relative to Adam's knowledge of the Trinity, has its parallel in the Author's Treatise on the Covenants,‡ where the same topic is discussed with some varieties of thought and expression.   Amyrault's assertion, that the doctrine of the Trinity so peculiarly respects the redemption of mankind,

---

* Sect. 15.

† His expression is,—" In qua non minus se manifestavit Trinitatis œconomia."

‡ Book i. ch. 2. sect. 5—8.

" that the knowledge of it cannot pertain to the state of innocence," was unquestionably rash; and the arguments brought forward by Witsius in opposition to that sentiment, it must be allowed, are at once ingenious and considerably satisfactory. To suppose that a revelation of the Three persons in the godhead was made to our first parents in Paradise involves, at least, nothing absurd or incongruous; and it is of great importance to maintain, that the personal distinctions in the Divine nature are not voluntary but necessary, and that these distinctions existed from all eternity.

Note XXXV. Page 138, line 23.

The venerable Author affirms, that " the same eternal life, which we obtain through Christ," was promised to Adam on condition of his perseverance in holy obedience; and refers his reader to another work, in which he has proved his assertion at large. He intends, no doubt, his *Economy of the Covenants,** where he treats particularly of the promises and seals of the covenant of works, and shows that everlasting happiness in the enjoyment of God was promised to Adam as the reward of perfect obedience. No one, however, can reasonably question, that Witsius, while he held that the life thus promised to Adam was in substance the same as that which we receive through Christ, would have cheerfully admitted, that the one falls short of the other in various respects. The very circumstance that the eternal life conferred upon fallen man is strictly an eternal *salvation*, creates a wonderful difference. Past experience of misery gives a double zest to happiness. The redeemed of the human race, having tasted the wormwood and the gall, their " soul hath them still in remembrance;" and the constant recollection of former guilt and wo cannot fail to make them, through eternity, drink, with a lively additional relish, of " the pure river of the water of life." The brighter the demonstrations, too, we receive of the love of God, and the stronger the motives we have to love him in return, and to repose an unsuspecting confidence in him, our felicity must be proportionally the greater; and redemption certainly exhibits at once more glorious demonstrations of the love of God to us, and more powerful motives to love him and trust in him, than any that were presented to Adam before the fall; or that could have been expected, although he had preserved his integrity, and been confirmed in bliss. By Christ's assuming our nature, in fine, a foundation was laid for a more intimate union and fellowship with the Supreme Being, than

* Book i. ch. iv. 6, 7.

we could have otherwise obtained. The Son of God is become our Brother, " bone of our bone, and flesh of our flesh ;" and through him we have also access to the Father under new and most endearing relations. " Go to my brethren," said Jesus to Mary, " and say to them, I ascend unto my Father and your Father, and to my God and your God." On this topic, the profound *Edwards* has some excellent remarks in his Sermons on the Wisdom of God in Redemption; and it is judiciously illustrated by the *Rev. John Robson* in a Discourse from Rom. v. 15.*

Note XXXVI. Page 142.

The expressions of our pious Author, as well as those of *Ignatius*, whom he quotes with approbation, relative to persons who deny the true divinity of the Son and Spirit, may to some readers appear harsh and uncandid. To others, however, they will seem capable of a fair vindication, from the awful rebuke of the Apostle Paul to Elymas, Acts xiii. 10.—from the solemn declarations of the Apostle John in his first Epistle, ii. 22, 23, and second Epistle 9—11.—and from various other passages of Scripture. The late Dr Witherspoon discovers a similar zeal, when he says ; " As to Socinians and Pelagians, - - - I never did esteem them to be Christians at all."† Not merely those whom some would stigmatise as " vulgar Theologians," but Divines who did not embrace the most evangelical sentiments, and who have been amply eulogised for superior gentleness of temper and moderation of conduct, have often, when employed in defending doctrines which they deemed fundamental, adopted a tone of equal severity in reference to those audacious inquirers, by whom they are denied. *Bishop Wilkins*, for example, a man of excellent temper as well as distinguished erudition, employs the following expressions with regard to those who deny the existence of God :— " And it were well if they might not only be reckoned among beasts (as they are by the Psalmist where he styles them *brutish*) but driven out among them likewise, and banished from all human society, as being public pests and mischiefs to mankind, such as would debase the nobility of our nature to the condition of brute creatures, and therefore are fit only to live among them."‡ If the benevolent and philosophical Bishop, from the impulse of a laudable zeal for the doctrine of the being of a God, expressed himself in such severe

---

* Discourses by Ministers of the (late) General Associate Synod, vol. ii. p. 180 *et seq.*

† Essay on Justification, page 75, note.

‡ Principles and Duties of Natural Religion, Book ii. ch. i. p. 292.

terms respecting its opposers, is it strange that Ignatius and Witsius, impelled by a similar zeal for the proper Divinity of the Son and Spirit of God, allowed themselves to represent the determined enemies of that important doctrine as blasphemers, and devils, or *false accusers?*

It is indeed with emotions of unfeigned sorrow that the Christian sees men rejecting essential articles of revealed religion; and " the wisdom which cometh from above" will teach him to guard against expressions calculated rather to irritate than to convince or reclaim them. It is much to be wished, that the friends of the Christian doctrines, while " contending earnestly for the faith once delivered unto the saints," were, in every instance, found, at the same time, " in meekness instructing those that oppose themselves, if God peradventure will give them repentance to the acknowledging of the truth." Indifference to truths of the first importance, however, it is to be regretted, not unfrequently assumes the sacred name of charity, and the fair semblance of meekness; and the decided enemies of the Christian Revelation are sometimes spoken of in such soothing and complacent terms as most unhappily tend to confirm their fatal security in the path of error, and to encourage others to adopt the same pernicious course. How unguarded, for instance, is the following sentence, which occurs in an extensive literary work of distinguished celebrity: " The sound Theist, who worships the same God, and cherishes the same hopes as the Christian, is a character whom no man ought rashly to condemn." No man, it is right to admit, ought to be accused or even suspected of infidelity without sufficient ground; and candour requires us to make a distinction betwixt those unbelievers whose outward morals are correct and who do not outrage society by a preposterous spirit of proselytism, and " the avowed infidel, who insults the public feeling by his vices, or shakes the public faith by his outrageous zeal." But to represent the Theist who rejects revelation, whether secretly or avowedly, as " worshipping *the same God* and cherishing *the same hopes* with the Christian," is obviously inconsistent with that reverence for the doctrine and authority of Sacred Writ which every " sound" Christian is bound to entertain. Every true Christian is fully aware, that the conceptions of God which the mere Theist entertains, if not totally different, at least come far short of those views of the Divine nature and character which the Scriptures supply; and that the vague, baseless, and self-righteous hopes of immortal felicity which are cherished by the votaries of Theism are quite dissimilar from the expectations of the followers of Jesus, and inexpressibly inferior in value, sweetness, purifying influence, and consoling energy, to that " good hope through grace," which anticipates the blissful presence and everlasting enjoyment of a Three-one God—rests on the sure basis of an infallible testimony—and springs from an humble dependance on that Divine Saviour, who " was dead, and is alive for evermore, and has the keys of hades and of death."

Note XXXVII. Page 144.

Our Author has no less clearly than concisely shown, that the sublime doctrine of the Trinity is not a point of barren speculation, but of vital importance to the comfort and sanctification of the Christian. Its enemies, indeed, have often boldly affirmed that, although it were true, it could be of no practical utility. But independently of other considerations, are there not certain devout regards and religious services due to the Son and Spirit as Divine Persons, if they are in reality Divine ? Our duty consists in conducting ourselves in a manner corresponding to those relations in which we stand to every one, and to the claims which every one has upon us, whether arising from his own dignity and excellence, or from the benefits he has conferred. Supposing, therefore, a man were to acquit himself faithfully of all other obligations, and at the same time habitually and pertinaciously, in spite of inspired instructions and warnings on the subject, to withhold that confidence, reverence, gratitude, and love, and those various acts of religious homage which are due to the Son and Spirit, would not this criminal neglect entitle him to the character, and subject him to the doom, of a wilful transgressor ? This is a consideration which merits the particular attention of those who profess indifference to doctrines but zeal for the commandments, and found all their hopes of salvation upon the careful performance of their duty.

The importance of the Trinity in a practical light has been amply illustrated by many writers, whose " praise is in the churches." Fuller's masterly performance on the comparative moral tendency of the Calvinistic and Socinian systems is well known. Dr Jamieson's " Vindication of the Doctrine of Scripture and of the primitive Faith concerning the Deity of Christ,"* contains an able refutation of Dr Priestley's objections to the Trinity as a useless mystery. Suffice it to add, that Dr Owen's treatise on " Communion with God, Father, Son, and Holy Ghost," has long been blessed as a guide to the exercise and a helper of the joy of those, whose supreme concern it is,

---

* Vol. i. pp. 551—567.

that they may be able to say with the beloved disciple, " Truly our fellowship is with the Father, and with his Son Jesus Christ."

NOTE XXXVIII. Page 147.

Witsius, in another Dissertation,* applies the words in Heb. ix. 14.—" who *through the eternal Spirit* offered up himself," to Christ's own Divinity. Yet here, not without some appearance of inconsistency, he observes that the expression, " the eternal Spirit," may, without any inconvenience, and even with great propriety, be understood of the Third Person in the godhead. This last interpretation has been adopted by several respectable interpreters, as Bishop Fell, and Dr Doddridge. It seems better, however, with Calvin, Beza, Pool, Fraser of Alness, and others, to consider the expression as referring to the divine nature, as subsisting in the person of the Son.

Some ancient manuscripts, it is true, instead of πνευματος 'αιωνιȣ, " the eternal Spirit," have πνευματος 'αγιȣ, " the Holy Spirit ;" and the Vulgate reads *per Spiritum Sanctum.* But according to Dr Owen, Dr Macknight, the Christian Observer,† and others, " the eternal Spirit" is the reading agreeable to the Syriac translation, and also to the great majority, as well as the most ancient, of the Greek copies. The Holy Ghost, it is readily admitted, is no less an *eternal Spirit* than the Deity of Christ. Yet it cannot escape attention, that when the Spirit is spoken of with reference to his personal agency, he is usually denominated the Holy Spirit.

That it might be said without impropriety, that Christ offered up himself through the Holy Spirit, it were vain to deny. To every admirer of the plan of redemption, it is delightful to contemplate the whole work of the third Person of the Trinity immediately relating to our Lord's humanity ; which was not only formed by his power, but enriched above measure with his gifts and graces, and animated by his influence amidst all his labours and sufferings on earth. The faith and patience, love and zeal, which " the man Christ Jesus" so vigorously exercised on the cross, are to be ascribed to the operation of the Holy Spirit resting upon him, according to ancient predictions. The idea, nevertheless, of Christ's offering himself through his own eternal Spirit—" through the divine nature acting in the person of the Son," is at least of equal importance in itself,

---

* Dis. xv. Sect. 6.

† See the Number for June 1809. It is suggested in the Observer that " the epithet 'αγιȣ (holy) is so constantly connected with the Spirit, that a scribe might inadvertently write it instead of 'αιωνιȣ (eternal.)

and seems more exactly to accord with the scope of the passage. "The design of the Apostle," as Dr Owen remarks in his Commentary on the place, "is to prove the efficacy of the offering of Christ above those of the priesthood under the law. Now this arose from hence, partly that he offered himself, whereas they offered only the blood of bulls and goats; but principally from the dignity of his person in his offering, in that he offered himself by his own eternal Spirit or Divine nature." Those excellent graces which, through the power of the Holy Ghost, he so nobly displayed amidst the shame of the cross, contributed, undoubtedly, their own share towards the merit and virtue of his offering. But his eternal Divinity was the altar which supported his mortal humanity under the tremendous load of infinite wrath; and which alone rendered the sacrifice of himself, a sacrifice of *boundless* worth and efficacy. "Christ suffered as man," says Calvin to the same effect with Owen, "but the saving virtue of his death was owing to the efficacy of the Spirit," by which he evidently intends his *divine nature*. "A sacrifice making an eternal expiation," he adds, "was a work which mere humanity could never have accomplished. The Apostle calls the Spirit an eternal Spirit, that we may know, that the reconciliation of which Christ is the author is eternal." This view of the passage might also be supported by referring to other parallel expressions in Rom. i. 4. and in 1 Pet. iii. 18. Dr Owen, who illustrates this text in his celebrated Treatise on the Spirit,* as well as in his Commentary on the Epistle to the Hebrews, seems unwilling to adopt either of these two senses to the exclusion of the other; but candidly admits, that the arguments for referring the expression to the divinity of Christ, preponderate.

Note XXXIX. Page 153, line 7.

In this section our Author speaks of the *communication* of the divine nature to the Son; in the thirteenth he speaks of its *communication* to the Spirit; and in various other passages, he makes use of similar expressions. Nor is this to be wondered at; for in the seventeenth century, the same language was in current use among the soundest Divines of the Protestant Church, not excepting Dr Owen. Even in subsequent times, the same, or similar, phraseology has been employed by writers who might have been expected to avoid it. *Archbishop Secker*, for example, speaking of our Saviour, says, "In respect of his Divine nature, he *derived his being* from the Fa-

* Book II. ch. iv. sect. 8, 9.

ther by an eternal generation ; not as creatures, who are made out of nothing and were made by him, but in a manner peculiar to himself, and inconceivable to us."* The late *Dr George Hill,* too, speaks of the *communication* of the Divine essence from the Father to him."†
But for a considerable time past, such expressions have, in general, been disliked, and laid aside by the friends of the truth,—partly because they bear some appearance of an attempt to explain what the Scripture has not explained ;—partly because they are extremely apt to be misunderstood, and have in fact been often misunderstood by plain Christians ;—and partly, in fine, because they have been egregiously perverted by the enemies of the necessary existence and supreme divinity of the Son and Spirit. That Witsius himself would have abstained from such expressions, had he been fully aware of the abuse to which they are liable, cannot be questioned by any one who perceives aright the prevailing spirit of his writings, or who will peruse with attention his observations on the word *create,*‡ or his reasoning against *Episcopius.*§

" As for the manner of the Father's eternal begetting of the Son," says Sir Peter King, " there are various similitudes used by the ancients to help our conceptions therein, as that the Father begat the Son as a fountain doth her streams, and the sun light, and a root the branches, and several other such like. But whether all of them will abide a strict scrutiny, I shall not here inquire : only this I will venture to affirm, that none of them doth yield us any adequate or satisfactory apprehension of this sublime and incomprehensible mystery. For which reason great caution is to be used in our searches thereunto and expressions therein, that we do not, with too great nicety and curiousness, dive into this profound and incomprehensible secret, lest while we endeavour to show our learning and knowledge, we betray our ignorance, and what is worse, conceive and utter things unbecoming the Divine and infinite Majesty."‖ The late venerable *Mr John Brown* of Haddington, in his " Compendious view of Natural and Revealed Religion,"¶ makes the following just remarks. " It being plainly evident from God's own word, that each of these three Persons is equally the Most High and only true God, no term or phrase must be admitted in the explication of their personal properties, which can in the least interfere with the Divine

---

* See his Lectures on the Creed in his Works, vol. iv. p. 278.
† Theolog. Institutes, p. 64. ‡ Dissert. viii. sect. 6.
§ Dissert. vii. sect. 18—23.
‖ Critical History of the Apostles' Creed, p. 134.
¶ Page 163.

equality or absolute independence of any of them. Subordinate godhead is no godhead at all, nor any thing but a mere chimera in men's brain. By calling the Father the Fountain of the Deity or of the Trinity, by saying that the Divine essence is *communicated,* or the Son and Spirit are *produced,* or that they have a *personal* though not an *essential* dependance on the Father,—learned men have inadvertently hurt this mystery, and given occasion to its enemies to blashpheme." " It is certainly absurd," adds the same author, " to attempt an explication of the personal properties, *Beget—Begotten,—Proceeding,*—by terms which are more unintelligible; and where to find clearer ones, I know not."—" Explaining a mystery," says Mr Bradbury with his usual vivacity, " must be quite wrong. It is best to keep it in its own language, and not utter words *hard to be understood.* It is at least a daring practice, not treating it as a mystery, but throwing it into a rumble of sounds. For these reasons, I could wish that saying had not obtained among Divines, that the Father is *the Fountain of the Deity.* This is a nicety that we have nothing in Scripture to lead us into. It is being *wise above what is written,* and *exercising ourselves in things too high for us.*"[*] To these quotations on this solemn and weighty topic, it may be sufficient to add, that Dr Campbell, after some keen remarks on certain Greek and Latin expressions which were employed by Christians in their early disputes on the subject of the Trinity, concludes with the following words; " It were to be wished that on topics so sublime, men had thought proper to confine themselves to the simple but majestic diction of the Sacred Scriptures."[†]

Note XL. Page 153, line 3 from the bottom.

Our venerable Author, in common with *Bishop Pearson,*[‡] and many other respectable Theologians of former times, seems to consider the expression in John v. 26. as having an immediate reference to that life which is essential to Christ as a Divine Person. But amongst Divines of the present day, who maintain the proper divinity and necessary existence of the Son of God, it is the prevailing, if not the universal sentiment, that our Lord, in this verse, speaks of the life which he possesses in his Mediatorial character. It is of importance indeed to remember, as Witsius suggests, that unless Christ had been originally possessed of the same Divine nature and life with the Father, he could never have had, as Mediator, a foun-

[*] Mystery of Godliness, vol. i. p. 97.
[†] Eccles. History, vol. ii. Lect. xiv. p. 4.
[‡] Exposition of the Creed, Art. i. pp. 34, 35. 8th edit.

tain of life in himself for quickening the souls or bodies of men.
But the question at issue here is this—Doth our Lord appear to affirm that it has *been given to him* by the Father to possess the Divine
life? Now, however consistent this view of the expression might
appear to Witsius and others to be with the essential independence
of Christ and his perfect equality with the Father, it seems much
more proper to adopt a different sense, if this can be done without
violating the rules of sound interpretation ; and whoever attends to
the connexion between the 26th and 27th verses may be expected to
conclude, that the sense now generally embraced by those who hold
the doctrine of Christ's proper divinity is not merely admissible, but
the most obvious and natural. " As the Father hath life in himself, so hath he given to the Son to have life in himself; and hath
given him authority to execute judgment also, because he is the Son
of man." The meaning is, that, because Christ is " the Son of man,"
and undertook to accomplish our redemption, the Father honoured
him as Mediator, both by appointing him a living and quickening head, and by giving him authority to execute judgment. In his
original character as a Divine Person, he has " life in himself" no
less originally and independently than he has " authority" to act the
part of Universal Sovereign and Judge. " Some judicious expositors think," says *Dr Guyse,* " that the Father's *giving to the Son to
have life in himself,* relates to the eternal and inconceivable generation of the Son, by which the same perfection of life was necessarily
communicated to him as is in the Father himself. But others understand it as an *œconomical* communication of life to the Son as man
and Mediator, founded upon and answerable to his original participation of the same divine life with the Father. And I rather incline to the last of these senses, because of the close connexion there
is betwixt this and what is said in the following verse about the Father's *giving him authority to execute judgment*—both of which are
brought in as proofs, not of what our Lord had said about his doing
all things in the same manner that the Father does them, (ver. 19.)
but of what he had said in the immediately foregoing verse about the
Son's quickening the dead in the administration of his kingdom ; and
because it seems to me that his being *the Son of man* is added at the
close of the next verse (v. 27.) as the reason of both those donations."*

Note XLI. Page 157.

Our Author allows that Calvin and some other Protestant Divines
have considered the expression, Acts xiii. 33. ἀναστησας Ἰησυν, as re-

* Practical Expositor, John v. 26. *Note.*

ferring to Christ's resurrection from the dead; and that this was the sense in which it was understood by the Translators of our authorised English Version, appears from their having rendered it—" He hath raised up Jesus *again.*" Witsius, however, with *Beza, Junius,* and others, seems to have been decidedly of opinion, that the expression refers to God's sending Jesus into the world, or to his exhibiting him as a Saviour; and accordingly he contends for this interpretation not only in these Dissertations on the Creed, but also in his " Conciliatory Animadversions."* Nor is this interpretation destitute of probability.

That the Greek word in question properly signifies, *to raise up,* or *cause to appear* in general, and that it is often applied to our Lord's manifestation in the flesh and his exhibition to mankind, is unquestionable. See Mat. xxii. 24. Acts ii. 30. iii. 22. vii. 37. Heb. vii. 11, 15. The term, it is allowed, frequently denotes also the *raising of persons from the dead,* as in John vi. 39, 40. Acts ii. 24, 32. But there is considerable force in the argument which the Author derives from the phrase at the beginning of verse 34th, " And as concerning that he raised him up from the dead,"—which seems to intimate that the Apostle makes a transition from speaking of the Father's having exhibited Christ as a Saviour to speak of his having raised him from the dead. Had Paul referred in verse 33d to the resurrection from the dead, it is probable that, with a view to render the meaning of ἀναστησας indisputable, he would have *there* added the expression ἐκ νεκρων, " from the dead." This seems much more likely, than that he would have added this expression to ἀναστησεν, " he raised him up," in verse 34th; if, in reality, he had already referred to our Saviour's resurrection in verse 33d.

To evade the force of this argument, it might indeed be alleged, that in verses 32d and 33d the Apostle speaks of God's raising Christ from the dead only in general; and that at verse 34th he proceeds to show that the Father raised him up " now no more to return" to the grave. This allegation, however, though somewhat specious, is not sufficient to invalidate our Author's argument. Nor is its force weakened by the notice taken of the resurrection in verses 30, 31. At the conclusion of verse 31st, the Apostle seems to pause; and having, in a preceding part of his discourse, announced God's raising up Jesus in both senses of the expression, first by exhibiting him as an incarnate Saviour verse 23d, and then by bringing him again from the dead verse 30th, he goes forward to show the corre-

* Chap. iii. Sect. 13.

spondence of both with the Old Testament Scriptures. Having formerly remarked, that " of this man's seed hath God, *according to his promise*, raised unto Israel a Saviour, Jesus," he, in the first place, in similar terms, adverts again to the exhibition of Christ in the flesh ; " And we declare unto you glad tidings, how that the *promise* which was made unto the fathers, God hath fulfilled the same unto us their children, in that he hath raised up Jesus ; as it is also written in the second Psalm, " Thou art my Son, this day have I begotten thee." The Apostle then shows, in the second place, verses 34—37, that in the Saviour's resurrection to immortal life, to which he had previously referred in verses 30th and 31st, we behold another striking instance of the accomplishment of ancient promises.

A difficulty with reference to the *eternity* of Christ's Sonship, it is commonly thought, arises from Paul's quoting Psalm ii. 7, in verse 33d, whether the verse be interpreted as relating immediately to his incarnation, or his resurrection. It is not intended, however, to protract this Note by a minute consideration of the supposed difficulty. Suffice it to observe, agreeably to the comment of Witsius himself in the Section now referred to, that whichever of these views be adopted, the Apostle ought not to be understood as intimating that the Messiah *became* the Son of God at a certain period, but only that his exhibition to mankind in the fulness of time, his wonderful incarnation, or his glorious resurrection from the dead, served to *manifest* his character as the Only-begotten of the Father, " whose goings forth have been from of old, even from everlasting."* The doctrine of the Sonship of Christ being in reality Divine and Eternal, is satisfactorily confirmed by *Dr Jamieson*, in that part of his elaborate work on the Deity of Christ, in which he considers the evidence of this momentous article arising from the use of that expression *the Son of God.*† It abounds with just and pertinent as well as ingenious and striking observations on the various testimonies borne to Jesus as the Son of God, by the Father, angels, devils, the enemies of Christ, and by our Lord himself and his Apostles. See also Dr Owen on Heb. i. 5.

The subject of this Note is briefly adverted to by the Rev. Mr Bell ;‡ and it may be just mentioned, that he shows at length, that the Apostle's quotation from Isaiah, " I will give you the sure mercies of David," although, at the first glance, it might appear to have

---

* Micah v. 2.
† A Vindication of the doctrine of Scripture, &c. Vol. i. pp. 347—492.
‡ Translation of the *Irenicum*, Note 6, p. 204, *et seq.*

no connexion with the subject of our Lord's resurrection, is equally appropriate and conclusive.

Note XLII. Page 169.

It has been generally admitted in the Christian Church, that the New Covenant is represented in Scripture under the metaphor of a Testament, and that amongst the numerous endearing designations Divinely given to Christ, the character of a Testator is entitled to a place. With what surprise then must the plain unlettered Christian be struck, when he is told, that the learned authors of the authorised English Version, and almost all the Translators of the Sacred Volume, from the writer of the *Syriac* Version to the most celebrated interpreters of the Protestant Churches, have been egregiously mistaken, in giving any such representation of the covenant or of Christ, and that the original expressions ought never to have been so rendered! This, however, is one of the boasted discoveries of modern criticism. Even the pious *Dr Doddridge*, in this instance following *Mr Pierce*, dismisses, in his Translation, the expressions *Testament* and *Testator* from the ninth chapter of the Epistle to the Hebrews; and the learned *Dr Macknight* reasons strenuously and confidently against the use of these terms. But although mere predilection in favour of certain figures and expressions, with which our ears are familiar, and which we have been long accustomed to deem sacred, should not make us deaf to the voice of sound instruction, or insensible to the force of solid argument, we ought not rashly to acquiesce in every pretended improvement, or without the most careful inquiry, to resign ourselves to the guidance and authority of a few writers, whatever be their merits, in opposition to the general current of respectable critics and translators. Nor should we allow ourselves to forget that, owing to the infirmities of human nature, those doctrinal sentiments to which men are attached, whether right or wrong, have often a very considerable influence, in many cases imperceptible and not avowed even to themselves, on the views which they adopt in their critical and philological researches. Impartiality demands, that every individual, so far as he is capable, should examine the passage for himself; and that such defences of the common translation as those found in the Commentary of the learned and faithful *Dr Owen*, and in the Notes of the pious and judicious *Bell*,* should be consulted with scrupulous attention, before the novel interpretation be finally embraced.

---

* Translation of the *Irenicum*, Note 25. p. 287 *et seq.*

The design of this Note is to throw out some hints calculated to show, at least, that the inaccuracy of the common translation of Heb. ix. 16, 17. is not yet sufficiently established. The original runs thus—Ὁπȣ γαρ διαϑήκη, ϑανατον αναγκη φερεσϑαι τȣ διαϑεμενȣ. Διαϑηκη γαρ ἐπὶ νεκροῖς βεϐαία, ἐπεὶ μή ποτε ἰσχυει, ὁτε ζῆ ὁ διαϑεμενος.— Our translators have thus rendered these verses: " For where a testament *is,* there must also of necessity be the death of the testator. For a testament *is* of force after men are dead ; otherwise it is of no strength at all while the testator liveth." Dr Macknight's version, on the contrary, is as follows : " For where a covenant, THERE IS a necessity that the death of the appointed SACRIFICE be brought in. For a covenant is firm over dead SACRIFICES, seeing it never hath force, while the appointed SACRIFICE liveth." * The capitals are his own, intended to distinguish the words which he supplies.

The term διαϑηκη, it is allowed, is generally rendered by our translators *covenant;* and it is the expression by which the *Seventy,* with very few exceptions, have uniformly translated the Hebrew word ברית, *berith.* This Hebrew term, however, about the derivation of which Etymologists are not agreed, although it is often employed to signify a *covenant,* is indisputably used also to denote a *sure promise,* and an *irreversible statute ;†* and according to Dr Owen, it is the only term by which a *testament* could have been expressed either in Hebrew or Syriac. The Greek word διαϑηκη literally signifies, in general, a *disposition, settlement, arrangement, dispensation.* That, in consequence of the manner in which this term is employed in the Septuagint, it was often considered among the Jews as synonymous with συνϑηκη, which is the proper Greek expression for a *covenant,* is readily granted. But what proof can be produced that they never understood διαϑηκη in any other acceptation ?—If the opinion of *Parkhurst* be entitled to any regard, *dispensation* would be a more eligible English word for it in most of the places where the term *covenant* is employed. " I am aware," says he, after having specified a number of instances in which it occurs, " that in most of the preceding passages our translators have rendered the word διαϑηκη by *covenant;* and a very erroneous and dangerous opinion has been built on that exposition, as if *polluted guilty* man could *covenant* or *contract* with God for his salvation, or had any thing else to do in this matter, but humbly to *submit* and *accept of* God's *dispensation* of purifi-

* A New literal Translation of all the Apostolical Epistles, with a Commentary, &c. *in loc.*
† See Witsius's Economy of the Covenants, Book i. ch. 1. sect. 3.

cation and salvation through the all-atoning sacrifice of - - - Christ Jesus." *

That διαθηκη usually signifies a *testament* in classical Greek, has been proved by several writers, and is conceded by Macknight. If, therefore, amongst the numerous passages in which it occurs in the writings of the Evangelists and Apostles, a few instances are found in which this is probably or certainly its meaning, the circumstance need not appear surprising. According to *Schleusner*, it is used in this acceptation in Gal. iii. 15. where our translators have rendered it *covenant*, and also in the passage under consideration, in which they have justly rendered it *testament*. The late *Dr Campbell*, too, who is generally esteemed the most eminent Biblical Critic that has ever yet adorned the Church of Scotland, and who, to say the least, was no zealous advocate for the peculiarities of Calvinism, whilst he urges the rendering of διαθηκη by the word *covenant* in most places where our translation has *testament*, makes an express exception with reference to Heb. ix. 16, 17. He admits that here the author of the Epistle " makes an allusion to the classical acceptation of the term ;" and that " it was necessary to give a different turn to the expression in that passage, in order to make the author's argument as intelligible to the English, as it is, in the original, to the Greek reader."†

According to the view which our translators have taken of the passage, the sense of both verses is clear and pertinent, their grammatical construction natural, and their several members are aptly connected. Τʊ διαθεμενʊ in verse 16th, and ὁ διαθεμενος verse 17th, correspond quite naturally with διαθηκη as well in signification as in etymology and sound ; and, in conformity with what *Mr Pierce* allows to be the usual meaning of the expression, signify *the person that bequeathes*, or the *testator*. Nor is the phrase ἐπι νεκροις improperly translated—"after men are dead." Dr Macknight indeed says—"Our translators have supplied the word ἀνθρωποις, and have translated ἐπι νεκροις *after men are dead ;* contrary to the propriety of the phrase." But νεκροι, be it observed, in its various inflexions, is employed at least upwards of sixty times in the New Testament to signify *dead men*, the word ἀνθρωποι being uniformly *understood*. After a somewhat careful search, we have not been able to discover a single instance of the kind, where ἀνθρωποι is expressed. See for example Mat. viii. 22. Acts x. 42. 1 Cor. xv. 12, 13, 15, 29, 35, 42. Heb. xi. 19, 35. xiii. 20. Rev. xiv. 13. Nor, in the gene-

---

* Greek Lexicon, on Διαθηκη, I. 1.
† Preliminary Dissertations, Dis. v. part 3, sect. 1.

rality of places, did the genius of the English language require, that
our translators should express the word *men*. It was better, for instance, to say, " Blessed are the dead that die in the Lord," than to
have said, " Blessed are the dead *men* that die in the Lord." In
a few passages, however, they have very properly expressed the word
men, as in the one before us, and in Mat. xxiii. 27, where they have
said—" full of dead *men's* bones." Νεκροι alone, it may be added,
without ἀνθρωποι, is used precisely in the same way in the Septuagint. See, for example, Psalm lxxxviii. 5, 10. cxv. 17. Eccles. ix.
5. Isaiah viii. 19. xxvi. 19. On supposition, therefore, that by
νεκροις the Apostle meant *dead men*, it would have been quite super-
fluous, and contrary as well to his own practice and that of the other
sacred writers as to the established idiom of the language, to have
added the word ἀνθρωποις.

No violence, besides, is done to the preposition ἐπι, when the
phrase is rendered " *after* men are dead." This preposition, when
governing the dative case, not unfrequently signifies *after*.* The
expression in Mark vi. 52, " For they considered not," ἐπι τοις
ἀρτοις, properly means, not *over* or *upon*, but *after*—" in consequence
of the loaves," i. e. having been miraculously multiplied. When we
read Acts xi. 19. of those that were " scattered abroad upon the persecution that arose," ἐπι Στεφάνῳ, the most natural rendering seems
to be, not " about Stephen," but *after Stephen*, i. e. in consequence
of Stephen's arraignment and death. In Philip. ii. 27, λυπην ἐπι
λυπη could not be more justly rendered than thus—*sorrow after
sorrow*. In like manner, the expression before us, ἐπι νεκροις, is correctly translated *after men are dead*. It thus forms a direct contrast, too, with the phrase in the last part of the verse, ὅτε ζῇ ὁ δια-
θέμενος, " *while* the testator liveth." The preposition ἐπι connected
with the dative, it may be added, is susceptible of another meaning,
equally or almost equally favourable to our present purpose. It may
signify *by, through, by means of*. If the expression, Philip. iii. 9.
" the righteousness which is of God," ἐπι τη πιστει, *by faith*," teaches
us that we are interested in the righteousness spoken of by means
of faith, ἐπι νεκροις might also import that it is *by the dead*, or *by
means of men becoming dead*, that a testament is valid, " firm," or
" of force."

Whilst these remarks seem to justify the conclusion that the version which our translators have given of these two verses is perfectly

* See Parkhurst's Greek Lexicon on ᾽ἐπι.

natural and just, that which the learned Doctor has ventured to substitute in their place, is quite the reverse. After τὸ διαθεμενῦ in verse 16th, he thinks proper to *supply* the word θυματος or ζωῦ, and to render the expression, " *the appointed* SACRIFICE." *But he produces no* PARALLEL *expression from any author sacred or profane, to vindicate the turn he thus gives to the phrase.** Besides, as Mr Bell

---

* The fact is, that neither διαθεμενος, nor any other part of the verb διατιθημι, appears to be at all employed by the Apostle Paul, who was most probably the inspired penman of this Epistle, or by any of the other writers of the New Testament, when they intend to take notice of persons, times, sacrifices, or other things, simply as *appointed*, *ordained*, or *determined*. It is various other terms that are made use of on such occasions. The expression in Heb. iii. 2. is ποιησαντι—in ch. v. 1. and viii. 3. καθισταται—in ch. ix. 6. κατεσκυασμενων—in verse 27. αποκειται. To notice the other Epistles of Paul, we have Rom. xiii. 1. τεταγμενα—1 Cor. vii. 17. διατασσομαι—Gal. iii. 19. διαταγεις—Ephes. ii. 10. προητοιμασεν—1 Thes. iii. 3. κειμεθα—ch. v. 9. ἐθετο—Tit. i. 5. καταστησης. In the same Apostle's discourses as recorded in the *Acts*, we find, ch. xiii. 48. τεταγμενοι—ch. xvii. 26. ὁρισας προτεταγμενους καιρους—verse 31. ἐστησεν ἡμεραν - - - ὡ ὡρισε. The reader, if he chooses to be at the trouble to consult the writings of the other sacred penmen of the New Testament, will obtain similar results; as in Mat. xxvii. 10. Mark iii. 14. Luke iii. 13. xxii. 22. John xv. 16. Acts i. 22, 23. iv. 28. vi. 3. x. 42. xvi. 4. In the Greek Version of the Old Testament, too, it is perhaps equally difficult to discover a passage in which διαθεμενος is employed to signify *appointed*. The following quotations may suffice. In Gen. xxx. 28. " *Appoint* me my wages," the expression is διαστειλον—Exod. ix. 5. " The Lord *appointed* a set time," ἐδωκεν ὁ θεος ὁρον—Numb. iv. 19. " *Appoint* them every one to his service," καταστησουσιν—ch. xxviii. 6. " *It is a continual burnt-offering which was* ORDAINED *in Mount Sinai*," γενομενη—1 Kings xii. 32, 33. " Jereboam *ordained* a feast," ἐποιησε—2 Chron. xxiii. 18. " to offer the offerings, as it was *ordained* by David διεστειλεν—Ps. xl. 6. " Burnt-offerings and sin-offerings *hast thou not required*" ουκ ἠτησας—xliv. 11. " Thou hast given us like sheep *appointed for meat*," προβατα βρωσεως. Phrases similar to this last are employed also in Ps. lxxix. 11. cii. 20. Nothing could justify the writer, he is aware, in producing so many quotations on this topic, except the importance of a correct interpretation of the sacred oracles, and the obvious tendency of these passages, as thus collected and compared, to support the authorised, which he conceives to be the just translation of Heb. ix. 16, 17. Let it not be thought that the expression Luke xxii. 29. " And I *appoint*, διατιθεμαι, unto you a kingdom, as my Father hath *appointed*, διεθετο, unto me,"—the *only* passage to which Dr Macknight has referred—is prejudicial to our argument ; for in that verse the word does not refer to *simple appointing*, but denotes a solemn *allotting* or *making over* of the kingdom by the Father to Christ, and by Christ to his disciples. In Dr Campbell's Version, accordingly, the word is rendered *grant*. The only other passages, beside the one before us, where διατιθεμαι occurs in the New Testament, are Acts iii. 25. Heb. viii. 10. x. 16, in all of which it signifies the *making* of a covenant.—Nor let it be alleged in defence of Macknight's Version, that although διαθεμενος be nowhere else used in the Scriptures to denote an *appointed sacrifice*, or any thing

observes, διαθεμενος, being the participle of the second Aorist of the Middle Voice, which has properly and most frequently an *active*, not a passive signification, if the word *appoint* is adopted at all, it should be rendered not *the appointed*, but the *appointer*. Accordingly, it may be worth while to state, that *Mr Pierce*, while he discards the idea of a *testator*, and employs the term *pacifier* in its room, still gives the original word an *active* signification; and that, in like manner, it is employed in an *active* sense in the only quotation which he

whatever merely as appointed, yet the Apostle having employed the term διαθηκη at the beginning of the verse, it was natural for him to use the word διαθεμενε at the close. If by διαθηκη he really meant a *testament*, and if, in accordance with that idea, he employed τε διαθεμενε to signify the *testator*, this was certainly the most appropriate term for his purpose, and it will be difficult to point out another at all suitable, not to say equally pertinent. But if he had no thought of a testament, —if by διαθηκη in these two verses he intended exclusively a *covenant*, and if he proposed to speak of an *appointed* sacrifice, nothing, it should seem, but a predilection for a jingle, could have induced him to employ the word διαθεμενε. On that supposition, he would, in all probability, have chosen some one of the other terms commonly used by himself and other sacred writers to express the idea of a thing's being appointed or required. Is it consistent with the accuracy, gravity, or dignity of an inspired writer, to sacrifice alike perspicuity and propriety to mere alliteration, or harmony of sounds?

The Greek scholar is requested further to observe, that, according to *Macknight*, θυματος a *sacrifice*, or ζωε an *animal*, should be supplied to agree with τε διαθεμενε verse 16th, while he supplies a different word—μοσχος, τραγος, or ταυρος, a *calf, goat,* or *bull,* to agree with ο διαθεμενος verse 17th. The truth is, that ο διαθεμενος is necessarily *masculine*, and τε διαθεμενε may be either *masculine* or *neuter*, as the structure of the sentence requires. In this passage both these expressions unquestionably refer to the very same person, or else the very same thing. To consider both therefore as masculine, as our translators have done, is, without doubt, most agreeable to nature. Why then does the Doctor entertain the unnatural supposition of a diversity of genders? The reason is manifest; the Lexicons could not readily furnish him with a Greek word in the *masculine* gender, that signifies an *animal, victim,* or *sacrifice;* and, in the estimation of an attentive reader, it might have thrown discredit on his version, had he alleged that τε διαθεμενε, verse 16th, must denote distinctly a *calf, goat,* or *bull.* It was equally impossible for him, on the other side, to compel ο διαθεμενος, verse 17th, to agree with θυμα or ζωον, and thus to signify in general a *sacrifice* or *animal;* and, in consequence, he sagaciously alleges, that a *calf, goat,* or *bull,* must be supplied, while, in order to make his version the more plausible, he takes the liberty to repeat the general term *sacrifice*. From *Griesbach's* edition of the New Testament it appears, that some ancient manuscripts have διατιθεμενε v. 16, instead of διαθεμενε; and that one Manuscript gives διατιθεμενος, v. 17. in place of διαθεμενος. But it does not appear, that any one ancient copy reads το διαθεμενον instead of ο διαθεμενος, or gives the least countenance to the notion that this word refers to a *sacrifice*, or to any thing except a *testator*.

produces in support of this interpretation, namely, a passage from *Appian*.* Unity and connexion, as *Mr Bell* particularly shows, require a correspondence betwixt διαθηκη at the beginning and διαθιμενȣ at the conclusion of the sentence. Were the one rendered a *disposition* or *appointment,* the other should be the *disposer* or *appointer.* If the one is a *covenant,* the other is the *covenanter;* and if the one is a *testament,* the other is of course the *testator.* Which of these different modes of rendering these two corresponding terms affords the best sense, it does not appear hard to determine. Those interpreters who have abandoned the natural translation of διαθεμενȣ, and διαθεμενος, have generally been much at a loss to fix upon another. *Dr Doddridge* seems not a little embarrassed, and accordingly, after stating both *Mr Pierce's* opinion and his own, has the candour to add; " yet I acknowledge considerable difficulties attend both these interpretations."

The new translation of επι νεκροις, which Doddridge renders *over the dead,* and Macknight " over dead SACRIFICES," seems equally indefensible. The preposition επι may indeed signify *over,* when this suits the connexion; but if it is wrong to interpret νεκροις as referring to *dead sacrifices, over* must be set aside, and give place to *after.* Macknight justly observes, that " νεκροις being an adjective, it must have a substantive agreeing with it either expressed or understood." But we have seen what substantive is understood, and how unnecessary, and how contrary to established practice, it would have been for the inspired writer to *express* the substantive. The Doctor alleges that θυμασι *sacrifices,* or ζωοις *animals,* is the substantive understood; but he does not produce a single example from the New Testament, or any other book, in which νεκροι, without a substantive expressed, is employed to signify dead sacrifices or animals. According to the sense in which our translators considered the passage, there was not the shadow of a necessity for *expressing* the substantive either after the participle διαθεμενȣ and διαθεμενος, or after the adjective νεκροις, the substantive understood being quite obvious to every one capable of reading Greek. But if the new translation be the just one, the substantive could *not* be obvious to the reader of the original, and the omission of it by the inspired writer in all these three instances was very singular, and has, in fact, rendered this a " hitherto ill understood passage," and involved it in almost impenetrable darkness—darkness to be dissipated only by the bright

---

* Διαθεμενος δε τους ενοχλουντας 'ως εδυνατο, " But having pacified them who troubled him," viz. his creditors, " as well as he could." - - *Lib.* ii. *De Bello Civili.*

lucubrations of the eighteenth century. This rare discovery appears indeed to have been in some degree anticipated, about the middle of the preceding century, in a Dissertation published by one *Codurcus.**

The translation, in short, of verses 16th and 17th given in our authorised Version, is so entirely natural and unexceptionable, that were the original seen any where as a *separate* or independent paragraph, no one acquainted with Greek, whether his knowledge of that language were superficial or profound, would ever think of its referring to any thing else than a *testament*, and its confirmation by the death of *the testator*. In this view, the expressions are correct, clear, and energetic ; and the sentiments conveyed, indisputably just. Add to this, that when the paragraph is contemplated in its *relative* position in this interesting portion of the sacred volume, the sense which our translators have preferred, receives powerful support. Although the Apostle, in the course of his reasoning in this admirable Epistle, borrows his illustrations chiefly from the typical institutions of the Mosaic ritual, it is by no means foreign to his manner to allude occasionally to well known usages founded in the law of nature, and generally observed alike among Jews and Gentiles. If in a preceding part of the work† he makes an allusion to the universal sentiments and practice of mankind with regard to the form, design, and effect of an *oath*, it should not appear surprising that he here refers to their universal sentiments and practice relative to the making of a *testament*, and the means of its becoming valid and unalterable.—The covenant of grace, besides, according to the doctrine of Paul throughout this Epistle, is a covenant of absolute and unconditional promises, ratified by the death of Christ.‡ What then could be more appropriate, better adapted to his purpose, or more directly calculated at once to enlighten the judgment and refresh the heart of the Christian, than to represent this covenant under the notion of a *testament*, and a testament confirmed by the death of the *testator* ? This representation of the matter was neither incorrect, nor utterly unprecedented. See Mat. xxvi. 28. Luke xxii. 29. John xiv. 27.

The immediate context, too, supplies arguments in defence of the common translation. At the close of the 15th verse we find the expression—" that they who are called might receive the promise of the eternal inheritance." The blessings of eternal life are thus exhibited as an *inheritance*—an inheritance *promised*, as was the

---

* See Pool's *Synopsis* on Heb. ix. 16.
† Ch. vi. 16—18.   ‡ See ch. viii. 8—12. x. 16—18.

earthly Canaan to the ancient Israelites, not merited by themselves —and an inheritance reserved for them who are *called ;* not, as some affirm, those who procure an interest in it by their own faith and virtue, but those whom God " hath called with an holy calling, not according to their good works, but according to his own purpose and grace." What could be more natural, in consequence, than for the inspired writer, in the sentence immediately following, to speak of a *testament* in which the whole *inheritance* is freely bequeathed by him who is at once the Mediator, the Priest, the Surety, the Testator, in a word, the " all in all" of this glorious and beneficent, arrangement, whether it be viewed as a *covenant* or a *testament ?*

It has been objected to our interpretation, that it is improper to speak of the *mediator of a testament ;* and that it is absurd to represent the Mosaic covenant, or dispensation, under the idea of a *testament*. But as this Note has already far exceeded its intended limits, let it suffice to refer the reader to the satisfactory replies which *Mr Bell* has made to these objections, in the Note alluded to above.

Dr Macknight's translation of the word φερεσθαι, it may be observed, is quite proper, and fully accords with the sense of the passage now contended for. The 16th verse, therefore, may be read thus : " Where a testament is, there is a necessity that the death of the testator *be brought in ;*" i. e. as the Doctor explains it from *Elsner, produced and proved,* or made apparent. The expression carries an allusion to the forms of a court of judicature.—In justice to the common version, it must be added, that it gives the same expression—*brought in,* on the margin.

It only remains, in conclusion, to advert to those sentences of *Witsius,* in which he speaks of God the Father as a Testator, and even says that he " did, by testament, intrust his Son Jesus Christ with this honour, that he should be the head of the elect," &c. The Scriptures, no doubt, represent God the Father as the Maker of that everlasting covenant on which our hopes depend, and as the original Giver of all its promises, whether relating immediately to Christ or to his spiritual seed. The Father, too, displayed his sovereign love towards " the man Christ Jesus," in expressly and particularly choosing him to be received into personal union with his dear Son, and exalted to subsequent honours ; and it was by a solemn and irreversible transaction, that he intrusted Christ with all his mediatorial offices and dignities. But when the covenant is viewed as a *testament,* it is more congruous, and more in unison with the phraseology of sacred writ, to speak of it merely as the *testament of Christ ;* of

whom alone it can be affirmed, that he died to ratify the testament.*
Our excellent Author seems to have been led to make use of the expressions referred to, principally by the view he took of Luke xxii.
29, which he somewhat improperly renders—" I appoint to you by
testament a kingdom, as my Father hath *by testament* appointed to
me." The truth is, that the verb διατιθημι, from which διαθηκη, the
term illustrated above, is derived, signifies in general to *dispose*,† or
to *make over*, to another some valuable possession. This verb can
refer either to a testament, or a covenant, or to a transaction somewhat different from both, as the connexion may require. Whilst
there are points of resemblance betwixt the manner in which the
Father has allotted a kingdom to Christ, and the manner in which
Christ allots a kingdom to his followers, there must, at the same time,
be circumstances of dissimilarity. Did the sound principles of interpretation render it necessary to express that difference in a version,
the one proposed by *Mr Bell* might perhaps be adopted ; " I *bequeath*
unto you, as my Father hath *covenanted* unto me, a kingdom."‡ But
it seems more consonant to accuracy and the dictates of good taste, to
employ a general term equally applicable, if possible, to both parts of
the sentence ; which has been attempted by our translators, the Vulgate, and several other Versions. *Dr Campbell's* Note on this and
the two subsequent verses, deserves, however, to be consulted.

Note XLIII. Page 172.

Our Author's illustration of *the possession of the whole world* as a
blessing of the testament is truly pious and consolatory. It is a comment on that striking expression, Rom. iv. 13. " For the promise
that he should be *the heir of the world* was not to Abraham, or to his
seed, through the law, but through the righteousness of faith."
Witsius appears to consider these words as relating immediately to
the competent share of earthly good secured to believers, the sanctified enjoyment of this world, and the subserviency of all the creatures to their spiritual advantage ; and as bearing an ultimate reference to " the new heavens and new earth, wherein dwelleth righteousness." Nor is he quite singular in this interpretation. *Calvin*,
Hammond, and *Macknight*, as well as the continuators of *Pool*, seem
to have understood the expression in nearly the same sense. These
interpreters, however, discover a greater inclination than our Author

---

* See *Dr Guyse's* last Note on Heb. vii. 22. and *Boston's* View of the Covenant
of Grace, Head iv. Christ the Testator of the Covenant.
† According to the Scottish dialect, to *disponc.*
‡ Translation of the *Irenicum*, p. 292.

to consider " the promise that he should be heir of the world," as
referring directly to the promise of the earthly Canaan, which was
an emblem of " the better country, even the heavenly." Yet there
are difficulties attending this view of the phrase. That Canaan was
promised to Abraham and his seed, is allowed. That the promise
included a still more extensive worldly inheritance, and that for some
time Abraham's natural posterity were in actual possession of it to
the full extent of the grant recorded in Gen. xv. 18—21, is also admitted. It is nowhere expressly said, nevertheless, in the Old Testament Scriptures, that Abraham was to be *the heir of the world*, and
none of these Commentators has pointed out any other passage in
holy writ where Canaan is styled *the world*. Had the Greek term
in Rom. iv. 13. been γῆς *of the land*, instead of κοσμυ *of the world*, it
would have been natural to conclude that the land of Canaan was
intended, or rather, as the whole context relates to the great blessing
of justification, which includes a title to eternal life, that the expression refers chiefly to the heavenly country, of which Canaan
was a type. But since the Apostle speaks of " the promise that he
should be heir of *the world*," it is not surprising that a somewhat
different view of the meaning has occurred to many attentive readers
and judicious interpreters. It is indeed affirmed that in the *Chaldee
Paraphrase* on Numbers xxiii. 13, the Israelites are said to *inherit
the world*.* It is urged also, that since *the world* is sometimes used
synecdochically to signify a part of the world, it might be very aptly employed to denote the land of Canaan, which was an important,
delightful, and highly-favoured portion of the globe. In spite of
these arguments, however, the idea recurs, that the sacred writers are
not accustomed to call Canaan the world, and that it was hardly to
be expected that Paul, in a plain didactic passage of an epistle, would
give it this designation. It is at least equally foreign to the usage
of the inspired penmen to speak directly of heaven under the general appellation of *the world*, accompanied by no distinctive epithet
whatever. To what else then can the expression be applied? *Chrysostome, Origen,* and other Greek fathers, were of opinion that the promise was given to Abraham that he should be " heir of the world" in
this respect, that it was promised to him that he should be the father of many nations, and that all the nations of the world should
be blessed in him ; and this interpretation has been adopted and defended by a considerable proportion of the most distinguished modern
Theologians, as *Beza, Parœus, Whitby, Doddridge,* and *Guyse.*

---

* *Glassius,* as quoted in Pool's *Synopsis* on the place.

Doddridge explains it as "his inheriting a seed out of all nations, whom he might be said to possess in such a sense as children are said to be a heritage, Ps. cxxvii. 3. Compare Gen. iv. 1. Prov. xvii. 6." The following comprehensive Note by Dr Guyse throws much light on the subject.

" This verse," says he, on Rom. iv. 13, " is apparently brought in as an argument to prove what had been said in the two foregoing verses about Abraham's being the father of all them that believe, whether they be Jews or Gentiles, through the righteousness of the faith which he had while he was uncircumcised; and therefore it seems inconsistent with the nature and design of the Apostle's reasoning to understand Abraham's being *heir of the world* literally of his being heir of the land of *Canaan :* For *that* was to be the inheritance of only his natural descendants, or of them that were circumcised; so that if the Apostle had any reference to the promised land, it could be only as it was a type of heaven. But I take Abraham's being heir of the world to be a phrase of much the same import with his being *the father of all them that believe,* whether they be circumcised or not, as he was called ver. 11. or with his being *the father of many nations,* as it is expressed by way of explication and further proof ver. 17. And as the heir is the head of the family, and signified, in *Jewish* language, the lord and possessor of its inheritance: So Abraham was the heir of the believing world that is scattered through all nations, as the promise of spiritual and heavenly blessings, as well as of a covenant-right to all temporal good things, was made first to him, and transmitted from him to them according to the covenant made with him; and so they are blessed with him as his *heirs according to the promise,*" Gal. iii. 8, 9, 29.

The writer cannot omit to mention, that the late *Dr George Lawson* of Selkirk, whilst he acknowledged the difficulty attending this expression, adopted materially the same views of its meaning with Dr Guyse. That truly learned and excellent man had occasion to notice this subject, in a course of Critical Lectures on the Epistle to the Romans which he delivered to his Students, and which, to their unfeigned regret, they never could prevail with him to publish.

The most plausible objection to this interpretation is, that the Apostle appears to state that the promise of the inheritance of the world belonged to Abraham's *seed* as well as to himself. This circumstance was not " forgotten," as Dr Macknight alleges, by *Beza.* That celebrated critic, on the contrary, expressly brings forward and replies to the objection. The substance of his answer is as follows.

—Abraham alone, strictly speaking, is *the heir of the world.* To understand the Apostle's expression, we must attend to the mutual relation between the father and the children. When God said to Abraham that he would make him " the father of many nations," the promise implied at the same time that a multitude of nations should have Abraham for their father, and be blessed with him, conformably to that gracious assurance, " I will be a God unto thee, and to thy seed after thee." Distinguishing favour was manifested at once to the father and his offspring. The Apostle, therefore, when he intends to show that all who possess the faith of Abraham, circumcised or uncircumcised, are to be considered his seed, has justly stated that the promise belongs not to Abraham only, but also to his seed. Yet in referring to the terms (the "*formula*") of the promise, he has expressed merely that which relates to the father, leaving what concerns the seed to be understood by the reader. Had he expressed the matter completely, it would have been to this effect ; " For the promise to Abraham that he should be the heir of the world, or to his seed, that they should be the inheritance of Abraham and share with him in the blessedness spoken of, was not through the law, but through the righteousness of faith."

Such is the sum of Beza's reply. Every inquirer can judge for himself ; and if the learned reader wishes to see a more ample account of the different opinions that have been entertained on this question, and of the arguments by which they are respectively supported, he may consult an instructive Dissertation on this subject by *Dr Marck,* the friend of Witsius and author of his Funeral Oration.*

Note XLIV. Page 173.

The venerable Author, after briefly stating his views with respect to the *Testament,* as having no stipulations or conditions, properly so called, but consisting of absolute and unmixed promises, refers the reader to another work, in which he has discussed this topic at greater length. He alludes, without doubt, to his Treatise *on the Covenants,* Book iii. ch. 1. sect. 8—20.—a passage well entitled to an attentive perusal. " The condition of a covenant," he observes, " properly so styled, is an action the performance of which gives a right to the reward. But that a condition of this nature cannot be required of us in the covenant of grace is self-evident ; because a right to life neither is nor can be founded in any action of ours, but

* *Scripturariæ Exercitationes,* Ex. xx. pp. 612—618.

in the righteousness of our Lord alone. The righteousness of the law having been perfectly fulfilled by him in our stead, nothing can in justice be required of us in order to procure a right already fully purchased for us. In this sentiment, indeed, all the Orthodox readily agree." To confirm this position, he illustrates the *testamentary* nature of the new covenant from Gal. iii. 15. Heb. viii. 10. ix. 15—20. Luke xxii. 29. He did not intend, he declares, to confound the notions of a covenant and a testament, but only to show that the covenant of grace partakes of the nature of a testament, and must be distinguished from a covenant which depends upon a compact or condition. He then quotes *Cloppenburg* and *Junius* as holding the same sentiments with himself. " The conditions being fulfilled," says the latter, " by Jesus Christ the angel of the covenant, the whole church, on his account, was appointed, without any condition, to inherit eternal life." The Author next shows from Jer. xxxi. xxxii. that " the Gospel strictly taken consists of pure promises of grace and glory ;" and that " whatever might be conceived to hold the place of a condition, is in reality comprehended within the range of those gracious and extensive promises." After these remarks, he proceeds to state, that none are admitted to heaven but those who believe in Christ, and, as opportunity is afforded, show their faith by their works. Faith and holiness, nevertheless, are not proper conditions of the covenant. They are, " on the part of God, the execution of previous promises and the earnest of future bliss; and on the part of man, the performance of those duties, which cannot fail to precede the full perfection of a soul that delights in God." At all events, they are not so much the condition of the *covenant*, as of the *assurance* that we ourselves stand in a new covenant relation to Jehovah as our God. After some further illustrations, he shows that faith, repentance, and newness of life, must by no means be considered as conditions of the covenant of grace in the same way in which perfect obedience was the condition of the covenant of works; and he accurately distinguishes betwixt the agency of faith as an instrument by which the meritorious righteousness of Christ, the only proper condition of the covenant, is received, and the importance of other spiritual graces and of good works, as evidences of faith and of union to Christ. Such is the scope of that passage in the Treatise on the Covenants to which the Author here refers.

Calvin, Mastricht, Guthrie, and many other excellent Divines, have styled faith the condition of the covenant. Even in the *Larger Catechism* compiled by the Westminster Assembly, it is said that faith in Christ is required of men as " the condition to interest them

in him."[*]   Evangelical Theologians, it must be observed, are far
from inculcating faith, repentance, and holy obedience, as *co-ordinate*
conditions of the covenant, or co-ordinate terms of salvation.   " To
represent repentance distinguished from faith," says Mr Fraser of
Alness, " as in a class of *co-ordinate* conditionality with faith in the
matter of justification, or attaining an interest in the covenant of
grace and blessings thereof, I cannot consider otherwise than as a
notion ill-founded, and of hurtful tendency."[†]   When the Divines
referred to speak even of faith as the condition of justification or
salvation, they by no means attribute our justification or salvation to
faith as a meritorious or procuring cause.   They are fully aware,
as the writer just quoted states, that " faith derives its virtue to
justify the sinner from its blessed object, and not from any thing
in a man previous, concomitant, or subsequent to his faith, however
certainly connected true unfeigned faith is with good dispositions and good works."[‡]   They consider faith merely as a condition
of *order* or *connexion,* as it is styled, and as an instrument by which
the justifying righteousness and complete salvation of Christ are received.   The Westminster Assembly, as Mr Bell remarks, seem to
have employed *condition* and *instrument* as synonymous or convertible
expressions ; for whilst, in the Question referred to above, they represent faith as the condition to interest sinners in the Mediator,
they affirm in the *Confession,* that " faith is the alone instrument of
justification ;"[§] and in reply to the 73d Question, they teach that
" faith justifies a sinner in the sight of God, only as it is an instrument by which he receiveth and applieth Christ and his righteousness."

It is doubtless incumbent on the teachers of Christianity to ap-
prise their hearers in the most explicit, earnest, and affectionate
manner, that without faith no man is vitally united to Christ, clothed with his justifying righteousness, or capable of serving him
aright ; and that without holiness in heart and practice, none shall
ever enter the abodes of eternal bliss.   Every part of the counsel of
God should be seasonably and faithfully delivered ; and every scriptural argument, calculated to repress that *antinomian* spirit, that
aversion to Christian purity and diligence which prevails among a
great proportion of the hearers of the gospel, should be zealously and
assiduously employed.   The doctrine of grace, however, although, in
common with other instances of the Divine benignity, it is sometimes
perverted by the depravity of man, must neither be entirely withheld,

* Quest. 32.   † Doctrine of Sanctification, p. 490.
‡ Ibid.   § Ch. xi. 2.

nor sparingly administered, nor exhibited in a feeble or mutilated form; and on this as well as other topics the prudent and faithful Preacher will study "to find out acceptable words," and to make use of "sound speech that cannot be condemned." The friends of truth indeed ought to "forbear one another in love;" and whilst on points of importance they cordially agree in sentiment, and differ only in modes of expression, no one of them should make another " an offender for" either scrupulously avoiding or solicitously retaining " a word." Yet since the term *condition*, as applied to the exercises or attainments of man with reference to matters of salvation, does not expressly occur in Sacred Writ, since it is confessedly susceptible of different acceptations, and since it is frequently employed and understood in an unsound and dangerous sense, it is not surprising that many warm admirers of evangelical truth have determined to shun this word, and have sometimes expressed their antipathy to it with considerable vehemence. " Faith does not justify us," says the Rev. John Brown, " as a preparing quality, or as a *condition* even of the lowest kind. - - - Faith, as a disposing qualification or condition, would be a work of the law, and so undermine and tarnish the free grace of God in our salvation."* " Faith," says the late Rev. John Russel, " is not the condition of our justification. Though the word *condition* be frequently used by pious writers, yet as it is confessed to be ambiguous, if we wish to rescue the *truth* from the imputation of *ambiguity,* the use of it ought to be laid aside. - - - Sometimes the word condition denotes a treaty of agreement, either proposed or accepted. - - - At other times it is taken in a judicial or law sense, denoting an article in any treaty, the fulfilling of which ratifies the treaty, and entitles to reward ; and, on the other hand, when any deficiency appears with regard to the performance of the stipulation, the treaty is supposed to be broken, and the person chargeable with that deficiency subjected to the penalty. - - - In this last sense faith cannot, with the least propriety, be represented as the condition of our justification. To admit a sentiment of this kind, would be in so many words to say that justification was the reward of our faith ; that we were possessed of power to perform this condition ; that in justification we had reason to glory before God ; and that the covenant of grace was turned into a covenant of works. What man is there who professes a belief of the revelation vouchsafed to us by God, who ought not to be ashamed of an attachment to such opinions as these ? Opinions which, if they were true, would render the Bible of no more use to

---

* Compendious View of Natural and Revealed Religion, Book v. ch. 2. last par.

us than the Alkoran of Mahomet.—See Mr Abraham Taylor on Faith."*

The doctrine of grace, it is well known, was zealously defended by the Rev. James Hog, Thomas Boston, Gabriel Wilson, Ebenezer and Ralph Erskine, and other Clergymen, who united in a Representation and Petition to the General Assembly of the Church of Scotland, respecting their Act of 1720 relative to the book entitled *The Marrow of Modern Divinity*. Whoever wishes to see an authentic account of the sentiments of these Divines with reference to the subject of this Note, will consult, with much advantage, a late publication, formerly noticed, by the Rev. John Brown, Whitburn, entitled, *Gospel Truth accurately stated and defended*, &c.†—The absurdity of making *sincere obedience* a proper *condition of salvation* is briefly but effectually exposed by the *Vicar of Everton*, an Author who communicates much important and salutary instruction with a vein of pleasantry which is evidently natural, but perhaps indulged occasionally somewhat to excess. ‡ The celebrated *Walker*, in fine, a Preacher equally admired by the man of taste for the simple elegance of his diction, and by the devout Christian for the evangelical spirit of his doctrine, often represents the call of the Gospel as expressed " in the most extensive and absolute terms." In the following passage, too, of a Sermon on 1 John v. 11. he has stated, very perspicuously, his views of what are called *conditions* of salvation. " Hence it appears how much they mistake the Gospel-constitution who represent eternal life as a distant reward suspended upon the performance of certain conditions on the part of the creature : whereas salvation through Christ, though perfected in heaven, is a present salvation ; of which the various particulars, which are commonly styled *terms* of acceptance with God, are in truth constituent parts, suited to the present state of Christians, and ought therefore to be considered as the genuine acting, and consequently the proper evidence of life received from Christ, but not as the conditions or means of obtaining it."§

Note XLV. Page 176.

Our Author teaches, that sincere love to his heavenly Father disposes the Christian, when conscious of a new offence, not only to

---

* The Nature of the Gospel Delineated, &c. a Sermon, p. 67. Note.

† Pp. 188, 216, 258, 259, 294, 295, 313, &c.

‡ The Christian World unmasked, by John Berridge, A. M. Vicar of Everton, late Fellow of Clare-hall, Cambridge, &c. pp. 24—39.

§ Sermons on Practical Subjects, by the Rev. Robert Walker, Vol. ii. Ser. 7.

implore pardon with unfeigned sorrow, but also " to *promise* greater circumspection in his future conduct." From this expression, and from similar phrases which occur in the course of this work, it appears, that Witsius did not object to the exercise of *vowing* under the New Testament dispensation: For what is a vow but a solemn promise to God with reference either to some specific service, or to the general course of our conduct. If it was lawful and proper for the saints in ancient times, both in a personal and social capacity, to vow to the God of Jacob, it seems difficult to conceive how the superior light and grace of the Christian economy should transform vowing into a superstitious and unwarrantable practice. The human will, when renewed and sanctified, cannot fail to cherish inclinations and form resolutions hostile to the interests of sin, and favourable to those of holiness. That such inclinations and resolutions should be deliberately and solemnly expressed by the Christian to his God, either in a distinct act of self-dedication, or else whilst he is employed in other religious exercises as prayer or partaking of the Lord's supper, —is in no way contrary to what the suggestions of reason and the natural tendencies of grace would lead us to expect. When the Psalmist strikingly contrasts certain moral and spiritual services of perpetual obligation with those ceremonial rites which were peculiar to the ancient economy, and abolished by the death of Christ, *paying our vows to the Most High* is expressly numbered amongst the former.[*]

The matter of our vows, it is of importance at the same time to remark, should be entirely consonant to the word of God. Nor is it to be forgotten, that we must vow in a right manner,—with knowledge, judgment and deliberation, with godly sincerity, and in particular, under the governing influence of evangelical views and feelings. When men secretly rely on the making or performing of their vows as in some degree the cause of their forgiveness and acceptance, they involve themselves in the guilt and danger of " going about to establish their own righteousness;" and when, instead of confiding in " the grace that is in Christ Jesus," they resolve or promise to conduct themselves with greater circumspection, inwardly depending on their own supposed energy, or on that superadded moral impulse they expect to derive from their solemn resolution or vow, they incur the designation and expose themselves to the disappointments and miseries of the " fool" mentioned by Solomon, " that trusteth in his own heart."[†]

[*] Psalm l. 8—15.　　　　　[†] Prov. xxviii. 26.

Witsius was far from directing any Christian to rely either on sorrow for the past, or on resolutions and promises of increased vigilance for the future, as the ground of pardon. It would have been equally abhorrent from his principles, to encourage resolutions of obedience formed, like those of Peter on a memorable occasion, in presumptuous dependance on human strength and determination. Vowing is so often resorted to by the ignorant and self-righteous as their sheet-anchor and supreme consolation, and owing to the misconceptions and legal propensities incident to real Christians themselves, their performance of this exercise has been so frequently debased by corrupt mixtures, that the exercise itself has fallen into considerable disrepute with many of the most sincere friends of evangelical religion.—" You may expect here," says a well-known writer, " something to be spoken of vows; but I shall only say this of them. Think not to bring yourselves to good by vows and promises, as if the strength of your own law could do it, when the strength of God's law doth it not. - - - The devil will urge you to vow, and then to break, that he may perplex your conscience the more."* The Rev. Andrew Fuller addresses the following caution to persons, to whom affliction has proved the means of impressing the mind in some measure with the importance of religion: " If you abound in vows and promises as to your future life, this is rather a sign that you know but little of yourself, than of a real change for the better."† A small Treatise of uncommon excellence by the late *Dr Haweis* contains this just and striking sentence; " One view of Christ in his transcendently gracious character as the dear Redeemer of lost souls, hath more power and efficacy to break the bonds of sin and urge us to obedience, than all the vows, promises, and resolutions wherewith we can bind our souls."‡ Even the Rev. *Adam Gib*, on grounds which to some of his readers may seem equally applicable to *public covenanting*, appears to recommend it as a more eligible form of *personal covenanting*, to intermingle it with prayer, than to perform it as a distinct and separate exercise. " There is a private covenant," says that writer, " made with God by individual persons separately; what is called personal covenanting." After remarking that this may be done by taking hold of God's covenant of grace, and vowing universal obedience to him, in a written and subscribed deed, he adds; " Yet there is reason to apprehend, that this way of personal covenanting has been often

* Marshall's Gospel Mystery of Sanctification, Direct. xiii. p. 244.
† A short Tract, " To the Afflicted," p. 8.
‡ The Communicant's Spiritual Companion, ch. vi.

mismanaged; and various forms of such a *personal covenant* have
been proposed by different writers of a tendency to mislead Christians as to their method of dealing with God about their souls."
Having adverted to the natural propensity of men to rest upon their
own covenant or exercise respecting it as the immediate ground of
peace, and having observed that a covenant is rightly made only
when the conscience is purged from guilt by faith's application of
the blood of Christ, and the soul sweetly constrained by the Saviour's love, he thus concludes: " Perhaps for guarding against
every old covenant way of it, personal covenanting may be more
properly reduced to the pouring out of the heart before God in
prayer."*

Note XLVI. Page 183.

Our Author's interpretation of the expression in Heb. xi. 3, rendered *worlds*, is clearly just, and coincides exactly with the remarks
which other men of erudition have made on the term. *Michaelis,*
for example, referring both to Heb. i. 2, and ch. xi. 3, has the following observations upon it. " 'Οι αιωνες is constantly used by the
Greek writers as a word expressive of *time*, or as denoting a succession of *ages*. But in the present instance, the context requires for
it a different sense, namely, that of *worlds*. Now the Jews used
their עולם in both senses; for though it literally denotes *sæculum,*
(an age,) yet they frequently applied it in the sense of *mundus,* (the
world.) For instance, they called the earth עולם השפל, that is the
lower world; to the middle regions they gave the name of עולם
התיכון; and the upper regions or the heavens they denoted by
עולם העליון. In no other instance," he adds, " either in the New
Testament or in the Septuagint, is this word used in the sense of
worlds."† Dr Owen‡ gives a similar account of the expression, and
in confirmation of the Jewish distribution of *the worlds*, refers to
Kimchi's comment on Isaiah vi. 3; in which that Rabbi thinks proper,
fancifully enough, to remark, that it is with a reference to the three
worlds that the word *Holy* is three times repeated by the Seraphim.
Grotius and others have strained the term *worlds*, at least in Heb.
i. 3, to signify the new creation, or the Church renewed by the

* Sacred Contemplations, Ch. ii. Sect. ii. p. 117. *et seq.*
† Marsh's Translation of the Introduction to the New Testament by the late
John David Michaelis, Professor in the University of Gottingen, Vol. iv. p. 235.
‡ Exposition of the Epistle to the Hebrews, Ch. i. 2.

evangelical dispensation. But the futility of this Socinian gloss is irrefragably proved by Owen, Whitby, and Dr *Magee*.*

Some writers, it may be noticed in fine, appear to consider ὁι αιωνες in Heb. xi. 3. as comprising not merely the whole system of the universe, but also the revolutions it has experienced, and the events of which it is the scene. Accordingly, Parkhurst on this Greek word observes, that " it seems in Heb. xi. 3. to denote the *various revolutions* and *grand occurrences* which have happened to this created system, including also the *system* or *world* itself." The system itself, however, is the subject at least directly intended; and this was, without question, the opinion of Macknight, to whom Parkhurst apparently refers as friendly to his own comment. " Τ ὒς αιωνας," says that author,—" literally *secula*, the *ages*. But the subsequent clause, *so that things which are seen were not made of things which did appear*, determines its signification to the material fabric of the worlds, comprehending the sun, moon, stars, and earth (called by Moses the heaven and the earth, Gen. i. 1.) by whose duration and revolutions, time, consisting of days, and months, and years, and ages, is measured."†

Note XLVII. Page 205.

The philosopher to whom our Author chiefly alludes in his discussion relative to the infinite extent which has been ascribed to the world, is no doubt *Des Cartes*. Of this celebrated man it has been justly said, " he obtained immortal honour by overthrowing the philosophy of Aristotle; but no doubt he indulged himself in a freedom of speculation not sufficiently restrained by a becoming regard to the dictates of revelation, or the principles of common sense." Dr Reid gives the following account of the manner in which he was led to entertain the idea of the world's *infinity*.

" It was probably owing to an aversion to admit any thing into philosophy of which we have not a clear and distinct conception, that Des Cartes was led to deny that there is any substance in matter distinct from those qualities of it which we perceive. We say that matter is something extended, figured, moveable. Extension, figure, mobility, therefore, are not matter, but qualities belonging to this something which we call *matter*. Des Cartes could not relish this obscure *something*, which is supposed to be the subject or

---

* Discourses and Dissertations on the Scriptural Doctrine of Atonement and Sacrifice, vol. i. Note 1. On the Pre-existence of Christ, and the species of arguments by which this article of the Christian Doctrine has been opposed, pp. 78, 79.
† A new literal Translation, &c. on Heb. xi. 3. Note 1.

substratum of those qualities ; and therefore maintained that extension is the very essence of matter. But as we must ascribe extension to space as well as to matter, he found himself under a necessity of holding that space and matter are the same thing, and differ only in our way of conceiving them ; so that wherever there is space there is matter, and no void left in the universe. The necessary consequence of this is that the material world has no bounds or limits. He did not, however, choose to call it *infinite,* but *indefinite."**

A similar conclusion has been deduced by some men of science from a very different set of premises. The astonishing discoveries supplied by the telescope have so delighted and overwhelmed them, that they can hardly find terms sufficiently strong to express the extent of the creation. *Dr Halley,* for instance, has advanced what he says seems to be a metaphysical paradox, namely, that the number of fixed stars must be more than finite, and some of them at a greater than a finite distance from others. *Addison,* after stating that *Huygenius* " does not think it impossible there may be stars whose light has not yet travelled down to us since their first creation," makes the following remark ; " There is no question but the universe has certain bounds set to it ; but when we consider that it is the work of infinite power, prompted by infinite goodness, with an infinite space to exert itself in, how can our imagination set any bounds to it ?"†

A living Preacher, who has pursued this lofty speculation with splendid eloquence and uncommon ardour, expresses himself in the following terms.—" The contemplation has no limits. If we ask the number of suns and of systems—the unassisted eye of man can take in a thousand, and the best telescope which the genius of man has constructed can take in eighty millions. But why subject the domains of the universe to the eye of man, or to the powers of his genius ? Fancy may take its flight far beyond the ken of eye or telescope. It may expatiate on the outer regions of all that is visible —and shall we have the boldness to say that there is nothing there ? that the wonders of the Almighty are at an end, because we can no longer trace his footsteps ? that his omnipotence is exhausted, because human art can no longer follow him ? that the creative energy of God has sunk into repose, because the imagination is enfeebled by the magnitude of its efforts, and can keep no longer on the wing through those mighty tracts which shoot far beyond what eye hath

---

* Dr Reid on the Intellectual Powers of Man, Essay ii. ch. 3.
† Evidences of the Christian Religion, &c. pp. 85, 86.

seen or the heart of man hath conceived—which sweep endlessly along, and merge into an awful and mysterious infinity ?"[*]

The arguments which Witsius adduces against the hypothesis of Des Cartes, who attributed to the creation an *absolute infinity*, have doubtless very great weight; and the reader who wishes to learn what a profound philosopher is able to advance on the same side of the question, may consult Locke's " Essay on the Human Understanding."[†] Dr Watts' "Philosophical Essays" also contain discussions on the nature and extent of space, the perusal of which will prove at least an entertaining exercise to those who take pleasure in abstract speculation.

Note XLVIII. Page 207.

The learned Author, in the short allusion which he makes to the disputes of chronologers regarding the number of years that has elapsed since the creation, obviously refers to that diversity of opinion upon this point amongst the friends of revelation, which has arisen in a great degree from the discrepancies betwixt the Hebrew copy of the Old Testament Scriptures, the Samaritan, and the Septuagint. The Hebrew copy, which Christians for good reasons now consider as the most authentic, appears to date the creation of the world 3944 years before the birth of Christ. The Samaritan Bible fixes it at 4305. The Septuagint makes it 5270. The calculations of historians and chronologers differ considerably from each other. *Josephus,* according to Dr Wells and Mr Whiston, makes the period between the creation and the Christian era 4658 years. *M. Pezron* extends it to 5872. But *Archbishop Usher,* whose chronology is generally received, makes it 4004.[‡]

It is a curious fact, that nearly all the celebrated writers in the Christian Church, both in the East and West, neglected the Hebrew computations and adhered to the Greek, till in the century before last some of the Roman authors adopted the Hebrew computations, —not because they were Hebrew, but because they tallied with the Latin Vulgate authorised by the Council of Trent. Jerome and Augustine were the only ancient writers of the Church who computed otherwise; and among the moderns, Beza was the first that questioned the correctness of the Greek chronology. For farther

---

[*] A series of Discourses on the Christian Revelation viewed in connexion with the Modern Astronomy, by Thomas Chalmers, D. D. Ser. i.

[†] Book ii. ch. 13. " Of space and its simple modes ;" and ch. 15. " Of duration and expansion considered together."

[‡] See Encycl. Britan. Art. *Creation.*

information respecting this controversy, in so far at least as it relates to the interval betwixt the creation and the deluge, and for an account of the manner in which *Cappel* has attempted to reconcile the difference between the Hebrew copy and the Septuagint, the reader may consult *Shuckford.**

Witsius, justly acquiescing in the Hebrew computations, lays it down as a fixed principle, that at the date of his writing this Treatise, viz. in the year 1681, the world had not reached the age of 6000 years. According to the received chronology, more than 170 years are still necessary to complete that period. But a far higher antiquity, it seems proper to mention, has on various pretexts been assigned to the world; and sceptics have, in consequence, urged the contracted limits of the Mosaic chronology, as a strong objection against the Divine inspiration and authority of Scripture. *Voltaire*, for instance, affirms that the sacred oracles are liable to a great degree of ridicule, because they represent the creation of the world, as having happened only 7000 years ago, while the Chinese trace it back to a much greater number of millions. *Halhed*, too, the Translator of the Code of Hindoo laws, after detailing the monstrous figments of the Indian Brahmins relative to their four Yugs, or grand periods of the world's existence, and the prodigiously long lives ascribed to their Menus, thus exclaims; " Computation is lost, and conjecture overwhelmed, in the attempt to adjust such astonishing spaces of time to our confined notions of the world's epoch: to such an antiquity the Mosaic creation is but as yesterday, and to such ages the life of Methuselah is but a span."†

The absurd superstition and ridiculous vanity of several nations, as of the Egyptians and Chaldeans, as well as the Indians and Chinese, have strikingly appeared in their bold pretensions to an astonishing antiquity. The degree of credit they have met with from some men of science in modern times, is a mortifying proof of human weakness and the power of prejudice. In several instances, however, individuals who were once disposed to admit such pretensions, have at last become ashamed of their credulity, and candidly acknowledged their error. Accordingly, *Maurice*, in his History of Hindostan,‡ after alluding to the admiration which *Mr Halhed* had at one time expressed for the Hindoo chronology, proceeds to say of that gentleman, he " has long been convinced of the futility of the claim to unfathomable antiquity of the presumptuous Brahmins."

* The Sacred and Profane History of the World connected, &c. Vol. i. Book 1.
† Quoted by Dr Tennant in his " Indian Recreations," Vol. i. sect. 16.
‡ Vol. i. ch. 2.

" It is by his immediate request," he adds, " that I announce to the public his altered sentiments on this point." The elaborate work of Maurice, from which this notice of Halhed's change of sentiment is taken, contains an ample refutation of the Brahminical pretensions ; and the Author shows particularly that their romantic calculations sprung from astronomical allegories, and that those allegories appear to be founded upon the basis of ancient facts, recorded by Moses, but distorted so as to suit their superstitious purposes. *Sir William Jones*, too, in his " Dissertation on the Chronology of the Hindoos," proposes the question, " Whether it is not in fact the same with our own, but embellished and obscured by the fancies of their poets, and the riddles of their astronomers ?" He inquires also, whether the story of the seventh *Menu* be not one and the same with that of Noah ? whether *Menu* comes from *Nuh*, the true name of that patriarch ? and whether the first *Menu* be Adam ?"*— Bishop Pearson has refuted, briefly indeed, but with ability and spirit, the claims of the Egyptians and Chaldeans, and brought forward cogent arguments for what he calls the *novity* of the world.† A passage of Shuckford also, in which he institutes a comparison between the Mosaic accounts and the short notices of ancient events, supplied by profane historians, as *Berosus* the priest of Belus at Babylon, *Sanchoniatho* the Phenician, and *Manetho* the Egyptian, deserves to be perused.‡

As one specimen of the success with which the annals of Moses are vindicated, and vain pretensions to an extravagant antiquity confuted, the following quotation from an excellent little work in defence of revelation may be here presented to the reader.—" The Chinese have carefully, from the earliest times, observed the motions of the heavenly bodies, and recorded in their calendars remarkable eclipses, and very singular conjunctions of the planets, as having happened in such and such an Emperor's reign. Now in this enlightened age, you know, we can calculate back and tell the year, day, hour, and minute and second when these eclipses, conjunctions, &c. happened at *Pekin ;* and from hence we evidently perceive, they have made many great and palpable mistakes in their so much boasted chronology. One in particular has been most satisfactorily demonstrated by the famous *Cassini*, from a very singular and most remarkable conjunction of the sun, moon, and several planets,

* See Dissertations and Miscellaneous Pieces, relating to the History and Antiquities of the Arts, Sciences, and Literature of Asia, Vol. i. pp. 279, 325. Vol. iii. p. 418.

† Exposition of the Creed, Art. i. pp. 58—63.

‡ Vol. i. Book 1.

mentioned in their annals as having happened almost at the very origin of their history. This celebrated astronomer, anxious to know the truth of this, calculated back, and from hence discovered an error in their chronology of only 500 years; and proved to demonstration, that such an extraordinary conjunction of the planets actually did happen at China on the 26th day of February, 2012 years B. C. i. e. in the fourth century after the flood, in the days of Noah and his sons, a little after the birth of Abraham. From all which it is clear that the boasted antiquity of the Chinese is forced, from proofs of its own recording, to contract itself within the compass of the Mosaic history, and to bring an additional proof of the veracity of the sacred records."*

The futile claims of nations to an extreme antiquity are not the only pretexts which scepticism has employed for the purpose of disparaging the chronology of Scripture. It has eagerly resorted also to various phenomena which the earth itself presents in its inferior strata or external productions; and which a vain philosophy readily misunderstands, or daringly perverts. Who has not heard, for instance, of the cavil of the Canon *Recupero,* somewhat lightly adverted to in *Brydone's* " Tour through Sicily and Malta ?" When digging a pit in the vicinity of *Jaci,* the canon informs us, he discovered no less than seven distinct layers of lava, each of which was covered with a bed of rich vegetable earth. He points out also a bed of lava, which *he conceives* to have been deposited about the time of the second Punic war, so thinly covered with soil as to be still unfit for producing either corn or vines. If a period of 2000 years, therefore, be required for converting lava into soil, 14,000, he alleges, must have elapsed since the formation of the lowest bed of the pit at *Jaci,* and consequently the mountain must have existed at a period still more remote.

The weakness of this argument has been clearly shown in a celebrated work. " Moses," says the writer of the article referred to, " professes to give an account of the history of mankind from the earliest period, and describes the manner in which the earth was prepared for our habitation, but he nowhere pretends to give the date of its formation. The earth therefore may have existed, and undergone various revolutions, previous to the period at which the Scripture narration commences." " But lest this mode of removing the difficulty," continues the writer, " should appear to some

* Major Gen. Burns' " Christian Officer's complete Armour," Dialogue i. p. 31.

of our readers not altogether satisfactory, we shall now examine the argument itself. Its whole force seems to depend upon two circumstances; upon the accuracy of the fact respecting the bed of lava which is said to have flowed from the mountain about the time of the second Punic war; and upon the correctness of the general assumption that all lavas require the same number of years to fit them for supporting vegetable life. With regard to the first point, we have no means of ascertaining what degree of credit is due to the opinion of Recupero. He indeed speaks of it as a matter clearly made out, but does not inform us from what principle he derived his conclusion.

" But admitting that this particular bed of lava did flow from the mountain about 2,000 years ago, and that it is still scarcely fit for the purposes of vegetable life, does it follow that all lavas are equally refractory ? If we were entitled to decide upon the qualities of lava from what happens in the parallel case of iron slag, we might, without hesitation, affirm, that lavas become fertile at very different periods, according to the nature of the substances from which they are derived, the consistency of their parts, the position of the bed, and their degree of exposure to those agents which produce a disintegration of their parts. But, fortunately, on this subject we are not under the necessity of having recourse to the doubtful argument of analogy. It is a fact well ascertained, that volcanic ashes and pumice vegetate much sooner than compact solid lava. But even lavas apparently in similar circumstances are covered with vegetable mould at very different periods. Chevalier *Gioeni* informs us that he found, in 1787, lavas which had been projected only twenty-one years before that period, in a state of vegetation; while others much more ancient remained barren. - - - - -

" The argument derived from the appearance of the pit at *Jaci* has no force, unless it can be demonstrated, that the thickness of the beds of vegetable earth corresponds exactly to the period betwixt the eruptions. But it must appear perfectly nugatory, if it can be shown that an appearance exactly similar has been produced within the limits of authentic history. The ruins of *Herculaneum* furnish us with a fact of this kind. The eruption which overwhelmed this once flourishing city is known to have happened in the reign of Titus, little more than 1700 years ago. Upon examining the ruins, it is found, that six different eruptions have occurred since that period, and that each of the strata of lava is separated by beds of rich soil."*

* Edinburgh Encycl. Vol. i. Art. ÆTNA, pp. 184, 185.

Note XLIX. Page 221.

The decided terms in which Witsius condemns and ridicules the opinion of those who deem it probable that the moon and the planets are the abodes of animal and intellectual life, may appear strange to some of his readers. But our surprise will cease, when we reflect that he flourished more than an hundred years ago, that the modern discoveries in astronomical science were then in their infancy, and that the most pious and learned members of the Protestant Churches were at that time almost universally hostile to a theory which struck them as at least seemingly repugnant to Scripture, and which was warmly espoused by a class of philosophers, some of whom in other respects discovered very little reverence for the authority of Divine revelation. The judicious *Mastricht* may be mentioned as furnishing another example of the unfavourable sentiments with which even well-informed Christians at first regarded the system maintained by the celebrated *Newton* (who, by the way, was a decided believer of the Scriptures) with his predecessors and followers. That excellent Theologian, when taking notice of the system of the world, has the following observation; " The Reformed ascribe the *lowest* place to this earth, which, according to the uniform tenor of sacred writ, is contradistinguished from the heavens and the stars, and which, *being in a manner the centre of the universe, remains immoveable,* Eccles. i. 4."* Even at the present time there are not wanting individuals of learning and worth who are invincibly attached to the exploded philosophy; or who, although they may perhaps admit the Newtonian doctrine so far as it relates to the revolutions performed by the earth and the other planets around the sun, are far from embracing the idea that the Moon, Mercury, Venus, and the other planets are inhabited, or that there are innumerable other systems of planets, peopled in like manner with worlds of intelligent beings. The late Mr Parkhurst makes the following remark : " The כוכבים, whether planets or fixed stars, were ordained by God to govern and enlighten the night. And the modern philosopher, who imagines the *moon* and *planets* to be *inhabited worlds,* and the *fixed stars, suns to other systems,* may perhaps find enough to awaken him from this amusing but delusive dream, in the excellent *Mr Baker's* Reflexions on Learning, ch. viii. (Compare Keill's Astronomy, sect. 10. towards the end) or in the learned *Calcott* on the *Creation,* p. 20," &c.†

* *Theologia,* lib. iii. cap. vi. sect. 19.

† Parkhurst's Hebrew Lexicon, on the word כבב, iii.

In order to prevent misconceptions of the venerable Author's meaning, it seems proper to make the following remarks on the passage to which this Note refers. 1st, He allows that the existence of a plurality of worlds is not, in the nature of things, impossible, and even reasons (sect. 75, 76.) in opposition to them who rashly affirmed that more worlds similar to this universe could not have been created by the Divine omnipotence itself. 2dly, Since the opinion, that the planets are the habitations of rational beings, how probable soever it may be deemed, is by no means demonstrably certain, our Author is right in so far as he impugns the hypothesis of those philosophers, if any such there were, who contended for its absolute certainty. Notwithstanding the overstrained expressions quoted from Kepler's *Selenographia*, it does not appear that the most powerful telescopes hitherto formed have enabled any astronomer positively to affirm, whatever conjectures he might entertain, that he actually *saw* inhabitants in the moon, or in any of the planets, exhibiting the natural symptoms of life and rationality. The reasonings on this point too from analogy, it is obvious, however specious or forcible they may seem, do not amount to demonstration. With regard to an express Divine testimony, in fine, in support of the opinion in question, it is confessedly wanting. 3dly, It was proper to combat the sentiments of those who asserted that the supposed inhabitants of the moon and the planets are not merely rational beings but *men*—creatures of the same or nearly the same nature with ourselves, though perhaps of a gigantic size. Whilst we profess to exalt the creative energy of God, why should we venture, with the same breath, to prescribe limits to his power? The amazing diversity of forms, instincts, and capacities, by which he has distinguished the numerous classes of animals in the various compartments of our own world, is calculated to give us the most elevated conceptions of the infinitude of his wisdom and might—of the *versatility*, if we may use the expression, of his plastic hand. Admitting that there is some general and even striking resemblance between the imagined inhabitants of other planets and ourselves with regard to rationality, moral agency, the social impulse, immortality, and capability of endless improvement, who can tell with what singular material organs or intellectual faculties, of which we can now form no idea, these distant families of the universe may have been endowed; what visible and beneficial shades of difference may subsist betwixt them all; and what characters of marked peculiarity may be traced in each by those angels, or other spirits, who are permitted to fly like lightning from world to world, in order to contemplate the mighty works

of Jehovah, and minister to the happiness of his countless offspring?
4thly, Witsius, in fine, is quite correct in holding, that this earth has
been the theatre of a most astonishing display of the Divine perfections and character, and that its inhabitants have been the objects
of the most distinguishing goodness and love.

In justice to our Author, these explanatory remarks have now
been suggested. Nevertheless, when, conformably to the prevailing
sentiments of the Christians of his own age, both illiterate and learned, he expressly denies the existence of intelligent beings in the
moon and the planets, and reprobates the opinion of those who maintain its probability as monstrous, and disgraceful to the Protestant
religion, it is frankly conceded that he proceeds too far. His arguments, however plausible, are not sufficient to justify his decided
condemnation of that opinion. From the profound silence of the sacred volume with regard to the existence, character, circumstances,
and history of beings resident in certain regions of the wide universe,
it doth not at all follow that those regions are utterly unpeopled, or
that any one of them is abandoned to perpetual solitude. The Bible
was not intended to furnish us with a system of universal knowledge,
but only to afford that portion of intelligence which was requisite to
enable us to attain the great end of our creation. Although the Almighty has, for purposes worthy of his wisdom and goodness, made
us in some degree acquainted, by means of the Scriptures, with the
nature, capacities, condition, and employments of Angels, both the
holy and the fallen, it cannot justly be inferred that it would have
been either proper or necessary to give us in our present mortal state
an equal measure of information, or any information at all, relative
to every other class of intelligent beings that may exist in the pla-
netary orbs, whether innocent or degenerate. Even on the supposition that some of those orbs contain multitudes of rational creatures
that have deviated from their original integrity, it is not for us to
inquire minutely into the course of the Divine procedure towards
them, lest we be found " intruding into those things which we have
not seen, vainly puffed up by a carnal mind." * But what should
hinder us from imagining, that whatever be the extent of the universe, and however numerous and varied its intelligent population,
devils and men are the only parts of the offspring of God, that have
ever cast off their allegiance to the Father of all, and that the rest
have universally persisted in the paths of obedience? And what
right have we, at the same time, to demand or expect explicit infor-

* Col. ii. 18.

mation relative to those numberless classes of rational and immortal beings, which may exist in unsullied innocence and consummate bliss? Whatever advantages might appear to us likely to accrue from a Divine communication on the subject, it does not become us peremptorily to conclude that such a communication could not have been withheld.

The enemies of Christianity, it is well known, have urged the magnitude of the visible creation as a powerful objection to the truth of the Scriptures, and in particular to their leading doctrine—redemption by the obedience and sufferings of incarnate Deity. That the Creator of innumerable worlds would lavish his goodness on this insignificant planet to such a degree as is taught in the Gospel,—that in the person of his Son he would assume the nature of its degenerate inhabitants, and shed his blood on the cross for their redemption,—they are pleased to represent as doctrines utterly incredible. On this topic there are some just remarks in a short essay by an anonymous Author, entitled, " The Philosophy of Divine Revelation no argument of imposture," and published in the year 1734. The subject has, however, been more copiously and satifactorily discussed in later productions. Dr Chalmers's able " Discourses on the Christian Revelation viewed in connexion with the Modern Astronomy," have been extensively read and highly admired. There is also a chapter in Fuller's " Gospel its own Witness,"* entitled, " The consistency of the Scripture doctrine of redemption, with the modern opinion of the magnitude of the creation," which has been justly esteemed by many competent judges,† a concise, solid, and masterly refutation of the objection referred to, as it is plausibly stated by a certain notorious deistical writer.

" All the reasoning," says Mr Fuller, " in favour of a multiplicity of worlds inhabited by intelligent beings amounts to no more than a *strong probability*. No man can properly be said to believe it. It is not a matter of faith but of opinion. It is an opinion, too, that has taken place of other opinions which in their day were admired by the philosophical part of mankind as much as this is in ours. - - - Now before we give up a doctrine, which if it were even to prove fallacious has no dangerous consequences attending it, and

---

* Part ii. ch. 5. p. 204. *et seq.*

† See the Christian Repository, Vol. ii. p. 560. where, at the close of a spirited review of Dr Chalmers's Discourses, the writer pronounces a warm encomium on this chapter of Fuller's work, and refers to a testimony in its favour, " by one who from a Deist has become a Christian and a Minister of the Gospel, in the RETROSPECT, No. vi. p. 59."

which if it should be found a truth, involves our eternal salvation, we should endeavour to have a more solid ground than mere opinion on which to take our stand.—But I do not wish," he adds, " to avail myself of these observations; for I am under no apprehension that the cause in which I engage requires them. *Admitting that the intelligent creation is as extensive as modern philosophy supposes, the credibility of redemption is not thereby weakened ; but, on the contrary, in many respects is strengthened and aggrandized."*

After adverting to the dignity of man as a creature destined to immortality, and to the incalculable importance of the salvation of one soul, Mr Fuller states and illustrates the following observations in proof that there is nothing in the Scripture doctrine of redemption, which is inconsistent with the modern opinion of the magnitude of creation. 1st, " Let creation be as extensive as it may, and the number of worlds be multiplied to the utmost boundary to which imagination can reach, there is no proof that any of them, except men and angels, have apostatized from God. - - - 2dly, Let creation be ever so extensive, there is nothing inconsistent in supposing that some one particular part of it should be chosen out of the rest as a theatre on which the great Author of all things would perform his most glorious works. - - - 3dly, If any one part of God's creation, rather than another, possessed a superior fitness to become a theatre on which he might display his glory, it should seem to be that part where the greatest effort has been made to dishonour him. - - - - 4thly, The events brought to pass in this world, little and insignificant as it may be, are competent to fill all and every part of God's dominions with everlasting and increasing joy. - - - An intellectual object requires only to be known, and it is equally capable of affording enjoyment to a million as to an individual, to a world as to a million, to the whole universe, be it ever so extensive, as to a world. - - - 1 Pet. i. 12. Eph. iv. 10. Ps. ciii. 22."

Having made these observations, the writer goes forward to vindicate the silence of Scripture, which neither teaches the doctrine of a multitude of inhabited worlds, nor affirms the contrary ; and to defend the popular style in which the Bible is written as best adapted to its great end. And he concludes his discussion by offering evidence in a series of particulars, that *the Scripture doctrine of redemption is even strengthened and aggrandized by the supposed magnitude of creation.* But instead of abridging these excellent remarks, it seems best to refer the reader to the work itself.

Note L. Page 235.

That the name Jesus is of Hebrew origin, and that it signifies a *Saviour*, cannot be questioned. Nor is there room to doubt that it is the very same name as *Joshua*—the designation which Moses, by the Divine direction, gave to the valiant and pious son of Nun. This is indisputably evident from Heb. iv. 8, quoted by our Author, and also from Acts vii. 45.; in both of which passages the Jesus spoken of is clearly Joshua, under whose conduct the Israelites obtained possession of Canaan, and " brought in" to that favoured country " the tabernacle of witness," which was erected in the wilderness.

To some readers, however, the Author may possibly appear to discover a taste for excessive refinement, when he represents this pleasant name as comprising in its signification something more than a Saviour. But he is at least by no means singular in this view of the expression. The same opinion is decidedly adopted by Bishop Pearson, Mr Parkhurst, and others, as well as by Eusebius and Gerhard; whose remarks on the term are quoted by Witsius. *Jerome*, too, as Pearson observes, a man much better acquainted with the Hebrew language than Eusebius, explains the word *Joshua* as meaning *the salvation of the Lord.* The arguments also in support of this opinion have considerable force.

When the name of the son of Nun was changed by Moses, at the command of God, from *Hoshea*, which signifies a Saviour, into *Jehoshua*, or, by a slight abbreviation, *Joshua*, the alteration must have been made for some important reason. On this subject there are two opinions. Some suppose that *Jehoshua* must be traced merely to the future tense of the same Hebrew verb from which *Hoshea* is derived, and that it intimated simply, that the successor of Moses was truly and effectually to save the people of Israel, and place them in the promised land. Others conceive that *Jehoshua* is a compound character, composed of his original name and part of the name Jehovah. The two following considerations appear to render this last opinion the most probable. In the first place, the composition of names with one or other of the names of God was exceedingly common among the Jews. Thus, Jehohanan signifies *the Lord is gracious*, Jehoshaphat—*the Lord is Judge,* and Eliezer—*my God is a helper.* In the second place, when the Lord honoured the successor of Moses with a new name, it is scarcely to be imagined that he would quite overlook the glory which belonged to himself. Whilst he was pleased to confer a new dignity on his faithful servant, he did not mean that the people should ascribe their deliverance to him independently of God. The name seems therefore to have been chosen and imposed with a view to direct their attention to the agency of Jehovah himself, and to impress them with the thought that the son of Nun was divinely appointed and qualified, and worthy of confidence as an adequate instrument in the hand of God, to accomplish for them a glorious deliverance.

The propriety of this name, according to the etymology now approved, is doubtless the more apparent, when it is considered that the son of Nun was a distinguished type of the Messiah, " the Captain of our salvation," to whom the true Israel are indebted for victory over the worst of enemies, and for the possession of the heavenly Canaan. It is obvious, at the same time, that *Joshua,* or *Jesus,* as applied to Christ, is calculated and probably intended to teach us, not merely that he is " God's salvation unto the ends of the earth," but also that he is in reality a *Divine* Saviour. The evangelist Matthew, appears to give countenance to this interpretation, as Pearson, in the following quotation, particularly shows.

" In the first salutation the angel Gabriel told the blessed virgin she should ' conceive in her womb and bring forth a Son, and should call his name *Jesus,*' Luke i. 31. In the dream of Joseph, the angel of the Lord informed him, not only of the nomination, but of the interpretation or etymology; ' Thou shalt call his name *Jesus,* for he shall save his people from their sins.' In which words is clearly expressed the designation of the person *He,* and the futurition of salvation certain by him, *he shall save.* Besides, that other addition of the name of God, propounded in Joshua as probable, appeareth here in some degree above probability, and that for two reasons. *First,* Because it is not barely said that *he,* but as the original raiseth it, ' *he himself** shall save.' Joshua saved Israel, not by his own power, not of himself, but God by him; neither saved he his own people, but the people of God: Whereas *Jesus* himself, by his own power, the power of God, shall save his own people, the people of God. Well therefore may we understand the interpretation of his name to be *God the Saviour. Secondly,* Immediately upon the prediction of the name of *Jesus,* and the interpretation given by the angel, the Evangelist expressly observeth; ' All this was done that it might be fulfilled, which was spoken of the Lord by the prophet, saying, Behold, a virgin shall be with child, and shall bring forth a Son, and they shall call his name *Emmanuel,* which being interpreted,

---

* 'Aυτος, ipse.

is, God with us.' Matt. i. 22, 23. Several ways have been invented to show the fulfilling of that prophecy, notwithstanding our Saviour was not called *Emmanuel ;* but none can certainly appear more
proper than that the sense of Emmanuel should be comprehended in
the name of Jesus; and what else is *God with us* than *God our Saviour?* Well therefore hath the Evangelist conjoined the Prophet and
the Angel, asserting Christ was therefore named *Jesus,* because it
was foretold he should be called Emmanuel; the angelical *God the
Saviour,* being, in the highest propriety, *God with us." ***

The name Jesus, it may be observed, was quite common amongst
the Jews in the apostolical age. This appears from the New Testament, as well as from Josephus. Paul makes honourable mention
of one Jesus, who is called Justus, as a fellow-worker with himself.†
We find also that Elymas the sorcerer, who was miraculously punished with blindness for perverting the right ways of the Lord,
was called *Bar-Jesus,* i. e. the son of Jesus. ‡ Nay, Jesus seems to
have been the proper name of Barabbas the malefactor whom Pilate
put in competition with our Lord. " No doubt can be made," says
Michaelis, " that the original reading Mat. xxvii. 16, 17. was 'Ιησυν
Βαραββαν. Origen - - - expressly declares it; and 'Ιησυν is found
in the Armenian, and in a Syriac translation which Adler discovered in Rome. The reading is probable in itself; for Jesus was at
that time a very common name, as we learn from Josephus; and
Barabbas was only an addition to the real name, signifying the son
of Abba or Rabba. The relation of St Matthew seems to be imperfect without it, and every impartial reader will prefer the following
to the common text; ' Therefore when they were gathered together,
Pilate said unto them, Whom will ye that I release unto you, Jesus
the son of Abba, or Jesus which is called Christ ?"§ But while it
is thus indisputable that this name, which in its proper sense belongs exclusively to our Saviour, has been given to others, it is not
on that account the less significant in itself, or the less delightful to
the ears of all who love our Lord Jesus Christ in sincerity. It is
with great propriety, at the same time, that Christians have long
forborne to make use of the name Jesus as a common appellation ;
and it were desirable that equal reverence and caution were discovered with regard to some other Divine names and titles, such as *Emmanuel.*

* Pearson's Exposition of the Creed, Art. ii. p. 71. 8th edit.
† Col. iv. 11.
‡ Acts xiii. 6.
§ Marsh's Trans. of Introduction to the New Testament, Vol. i. p. 314.
2d edit. See also p. 520. note 23.

Note LI. Page 239.

The doctrine of the cross, with whatever vehemence it has been opposed in former days, or at the present time, is unquestionably founded in the word of God. To every impartial reader indeed it is obvious, that the sacred oracles not only contain this doctrine, but teach it in the most explicit and perspicuous manner, and uniformly represent it as of vital moment to the peace, holiness, and eternal happiness of fallen mankind. Our Author very justly maintains, in opposition to the *Remonstrants*, not merely the *reality*, but the *necessity* of the atonement of Jesus Christ. " God cannot deny himself." If " it is impossible for God to lie," it is equally impossible for him to perform any deed, or to adopt any line of conduct, contrary to his holiness, righteousness, and other essential attributes. His devising and appointing an adequate satisfaction to his punitive justice, as the medium through which his boundless mercy might flow to the guilty and perishing children of men, ought not, according to the numerous intimations of Scripture, to be resolved into his mere good pleasure, but to be referred also to his pure and righteous nature. This, however, is a grave and weighty topic, which it would be difficult or impossible to illustrate to advantage, within the limits of a short Note. Suffice it therefore to mention, that it is ably and concisely treated by Witsius himself, in his *Economy of the Covenants,** and that it is discussed by Dr Owen at great length, and with much energy, both in the *Exercitations* prefixed to the second Volume of his Exposition of the Epistle to the Hebrews, † and in a separate Treatise. ‡ Several modern publications on the subject, also, deserve an attentive perusal; as Moir's Scripture Doctrine of Redemption, the Rev. George Stevenson's Dissertation on the Necessity of the Atonement, and the 55th Sermon of Dwight's Theology.

Note LII. Page 245.

The evangelical doctrine of Christ's fulfilling on behalf of his people, the whole obedience required by the law in the form of a covenant, as well as suffering the punishment due to their offences, is a highly important and interesting topic. But for the same reason assigned in the Note immediately preceding, a particular illus-

* Book ii. ch. 8. On the Necessity of the Satisfaction of Christ.
† See, in particular, the 5th, 6th, 7th, and 8th Exercit.
‡ " A Dissertation on Divine Justice, or the Claims of Vindicatory Justice asserted and clearly defended against Socinus and his followers," originally written in Latin, and translated by Mr Hamilton.

tration of it cannot here be attempted. The Author states, and supports his sentiments respecting it, more fully in his work on the Covenants.* It is well defended also by many other valuable writers, as by Dr Owen, † Rawlin, ‡ Dr Erskine, § President Dickenson, ‖ and Dr Dwight. ¶ One of its ablest and most determined opposers, is Dr Whitby, who reasons keenly against it, in a long dissertation " concerning the imputation of Christ's perfect righteousness and obedience to the law for us, for righteousness or justification," subjoined to the first Volume of his " Paraphrase and Commentary on the New Testament." Whitby points his artillery, chiefly against Bishop Beveridge's statement of this topic, in his " Private Thoughts on Religion," Art. viii. He attempts to prove that the doctrine of our Lord's active and perfect obedience being imputed to us, has not the least foundation in Scripture, and propounds a series of arguments, which, in his apprehension, fully confute it. But the intelligent reader will easily perceive that Whitby's usual good sense visibly fails him on such subjects; that although some parts of his reasoning are specious, they are void of solidity; and that many of his arguments are extremely futile.

One of his proofs, for instance, is, that justification consists merely in the remission of sin; whereas it is undeniably clear, from Rom. v. 18—21, and many other passages, that a title to eternal life, as well as remission of sin, is included in justification. Another of his arguments is thus expressed : " It is impossible that by the obedience of another imputed to us we can obtain a title to the life promised by that law which saith, *Do this and live ;*" and in illustration of this he remarks, that the law requires personal obedience. But was he not aware that the law says, " Cursed is every one that continueth not in all things which are written in the book of the law to do them ;" and that accordingly it requires personal suffering from its transgressors, as well as personal obedience from its subjects ? And since he allows that, in consequence of the counsels of Divine mercy, Christ " was made a sin-offering or expiatory sacrifice for us," that we might be delivered from the guilt and punishment of sin, why should he deem it incredible that Christ, being made under the law, rendered a perfect obedience to its precepts in the room of his people, that he might procure for them a title to life ? If substitution was

---

* Book ii. ch. 3. sect. 9—14. Book iii. ch. 8. sect. 46. and *passim.*
† The Doctrine of Justification, &c. ch. 13.
‡ Sermons on Christ, the Righteousness of his people.
§ Discourses, Vol. i. Dis. 9.
‖ Familiar Letters, Let. 12.
¶ Theology, Ser. 56.

admissible in the one case, was it not equally so in the other?—In his remarks on Rom. v. 19. he observes, that "freedom from condemnation could not be obtained by Christ's active obedience." Now, it is by no means denied, but expressly taught by Bishop Beveridge and others, whose doctrine Whitby opposes, that our Lord's sufferings and death were necessary to expiate guilt, and obtain our freedom from condemnation. But it may be asked, Could deliverance from condemnation have been procured without Christ's active obedience? Did he not obey the will of God, even in submitting to humiliation, sorrow, and death? Nay, could his sufferings and death have proved at all acceptable to the Father and satisfactory to justice, unless they had been undergone from a principle of obedience, and in the exercise of that love which is the fulfilling of the law? The obedience and sufferings of our Divine Surety, though they may be distinguished from each other in our ideas, are not divided. They were closely connected, as has just been suggested, in their very operation, during the whole period of his abasement; they are inseparably joined, also, in their meritorious virtue and blessed effects; and, as Dwight observes, " the attempts made to discriminate between these parts of Christ's mediation, and to assign to each its exact proportion of influence in the economy of redemption, seem to have been very partially successful." This view of the subject, however, clearly exposes the absurdity and incongruity of the sentiments of those who hold that Christ suffered in the room of his people, and yet deny that he obeyed in their stead. His obedience and sufferings were, in reality, so mixed and blended, that if the one was vicarious, the other must necessarily have been so too.

With regard to the hackneyed objection against this doctrine, that it supersedes the necessity of holy obedience on our part, and is injurious to the interests of morality, it was anticipated and obviated by the Apostle Paul himself, in the 6th chapter of his Epistle to the Romans. Let it suffice to refer to the able exposition of that chapter by Fraser of Alness in his Treatise on Sanctification, and to Dr Witherspoon's excellent " Essay on the connexion between the Doctrine of Justification by the imputed righteousness of Christ and holiness of life."

Note LIII. Page 251.

From the concluding sections of the Dissertation on the name *Jesus,* and from the uniform scope and spirit of this Treatise, it is clear that the Author was none of those who wish to discard the human affections from the concerns of Religion. With him it was an established maxim, that not only should the understanding be enlightened, but the heart impressed; and in particular, that the desires and affections of the soul should go forth with an holy ardour to the great Redeemer.

If our religious affections indeed are not under the guidance of a sound judgment and a renovated will, and if they are not accompanied with a tender conscience and a consistent practice, they are vain and delusive. But is not the understanding liable to perversion as well as the heart? And if no man proposes to degrade the understanding from its proper place and office in the grand business of religion, on account of the weakness and obliquity which it often discovers in its manner of thinking and judging with reference to sacred subjects, ought not every one to esteem it unjust and preposterous to denude the heart of its legitimate sphere and influence in the deeply interesting matters of God and eternity, because its passions and affections, in some instances, operate irrationally and enthusiastically?

Many celebrated authors have shown the vast importance of having the affections decidedly engaged in the cause of God and holiness. President Edwards, in his admirable Treatise on this subject, makes it his principal object to discriminate between religious affections that are spurious, and those which are truly gracious; but, at the beginning of the work, he proves, by a series of incontestible arguments, that " true religion consists very much in the affections." The amiable M'Laurin adverts to the same subject in the course of his Essay on the Scripture Doctrine of Divine Grace. Mr Wilberforce has a chapter containing valuable observations " on the use of the passions in religion," in his excellent publication, entitled, " A Practical View of the prevailing Religious System of professed Christians, contrasted with real Christianity." Even the incidental remarks of pious writers bearing on this point, clearly mark the importance they attach to sanctified affections. Dr Bryce Johnston, for instance, when referring to the glories of the millenial period of the Church, has these expressions: " That spirituality, elevation, and ardour of affection, which, in the present age, would be looked upon by many as enthusiasm, would fall quite short of that refinement and elevation of affection which is suited to that period in which the kingdom of God, which is not meats and drinks, but truth and righteousness, and peace and joy, shall come."*—The following passage from Dr Owen, which immediately relates to the state of our affections towards the

---

* Commentary on the Revelation, Vol. i. ch. iv. 7.

Saviour, is so weighty and impressive, that it must not be kept back from the reader.

" They know nothing of the life and power of the Gospel, nothing of the reality of the grace of God, nor do they believe aright one article of the Christian faith, whose hearts are not sensible of the love of Christ herein. Nor is he sensible of the love of Christ, whose affections are not thereon drawn out unto him. I say they make a *pageant* of religion, a fable for the theatre of the world, a business of fancy and opinion, whose hearts are not really affected with the love of Christ in the susception and discharge of the work of mediation, so as to have real and spiritually sensible affections for him. Men may *babble* things which they have learned by rot ; they have no real *acquaintance* with Christianity, who imagine that the placing of the most intense affections of our souls on the person of Christ, the loving him with all our hearts because of his love, our being overcome thereby until we are *sick of love*, the constant motions of our souls towards him with delight and adherence, are but *fancies* and *imaginations*. *I renounce that religion*, be it whose it will, that teacheth, insinuateth, or giveth countenance unto such abominations. That doctrine is as discrepant from the Gospel as the *Alkoran*, as contrary to the experience of believers as what is acted on and by the *Devils*, which instructs men unto a contempt of the most fervent love unto Christ, or casts reflexions upon it. I had rather choose my eternal lot and portion with the *meanest believer*, who, being effectually sensible of the love of Christ, spends his days in mourning, that he can love him no more than he finds himself on his utmost endeavours for the discharge of his duty to do, than with the best of them whose vain speculations, and a false pretence of reason, puff them up unto the contempt of these things."*

If devout affections towards the Lord Jesus thus form an essential part of religion, the means of exercising and improving these affections ought not to be neglected. Nor can it admit of a doubt, that the ordinance of praise is particularly calculated to animate the feelings of confidence, admiration, gratitude, love, and joy. Amongst the compositions to be employed in this heavenly service, those psalms and hymns and spiritual songs with which we are supplied by the sweet Singer of Israel and other inspired writers, are unquestionably entitled to the highest place. Yet, whatever difference of sentiment

---

* Declaration of the glorious Mystery of the Person of Christ, Ch. xiv. pp. 206, 207.

may prevail with regard to singing hymns of human writing in public assemblies, few Christians, it is presumed, would dispute the
propriety of employing for their assistance in *personal* devotion, any
song or hymn, characterised by correctness of sentiment, and scriptural simplicity of diction. To this Witsius appears to refer, when
he recommends the frequent use of Bernard's Song.—The late Dr
Haweis, it may be mentioned, in a short and lively Essay on " Psal-
mody," vindicates the exercise of praise from the contempt which
has been thrown upon it, and points out its pleasures and advantages.*

Note LIV. Page 257.

That the name *Chrest,* instead of Christ, was given to our blessed
Saviour by some of the heathens from malice or contempt, is highly
probable. It is possible, however, that *Suetonius* thus expressed the
name from ignorance or inadvertence. Michaelis remarks, that he
commits a mistake respecting the name Christ, and that he refers
not to the person of Jesus Christ, but to the Messiah expected by
the Jews, upon whom they depended for support in their sedition.
Upon the supposition, however, that Suetonius did refer to Jesus
Christ, either that respectable historian, as some allege, must have
been led into an anachronism, and thought that Jesus was alive on
the earth while Claudius wore the purple, whereas he was crucified
during the reign of Tiberius; or his meaning, as Witsius imagines,
was merely that the doctrine of Christ, being disseminated at Rome
by his disciples, was the occasion not of an insurrection, but of mutual contentions among the Jews residing in that city.

Although some writers apprehend that Suetonius refers to a certain seditious Jew whose real name was *Chrest,* and although Michaelis supposes that he intends only an expected Christ or Messiah,
while he mistakes the name,—it is not unlikely that the edict issued
by Claudius about the eighth year of his reign, enjoining all Jews
to leave Rome, did originate in an alarm taken by that jealous and
unhappy Emperor at the propagation of Christianity, and the dissensions which took place among the Jews relative to the character
and doctrine of Jesus Christ. It was in consequence of that decree
that Aquila and Priscilla, as we read Acts xviii. 1, 2., removed from
Rome to Corinth. Yet it was not as *Christians,* but as *Jews,* that
these worthy individuals, in common with others of the same na-

* Essays on the Evidence, Characteristic Doctrines, and Influence of Christianity, Ess. xvi.

tion, at that time suffered banishment. Nero, the successor of Claudius, was the first Roman Emperor that expressly made Christianity a crime, and unsheathed the sword of persecution against its professors. This edict of Claudius too, it appears, was speedily repealed, or at least expired with himself; for Aquila and Priscilla had returned to Rome previously to the date of Paul's Epistle to the Romans, which was probably written in the year of Christ 58, being the fourth year of Nero's reign.* See Dr Doddridge's Note b on Acts xviii. 2, and Dr Hammond's Note a on Acts xxvi. 31.

Note LV. Page 260.

It is with full propriety that the Author applies the 7th verse of the 45th Psalm to our anointed Saviour. The whole of that sacred song refers to the Messiah and the Church; and nothing can be more absurd than the interpretation of *Wakefield* and others of the same class, who explain it as relating merely to Solomon's marriage with Pharoah's daughter. Calvin, and some other respectable interpreters, have conceded that Solomon's marriage is the immediate subject of this Psalm, while they consider it as ultimately and principally referring to the spiritual union between Christ and his Church. But it seems much more correct to regard it as descriptive exclusively of the latter. In this way it is understood, not only by *Bishop Horne* in his beautiful Commentary on the Book of Psalms—a commentary which may possibly be thought to verge to the extreme of applying every Psalm and every expression to spiritual and evangelical topics—but also by *Dr Owen* and *Bishop Horsley*.

Dr Owen is decidedly of opinion that the Messiah is the only subject of this Psalm. " Most of the things mentioned," he observes, and the expressions of them, " do so *immediately* belong to Christ, that they can in no sense be applied to the person of Solomon."†

Bishop Horsley pronounces a severe censure on those who allow that Solomon is at all referred to in this Psalm. It is most certain, he admits, that in the prophetic book of the Song of Solomon, the union of Christ and the Church is described in images taken from the early loves of Solomon and his Egyptian bride. But this Psalm, he remarks, is of a different cast. We nowhere read of Solomon's comeliness of person or affability of speech, ver. 2. He was no warrior, ver. 3—5. He was not distinguished by antipathy to wickedness, in the large sense of the word, ver. 7. Nor had he a numerous

* Rom. xvi. 3, 4.
† Exposition of the Epistle to the Hebrews, on Ch. i. 8, 9.

progeny, ver. 16. Thus there are circumstances particularly inapplicable to Solomon; and there are others which clearly exclude not only Solomon, but every earthly king, ver. 6. The Bishop derives an argument also from that expression, ver. 1, " I speak of the things which I have made touching the King," or *unto the King ;* or *I address my performance unto the King.* " It is a remark of the Jewish expositors," he observes, " and a just one, (and very weighty, coming from them,) that the appellation of *the King* in the book of Psalms is an appropriate title of the Messiah, in so much that, wherever it occurs, unless the context directs it to some special meaning, you are to think of no earthly king, but of the King Messiah. By this admission, then, Christ is the immediate subject of this Psalm."— Horsley's four sermons on the whole of this Psalm are uncommonly able and ingenious. For the sake of those readers who have not an opportunity of seeing them, this Note may be properly concluded with his illustration of the latter part of the 7th verse.

" —' God, even thy God, hath anointed thee with the oil of gladness above thy fellows,' i. e. God hath advanced thee to a state of bliss and glory above all those whom thou hast vouchsafed to call thy fellows. It is said, too, that the love of righteousness and hatred of wickedness is the cause that God has so anointed him, who yet in the 6th verse is himself addressed as God. It is manifest that these things can be said only of that person in whom the godhead and manhood are united—in whom the human nature is the subject of the unction, and the elevation to the mediatorial kingdom is the reward of the man Jesus: For Christ, being in his divine nature equal with the Father, is incapable of any exaltation. Thus the unction with the oil of gladness, and the elevation above his fellows, characterize the manhood; and the perpetual stability of the throne, and the unsullied justice of the government, declare the godhead. It is, therefore, with the greatest propriety, that this text is applied to Christ in the Epistle to the Hebrews, and made an argument of his divinity ; not by any forced accommodation of words, which in the mind of the Author related to another subject, but according to the true intent and purpose of the Psalmist, and the literal sense and only consistent exposition of his words."*

NOTE LVI. Page 271, line 3 from the foot.

The Author, after having affirmed, that when Christ suffered for us in the human nature, the sacrifice derived worth and dignity

---

* Horsley's Sermons, Vol. i. p. 117. 2d edit.

from the divine nature to which it was personally united, quotes, without scruple, Acts xx. 28, as teaching us, that not the blood of a mere man, but " the blood of God," was shed for our redemption. It may not be improper, however, to state that the authenticity of this expression has been questioned by several biblical critics. The celebrated Griesbach, in particular, has received into the text the phrase *Church of the Lord,* instead of *Church of God,* and written a long note in defence of this reading. He compares six or seven different readings; and produces the evidence, so far as his very laborious researches extended, in favour of each. The Note is certainly worthy of attention. A great number of excellent Manuscripts and Versions, as well as quotations from the fathers, give countenance, it must be acknowledged, to the reading he prefers. He appears, however, rather to under-rate the proofs by which the common version is supported, and some of his objections to it are of no weight. The advertisement, too, prefixed to the London edition of 1818, states a circumstance particularly deserving of notice, namely, that from a recent and careful inspection of the *Vatican Codex,* it appears that this singularly ancient and valuable Manuscript, which some critics prefer even to the *Alexandrian,* clearly supports the received version. It is justly alleged in that advertisement, which contains a *fac simile* of Acts xx. 28. in the original, as it stands in the Vatican, that Griesbach would probably have formed a somewhat more favourable judgment of the reading—*Church of God,* if he had learned that the reading is such in the *Codex Vaticanus.*

It seems proper also to request the attention of the reader to the following appropriate remarks of Michaelis, which occur in a Section containing " general rules for deciding on the various readings." " In comparing two different readings," says that ingenious critic, " we must always examine which of the two could most easily arise from the mistake or correction of the transcriber; readings of this kind being generally spurious, whereas those which give occasion to the mistake or correction, are commonly genuine. Of the following different readings, Acts xx. 28. θεȣ, κυριȣ, χριστȣ, κυριȣ θεȣ, θιȣ και κυριȣ, κυριȣ και θιȣ, the first is probably the true reading, and all the others are to be considered as corrections or *scholia;* because θιȣ might easily give occasion to any of these, whereas none could so easily give occasion to θιȣ. If St Luke wrote θιȣ (*of God*), the origin of κυριȣ and χριστȣ may be explained either as corrections of the text or as marginal notes, because ' the blood of God' is a very extraordinary expression; but if he had written κυριȣ (*of the Lord*), it is inconceivable how any one could alter it into ἐις, and on this latter supposition, the great number of different readings is inexplicable. It seems as if different transcribers had found a difficulty in the passage, and that each corrected according to his own judgment."*

Beza too, long before Michaelis flourished, expressed his opinion in words to this effect. " I suspect that the expression *the Lord* had been added on the margin by some one who thus explained the word *God*, in opposition to the *Anthropomorphites*, lest Paul should seem to attribute blood to the Divinity itself;—and had afterwards crept into the text."† Since, in the early ages of Christianity, heretics appeared, who ascribed human infirmities and a capacity of suffering to the Divine essence, it was not unnatural for the orthodox to apprehend that the expression *God* in this verse might be adduced by them, with some appearance of reason, as an argument in support of their heresy ; and such apprehensions possibly gave occasion to a marginal note which was subsequently introduced, perhaps by accident, into the text, and ultimately employed in many copies to supplant entirely the authentic expression. But the absurd errors of the *Patripassians* and *Anthropomorphites* are nearly, if not completely, extinct; and no one who is at all acquainted with the first principles of the Christian system can readily misunderstand the phrase—" the blood of God." This expression is indeed extraordinary, but it is intended to denote an extraordinary, yet most certain and momentous truth. It was only in the human nature, that Christ had blood to shed. " The Divine nature," as a certain preacher remarks, " is impassible and immortal ;" and, amidst all the debasement and sorrow of our Lord's manhood, " it remained in the immutable possession of infinite glory and felicity." But in consequence of the personal union constituted between the Divine nature in the person of the Son and the human nature which he was pleased to assume, it may be justly said that God suffered and died ; and without question, the dignity of the one nature gave boundless worth and efficacy to the sufferings and death of the other.

The same sublime topic is frequently illustrated, in other parts of the sacred volume, by expressions equally paradoxical, and, at the same time, equally just, weighty, and instructive. The inspired writers dwell with peculiar pleasure on the mysteries of redeeming love, and delight to recognise at once the infinite distance between

---

* Marsh's Translation of Michaelis's Introduction to the New Testament, Vol. i. Part i. ch. 6. sect. 13. rule 11.

† See Beza's Note on Acts xx. 28.

the divinity and humanity of Christ, their wonderful union, and their surprising and effectual co-operation in the scheme of redemption. Compare in the Epistles of Paul himself, by whom the valedictory Address recorded, Acts xx. 18—35, was delivered to the presbyters of Ephesus, Rom. ix. 5. 1 Cor. ii. 8. 1 Tim. iii. 16. Col. i. 14—17. Tit. ii. 13, 14. Heb. i. 3.;—and in the writings of other sacred penmen, Isaiah ix. 6. Zech. xiii. 7. John i. 14. iii. 13. Acts iii. 15. 1 John i. 7. iii. 16. Rev. v. 12.

Those who prefer the reading, *Church of the Lord*, have suggested, that as *Church of God* is an expression of frequent occurrence in Scripture, a transcriber might inadvertently have written it in place of *Church of the Lord*, and that being once introduced, it might, for various reasons, prove acceptable to many, and secure its credit. But if the sacred historian in reality wrote *Church of God*, it is still more easy, as Michaelis shows, to account for the introduction of other readings, and the countenance which they received. The truth is, that *Church of the Lord* being quite an unusual expression, it was not so likely, at least humanly speaking, to occur to the Apostle himself, as *Church of God*; and it was completely in unison with Paul's accustomed energy of thought and expression, to illustrate the dignity and value of the Church, and the consequent importance of pastoral fidelity, by describing it as a society which " God has purchased with his own blood." The writings of no inspired author are so remarkably characterised as those of this ardent Apostle, by unexpected turns of sentiment, paradoxical representations, and striking contrasts. This peculiarity appears not merely in statements which immediately respect the person and work of " the great God, even our Saviour Jesus Christ," but also in passages relating to other topics, as the privileges and experience of Christians, and the character, attainments, and circumstances of the Apostles of Christ. See for example, 1 Cor. xiii. 10—12. Gal. ii. 19, 20. Eph. ii. 1—7. Col. iii. 3, 4. Philem. ver. 15, 16. 1 Cor. iv. 12, 13. 2 Cor. iv. 8—12. vi. 8—10. xii. 10.

Note LVII. Page 271. line 2 from the foot.

From the *Dutch Annotations* referred to by our Author, as well as other publications that might be quoted, it appears that even some Protestants admit, that the cross may be considered as the altar, on which Christ offered up his sacrifice. Witsius himself, in our apprehension, seems to speak too favourably of this idea, when he allows that, as the altar was intended to support the victim, the cross, in that respect, may, *and even ought* to be called the altar. Although

our Lord was indeed suspended on the accursed tree, that tree was rather the engine of torture, and the instrument of death, than the means of support. In strict propriety of speech, the sacrifice was sustained, as well as sanctified, and rendered inconceivably valuable, by his own eternal divinity, Heb. ix. 14. The offering up of this great oblation, besides, occupied not merely the few hours he hung on the cross, but the whole period of his abasement. " The sacrifice was *laid* on the altar," as it is stated in an useful and well-known Catechism, " in the first moment of his incarnation, Heb. x. 5. *continued* thereon through the whole of his life, Is. liii. 3.; and *completed* on the cross and in the grave, John xix. 30. Is. liii. 9." *
For these reasons, our Lord's Divine nature is generally represented by the Protestant Theologians, in their systems and discourses, as *the only proper altar* on which this grand atoning sacrifice was offered. The following specimen from the instructive and lively M'Ewen may suffice.

" The altar, what was it? His cross, say some. Nay, it was rather his divine nature, which, like the altar, supported, and, like the altar, sanctified his holy humanity, which alone was destroyed. This the cross can scarce be said to do, which was but the instrument of man's cruelty, and a despicable piece of timber, which neither sanctified the body which it carried, nor received sanctification from it. Where then are they who address it with divine honours, and pay even to its picture that homage, which is due to him alone, that expired in agonies on that shameful tree." †

Note LVIII. Page 274.

The intercession of Christ, without question, differs widely from those petitions which sinful men present unto God for themselves and others. Owing to the glory of his person, and the merit of his righteousness, it has a dignity, authority, and efficacy, altogether peculiar to itself. Even " in the days of his flesh," he could say, " I knew that thou hearest me always;" ‡ and in his present exalted state, he intercedes for his people in a manner becoming his glorious elevation, as " a Priest upon his throne." § Christ has, no doubt, purchased a people for himself with his own blood, and fully merited on their behalf all those inestimable blessings which he solicits for them. Yet there is cause to question the accuracy of the

---

* Explication of *the Shorter Catechism*, by the Rev. James Fisher and other Ministers of the Associate Synod, Qu. xxv.
† Treatise on the Types of the Old Testament, Book ii. ch. 8.
‡ John xi. 42.   § Zech. vi. 13.

interpretation which our excellent Author, in common with Doddridge and many other Theologians, puts upon Θελω, John xvii. 24.
which is rendered in our authorised Version, *I will.* Dr Campbell
renders it *I would,* and vindicates this translation in a Note.

" Θελω expresses no more," says that acute writer, " than a petition, a request. It was spoken by our Lord in prayer to his heavenly
Father, to whom he was obedient, even unto death. But the words
I will, in English, when *will* is not the sign of the future, express
rather a command. In Latin, *volo,* though not so uniformly as the
English *I will,* admits the same interpretation; and, therefore,
Beza's manner here, who renders the word used by John *velim,* is
much preferable to that of the Vulgate, Erasmus, the Zuric Translation, and Castalio, who say *volo.* That the sense of the Greek
word is, in the New Testament, as I have represented it, the critical reader may soon satisfy himself, by consulting the following passages in the original: Mat. xii. 38. xxvi. 39. Mark vi. 25. x. 35.
In some of these, the verb is rendered *would,* by our Translators; it
ought to have been rendered so in them all, as they all manifestly
imply request, not command. In most of the late English translations, this impropriety is corrected. Doddridge and Wesley have,
indeed, retained the words *I will;* nay, more, have made them the
foundation of an argument, (one in his Paraphrase, the other in his
Notes,) that what follows *I will,* is not so properly a petition,
as a claim of right. But this argument is built on an Anglicism in
their translations, for which the sacred author is not accountable.
Augustine, in like manner, founding on a Latinism, argued from
the word *volo* of the Italic version, as a proof of the equality of the
Father and the Son. He is very well answered by Beza, whose
sentiments on this subject are beyond suspicion. See his Note on
the place. The sons of Zebedee also use the word Θελομεν, Mark x.
35. in making a request to Jesus; but it would be doing great injustice to the two disciples, to say, either that they claimed as their
right what they then asked, or that they called themselves equal to
their Lord and Master. - - - I shall conclude this Note with the
words of Castalio, (*Defensio,* &c.): " Ego veritatem velim veris
argumentis defendi, non ita ridiculis, quibus deridenda propinetur
adversariis."*

Before concluding this Note, it seems right to add that a remark
somewhat similar to that which Campbell makes on the Greek word

---

* This Latin sentence, turned into English, is as follows: " I wish to see the
truth defended by arguments that are true and solid, and not so ridiculous, as to
expose it to the derision of adversaries." T.

θιλω, John xvii. 24. may be made on the Hebrew term שאל,
Psalm ii. 8. Our Author renders it *posce*, (demand;) and *Pagninus*
employs the corresponding term *postula*. But in the version by
Tremellius and *Junius*, it is translated *pete*, with which the word
ask, employed by our translators, coincides. The original expression,
it is admitted, sometimes signifies *to require, to demand;* but probably its more frequent acceptation is *to ask, to crave.* This is the
meaning, for example, Josh. xv. 18. where we read that Achsah,
the daughter of Caleb, moved Othniel to *ask* of her Father a field;
—Judg. v. 25. (compare ch. iv. 19.) where it is said of Sisera,
" He *asked* water, and she gave him milk;"—and 1 Sam. i. 20.
where we are informed of Hannah, that " she bare a son, and called
his name Samuel, saying, Because I have *asked* him of the Lord."
—However valid, therefore, the claim to the possession of the heathen for his inheritance, which our Lord has established by his obedience unto death, the word rendered *posce* by Witsius, does not
necessarily imply his *demanding* that inheritance as a matter of
right.

NOTE LIX. Page 279. line 5.

With great propriety our Author teaches that Christ is not our
Lawgiver, by promulgating a *new law*, that is purer than the law
of Moses, and to which as more perfect, the promise of eternal life
is annexed." Our Lord has, indeed, introduced a new dispensation
of the true Religion, greatly superior, in many respects, to the Mosaic
economy; but the moral law, which was published from Mount
Sinai, is spiritual, perfect, and eternal in its obligation and utility.
Christ's meritorious obedience to that law, is the justifying righteousness of his people, and the foundation of their title to everlasting
life; and at the same time, that law, in all its extent, is the authoritative and unalterable rule of conduct prescribed to his followers,
by their real and progressive conformity to which, they are required
to evince the sincerity of their faith, and to manifest their gratitude
for redeeming love.

Our Lord, no doubt, during the course of his ministry on earth,
acted the part of an incomparable Interpreter and Vindicator of that
sacred law which he had originally inscribed on the human heart,
and published from Sinai with awful majesty. He defended its authority, demonstrated the spirituality and extent of its commands,
placed them in a striking light, and enforced them by new and most
endearing motives. Yet he cannot justly be said to have added any
new precepts to the moral law. This is clearly and concisely shown

by *Rüssenius* in his excellent *Compendium* of Turretine's Theology.*

The precepts of the Gospel is an expression which is not only employed by the enemies of the evangelical system, but for which a considerable number of its friends, owing, probably, in a great degree, to their not adverting to its ambiguous nature, seem to entertain a strong predilection. If any of those who make use of this phrase intend to insinuate, that Christ made additions to the moral law, and remedied certain defects which have been imputed to it, their notion of that law, agreeably to what has just been said, is quite erroneous: Or, if, by *the precepts of the Gospel,* they mean certain precepts delivered by Christ and his Apostles, our obedience to which procures an interest in the blessings of the Gospel, they assuredly swerve from the simplicity of Christian truth, and really, although perhaps unintentionally, take part with those teachers, who inculcate the doctrine of Christ's having published *a new law of grace,* by which men acquire for themselves a title to eternal life on easier terms than those which were at first proposed in the covenant of works.

The term *Gospel* occurs in the sacred volume, it is allowed, in two acceptations. It is sometimes employed extensively to signify all that is taught in the New Testament, including histories, doctrines, and precepts, if not also a great proportion at least of the various contents of the Old Testament, which is not superseded, but confirmed by the New; as 2 Cor. ix. 13. 2 Thes. i. 8. 1 Pet. iv. 17. Rev. xiv. 6. 7. In this sense it is nearly synonymous with the word *Law,* when used in a large sense, as Psalm i. 2. xix. 7. Is. viii. 20. But *Gospel* is undeniably, and, it may be added, generally, made use of by the sacred writers, in a more precise and limited acceptation, to denote the doctrine of the grace of God,—the glad tidings of the birth of a Saviour, and of reconciliation by the blood of the cross,—in contradistinction to the law, strictly so called. In this sense, the Gospel, it may be unblushingly affirmed, has no precepts whatever.

" If we take the word *Gospel* in a strict sense," says our venerable Author in another work, " as it is the form of the Testament of grace, which consists of mere promises, or the absolute exhibition of salvation in Christ, then it properly prescribes nothing as duty, it requires nothing, it commands nothing—no, not so much as to believe, trust, hope in the Lord, and the like. But it relates, declares, and signifies to us, what God in Christ promises, what he willeth, and is about to do. Every prescription of duty belongs to the law, as the venerable *Voetius*, after others, has inculcated to excellent purpose: *Disput. tom.* 4, *pag.* 24, &c. And this we must firmly maintain, if with all the Reformed, we would constantly defend the perfection of the law, as containing in it all virtues, and all the duties of holiness. Yet the law, as adapted to the covenant of grace, and, according to it, written in the hearts of the elect, commands them to embrace, with an unfeigned faith, all things proposed to them in the Gospel, and to order their lives agreeably to that grace and glory. And therefore, when God, in the covenant of grace, promises to an elect sinner faith, repentance, and, consequently, eternal life; then the law, whose obligation can never be dissolved, and which extends itself *to every duty*, obliges the man *to* assent to that truth, highly to esteem the good things promised, earnestly to desire, seek, and embrace them," &c.*

This Note may be concluded with a few remarks on a point somewhat connected with its subject. Near the beginning of this Dissertation on the name *Christ*, the Author speaks of our Lord's offices as so mixed and blended together in their execution, that, provided their nature be rightly illustrated, it is of no great moment to ascertain the order in which they should be considered. This observation requires to be explained. The offices of Christ are, without doubt, blended in their exercise; and it is possible to contend too eagerly with regard to the arrangement which, in treating them, it is most proper for a Christian teacher to adopt. A distinction has been made, and not without reason, betwixt the *natural* order, and the order *of execution;* and sound Theologians, in discoursing on the subject, sometimes prefer the former, sometimes the latter. According to the *natural* order, the priestly office holds the precedency; for the Redeemer's atoning sacrifice laid the foundation, not only for his making intercession for us, but also for his discharging towards us every part of his Prophetical and Kingly offices, in a manner consistent with the perfections and moral government of God. According to the order of *execution*, Christ first illuminates our under-

---

* Mr Bell's Translation of the *Irenicum*, Ch. xvii. sect. 9. See also that Translator's Note 13, pp. 229—232, which relates to *the precepts of the Gospel;* and Note 33, pp. 328—336, where he combats the notion of a new, mild, and remedial law, and quotes a judicious passage from *Du Moulin*, which happily illustrates the manner in which the moral law binds the sinner to faith and repentance. Those who wish to study this subject maturely, may consult also the Answers to the Twelve Queries; Dickenson's Familiar Letters, Let. 13, entitled, " The New Law of Grace examined and disproved;" and the late Rev. William Arnot's Sermons on the Harmony of the Law and Gospel, pp. 158—170.

standings as a Prophet, then applies his blood to our consciences as a Priest, and finally subdues us to himself, and secures our cordial submission to his authority as a King. It is only when we are justified by his righteousness, and enabled to rely on that mercy which, through his sacrifice and intercession is extended to the guilty, that we are prepared to render a cheerful and acceptable obedience to his ordinances and laws. To maintain thus far, that such is in reality the order in which Christ executes his offices, is a matter of no slight importance. But this order is obviously inverted by those who hold that it is by compliance with *the precepts of the Gospel,* and by obedience to a *new law of grace,* that men become entitled to remission and acceptance; and the undoubted principles of our Author are evidently incompatible with this unscriptural and dangerous inversion.

Note LX. Page 279, line 11.

Men of learning are not yet fully agreed with respect to the precise signification of " the gates of hell," i. e. *hades,* mentioned Mat. xvi. 18. Schleusner, in his Greek Lexicon, represents the word *ᾅδης* as sometimes meaning *hell,* the place of punishment, or the condition of the damned, as 2 Pet. ii. 4. Luke xvi. 23. To these passages he adds Mat. xvi. 18, and observes, that by " the gates of *Hades*" he understands the violence and power of the Devil, and of all the fierce adversaries of Christ, whose efforts against the Church shall be rendered abortive. He remarks, too, that the expression was considered in this light by Chrysostome. This modern and foreign lexicographer thus lends his support to the same interpretation which is given by the pious *Matthew Henry,* and the generality of English Expositors. Dr Campbell, on the contrary, contends, that *hades* should never be rendered *hell,* and that it always refers merely to the state of the dead in general. By " the gates of hades," he understands death, which is, so to speak, the gate by which men enter the invisible world; and he regards the promise of the Saviour, that the gates of hades shall never prevail against his Church, as equivalent to the expression, " It shall never die," " It shall never be extinct."* It is clear, however, that, even admitting the justness of this criticism, the Saviour's promise still involves the idea, that the utmost efforts of devils and ungodly men to accomplish the ruin of the Church shall prove ineffectual.

* Preliminary Dissertations, Diss. vi. Part 2. sect. 17.

An opportunity of inquiring more particularly into the import of the term *Hades* will afterwards occur. It may gratify the reader, in the mean time, to compare Campbell's view of the expression in question with the turn which Horsley gives it in a Sermon on Mat. xvi. 18, 19.—" In the present state of sacred literature," says that learned Bishop, " it were an affront to this assembly to go about to prove, that the expression of ' the gates of hell' describes the invisible mansions of departed souls, with allusion to the sepulchres of the Jews and other eastern nations, under the image of a place secured by barricadoed gates, through which there is no escape, by natural means, to those who have once been compelled to enter. Promising that these gates shall not prevail against his Church, our Lord promised not only perpetuity to the Church to the last moment of the world's existence, notwithstanding the successive mortality of all its members in all ages, but what is much more, a final triumph over the power of the grave. Firmly as the gates of hades may be barred, they shall have no power to confine his departed saints, when the last trump shall sound, and the voice of the archangel shall thunder through the deep."*

Note LXI. Page 287.

The sentiments of our venerable Author with reference to the duration of the mediatorial kingdom of Christ, are similar to those which have been entertained by many worthy and respectable Divines. It seems difficult, however, to reconcile some parts of his comment on 1 Cor. xv. 24—28. with what he had stated in section 41.; and even authors who hold materially the same views of the subject with Witsius, have been surprised at some of his expressions. Doddridge, for example, in his Paraphrase on that contested passage, teaches, in language sufficiently clear, that, by some publick act, Christ shall give up his commission to preside as universal Lord in the mediatorial kingdom, and that his redeemed shall no longer need a Mediator. Yet in a Note on ver. 28. he says; " It is surprising to find authors of such different sentiments as *Witsius* and *Crellius*, agreeing to speak of Christ as returning, as it were, to a *private* station, and being ' as one of his brethren,' when he has thus given up the kingdom." " The union of the divine and human natures," adds Dr Doddridge, " in the person of the great Emmanuel, the incomparable virtues of his character, the glory of his actions, and the relations he bears to his people, with all the *texts* which assert

* Horsley's Sermons, Ser. 13.

the perpetuity of his government, prohibit our imagining that he shall ever cease to be illustriously distinguished from all others, whether men or angels, in the heavenly world, through eternal ages."—Justice to our Author requires us to observe, that, although he does speak of Christ, in human nature, becoming " as one of the brethren," he describes him, in the words immediately following, as still " possessing manifold and most excellent glory, without any diminution of the glory which he now enjoys;" and that, in a preceding section, he had affirmed, that Christ will always be " by far the most noble member of the Church, and as such will be recognised, adored, and praised."

The translator, while he urges a fair interpretation of his Author's expressions, ought not to vindicate him in any point in which he humbly presumes to consider him mistaken. He certainly agrees with those Divines, who maintain that our Lord's mediatorial kingdom, as well as his prophetical office and priesthood, is eternal; and who put a different, and, in his apprehension, a much more just and natural interpretation upon the passage just referred to in 1 Cor. xv. than that which is given by our Author, Doddridge, Whitby, and others. It appears to him also a matter of some consequence, that every reader should be furnished with an antidote against misconceptions on this subject; and as he knows nothing better calculated to serve this valuable purpose than the following comprehensive and satisfactory statement of the late Dr Erskine, he takes the liberty to quote it without further apology.

" Christ's power over all flesh," says that able and excellent man of God, in a Discourse on John xvii. 2. " shall appear in ruling his Church in heaven, and imparting to them the blessings of glory. ' He shall reign over the house of Jacob for ever, and of his kingdom there shall be no end,' Luke i. 33. It seems absurd to suppose that he who is emphatically termed ' the Prince of Peace' shall enjoy his power, only, when war and opposition remain, and shall be divested of it, when enemies are conquered, and peace established by their destruction. No; my Brethren, he shall for ever continue the King of his Church, the channel through which all their bliss is conveyed, the bond of their union with God, and the medium of their access to him.—The spring and security of all the happiness of saints in heaven, is shortly this; ' The Lamb which is in the midst of the throne shall feed them, and shall lead them unto living fountains of waters.' Every enjoyment will be enhanced to them, and doubly relished, when received from the hands which, for their redemption, were nailed to the accursed tree. Scarcely could Christ be said to give eternal life to as many as were given him by the Father, if he only bestowed on them the first-fruits of that life, not the full harvest. Imagine not that when Christ has conducted you to the palace of the Father, his relation to you as Mediator, and his acts of kindness to you in consequence of that relation, cease. No; he ever liveth to make intercession for us. His throne is for ever and ever; and it is the everlasting kingdom of our Lord and Saviour Jesus Christ, into which an entrance shall be ministered abundantly to his faithful subjects. Christ is called our Life, (Col. iii. 4.) which, as is evident from the context, must mean that, as he now imparts to us the blessings of grace, so hereafter he will impart to us the blessings of glory. When the marriage of the Lamb is come, the Church will not receive less from her heavenly Husband, than when she was only espoused to him. And when the redeemed shall reign for ever and ever, the Redeemer shall not cease to reign.

" I know that many learned and pious Divines have taught a different doctrine, and argued speciously in support of it from 1 Cor. xv. 24, 25, 28. But in matters of faith, calling no man Master, we ought to bring every opinion to the touchstone of the sacred oracles, and to explain what is more dark and obscure in a way consistent with what is more clear and explicit. *Christ shall deliver up the kingdom to God, even the Father.* But as the Father did not cease to reign, when all power was given to Christ in heaven and in earth; so neither shall the Son cease to reign, when he delivers up the kingdom to the Father. As the Father's reign shall not then begin, so the Son's reign shall not then terminate. The kingdom, therefore, in this passage, means the subjects of the kingdom. Christ, having completed the salvation of every one of them, shall present them all to the Father, saying, ' Behold I and the children which God hath given me.' He shall give an account of what he did on earth in consequence of the trust committed to him, and shall claim that the purchase of his blood, and the conquests of his grace, may inherit the kingdom to which they are thus entitled, and for which they have been thus prepared.

" The King of Zion must reign till he hath put all his enemies under his feet. But to infer from this, that he must reign no longer, is as absurd as it would be to infer from Michal the daughter of Saul having no child until the day of her death, that after her death she had a child. David says, ' The Lord said unto my Lord, Sit thou at my right hand, till I make thine enemies thy footstool.' Lest this should lead to false notions of the duration of Christ's kingdom, we are told that he *for ever* sat down on the right hand of God.'

" We are informed that when all things shall·be subject to him,
*then shall the Son also himself be subject to him that put all things
under him, that God may be all in all.* But this neither proves that
Christ's power over all flesh ends, or that his subjection to the Father commences with the general resurrection. Both in the purchase and application of salvation, Christ always acted as the Father's righteous servant. And in Scripture, things are often said to
happen, when they are known and made manifest. We have three
instances of this in one Chapter, Rom. iii. 4. ' Yea, let God be true,
but every man a liar,' i. e. Let God be acknowledged true, and every
man accounted a liar, who arraigns the Divine faithfulness. Ver. 19,
' What things soever the law saith, it saith to them, who are under
the law, that every mouth may be stopped, and all the world may
become guilty before God,' i. e. may appear to be guilty, may have
their guilt manifested. Ver. 26. ' That God might be just, i. e.
might appear to be just. Let me apply these observations to the
present subject. The Apostle to the Hebrews, having told us
that God hath put all things under Christ's feet, yea, left nothing
that is not put under him, immediately adds, ' But now we see not
yet all things put under him.' In like manner, if we know the
Mediator's subjection to the Father, it is now by faith, not by
sight : but after the resurrection, when Christ shall give an account
of all he hath done for the salvation of those given him by the Father, that subjection shall be more fully manifested to the whole
rational creation. Thus the spirits of the prophets are said to be
subject to those other prophets, who judge what they have spoken,
(1 Cor. xiv. 32. compared with ver. 29.) Indeed the Son as Head
of the redeemed, shall through all eternity acknowledge, that in the
glorious scheme of man's redemption, all things are of God ; and
shall lead the worshippers of the higher house, in their expressions
of reverence, love, and subjection, to his Father and their Father,
his God and their God.

" Thus there is nothing in this passage inconsistent with the clear
declarations in other passages of Scripture, that Christ's mediatorial
relations to his people shall continue for ever, and that he will
eternally exert his power in consequence of those relations for their
benefit."*

Note LXII. Page 290.

It is not in vain that the Author urges the necessity of receiving
Christ in all his offices. The human heart is naturally averse to

* Dr Erskine's Sermons, Vol. ii. Disc. 16. pp. 492—496.

him in his whole mediatorial work; and those only who are enlightened and renewed by the Spirit, are capable of discerning aright the glory and importance of every gracious character which he sustains. The reader must be careful, at the same time, not to misunderstand the Author's remark—that if men have no inclination to submit to the Saviour's instructions as a Prophet, and to obey his laws as a King, their glorying in him as a Priest is merely presumptuous. It is, doubtless, his design, to inculcate, that an unfeigned dependance on Christ as a High Priest who has expiated our sins by the sacrifice of himself, is always accompanied and manifested by a sincere reliance upon him as a Teacher and King, and by a cordial submission to his prophetical and royal authority; and to reprove the temerity of those who pretend to have " faith in his blood," while they continue indisposed to hear him as their Prophet, and obey him as their Lawgiver. A readiness to acquiesce in the instructions, and to keep the ordinances and commandments of Christ, is a fair and necessary test of a personal interest, by faith, in his atonement. The meaning of Witsius, however, cannot be, that men, by subjecting their judgment to his teachings, and their will to his authority, *procure for themselves* an interest in his atoning sacrifice and prevailing intercession. Nor is it probable that he intended to intimate, that the inclinations of the human heart are less inimical to Christ's priestly character than to his other offices. A great number of mankind, indeed, *make a profession* of confidence in the blood and righteousness of Christ, while their habitual conduct discovers an inveterate disaffection to his authority and laws. But are there not many, who, whilst they profess high admiration for the precepts of the Christian Religion, are avowedly hostile to the Christian atonement, and to justification by the righteousness of the Mediator? And is it not certain, that fallen man, proud amidst the ruins of his nature, and arrogant amidst the moral pollutions by which he has rendered himself inexpressibly abominable in the eyes of infinite purity,—has a deep-rooted backwardness to be indebted for pardon and acceptance, to the propitiation brought near by the Gospel? All, it is true, are averse to misery; and whoever is persuaded of the existence of a hell, is desirous to escape that place of torment. But it requires Divine illumination to convince a man effectually, both that his sins deserve everlasting misery, and that for deliverance from it, he must be entirely indebted to the free grace of God, and the vicarious sacrifice of Jesus Christ. The same base and criminal pride, which has induced some to prefer the loss of natural life to coming under obligations to the hand of charity for the means of its support, has prompted thousands of the human race to choose rather to expose their immortal souls to eternal ruin, than to stand indebted to the grace of God reigning through the righteousness of Christ, for pardon and eternal life. See Mat. xix. 16—22. Luke xviii. 11, 12. Rom. ix. 31—33. x. 1—4.

On this subject, the remarks of an evangelical writer formerly referred to,* are worthy of notice. " Many think," says he, " and will often say, that sinners are *willing* to have Christ as a *Saviour,* but not as a *King and Lawgiver.* To speak freely, I verily think as to great numbers in the professing world, the contrary is *rather* true. They would have Christ as a *Lawgiver,* and are not willing to have him as a *Saviour.* The *Papists* contend, that Christ is a Lawgiver, and they must be saved by keeping his law. The *Socinians* and *Arminians* are all of them also agreed in this. But (sure I am not mistaken!) they are enemies to all that free grace whereby he saves sinners; and so is *every man* by nature. True, indeed, they would be saved; but they would not have *Christ* to be their Saviour. They would be saved by *the law,* and so by obedience of their own performing. And whatever man he is, of whatever profession, that setteth up his own righteousness and puts any trust therein, - - - - he would have Christ to be a Lawgiver (if it may be said he would have Christ at all;) but Christ as a Saviour by his righteousness, he would not, he will not have, John v. 40. *Mr Mowsley's* experience is a confirmation of this.† He thought verily he desired the destruction of sin, and loved to hear of a holy life mightily; but the doctrine of denying self-righteousness was a hard saying, and he could not, a great while, tell how to suppose one should be justified by *another's* righteousness. It is at least as great a point, and as difficult, to submit to Christ's *righteousness,* as to submit to his government." - - -

" The way of receiving Christ in truth as a Saviour," adds Mr Beart, " is for a sinner who has neither righteousness nor strength, nor any thing that is good, who sees all is lost, that there can be no repairing of ruined nature, to seek his whole salvation from the Lord Jesus Christ, by believing; not only to seek sanctification, as a legal professor may think he doth, but to seek it from Christ as the alone author and fountain of it, in a way of believing. This is the

---

* Beart's Eternal Law, and Everlasting Gospel, Part first, Pref. pp. 30—32.

† The Author here refers to page 100. *et seq.* of an account of his own religious experience, left by a *Mr Thomas Mowsley,* Apothecary, who died 1669; and published at the end of his Funeral Sermon, entitled *Death Unstung,* by Mr James Janeway, 1672.

soul that desires to have Christ in his kingly office. *Again,* not only to follow after a justifying righteousness, but to receive Christ for righteousness, as the *matter* of his justification, Rom. ix. 30—33. Otherwise, seeking righteousness by the works of the law, they stumble at *that stumbling-stone,* where so many professors have stumbled—men that seemed *not far from the kingdom of heaven,* and yet so far as never to obtain it."

The prevalence of *Antinomian* sentiments among some classes of professed Christians is much to be deplored. " Is Christ the minister of sin ? God forbid." To many who once made a specious and imposing profession, he will thus address himself in the great day of judgment—" I never knew you; depart from me, *ye workers of iniquity.*"* The Ministers of the Gospel ought certainly to employ their strenuous and united efforts for the destruction of " the hydra of Antinomianism." It is not, however, by the relaxation of their zeal in preaching the pure gospel of the grace of God—by an infrequent, scanty, and timid exhibition of evangelical doctrine—or by adopting statements and expressions that are in any degree contrary to the truth as it is in Jesus, or inconsistent with its simplicity and purity, that they can justly expect to subdue this hideous monster. The same " battle-axe and weapon of war" which was wielded with astonishing success by Apostles and their coadjutors in the primitive days of Christianity, must still be employed in this sacred warfare. Whilst the duties of holiness are explained and inculcated in all their extent, and whilst the criminality and folly of sin in its various forms are faithfully exposed, the doctrine of grace must be clearly and earnestly exhibited, and the cross uniformly presented to the attention of men, as supplying by far the most influential motives to repentance and " newness of life."

Paul is, without doubt, a pattern to all who are invested with the sacred office. When this great Apostle, in his Epistle to Titus, had adverted to the lamentable conduct of the Antinomians of that age, men who " professed that they knew God, while in works they denied him," what measures does he recommend to the adoption of the young Evangelist, for repressing their detestable and ruinous errors ? Doth he at all insinuate that Titus should become somewhat more sparing than formerly, in publishing the riches of Divine mercy, or that he should adulterate the Gospel by a neutralizing mixture of legal doctrine ? By no means. He directs him, on the contrary, to

* Gal. ii. 17. Mat. vii. 23.

persist in testifying " the grace of God which bringeth salvation"—
not omitting, at the same time, to point out minutely and impres-
sively its practical bearings and tendencies; and after laying before
him a beautiful summary of the doctrine of a free salvation,* he immediately adds : " This is a faithful saying ;" i. e. This doctrine, of
which I have just sketched an outline, is incontestably certain, and
entitled to the most cordial credit—" and these things I will that
thou affirm constantly," these precious truths respecting the sovereign love and mercy of God to depraved and perishing men, the
righteousness and mediation of Christ, and the regenerating agency
of the Holy Spirit, must be strongly and unceasingly affirmed—
" that they who have believed in God, might be careful to maintain
good works," i. e. in order that believers, sweetly constrained by the
grace of God, and drawn by the cords of his love, may be effectually
incited to adorn their profession, and glorify God, by a pure and exemplary practice.

In addition to the valuable writings mentioned in some preceding
Notes, the reader will find much instruction on the sanctifying influence of the Gospel, and the connexion subsisting betwixt the renunciation of legal hope and the cultivation of true holiness in
heart and life, in the following Sermons; the Rev. Ralph Erskine's,
entitled, " Law-death Gospel-life," from Gal. ii. 19.†—the Rev. Ar-
chibald Hall's from the same text, entitled, " Believers' death to the
law, a doctrine according to godliness ;"—the Rev. John Brown's,
(late) Biggar, bearing the title of " the Christian doctrine of Sanctification," and founded on Rom. viii. 3.‡

Note LXIII. Page 291.

In this interesting Dissertation on the name Christians, the
Author strikingly adverts to the time, and the place, in which this
appellation was first given to the followers of Jesus, and copiously
illustrates its import. There is one question, however, connected
with the subject, ...e discussion of which he has thought proper to
omit, viz. To whom they were originally indebted for this name ?
Whether it was contrived by their enemies, assumed spontaneously
by themselves, or taken by the special direction of God? Witsius, however, makes use of expressions, from which it appears that he approved
of the last of these opinions ; for he says, section 4th,—" *It seemed*

---

* Tit. iii. 3—7.
† Vol. i. pp. 131—166. 1st edit. folio.
‡ Sermons by Ministers belonging to the (late) Associate Synod, pp. 123—164.

proper to the Holy Spirit, that the disciples of Christ should henceforth be termed Christians, from Christ himself." This, too, appears to have been the prevailing opinion among respectable Divines. It was probably embraced by Pearson. He does not, at least, entertain the idea that this designation was invented by the enemies of Christianity; and he informs us from the writings of *Joannes Antiochenus,* that it was first given by *Euodius,* a Bishop of the Church of Antioch.* In Pool's Annotations on the place, it is expressly affirmed that this name was " given them by divine authority, for the word implies no less." Dr Guyse, in his Paraphrase, thus comments on Acts xi. 26. " Not without warrant from divine intimations, they publicly and solemnly took upon themselves the name of Christians, in opposition to unbelieving Jews and Heathens." Dr Whitby remarks, that some think the giving of this name to believers, the fulfilment of the promise in Is. lxv. 15. - - - " The Lord God shall - - - - call his servants by another name." The pious Mr John Newton, in his sermon on the passage, makes the following observations.

" There is an ambiguity in the original word χρηματισαι, which our Translation renders *called;* for although that is the more general sense it bears in heathen writers, wherever it occurs in the New Testament, except in this passage and in Rom. vii. 3. it signifies to be taught or warned by a revelation from heaven. Thus it is spoken of Joseph and the wise men, Mat. ii. Simeon, Luke ii. Cornelius, Acts x. Noah, Heb. xi. and elsewhere. It does not, therefore, appear quite certain from the text, whether the disciples chose this name for themselves; or the wits of the time fixed it upon them, as a mark of infamy; or lastly, whether it was by the special direction of the Spirit of God, that they assumed it. But I incline to the latter supposition, because in those happy times, it was the practice and the privilege of the disciples to ask and to receive direction from on High on almost every occurrence, but chiefly on account of the excellent instructions couched under this emphatical name - - -." No writer, however, seems to have gone farther on the same side of the question, than Dr Doddridge, who thus *translates* the expression—" The disciples were, by divine appointment, first named Christians at Antioch."

The opinion of Dr Campbell on this point is quite the reverse. " It is not unreasonable," says he, " to think, that a name which had its rise among their enemies might afterwards be adopted by

* Exposition of the Creed, pp. 103, 104.

themselves. The name Christians first used at Antioch, seems, from the manner in which it is mentioned in the Acts, (xi. 26.) to have been at first given contemptuously to the disciples, and not assumed by themselves. The common titles, by which, for many years after that period, they continued to distinguish those of their own society, as we learn both from the Acts, and from Paul's Epistles, were the *faithful* or believers, the *disciples*, and the *brethren*. Yet before the expiration of the Apostolic age, they adopted the name *Christian*, and gloried in it. The Apostle Peter uses it in one place, 1st Ep. iv. 16. the only place in Scripture wherein it is used by one of themselves."*

The fact is, that χϱηματισαὶ is a term so extensively applied, as to leave it undetermined, whether the name in question was imposed by divine authority, or invented by human wisdom or wit. Beza considers it as synonymous with ὀνομαζεσθαι, and renders it *nominarentur*. The Vulgate, in like manner, makes it *cognominarentur;* Castalio, *appellarentur ;* and our authorised English Version, *called*. The word, it is granted, according to the remark just quoted from Mr Newton, often occurs in Scripture with reference to revelations from God; and although our translators have acted differently in the verse under consideration, they have in several other passages rendered it as if it completely implied that idea. Thus in Heb. viii. 5. they say, *Moses was admonished of God ;* and Mat. ii. 12. *Being warned of God*. The corresponding noun χϱηματισμος, Rom. xi. 4. is also rendered *the answer of God*. But on this subject, Dr Campbell's Note, Mat. ii. 12. deserves attention. Having rendered the expression simply, *being warned in a dream*, he says, " E. T. *Being warned of God in a dream*. With this agree some ancient, and most modern, translations, introducing the term *response, oracle, divinity*, or something equivalent. The Syriac has preserved the simplicity of the original, importing only *it was signified to them in a dream ;* and is followed by Le Clerc. That the warning came from God, there can be no doubt; but as this is not expressed, but implied, in the original, it ought to be exhibited in the same manner in the version. What is said explicitly in the one, should be said explicitly in the other ; what is conveyed only by implication in the one, should be conveyed only by implication in the other. Now that χϱηματιζειν does not necessarily imply *from God*, more than the word *warning* does, is evident from the reference which, both in sacred authors and in classical, it often has to inferior agents. See Acts 22.

---

* Preliminary Dissertations, Diss. ix. Part 1, § 10.

where the name of God is indeed both unnecessarily and improperly introduced in the translation; xi. 26. Rom. vii. 3. Heb. xii. 25. For Pagan authorities, see Raphelius."

On the whole, Campbell appears to be correct in the interpretation of the *term*. But, notwithstanding the arguments he suggests in support of his opinion, and those of *Wetstein*, quoted by Parkhurst,* he is possibly wrong in ascribing the invention of the name *Christians* to the enemies of the Christian faith.

Note LXIV. Page 293.

While the Author gives the name of *Græci* to those inhabitants of Antioch, to whom " the men of Cyprus and Cyrene," as we read, Acts xi. 20, 21. preached the Gospel with remarkable success, the Translator has not scrupled, in conformity with the common version, to call them *Grecians*. He considers *Greeks* and *Grecians*, indeed, as synonymous terms. The latter is, at least, often employed in the same sense with the former. In this acceptation it seems to be used by our Translators themselves, Joel iii. 6. " The children also of Judah, and the children of Jerusalem, have ye sold (marg.) *unto the sons of the Grecians ;*" where the expression in the Septuagint is— τοις υιοις των 'Ελληνων. In the New Testament, however, our Translators carefully distinguish between *Greeks* and *Grecians*. By the former they obviously understand Greeks, or Gentiles, by birth ; whilst they represent the latter as a different class of people, without determining, at the same time, whether they were converts from heathenism to the Jewish Religion, or Jews by birth who spoke the Greek tongue. In this instance, our English version is more exact than either the Vulgate, or Beza's translation ; in which both 'Ελληνες and 'Ελληνισται are uniformly rendered *Græci*. Yet the term *Hellenists* seems more eligible than *Grecians*.

Notice was formerly taken † of the diversity of sentiment among critics with regard to the *Hellenists* mentioned in the Acts, and reasons were very briefly stated for preferring the opinion that they were Jews who spoke the Greek language. Besides the Authors there referred to, the reader may consult a judicious Note by Whitby on Acts vi. 1. Many able writers contend, that it is manifestly Jews that are intended in Acts xi. 20. Hammond, Whitby, and Campbell, for example, concur in this opinion. Whitby, in his Note on that verse, censures Grotius for making the *Hellenists* Greeks, although he had acknowledged that it is Jews that are meant by this ex-

---

* Greek Lexicon, on the word Χριστιανος.
† See Note XXII.

pression in ch. vi. 1. And, after observing that it was thus understood by *Chrysostome* and *Œcumenius*, he adds: " It seems necessary
to understand the Jews using the Greek language, and reading the
Scriptures in that tongue, (as Buxtorf says they did,) 1st, Because
these persons preached to the Jews only, ver. 19. 2dly, Because
they of the Church of Jerusalem sent to them Barnabas, whom they
would scarce send to the uncircumcised."—Campbell, after having
adverted to two passages in which the word *Hellenists* occurs, viz.
Acts vi. 1. and ix. 29, thus proceeds : " The only other passage is
where we are told (Acts xi. 20.) that some of those, being Cypriots
and Cyrenians, who were scattered abroad on the persecution that
arose about Stephen, *spake unto the Grecians* (προς τας Ἑλληνιστας) at
Antioch, *preaching the Lord Jesus.* Whether this was before or after the baptism of Cornelius recorded in the foregoing chapter, is not
certain : but one thing is certain, that it was before those disciples
could know of that memorable event. Concerning the others who
were in that dispersion, who were probably *Hebrews,* we are informed in the verse immediately preceding, that in all those places, Phe-
nicia, Cyprus, and Antioch, through which they went, they preached the word to none but Jews." *

There are, nevertheless, respectable authors who prefer a different
interpretation. Beza, while by *Hellenists* in Acts vi. 1. he understands Gentiles that were circumcised, and complete proselytes to
the Jewish religion, imagines that *Hellenists* in Acts xi. 20. are the
σεβομενοι of the Gentiles, persons who, though they had not submitted to the rite of circumcision, allowed the inspiration of Moses and
the Prophets, and worshipped exclusively the God of Israel. Dr
Guyse and the continuators of Pool, in like manner, apply the expression to the devout Gentiles. Dr Doddridge is decidedly of opinion, that, while a contrast is stated betwixt the conduct held by
the generality of the disciples mentioned ver. 19. and the measures
adopted by the men of Cyprus and Cyrene ver. 20, these last preached the Lord Jesus even to *idolatrous* Gentiles. In the passage to
which this Note refers, Witsius, without entering into the question
relative to their proselytism, considers the preaching of these disciples of Cyprus and Cyrene as a service performed to Greeks, or
Gentiles, by birth.

The just determination of this point seems to turn upon the authenticity of the word Ἑλληνιστας in Acts xi. 20. If this term, which
occurs in the majority of Manuscripts and Versions, be authentic, and

* Preliminary Dissert. Diss. i. part i. § 6.

if it is sufficiently clear that in Acts vi. 1. and ix. 29. it necessarily refers to Jews by birth, it may be reasonably deemed a rather violent interpretation to apply it to any others than Jews in ch. xi. 20. Ἕλληνας, however, is the word in the Alexandrian Manuscript; and this reading is supported by the Syriac, Arabic, Coptic, and Ethiopic versions, and by the authority of Eusebius, Chrysostome, Theophilus of Antioch, and some other fathers. Griesbach has admitted Ἕλληνας into the text; and if this be the genuine reading, the sense which our Author has adopted must be correct.

It is hardly necessary to state, that as the Greeks were the most celebrated of the Gentiles in the neighbourhood of Judea, and as, after the conquests of Alexander, their language was generally introduced amongst other nations, it was quite customary for the Jews to employ the name *Greeks* as a general designation for *Gentiles*. Compare John vii. 35. xii. 20. Rom. x. 12. 1 Cor. xii. 13. Gal. iii. 28. Col. iii. 11.

Note LXV. Page 298.

The account which our Author here gives of the contemptuous designations with which the Christians were branded by the heathen, is illustrated and confirmed by a passage of Tertullian's Apology, quoted by Bingham. " Tertullian," says that historian, " mentions another name which was likewise occasioned by their sufferings. The martyrs, which were burned alive, were usually tied to a board or stake of about six feet long, which the Romans called *Semaxis,* and then they were surrounded or covered with faggots of small wood, which they called *Sarmenta*. From this their punishment, the heathen, who turned every thing into mockery, gave all Christians the despiteful name of *Sarmentitii,* and *Semaxii.*"*

Note LXVI. Page 306.

The *Maronites* are a sect of professed Christians in Palestine, dissenting in certain articles from the Greek Church. They derive their name from *Maroun,* a hermit, who flourished towards the close of the sixth century, resided on the banks of the river Orontes, was respected for his austerities and supposed miracles, and strenuously supported the western Christians in their disputes with those of the east. Their country is about 150 leagues square, including great part of Lebanon, of which they took possession so early as about the year 677. Near the beginning of the thirteenth Century, after a tem-

* See Bingham's Antiquities of the Christian Church, Book I. chap. ii. sect. 10. The Latin of Tertullian is quoted from *Apol.* c. 50.

porary separation, they effected a reunion with Rome, which still subsists. Although they acknowledge the supremacy of the Pope, they elect a Patriarch for themselves, and they observe certain rites of their own in addition to those which they have borrowed from the Church of Rome. Some of their devotional books are in Syriac, but they celebrate divine service in Arabic. While they pay tribute to the Pacha of Tripoli, they keep themselves quite distinct from the Mahometans, and will suffer none of that religion to live among them. For further information relative to this interesting people, see Mosheim,* Russell's History of Aleppo,† and Volney's Travels through Syria and Egypt.‡

Note LXVII. Page 309.

The Author, with his usual caution, does not presume to determine precisely the time when the extraordinary gift of prophecy was withdrawn from the Church. He regarded this gift, however, it is evident, and some other miraculous gifts,§ as having been continued to a certain extent, considerably beyond the Apostolic age. Our limits do not permit us to essay a particular discussion of this subject. Suffice it, therefore, to refer those who are disposed to examine it minutely to Whitby's General Preface to the Apostolical Epistles, and to the Treatise by Witsius himself " On Prophets and Prophecy, chap. 24. On the continuance of Prophecy after the death of the Apostles." ||

With respect to revelations of future events alleged to have been made to certain individuals in modern times, such as those ascribed to Archbishop Usher, and to John Knox that great Reformer, and some other Scottish Ministers, it is generally believed that such intimations are at least extremely rare. There are strong objections against admitting the reality of these modern revelations at all.— The reader will find some ingenious remarks on this subject, by the learned Dr M'Crie, in his Life of John Knox.¶

It may not be improper to record here the following instance of the venerable Author's characteristical modesty and candour. In the Treatise on Prophecy just referred to, having detailed arguments both for and against prophetic powers in latter times, he leaves the

---

* On the 7th. and also the 16th Century.
† Vol. ii. pp. 28, 34, 395, 396. 2d edit.
‡ Vol. ii. ch. 24. sect. 2.
§ See Diss. xi. sect. 36.
|| *De Prophetis et Prophetia*, cap. 24. *De continuatione Prophetiæ post excessum Apostolorum*. Miscellan. Sacra. Tom. I.
¶ Vol. ii. per. 9. p. 262. *et seq.*

question in a great degree undecided. While he rejects not merely all modern prophecies that are contrary to sacred writ, but also those which pretend to be a rule of faith and practice to the Church, he allows that good men, through intimate fellowship with God, may sometimes have premonitions of future events, though given merely for the purpose of regulating their own personal conduct on occasions of singular importance and difficulty. He then makes an apology for this admission, part of which is expressed in the following terms: " I have myself, however, I acknowledge, no experience of the gift of prophecy. Besides the careful study of the sacred volume, than which nothing affords me greater pleasure, I deem it quite sufficient to receive that unction from the Holy One, which teacheth all things, and a portion of which it pleases God, in his great liberality, to impart to every individual of them that fear him."*

Note LXVIII. Page 326.

The original term κεκληρονομηκεν, Heb. i. 4. which our translators render, *He hath by inheritance obtained,* is rendered by the Vulgate, *hæreditavit;* by Beza, *sortitus est;* and by Doddridge, *he has inherited.* The word properly signifies to obtain any thing by lot, as when Palestine was divided among the Israelites, so that a certain part fell by lot to each tribe and family, the share of each individual being called גורל and κληρος, as Num. xxvi. 55. Josh. xiv. 1, 2.† It is used extensively, however, as Dr Campbell observes,‡ to " denote possessing by any title, by lot, succession, purchase, conquest, or gift." The following remarks, too, are exceedingly just. " A single word is sometimes used with energy and perspicuity, as a trope. But if we substitute a definition for the single word, we destroy the trope, and often render the sentence nonsensical. To say, *the meek shall inherit the earth,* is to employ the word *inherit* in a figurative sense, which can hardly be misunderstood by any body, as denoting the facility with which they shall obtain possession, and the stability of the possession obtained. But if we employ circumlocution, and say, in the manner of some interpreters, *The meek shall succeed to the earth by hereditary right,* by so explicit, and so

---

* " Non dissimulo autem, nihil mihi unquam prophetici contigisse. Præter diligens sacrarum literarum scrutinium, quo nihil suavius jucundiusque, sufficit mihi unctio a Sancto illo profecta, quæ docet omnia, et cujus portionem aliquam singulis sui reverentibus impertit Divini numinis benignitas."

† See Parkhurst on the word, and the *Lectiones Academicæ* of *Ernesti* on the Epistle to the Hebrews, ch. i. 4.

‡ See his Note on Mat. v. 3.

formal, a limitation of the manner, we exclude the trope, and affirm what is palpably inapplicable, and therefore ridiculous; for to obtain by hereditary right, is to succeed in right of consanguinity to the former possessor, now deceased."*

On the same principle, thus applied to Mat. v. 5. the rendering by the Vulgate and Doddridge in Heb. i. 4. as quoted above, is preferable to that which is adopted in our authorised version. Accordingly, *Ernesti* and his Annotator *Dindorf* concur in the opinion, that the expression should be translated simply, *he has received,* or *obtained.* At the same time, κεκληρονομηκε, ver. 4, may be considered as probably referring to κληρονομον, ver. 2. Christ being *naturally* and *independently* " Heir of all things" as a Divine Person, the Father *appointed* him as Mediator to be the Heir and Lord of all—of every possession, and every dignity. In like manner, Christ being originally and eternally " the Son of God," the Father, upon occasion of the honourable performance of his mediatorial work on earth, solemnly pronounced and declared him to be his Son, in a sense altogether peculiar to himself, Rom. i. 4. Thus he has *inherited* a more excellent name than angels—he has obtained it as the natural and the appointed Heir of all things, and, as Witsius remarks, his title to this glorious designation is " indisputable and unalienable." See Dr Owen's Exposition, and Guyse's Paraphrase on the place. Dindorf, after Erasmus and others, observes that κεκληρονομηκε, in the perfect tense, has the force of the present, and denotes the perpetuity of the possession; and that in this view, it is parallel to κεκοινωνηκε, Heb. ii. 14, and to τετελειωκε, ch. x. 14.

Note LXIX. Page 330.

That the Messiah is chiefly and ultimately intended by the Wisdom which most earnestly and affectionately solicits the attention of mankind in the 8th Chapter of the Book of Proverbs, has been generally held by the best interpreters, ancient and modern. Whatever ridicule the enemies of the truth may throw upon the *orthodox* interpretation, this chapter exhibits a sublime and interesting testimony to the Divine dignity of Christ, and to the eternal relation subsisting between the Father and Him, while it presents the most endearing view of his ardent and everlasting love for the sons of men. It is with sincere pleasure that the Translator lays before the reader the following quotation on this subject from a learned and penetrat-

* Preliminary Dissertations, Diss. xii. part i. § 17.

ing writer, who well knew how to think for himself, on subjects of sacred criticism.

" For my part," says Dr Campbell, when discussing the import of the term Λογος in a Note on John i. 1. " I entirely agree with those who think it most likely, that the allusion here is to a portion of holy writ, and not to the reveries of either Philo or Plato. The passage of holy writ referred to, is Prov. viii. throughout. What is here termed ὁ λογος, is there ἡ σοφια. There is such a coincidence in the things attributed to each, as evidently shows, that both were intended to indicate the same Divine personage. The passage in the Proverbs, I own, admits a more familiar explanation, as regarding the happy consequences of that mental quality, which we may call true or heavenly wisdom. But it is suitable to the genius of Scripture prophecy to convey, under such allegorical language, the most important and sublime discoveries."

NOTE LXX. Page 333.

The expression in Micah v. 2, " whose goings forth have been from of old, even from everlasting," ought certainly, and perhaps entirely, to be referred to the eternal generation of the Son of God, which supplies the most perfect contrast with his birth in human nature in the fulness of time. Although the phrase מימי עולם *from the days of old* is usually employed with reference to a limited duration, yet עולם itself is often applied to an absolute eternity, both with reference to the past and the future, as in Gen. iii. 22. Ps. ix. 8. Gen. xxi. 33. Ps. xli. 14. Prov. viii. 23. Is. xl. 28. Calvin remarks, that קדם and עולם when used separately, frequently mean a limited period, but when conjoined, as in this verse, strongly denote an absolute eternity.*

It is somewhat surprising, that our Author seems to refer to the expression, Tit. i. 2, πρὸ χρονων αἰωνιων, rendered by himself *ante tempora secularia*, and by our Translators " before the world began," as if it related merely to the time of the making of the first Gospel promise recorded, Gen. iii. 15. In spite of what Locke, Macknight, and others have alleged to the contrary, that expression in Tit. i. 2, which occurs also 2 Tim. i. 9. refers without doubt to the promises *made from all eternity* by the Father to the Son as the head of his people. See Beza, Guyse, and Doddridge on these two places.

* Comment. on the place.

NOTE LXXI. Page 335.

The Hebrew word פָּנַי in Exod. xxxiii. 14, 15. rendered in our English translation *my presence*, literally signifies *my face;* and our Author is by no means singular in applying it to the Son of God. In Pool's Annotations on the place, it is thus explained : " My presence, Heb. *my face*, i. e. I myself—by comparing this with 2 Sam. xvii. 11. The Angel of my presence, Is. lxiii. 9. - - - And I will not turn thee over to an angel, as I threatened, ver. 2." Calvin views the expression in the same light, and regards it as a proof " of the eternal divinity of Christ." " These words," says he, " *My face shall go before thee*,* are of the same import as if he had said, ' I will so go before thee, that you may be truly sensible that I myself am present with thee, as if you beheld my face in a mirror placed before your eyes.' Now, since that was to be fulfilled in Christ, it follows that he is the eternal God, whose glory, power, and majesty transcend all creatures."†

It is necessary only to add, that the reader has no reason to be surprised at the 14th verse appearing in the form of a question, instead of an express promise. The original words are quite susceptible of this mode of interpretation. It is not unsuited to the scope of the passage ; and it is the mode adopted in the Latin Version of the Old Testament by Tremellius and Junius, from which the words are quoted by Witsius.

NOTE LXXII. Page 354.

Our Author's critical examination of the term Δεσποτης is able and satisfactory. Although Dr Whitby, Dr Clarke, and others have affirmed that this title is never given to our Saviour in the New Testament, the contrary is sufficiently established by Witsius, and by later writers. See, in particular, Parkhurst's reasonings against Clarke.‡ Even Schleusner admits that Christ is intended by δεσπο-την, 2 Pet. ii. 1. The following quotation from a learned writer lately deceased, serves also to confirm the remark quoted by our Author from Beza and Bisterfeld, respecting the use of the Greek article in Jude, ver. 4. " Supposing the common reading to be the true one, I see no reason to doubt the proposed interpretation which explains δεσποτης θεος and κυριος as one Person, Jesus Christ : for had *two* persons been meant, we should have read ΤΟΝ Κυριον ημων. That the Syriac Translator understood the passage of one Person is most

* Facies mea præcedet.   † See Calvin on the place.
‡ Greek Lexicon on the word Δεσποτης.

certain: he puts Κυριον in *apposition* with δεσποτην θεον, and renders 'the only Lord God (viz.) our Lord Jesus Christ." The Coptic does the same.*

NOTE LXXIII. Page 369.

What our venerable Author intends by representing the heathen moralists as "unjust possessors" of those choice sentiments which he produces from their writings, may be collected from his own expressions in another work. In his Dissertations on the Lord's Prayer, after quoting passages from Epictetus and Marcus Antoninus, that relate to the importance of performing every duty with pious respects to God, he adds: " By these quotations, it is not intended to intimate, that the mysteries of our Religion with regard to the hallowing of the name of God, may be learned equally well from the maxims of Philosophers, as from the books of Sacred Scripture. Their most excellent sayings come far short of the sublimity of holy writ, and have possibly been derived from that source: for it is difficult to find such noble sentiments in the writings of Philosophers till after the publication of the Gospel. Yet instructions and examples, so devout, furnished by the heathen, ought surely to excite Christians to emulation."†

The incomparable superiority, in all respects, of true Christian morality to the best systems of morals devised or practised by the heathen, is an important topic, on which our limits do not permit us to enter. It is excellently illustrated by Dr Owen in his Treatise on the Spirit, ‡ and by Witsius himself in his Economy of the Covenants. § Leland has treated this subject in a most elaborate and satisfactory manner; ‖ and it is adverted to with brevity, but with her accustomed elegance and spirit, by Mrs Hannah More, in her interesting " Essay on the Character and Practical Writings of St Paul."¶

* Dr Middleton's Doctrine of the Greek Article, p. 658.
† Exercit. viii. sect. 19. ‡ Books iv. and v.
§ Book iii. ch. 12. sect. 59—103. ‖ Vol. ii. part. ii. ch. 1—13.
¶ Vol. i. ch. 1.

END OF THE FIRST VOLUME.